Teen Genreflecting

Recent Titles in Genreflecting Advisory Series

Diana Tixier Herald, Series Editor

Urban Grit: A Guide to Street Lit
Megan Honig

Historical Fiction for Teens: A Genre Guide
Melissa Rabey

Graphic Novels for Young Readers: A Genre Guide for Ages 4–14
Nathan Herald

Make Mine a Mystery II: A Reader's Guide to Mystery and Detective Fiction
Gary Warren Niebuhr

Mostly Manga: A Genre Guide to Popular Manga, Manhwa, Manhua, and Anime
Elizabeth Kalen

Romance Fiction: A Guide to the Genre, Second Edition
Kristin Ramsdell

Reality Rules II: A Guide to Teen Nonfiction Reading Interests
Elizabeth Fraser

Genreflecting: A Guide to Popular Reading Interests, Seventh Edition
Cynthia Orr and Diana Tixier Herald, Editors

Women's Fiction: A Guide to Popular Reading Interests
Rebecca Vnuk and Nanette Donohue

Encountering Enchantment: A Guide to Speculative Fiction for Teens, Second Edition
Susan Fichtelberg

Graphic Novels: A Guide to Comic Books, Manga, and More, Second Edition
Michael Pawuk and David Serchay

Genreflecting: A Guide to Popular Reading Interests, Eighth Edition
Diana Tixier Herald and Samuel Stavole-Carter

Teen Genreflecting

A Readers' Advisory and Collection Development Guide

Fourth Edition

Sarah Flowers and Samuel Stavole-Carter

Foreword by Diana Tixier Herald

Genreflecting Advisory Series

LIBRARIES
UNLIMITED®
An Imprint of ABC-CLIO, LLC
Santa Barbara, California • Denver, Colorado

Copyright © 2020 by Sarah Flowers and Samuel Stavole-Carter

Library of Congress Cataloging-in-Publication Data

Names: Flowers, Sarah, 1952– author. | Stavole-Carter, Samuel, author. | Herald, Diana Tixier. Teen genreflecting.
Title: Teen genreflecting : a readers' advisory and collection development guide / Sarah Flowers and Samuel Stavole-Carter ; foreword by Diana Tixier Herald.
Description: Fourth edition. | Santa Barbara, California : Libraries Unlimited, [2020] | Series: Genreflecting advisory series | Includes index.
Identifiers: LCCN 2020006218 (print) | LCCN 2020006219 (ebook) | ISBN 9781440872723 (cloth) | ISBN 9781440872730 (ebook)
Subjects: LCSH: Young adult fiction, American—Bibliography. | Young adult fiction, American—Stories, plots, etc. | Fiction genres—Bibliography. | Teenagers—Books and reading—United States. | Young adults' libraries—Collection development—United States.
Classification: LCC Z1232 .H47 2020 PS374.Y57 (print) | LCC Z1232 PS374.Y57 (ebook) | DDC 016.813008/09283—dc23
LC record available at https://lccn.loc.gov/2020006218
LC ebook record available at https://lccn.loc.gov/2020006219

ISBN: 978-1-4408-7272-3 (hardcover)
      978-1-4408-7273-0 (ebook)

24 23 22 21 20   1 2 3 4 5

This book is also available as an eBook.

Libraries Unlimited
An Imprint of ABC-CLIO, LLC

ABC-CLIO, LLC
147 Castilian Drive
Santa Barbara, California 93117
www.abc-clio.com

This book is printed on acid-free paper ∞

Manufactured in the United States of America

Contents

Acknowledgments vii

Foreword by Diana Tixier Herald ix

Introduction xi

Chapter 1—Contemporary Life 1

  Identity 1

    Ethnic and Racial Identity 5

    Gender and Sexual Identity 8

    Faith 10

    Passions 13

      Art, Poetry, Writing 13

      Music 14

      Sports 16

      Theater and Dance 19

      Games 20

      Social and Political Activism 21

      Cooking 22

  Coming of Age 23

  Relationships 29

    Friends 29

    Families 33

      Teen Pregnancy and Parenting 37

      Fostering Arrangements 39

      Homelessness and Runaways 40

  Death, Disability, Disease 42

  Sarah's Picks 46

Chapter 2—Historical Fiction 47

  North American Historical Fiction 47

    North American Fiction before 1900 47

    20th-Century North America 52

  World Historical Fiction 60

    World Historical Fiction before 1900 60

    20th-Century World Historical Fiction 67

  Sam's Picks 75

Chapter 3—Romance 77

  Contemporary Romance 77

  Chick Lit 88

  LGBTQIA+ Romance 90

  Collections of Romance Short Stories 94

  Sarah's Picks 95

Chapter 4—Adrenaline 97
  Mystery 97
    Contemporary Mysteries 97
    Historical Mysteries 103
  Suspense 107
  Adventure/Thrillers 113
    Action-Adventure 114
    Survival Stories 115
    Espionage and Terrorism 118
  Sarah's Picks 123

Chapter 5—Speculative Fiction 125
  Paranormal and Horror 125
    Occult 126
    Ghosts 129
    Monsters 132
    Vampires, Werewolves, and Shapeshifters 135
    Zombies 142
    Witchcraft 145
    Unexplained Phenomena 148
    Superheroes 152
    Sam's Picks 154
  Science Fiction 154
    Action Adventure 155
    Bioengineering 159
    Virtual Reality 163
    Alternate Worlds and Parallel Worlds 165
    Steampunk 167
    Time Travel 169
    Aliens 170
    Utopia/Dystopia 172
    Postapocalyptic 177
    Sam's Picks 181
  Fantasy 181
    Epic 182
    Heroic 191
    Magic and Wizards 193
    World of Faerie 197
    Urban Fantasy 200
    Magical Realism and Mythic Reality 205
    Myth and Legend 209
    Fairy Tales 214
    Alternate and Parallel Worlds 215
    Sam's Picks 217

  Appendix A: Alternate Formats 219
  Appendix B: Multicultural Interest 223
  Author/Title Index 229
  Subject Index 247

Acknowledgments

First and foremost, we would like to thank Diana Tixier Herald, author of six books in the original *Genreflecting* franchise, and originator and author of the three previous *Teen Genreflecting* books. We are grateful to her for entrusting us with this book and for encouraging us along the way. Without all of her earlier work, this book would not have been possible. Thanks also to Di for providing information on teen book clubs (see Introduction) and writing the Foreword for this book.

Thanks to Emma Bailey at Libraries Unlimited for taking on this project after it had already started.

Thanks to the YA book industry—authors, publishers, agents, and editors—who keep us well supplied with engrossing, thoughtful, entertaining stories.

Foreword

If you have even been a parent, you know the trepidation one faces the first time you hand your baby off to someone else. Well, *Teen Genreflecting* was my "baby." Even though I wrote or worked on six editions of *Genreflecting*, I didn't conceive it or originally bring it into the world. That was done by the godmother of contemporary reader's advisory, Betty Rosenberg. I am so happy Sarah Flowers and Samuel Stavole-Carter were willing to take *Teen Genreflecting* up and carry it forward into the next decade.

As a child I had two obsessions: the first with reading and the second with teenagers. I wanted to be a teenager when I grew up. When I joined ALA, I discovered the only division that had any committees focused on the kinds of reading I love: science fiction, romance, fantasy, mystery, and horror. This was YASD, now YALSA. The most wonderful thing about YALSA was discovering the richness, humor, and beauty to be found in teen literature and the passionate, smart librarians who were connecting adolescent patrons in their libraries to those books.

My adolescence was difficult, and I survived it only because of books, libraries, and the librarians who helped me find the books that let me know I wasn't alone, that anything was imaginably possible, and that the future could be brighter than the past. That is why it is so important to connect teens to the books that may save them or may just make their day better or more interesting. Because it is an important mission, it is a real boon to have Sarah and Sam, two librarians who are experts not only in YA literature but also in connecting with teens, write this edition of *Teen Genreflecting*.

I first met Sarah Flowers in 2001 when we served on the YALSA preconference planning committee for a workshop called SF in SF. At that time, seeing actual teens at an ALA conference was fairly rare, but we decided that because the workshop was about speculative fiction—science fiction, fantasy, horror, and paranormal—for teens, we should also hear from teens. The teens also introduced the authors who were speaking. Sarah was one of the California librarians who brought knowledgeable, articulate teens for the panel. She not only was knowledgeable about YA lit but also had great organizational skills and a thorough understanding of and connection to teens.

When I rejoined the staff at Mesa County Libraries a couple of years ago, Sam Carter was working in youth services as a library assistant and attending library school. We bonded over a shared delight in science fiction and young adult lit. After he edited a few of the blog posts I wrote for the library's website, I asked him to team up with me on the eighth edition of *Genreflecting*, which was published in 2019.

I am thrilled that Sarah and Sam combined their skills and knowledge to bring forth a great guide that will help librarians, bookseller, teachers, and anyone else who wants to connect teens to the books they will find enjoyable.

While all genres change over time, with new ones emerging and others dropping in popularity, trends in the books teens read are especially volatile. Some erupt onto the scene and burn brightly for a time before flaming out almost overnight. This edition of *Teen Genreflecting* is quite different from the last edition, not only in that it features hundreds of new titles, but the organization corresponds to how today's teens are looking at what they like to read. Popular fiction reflects contemporary culture, and Sam and Sarah, with their connections to young adult readers, have organized this guide in a way that works for guiding today's readers to the books they need.

This edition reflects some of the very positive changes that have taken place in society and publishing since the first edition of *Teen Genreflecting* was published in 1997 with different categories and groupings.

Many of my personal favorite books of past years that are still popular are included, such as *Anna Dressed in Blood* by Kendare Blake, *Tithe* by Holly Black, Graham McNamee's *Acceleration*, *Anna and the French Kiss* by Stephanie Perkins, Kenneth Oppel's *Airborn*, and Angela Johnson's *First Part Last*, as well as the very best newly published books.

Be sure to read the introduction as it features smart insights into creating responsive young adult collections and providing teens with great reader's advisory service and programs. Readers will find books in these pages that reflect who they are and the world they inhabit, as well timeless adventures in other worlds. In addition to being a great overview of what teens enjoy reading, *Teen Genreflecting* is a great resource for experiencing the breadth and richness of genres of fiction. If you want to read in genres you don't regularly read, you will find Sarah's Picks and Sam's Picks at the ends of each chapter a great place to start.

Happy reading!

—Diana Tixier Herald

Introduction

Young adult or teen fiction continues to be one of publishing's biggest markets. Teen books are best sellers, they are being made into movies, and adults are reading them voraciously, as are the target audience of readers aged 12 to 18.

Today's Teen Readers

Today's teens fall into the post-Millennial or Gen Z generation. This is a large, diverse group and among the most ethnically and racially diverse in U.S. history. According to the Pew Research Center, over the whole age range (from 6 to 21) only 52% are non-Hispanic white, with 25% Hispanic, 14% black, 6% Asian, and 4% mixed race or other. Of course, those are only composite numbers. In many areas, the percentages may vary widely. In the San Francisco Bay Area, for example, for all age groups, according to the Association of Bay Area Governments (ABAG), about 41% are (non-Hispanic) white, with 24% Hispanic, 6% black, 24% Asian, and 5% in the ever growing category of "two or more races."

According to Pew, post-Millennials are on track to be the most highly educated generation. In part this is because their parents are more likely to have college degrees than people in earlier generations (43% of Gen Z kids have at least one parent with a bachelor's degree, compared with 32% of Millennials). Although only the first post-Millennials have finished high school, their completion rate (80%) is higher than that of previous generations.

About 65% of post-Millennials live in a household with two married parents, which is down slightly from earlier generations, but most of those are dual-earner households, with the result that their level of affluence is somewhat higher than previous generations'.

Fully 95% of teens now have access to a smartphone, according to a 2018 Pew Research Center report, and this crosses all gender, ethnic, racial, and socioeconomic lines. Interestingly, those of lower socioeconomic status are more likely to have a smartphone than to have access to a laptop or desktop computer at home. Some 45% of teens say they are online "almost constantly," and another 44% say they go online "several times a day." Half of girls are near-constant Internet users, compared to 39% of boys. Hispanic teens are more likely than whites (54% versus 41%) to claim "near-constant" Internet use. YouTube, Instagram, and Snapchat are the top online platforms for teens.

Teens and Reading

So what does that mean for reading? Well, as David Denby put it in a 2016 *New Yorker* article, "It's very likely that teenagers, attached to screens of one sort or another, read more *words* than they ever have in the past. But they often read scraps, excerpts, articles, parts of articles, messages, pieces of information from everywhere and from nowhere." But are they reading books? Certainly young adult books are selling as well as or better than ever, although some estimate that as many as 80% of young adult books are bought *by* adults *for* adults. According to a study by professors at San Diego State University, "In the 1970s, about 60 percent of high school seniors reported reading a book, magazine or newspaper every day. Four decades later, in 2016, 16 percent of high school seniors reported doing so."

Young adult books are being made into popular movies at a faster rate than ever. The year 2018 alone saw the release of movies based on Jenny Han's *To All the Boys I've Loved Before*, Becky Albertalli's *Simon vs. the Homo Sapiens Agenda* ("Love, Simon"), James Dashner's *Maze Runner: The Death Cure*, David Levithan's *Every Day*, Angie Thomas's *The Hate U Give*, Ernest Cline's *Ready Player One*, Julie Murphy's *Dumplin'*, Emily Danforth's *The Miseducation of Cameron Post*, *Between Shades of Gray* by Ruta Sepetys (*Ashes in the Snow*), and Philip Reeve's *Mortal Engines*.

Readers' Advisory for Teens

Joyce Saricks, the guru of readers' advisory and author of *Readers' Advisory Service in the Public Library*, says, "A successful readers' advisory service is one in which knowledgeable, nonjudgmental staff help fiction and nonfiction readers with their leisure-reading needs." Jessica Moyer and Kaite Mediatore Stover remind us, "Readers' advisory encompasses many different leisure reading formats and means of communication, and working with patrons of all types and ages, in and outside the library." Heather Booth says, "[Readers' advisory] is a skill that is part science, part art, with a healthy dash of mind reading."

All of those things are true, and readers' advisory with teens is even more complicated. For one thing, suggesting books for teens may involve more than leisure reading. Teens often have to read specific types of materials ("a science fiction book," "a novel in verse," "historical fiction," or something else) for school assignments, and helping them find a book that will meet their assignment needs while also appealing to them can be a challenge. Plus, readers' advisory with teens may often include suggestions of materials from the YA collection, the adult collection, and/or the children's collection, depending on the age and the abilities and interests of the teen. In addition, teens are open to a variety of formats, including print and e-books, graphic novels, audiobooks, podcasts, and more.

Young adult literature is a relatively new concept, just as "teenager" is a relatively new concept. Both ideas really began to flourish in the mid-20th century, when adolescents began to stay in school longer and live at home until they were in their late teens. The first YA books were primarily "problem novels"—realistic fiction that focused on the particular issues of adolescence, including coming of age and dealing with sex, alcohol, drugs, family situations, and other challenges. Today the field of young adult literature has expanded to include a vast array of fiction and nonfiction, and it covers every subject, genre, theme, and topic imaginable. In truth, the only thing that makes a book a "YA book" is the fact that its publisher has designated it for readers between the ages of, roughly, 12 and 18.

Diversity

A real challenge in readers' advisory with teens can be finding books and other materials that match the diversity of the community—or even materials that provide windows for local teens into diverse cultures. At various times, teens want to read about "people just like me" and about those whose lives they see as exotic and different. What those two extremes will look like will depend, naturally, on what the individuals themselves are like. Marc Aronson points out that in "the Jewish, black, and Hispanic high school I went to . . . there was nothing more exotic than Irish Catholics." However, most of the time, looking for diverse materials means looking for books that represent cultures and identities other than white, American, straight, and cisgender.

In June 2013, using statistics from the U.S. Census and the Cooperative Children's Book Center, Lee & Low Books demonstrated that while 37% of the U.S. population are people of color, only 10% of the roughly 3,500 children's books (including YA) that are published each year contain characters of color. What's more, in 2015, 60% of the books published about people of color were created by people outside of those cultures. Lee & Low Books has been tracking these numbers, which are showing some improvement. In 2018, they noted:

> Starting in 2014, the number of diverse books being published increased substantially. And in 2016, the number jumped to 28%. This year shows that number is steadily increasing, hitting 31%—now the highest year on record since 1994. Like 2016, there were major award wins for authors of color in 2017, including a Newbery Medal for Erin Entrada Kelly, a Newbery Honor for Jason Reynolds, Renée Watson, Derrick Barnes, and Gordon C. James, and a Morris Award and Printz Honor for Angie Thomas.

It is easy to fall into the trap of deciding that you do not need to be concerned about materials about an ethnic group or other identity because no one in your community fits that particular profile. But consider this story from author Matt de la Peña in his 2016 Newbery Medal acceptance speech:

> At one of the big national conferences, a librarian approached me outside an event space and excitedly introduced herself. "I want you to know," she told me, "that I really like your books. I mean, we don't have those kinds of kids at our school, so we don't stock many of them, but I want you to know how much I appreciate your work."
>
> "No, I totally get it, ma'am," I said. "Out of curiosity, though, how many wizards do you have at your school?"

The Whole Library (or Bookstore)

One of the interesting things about teens is that, unlike most children, who stay in the children's room, and most adults, who never venture out of the adult department, teens often freely use the entire library for both recreational and informational needs. Teens are neither children nor adults, but they have characteristics of both. This means that in doing readers' advisory with teens, it is not possible to focus on a single, small, teen collection. Rather we need to be aware of materials that teens may need or want and that may be found in every part of the library.

By the age of 12 or 13, many young people have already begun to read adult books. In many cases, the books they are assigned in school are books that were published for adults—books like *To Kill a Mockingbird*, *The Adventures of Tom Sawyer*, and Anne Frank's *Diary of a Young Girl*. Teens who like fantasy and science fiction are almost always reading adult books by their early teens, mainly because that's where they can find enough books to fill their need to read. Nonfiction readers are also moving to adult books by the early teenage years, although the recent surge in strong YA nonfiction is helping to fill that gap.

In addition, there is the relatively new genre of "new adult" fiction: stories that feature young people who are in college or newly out on their own. Some of these books are published as adult books; others are YA books, and their readership crosses over between adults and teens.

Teens may also still read from the children's section, especially if they are still following a favorite author. Think of the teens who started reading the *Harry Potter* books when they were 11 or 12 and followed the series through to its finish (and beyond!). They were well into college by the time the seventh book in the series came out, and even though many libraries shelved the book in the children's section, followers wouldn't have missed reading it for the world.

Approaches to Teens

If a teen approaches you to ask for help in finding a book, you're off to a good start. However, many teens are not even aware that library staff can help them find recreational materials, so be alert to signals that a teen is looking for something to read. If teens are wandering around the stacks, picking up books occasionally or talking about books with a friend or parent, they might be open to a discussion about other books to read. On the other hand, if a teen is engrossed in reading or in chatting with friends, avoids eye contact, or is otherwise sending "leave me alone" signals, back off until another time.

Generally speaking, though, you want to start a conversation, and that will give you a chance to think about books that might meet the teen's interests. Be aware of the teen's reactions during this conversation. Try to pick up on expressions of interest, but match your level of energy with theirs so that you don't scare them away.

Keep in mind, too, that teens go through a period, while the brain is growing and changing, in which they are less able than either adults or children to correctly gauge the emotions of others. This means they are not as good at decoding facial expressions and are more likely to regard your neutral face as "mean" or "angry." So it's important to present a friendly face to teens in the library, if you hope to be able to help them.

Some teens, especially boys, may find it difficult even to have a straightforward conversation about books in a face-to-face setting. These teens may be more comfortable sharing their thoughts and ideas if you are standing next to them instead of in front of them. If you are looking at the books and library materials instead of directly at the teen, he may find it less intimidating and invasive. Watch for nonverbal cues to help you determine the best approach.

Appeal

Anyone who has done readers' advisory work for any length of time is well aware that when a reader wants a book that is "like" another book, it is not enough to suggest a book on the same topic. Two books with the same catalog subject heading may be wildly different in terms of the "feel" of the book. This "feel" is what we mean when we talk about appeal.

There are many ways of looking at appeal. If you have ever been in a book discussion group, you are probably aware that people look for different things in a book. Some read only for plot and get bored by long descriptions of characters or places. Others love to be able to sink into a book's setting and are perfectly happy when not much happens. Others want to read a book only if it has characters that they can care about. Still others get most excited about a book that really makes them think—it looks at something in a new or different way, explores ideas, or speculates about life or the future in some way.

None of those factors have anything to do with the subject of a book. Markus Zusak's *The Book Thief* has a subject heading of "Death—Fiction" because the narrator of this book about the holocaust is Death. John Green's *Looking for Alaska* also has a subject heading of "Death—Fiction," both because a main character dies and because the narrator has an obsession with death. Yet these two books have very different appeal factors. Although both have strong characters, *The Book Thief* has a leisurely pace, and its tone is haunting and melancholy. *Looking for Alaska*, on the other hand, is more of a quick read, with a tone that is sometimes humorous, sometimes thoughtful, and always witty. In this book, we try to include both subjects and appeal factors in our descriptions and tags.

If a teen asks for help finding a particular book, you can also use that as an opportunity for some readers' advisory. Asking how they heard about the book can lead to an interesting conversation. If, for example, they are reading everything they can find by that particular author or on that particular topic, you have a chance to suggest similar authors or other books on the topic. If, on the other hand, it was a recommendation from a friend, you can ask whether the friend's recommendations are usually on target. If not, perhaps you can steer the teen toward something he or she would rather read.

Listening is an important part of the readers' advisory interview. As you are talking (and listening!), consider the following:

- Is the reader looking for a particular type of story, book genre, or topic?

- Does the reader want to achieve a certain mood (to cry, to laugh, to feel "warm and fuzzy")?

- Does the reader want to stay with the known or meet the unknown?

Don't assume you know what teens want, but keep them talking until you think you have a mutual understanding. Then, consider where to go next: the catalog, a tool like NoveList, annotated book lists, or just your own brain.

Once you have come up with a few books, it's time to back away. Let teens know that these are just suggestions and that they should feel free to take one or more but that they are under no obligation to take any of them. You can ask them to let you know later if they liked any of the books, but give them the time and the space to look at the items you've suggested. And don't be hurt if they just leave the entire stack of books on the table. Better luck next time!

Purpose and Audience of This Book

This guide is intended to help readers' advisors to connect readers who like teen or young adult literature to the books they will most enjoy. It organizes and describes more than 1,000 fiction titles by genre, subgenre, and theme, grouping them according to specific appeals and reading tastes. In addition to the annotations, you will also find subject and appeal and notes on the various genres.

This guide is not intended to be an all-inclusive compendium of authors who write genre fiction for teens. It is not a scholarly or historical treatise on the subject of young adult genre fiction. Nor is it meant to provide a comprehensive list of titles by specific authors. It is merely a guide to help readers' advisors and others understand the genres as they currently appear in young adult or teen fiction and assist readers to find the books they want to read. The authors hope that public and school librarians, educators, booksellers, and other adults who work with teen readers will find it a valuable professional resource.

Genre Blending or Mash-ups

Sorting books into genres gets more complicated all the time. In the past decade or so, there has been a real upsurge in books that do not fit neatly into any one genre. Historical romances and historical mysteries have been around for a long time, but paranormal romance took off with the *Twilight* series. Steampunk combines science fiction or fantasy with historical fiction. A book like *Code Name Verity* is historical fiction, a spy story, action-adventure, a mystery, suspense, and a story about friendship. In this book, the authors made subjective decisions about where to classify these mash-up or genre-blending books, but we have always tried to give you plenty of means to access them through the indexes and subject terms. In some cases, such books are listed in more than one section in order to emphasize the various appeal factors.

Scope, Selection, Criteria, and Methodology

Major fiction genres popular with readers of teen fiction are represented in this book, including contemporary fiction, historical fiction, speculative fiction, and more. It covers books published specifically for the teen audience, as well as books published for children and adult readers that are also popular with teens. Most of the titles in this book were published in the last 10 years, since the third edition of this book, but some classics and older but highly popular titles are included, as they are commonly available in library collections. Those interested in learning more about older titles are encouraged to consult the previous three editions of this guide.

New in This Edition

In addition to many, many new titles since the last edition of *Teen Genreflecting*, a few major organizational changes have been made. Certain "genres"—"Issues," "Alternate Formats," and "Multicultural"—were eliminated entirely. The authors felt that these were not really genres but rather appeal factors and topics that fit into various other genres. These have been noted in the annotations and subject headings. Formats such as verse novels, epistolary novels, and graphic novels are not in a separate section but rather included in their appropriate genres: contemporary, historical, fantasy, and so on. Likewise, diverse and multicultural fiction spans the genres of contemporary, historical, adrenaline, science fiction, and fantasy. As more and more diverse books are being published, it seemed unfair to relegate them to a single chapter. Likewise, "issues," such as death, abuse, bullying, and the like, cut across genres. Books featuring LGBTQIA+ (lesbian, gay, bisexual, trans, questioning/queer, intersex, asexual, and more) teens are now in the mainstream and appear in all genres. In fact, this edition now has a new subgenre for LBGTQIQ+ Romance.

Mystery, suspense, adventure, and thrillers have all been consolidated under the genre of adrenaline, with the individual types as subgenres. Likewise, science fiction, fantasy, and paranormal/horror are now subgenres under the overall genre of speculative fiction.

Organization and Features

As noted previously, the titles for this book are arranged according to genres, subgenres, and themes. The chapters, sections, and subsections are meant to group books with similar appeal together, so that users can readily identify readalikes. Chapters include broad sections for specific types, common themes, or both.

In many cases, an argument can be made to place a specific title in more than one category, and in some cases you will find the same book in more than one place. Obviously, the final decision of where to place a book in a guide like this involves some subjectivity. The judgments made here are based on publisher information and on the authors' personal experiences as readers' advisors. Indeed, in some cases, the same book appears in more than one genre, which the authors hope will improve the chances for the right reader to find the right book. Appendices of special lists and a detailed subject index provide additional access points for users.

Books in series are listed under the author's name and series title. In cases in which multiple authors have contributed to a series, the series is placed alphabetically by series title rather than by author. Individual titles within a series are placed in series (chronological) order, rather than alphabetical order, because readers usually wish to read the titles in series order.

Author, title, and original U.S. publication date are provided for all titles, along with an indication of interest level. Designations are used as follows:

> **M** middle school, grades 6 through 8
> **J** junior high school, grades 7 through 9

S   senior high school, grades 9 through 12

O   mature teens, senior high school, grades 11 and 12

These designations are based on reviews, library catalogs, and, again, personal experience and judgment. The overlap reflects the developmental pace of readers and rapidity of change at the younger end of adolescence. Users should also keep in mind that these designations are subjective. Often one resource recommends a title for grades 5 through 8, while another recommends the same title for ages 14 and up. It cannot be overemphasized that teens should read whatever they are comfortable with and whatever they find interesting and exciting, regardless of the assigned grade range.

Major awards and honors are one way to find the best of the best each year for different audiences. The following awards and honors are noted in the annotations:

Alex	The Alex Award is for books published for adults but of interest to teens. Ten titles are honored each year. Given by YALSA, the Young Adult Services Association, a division of the American Library Association (ALA).
Bloomer	The Amelia Bloomer Project, a committee of the Feminist Task Force of the Social Responsibilities Round Table of the American Library Association, compiles the Amelia Bloomer List, an annual annotated book list of well written and well illustrated books with significant feminist content, intended for young readers (ages birth through 18).
BBYA	Best Books for Young Adults is a list created by a committee of YALSA. The list was retired in 2010 and replaced by BFYA.
BFYA	Best Fiction for Young Adults is a yearly list created by a YALSA committee.
GGN	Great Graphic Novels for Teens is yearly list created by a YALSA committee.
Golden Kite	The Golden Kite Awards are given annually by the Society of Children's Book Writers and Illustrators to recognize excellence in children's literature.
Morris Award	The William C. Morris YA Debut Award goes to books by a first-time author, which are selected by a YALSA committee. It was first awarded in 2009.
Morris Finalist	One of the four runners-up to the Morris Award.
LA Times	The LA Times Books Prize–Young Adult Category is selected by a committee of authors and librarians and includes the winner and four short-listed finalists.

Printz Award and Honor Books   The Michael L. Printz Award, selected by a YALSA committee, goes to a book that exemplifies literary excellence in young adult literature. Up to four honor books are also selected.

Rainbow   The Rainbow Book List presents an annual bibliography of quality books with significant and authentic GLBTQ+ content, recommended for people from birth through 18 years of age. It is administered by the Rainbow Round Table (formerly the Gay, Lesbian, Bisexual, and Transgender Round Table) of the American Library Association.

Stonewall   The Stonewall Awards are presented to English language books that have exceptional merit relating to the gay/lesbian/bisexual/transgender experience. Selected by a committee of the Rainbow Round Table (formerly the Gay, Lesbian, Bisexual, and Transgender Round Table (GLBTRT)) of the American Library Association.

Walden   The Amelia Elizabeth Walden Award goes to a book that exemplifies literary excellence, widespread appeal, and a positive approach to life in young adult literature. Selected by a committee of the Assembly on Literature for Adolescents (ALAN) of the NCTE (National Council of Teachers of English), it was first awarded in 2009 and includes the award winner and four short-listed finalists.

The annotations also include mention of other awards that are not specifically for teen books or that have a narrower focus:

Coretta Scott King   This award recognizes outstanding books for young adults and children by African American authors and illustrators that reflect the African American experience. The award is administered by EMIERT, the Ethnic and Multicultural Information Exchange Round Table of the American Library Association.

Edgar   This is an annual award by the Mystery Writers Association for the young adult category.

Lambda   Lambda Awards are judged principally on literary merit and content relevant to lesbian, gay, bisexual, transgender, and queer lives, and there is a Children's/Young Adult category. A panel of literary professionals does the judging.

Mythopoeic   Awarded annually by the Mythopoeic Society, this award for children's literature considers books from picture books to young adult novels. It is occasionally awarded to an entire series rather than to individual books.

NBA   The National Book Award is awarded by the National Book Foundation and selected by a five-member panel of respected authors for each of four categories, one of which is Young Peoples' Literature. It includes the award winner and four short-listed finalists.

Norton Nebula   The Norton Nebula Andre Norton Award, first given in 2005, is awarded by the Science Fiction and Fantasy Writers of American for a young adult novel, as part of the Nebula Awards.

Schneider Family Book Awards   This award, administered by the American Library Association, honors an author or illustrator for a book that embodies an artistic expression of the disability experience for child and adolescent audiences.

Sydney Taylor Award   This is presented annually by the Association of Jewish Libraries to outstanding children and teen books that authentically portray the Jewish experience.

Other Resources for Finding Books Popular with Teen Readers

- **Book Riot** (bookriot.com): Book Riot is packed with articles, podcasts, videos, and more—in fact, probably far more than anyone could ever keep up with. Fortunately, you can filter the articles by genre, and they include young adult literature as a genre.

- **Epic Reads** (www.epicreads.com/books): Epic Reads is a great place to keep up on new YA books. The site includes information about new and upcoming books, plus lots of fun things like quizzes, booklists, readalikes, book trailers, and more.

- **The Hub** (www.yalsa.ala.org/thehub): The Hub is YALSA's Teen Literature blog. It contains reviews and analysis, readalike lists, and much more. It now also contains reviews of nominated titles for YALSA's selected lists: Best Fiction for Young Adults, Great Graphic Novels for Teens, Quick Picks for Reluctant Readers, and Selected Audiobooks.

- **No Flying, No Tights** (www.noflyingnotights.com): This is a graphic novel review site, featuring reviews from librarians of graphic novels for children, teens, and adults. They review only graphic novels that are available to libraries via standard library book jobbers, such as Baker & Taylor, Ingram, and Follett. They also have staff picks for various ages and lists of "Must Haves" and "Classic Fantastic."

- **Stacked** (stackedbooks.org): Stacked is a blog by a YA librarian and former YA librarian that does a good job of keeping up-to-date on YA books and providing in-depth looks at YA literature. One especially nice feature is the frequent lists of upcoming debut novels.

- **Teen Reads** (www.teenreads.com): Teen Reads is part of the online "magazine" *The Book Report Network*. It contains reviews and articles of YA books, author interviews, polls, contests, and more. Teen Reads has a Teen Board of about 30 teens from around the United States who write reviews, submit blog posts, and answer questions.

- **Teen Services Underground's Booklists** (www.teenservicesunderground.com /features/booklists): Booklists are contributed by librarians who work with teens. The website also includes a section with tips and techniques for doing readers' advisory with teens.

- **We Need Diverse Books** (weneeddiversebooks.org): A great first stop in the search for diverse books, WNDB is, in their words, "a grassroots organization of children's book lovers that advocates essential changes in the publishing industry to produce and promote literature that reflects and honors the lives of all young people." The website contains a wealth of resources for librarians and others who are looking for books about diverse cultures, ethnicities, sexual identities, genders, disabilities, and more. They link to review sources and maintain a blog to discuss current issues and new books.

- **YALSA's Book Awards and Booklists** (www.ala.org/yalsa/bookawards /booklists/members): Selected by YALSA members, these lists are essential for anyone selecting teen materials or doing readers' advisory with teens. YALSA also has a searchable database of all of its awards and selected lists, called the Teen Bookfinder (http://booklists.yalsa.net).

- **We Are Kid Lit Collective** (https://wtpsite.wordpress.com): The Collective creates an annual summer reading list of books by and about IPOC (Indigenous and People of Color), people with disabilities, and people from the LGBTQIA+ communities.

Journals

All of the standard print review journals include reviews of teen books, including graphic novels and books published for adults but with appeal to teens. Keeping up with journal reviews is one of the best ways to expand your knowledge of teen books. Journals to follow include *Booklist*, *The Horn Book*, *Kirkus Reviews*, *Publisher's Weekly*, *School Library Journal*, and *VOYA* (*Voice of Youth Advocates*).

Databases

Your library may subscribe to some readers' advisory databases. It is worthwhile to explore these and learn how to use them effectively. EBSCO's NoveList database, BookBrowse, and Booklist Online all allow searching by various settings, genres, and subjects. NoveList has a K–8 version as well as NoveList Plus, which includes both adult and YA books. NoveList Plus gives you the opportunity to search using appeal factors. The content is definitely more robust when it comes to adult books, but it can be a good starting place for YA books too.

Book Clubs for Teens: A Special Feature by Diana Tixier Herald

Choose Your Own Book Clubs

The best way to discover the stories, authors, and genres that really impact teen readers are to talk to teen readers and build professional relationships around their reading interests. Teen book clubs that give the readers the opportunity to freely choose what they read is a great way to build those relationships and garner the most up-to-date information on the current reading interests of adolescents in your community.

Book clubs provide a forum for participants to talk to one another about the books that excite them, bore them, or fascinate them. It opens up a way to learn the language of describing books in ways that enable others to understand the reader's experience. Book clubs also allow readers to communicate with a larger community about their likes and dislikes by posting reviews that may be shared in a library's blog, on a website, and even sometimes in print. If teens' opinions are shared with members of book award or notable books committees, they can even have an impact on the broader world of what books are found in bookstores and libraries. Book clubs can give validation and power to the opinions of teens, something teens do not always have other avenues to reach.

Starting a Teen Book Club

Working the desk in the teen or children's area of the library is the first step in meeting possible participants. People like to be asked their opinions, and many teens are more than happy to provide them. Surveys can also be popular with potential club members. When you encounter a teen (or soon to be teen, anyone of middle school or high school age) ask whether they would be interested in sharing their book recommendations with other teens and librarians. Ask what would be convenient meeting times, and, when you find a time and day that works best for those who answered, start your publicity for the first meeting. Personally invite to the first meeting every teen you talked to in the weeks leading up to it. If you are in a public library, contact school librarians; if you are starting your club in a school, notify all the teachers and counselors, and ask them to extend invitations to students they suspect may be interested. Some avid readers have never interacted with library staff, or even discovered the school library, but teachers or counselors may know who they are.

Another great way to promote your book club is to take your show on the road. Visiting schools to book-talk and get students excited about books is a great time to invite readers. Book-talking to teens in shelters and other youth facilities is another great outreach opportunity to find additional book club members.

It is important to emphasize to potential participants that it is a no-stress book club. The purpose is to have fun with reading. It is all about choice. Readers pick what they want to read. Nobody is required to read specific books. Readers are invited to come to all the meetings they can but not to worry on the occasions they cannot attend, even if they will be out for several weeks for play practice, a sports season, or other activity.

Carrots to induce teens to attend may include the opportunity to win ARCs (advance reader copies) of books they review, the opportunity to have their reviews published in the library or on the library website, or even just first crack at reading new books purchased for the collection before they go out on the shelves for the general public. Snacks are another enticement that often encourage teens who are hanging out in the library to join in.

Have a book truck or table full of books. Librarians who attend conferences often have ARCs to make available, but new books from the library collection or even old favorites can be used.

Keys to Success

Start out with clear expectations. We start our book clubs stating our goals and expectations.

Goal of the Book Club

- Celebrate the joy of reading in the company of other readers.

- Share books we like.

- Discover books we want to read.

Rules of the Book Club

- Respect one another.

- No two people ever read the same book. Reading is a personal interpretation of the marks on a page (or screen) made by the writer. So everyone's opinion about a book is valid, and a book isn't good or bad but is a different experience for each reader and affects each one differently.

- Reading is a creative exercise. Readers turn letters and words into the world they imagine it to be. As Mo Willems has said many times, "I only write 49 percent of the book and the audience puts in the rest."

- "Never apologize for your reading tastes," says Betty Rosenberg.

- If you start reading a book and aren't enjoying it, *stop*! There are too many books you will love to waste time on one you don't like. (Caveat: This only applies to pleasure reading, not to books required for class or work.)

- Take more books than you think you can finish in case you discover you aren't enjoying one or are not in the mood for it.

Agenda Example

- State the goal.

- State the rules.

- Participants introduce themselves (often mentioning their preferred pronouns).
- The facilitator book-talks a YA title.
- Participants are invited to book-talk a title.
- Participants are offered tablets to write reviews.
- The facilitator makes general announcements.
- There is time for book browsing.
- Socializing is definitely encouraged.

Book Review Form

It's easy to create a Google Form and see results in Google Sheets, but paper forms work well too. If you have a supply of ARCs or review copies, they are a great enticement as prizes for teens writing reviews.

Information to Request on the Review Form

- **Reader's name or alias**: For confidentiality, especially when publishing reviews, use only the reader's first name, initials, or an alias.
- **Grade**: It's easy to set up radio buttons with grade levels included in your book club.
- **E-mail**: This will be confidential and not be shared. It will be used only on rare occasions by the librarian to contact you about your reviews. (I added this question after being contacted by publishers about quoting teen reviews in publicity materials, articles, or books about YA literature.)
- **Author**
- **Title**
- **Publisher**
- **Publication Year**
- **Review**: Please write a review of the book. You might include in your review whether you would recommend this book, what the most compelling aspect of it is, and/or what makes it good. Be sure your comments don't 'spoil' the book!
- **How would you rate this book?** (The following scale was originally adapted from a scale used by Adela Peskorz with her teen book clubs.)
  - 5 = Hard to imagine a better book
  - 4 = Better than most
  - 3 = Readable
  - 2 = Needs work
  - 1 = How did it ever get published?
  - Additional Comments: Anything else you want to say?

- **I would like a copy of this book**: [Radio buttons for yes or no] Make sure your review tells why you like the book enough to be entered in a drawing to win a copy.

Rewards of Reviewing

Reviewing books for Choose Your Own Book Clubs has many benefits for teen reviewers. In addition to honing their writing skills, it allows them to share their opinions with others. When the reviews are used by someone serving on an award or notables committee, it is a community service to teen readers across the continent who will benefit from books added to library collection because of the lists and awards. Some schools with community service requirements have given students credit for the reviews submitted.

Occasionally, when shared on social media with the author or publisher tagged, a response will turn up. What teens don't love it when a favorite author responds to, shares, or retweets their comments?

Benefits for Librarians and Book Sellers

By hosting a teen book club, you have a built-in focus group that helps identify current trends in what teens like to read, authors rising in popularity, debut novels that resonate with readers, and much more. The information is not only useful for collection development but also for identifying various genres and subgenera for reader's advisory.

How to Use This Guide

This guide may be used in a number of ways. Perhaps the most common way is in identifying readalike books. Books with similar characteristics and themes are grouped together. When the reader is looking for another book just like the one he or she has read, look for the title in the title index, and you'll find similar titles in the same section. Once the user finds a genre or subgenre of interest, a quick scan of the annotation indicates whether a specific title will be of interest to the reader. Additionally, the subject index and the appendices will be useful starting places. There are two appendices:

Appendix A. Alternate Formats: Verse, graphic, epistolary, scrapbook, and so on.

Appendix B. Multicultural Titles: Listed in the book under their appropriate genre but collected in a list here: Latinx interest, black interest, Asian interest, international.

Of course, the book may also be used to familiarize readers' advisors with genre fiction for young adults. Book lists and narrative material help clarify the genres and the books and authors they contain.

Librarians wishing to expand their genre fiction collections for teens may find some of the newest and most popular titles in this guide. It may also be used as a source for book lists, displays, and other passive readers' advisory techniques. Whatever the specific application, this book should be used to share the joy of reading and books.

Closing

Use this guide to put teens together with the books that they will enjoy, that will entertain them, make them laugh or cry or shiver, that will help them shape their own lives. Use this guide to find books you will enjoy, and remember that not all readers of teen lit are teens. More and more adults are finding the pleasures of tightly plotted novels published as teen novels. Good books are good books, no matter the originally intended audience. So we hope that this book will help you share the pleasures of teen books with everyone—teens and adults alike.

References

Aronson, Marc. *Exploding the Myth: The Truth About Teenagers and Reading.* Scarecrow Press, 2001.

Booth, Heather. *Serving Teens through Readers' Advisory.* ALA, 2007.

De La Peña, Matt. "2016 Newbery Acceptance Speech." *The Horn Book,* June 27, 2016. (https://www.hbook.com/?detailStory=2016-newbery-acceptance-by-matt -de-la-pena.) Accessed August 16, 2019.

Gilmore, Natasha. "Nielson Summit Shows the Data behind the Children's Book Boom." *Publishers Weekly,* September 15, 2015. (https://www.publishersweekly .com/pw/by-topic/childrens/childrens-industry-news/article/68083-nielsen -summit-shows-the-data-behind-the-children-s-book-boom.html.) Accessed August 16, 2019.

Lee & Low Books. "The Diversity Gap in Children's Book Publishing, 2018." (https:// blog.leeandlow.com/2018/05/10/the-diversity-gap-in-childrens-book -publishing-2018/#more-15863.) Accessed August 16, 2019.

Moyer, Jessica, and Kaite Mediatore Stover, eds. *The Readers' Advisory Handbook.* ALA, 2010.

Saricks, Joyce. *Readers' Advisory Service in the Public Library,* 3rd ed. ALA, 2005.

Chapter 1

Contemporary Life

The books in this chapter are often called *realistic fiction* or *mainstream fiction*. This genre is characterized by a recognizable contemporary setting with situations the reader can actually see happening. Sometimes, as in *I Woke Up Dead at the Mall*, by Judy Sheehan, the premise falls outside contemporary reality, but readers identify with the realistic setting despite the fantastical premise. This genre features teen protagonists trying to live their lives and figure out who they are and who they want to be. This genre also includes novels about "issues"—from learning disabilities to drugs, from death to stepparents.

Readers who like contemporary fiction often also enjoy *romance fiction* that takes place in the identifiable here and now.

Identity

Finding one's identity is one of the primary jobs of the teenage years. Adolescence is a time of trying on new personas, trying out new ideas, and forming new relationships. Some teens have a hard time figuring out who they are, while others just sail through. Sometimes one's identity is tied closely to one's ethnic or racial background, gender or sexual identity, or faith.

Acevedo, Elizabeth.

The Poet X. 2018. 9780062662804. **J** **S**

Xiomara is a Dominican American girl who lives in Harlem. She feels that no one understands her, especially her mother, who insists that Xiomara go to Confirmation classes at their parish church. Xiomara writes her thoughts in a battered journal she carries around with her. Then she is invited to join her school's slam poetry club, and she begins to find new ways to express herself, even though it means hiding her true self from Mami. (BFYA, Printz Award, NBA, LA Times)

Subjects: Catholic Church; Faith; New York, Harlem; Slam Poetry; Verse Novels

Alexander, Kwame, with Mary Rand Hess.

Solo. 2017. 9780310761839. **J** **S**

Blade Morrison is the son of an aging rock star who spends more time in rehab than he does making music. Blade is himself a musician and songwriter, but he wants nothing more than to get away from his father and go to college across the continent—especially when his dad shows up wasted at Blade's high school graduation. Blade's sister Storm is also trying to make it as a musician, and their mother died when Blade was seven. But when his sister reveals that he was adopted as a baby, Blade sets out for Ghana to find his birth mother and figure out who he really is.

Subjects: Adoption; African Americans; Fathers and Sons; Ghana; Hollywood; Rock Music

Ali, S. K.

Saints and Misfits. 2017. 9781481499248. **J** **S**

Janna considers herself a misfit. Her mother seems to prefer Janna's older brother, Muhammed, a college student who is about to marry the perfect Muslim girl, "Saint Sarah." Her father has moved away and remarried, and he thinks Janna is overdoing it by wearing hijab. She is falling for a non-Muslim boy, who seems to like her back, but she isn't sure how being with him could work. And most of all, she is suffering after being attacked at a party by the cousin of a friend, a young man who everyone else thinks is a pillar of the Muslim community. Relationships with an elderly Indian man, her new soon-to-be sister-in-law, a kind young man, and a niqabi friend all help Janna find her voice and her place in the world. (Morris Finalist, BFYA, Bloomer)

Subjects: Family; Friends; #MeToo; Muslims; Sexual Abuse

Benway, Robin.

Audrey, Wait! 2008. 9781595141927. **J** **S**

Audrey used to date Evan, who is in a band called the Do-Gooders. When Audrey breaks up with Evan, Evan is inspired to write "Audrey, Wait!" aka "The Song" that changes Audrey's life forever. Audrey never wanted to be famous, but now she has people discussing her life on Internet message boards and following her around with cameras. Singers from other bands want to date her, just for the song inspiration. Audrey is quickly losing control of her life. What Audrey needs is to learn to start making her own choices, and with the help of her best friend Victoria and the guy she works with at the Scooper Dooper, James (why did she never notice him before?), she just might make it through her more than 15 minutes of fame.

Subjects: Fame; Rock Music

Dessen, Sarah.

What Happened to Goodbye. 2011. 9780142423837. **S**

McLean is constantly reinventing herself, every time she and her father move. She has been Beth, and Eliza, and Lizbet, and Liz. But now that her father has started up a new restaurant in Lakeview, she almost accidentally gives her real name to the boy next door, which is just the start in building a whole new community and finding her own place in the world. (BFYA)

Subjects: Divorce; Friends; High School; North Carolina; Restaurants

Gilbert, Kelly Loy.

Conviction. 2015. 9781423197386. **J** **S**

Sixteen-year-old Braden lives in the Central Valley with his Dad, who is a popular Christian radio host. Braden is a star pitcher on his high school team. He has a brother, Trey, who is about 10 years older and who has not had anything to do with Braden or his father in years. Then Braden's father is arrested for aggravated first-degree manslaughter in the death of a police officer and held without bail. Trey comes back to stay with Braden. As he awaits his father's trial, Braden has the opportunity to examine his relationships with his father, with Trey, with a girl, with baseball, and with God. These relationships often play off one another as he begins to realize how his relationship with his father affects his relationship with Trey and how his feelings about God affect his feelings about baseball. (Morris Finalist, BFYA)

Subjects: Baseball; Brothers; California; Fathers and Sons; Religion

Lockhart, E.

The Disreputable History of Frankie Landau-Banks. 2008. 978078683189.
J **S**

Turning gorgeous and curvy during the summer between her freshman and sophomore years, Frankie attracts the attention of Matthew, a popular senior. When she discovers he is a member of an all-male secret society at their elite boarding school, she figures out a way to infiltrate it. (BBYA, Printz Honor, NBA)

Subjects: Boarding Schools; Pranks; Secret Societies

Moskowitz, Hannah, and Kat Helgeson.

Gena/Finn. 2016. 978145213898. **S**

Gena, a senior at a posh boarding school and Finn, newly graduated from college, are both members of the fandom for *Up Below*, a television show about two firefighters named Jake and Tyler. Gena (Genevieve) and Finn (Stephanie) are both "Jake girls" who have made names for themselves on the fan boards. Their e-mails, texts, fanfiction, and blog posts reveal information about their lives bit by bit. For each of them, the fandom is important but not really integrated with their "real" lives, and they are drawn more and more to each other. Their relationship intensifies, and they both struggle to figure out what it means to "love" the person on the other side of the computer. Meanwhile, their real lives begin to get more complicated, as they meet in person, and as Gena's mental health issues and Finn's relationship with her boyfriend begin to intrude on Gena and Finn's fan-based rapport. These two young women are growing up and struggling to figure out who they are and what is important in their lives and learning that the answers aren't necessarily easy or clear-cut. (Rainbow)

Subjects: College; Epistolary Novels; Fanfiction; LGBTQIA+; Mental Illness

Murphy, Julie.

Puddin'. 2018. 9780062418388. **J** **S**

In this companion novel to Murphy's *Dumplin'* (see Chapter 3), Willowdean's classmates Millie and Callie tell the story in alternating chapters. Millie is giving up on fat camp (not that it ever worked anyway) and applying to a broadcast journalism program at The University of Texas at Austin. Callie hopes to become captain of Clover City's dance team and make it to a big tournament. When Millie's family's boxing gym can't afford to continue to sponsor the dance team, Callie and others vandalize the gym. When Callie is caught, she is sentenced to work at the gym alongside Millie. As the girls get to know each other, they come to see that each is more complex than the other had realized.

Subjects: Body Image; Dance; Friendship; Journalism; Texas

Norton, Preston.

Neanderthal Opens the Door to the Universe. 2018. 9781484790625. **J** **S**

Cliff is known as Neanderthal because of his size—a hulking 6-foot 6 inches. He doesn't really have any friends at school and has been more or less alone since his older brother's suicide. But now he has been approached by the popular and uber-cool Aaron Zimmerman, quarterback and big man on campus at Happy Valley High School (HVHS). But then Aaron is injured in a football game, is in a coma for a few days, and when he returns to school, he approaches Cliff with an astonishing claim: While in the coma, he saw God, and God gave Aaron a list of things that need to change at HVHS. Oh, and God also told Aaron that Cliff is supposed to help him. Cliff isn't too sure about this, but Aaron is persistent, and Cliff is certainly in agreement that some things about HVHS need to change. So he is drawn into Aaron's crusade, which ultimately causes his whole life to change. (BFYA)

Subjects: Family; Faith; Friends; Grief; LGBTQIA+; Suicide

Rubin, Lance.

Crying Laughing. 2019. 9780525644682. **J** **S**

Winnie Friedman was raised on comedy. Her father is a former comedian who, as a stay-at-home dad, made sure that Winnie saw every classic comedy routine and movie. The two of them trade quips constantly. But after a disastrous attempt at stand-up comedy at her Bat Mitzvah, Winnie is determined never to perform in public. Then Evan, by all accounts the funniest guy in school, laughs at Winnie's lunch-line comments and suggests that she join the school's improv troupe. Winnie decides to take the leap, but at almost the same moment, her dad is diagnosed with ALS—not funny in the least. As Winnie explores improv, she begins to learn what really matters to her, and her friendships and her family relationships shift and change.

Subjects: ALS; Comedy; Fathers and Daughters; Humor; Improv

Smith, Jennifer E.

Windfall. 2017. 9780399559372 **J** **S**

Alice and Teddy have been friends since they were nine, when Alice's parents died and she came to live with her aunt and uncle and cousin Leo. Leo, Teddy, and Alice are best friends, although Alice is also secretly in love with Teddy. For his 18th birthday, during their senior year, Alice buys Teddy a lottery ticket. When the ticket brings home $140 million, life changes for all of them.

Subjects: Chicago; Lottery

Solomon, Rachel Lynn.

You'll Miss Me When I'm Gone. 2018. 9781481497732. **J** **S**

Adina and Tovah are twins, but they don't have much in common anymore. Tovah finds comfort in their Jewish faith; Adina rebels against it. Tovah wants to be a scientist; Adina is a viola player. Tovah is shy; Adina is outgoing. And now that they are turning 18, an even bigger divide awaits them: Tovah wants to take the test that will tell them if they have inherited their mother's Huntington's disease. Adina would just as soon not know, but she promised Tovah they would find out together. They have always competed with one another, argued with one another, and tried to emphasize their differences. Now they really are different, as one twin has the disease and the other doesn't. The news pushes them farther apart but also helps them accept their differences. (Sydney Taylor Honor)

Subjects: Huntington's Disease; Israelis; Jews; Self-Harm; Sisters; Viola Players

Ethnic and Racial Identity

Dealing with ethnic and racial identity can be a major issue in life and one that many teens must deal with. Especially when their racial or ethnic background conflicts with that of the society in which they live, teens are forced to look more deeply into their own backgrounds to discover who they are and how they will live.

Capó Crucet, Jennine.

Make Your Home among Strangers. 2015. 9781250059666. **O**

Lizet is the daughter of Cuban immigrants and the first in her family to attend college—and it's not Miami–Dade Community College, either; it's Rawlings College, an elite liberal arts school in upstate New York, where Lizet has received a full scholarship. While Lizet is away from home, experiencing snow for the first time and finding out just how poorly Hialeah Lakes High School has prepared her for higher education, her family and her boyfriend Omar continue their lives in Miami and don't understand what Lizet is doing. Lizet's trips home at Thanksgiving, Christmas, and Easter reveal the growing distance between where she came from and where she is now, and she realizes she must decide whether she wants to make her home among strangers.

Subjects: College; Cuban Americans; Family; First-Generation College Students; Latinx; New York State; Miami

Gilbert, Kelly Loy.

Picture Us in the Light. 2018. 9781484726020. **S**

Danny Cheng is a second-generation Chinese American teen, living in Cupertino, California. He is an artist, and he is thrilled not only to have been accepted to the Rhode Island School of Design but also that his parents approve of his art. Unlike many of his Chinese American friends' parents, they are not pushing him into a tech career. Then he uncovers a box in the closet that seems to indicate that his parents are not who he thinks they are. At the same time, Danny is dreading going away to school without his best friend, Harry Wong. Harry seems perfectly happy with his girlfriend—but is he really? And can Danny go off to college with all this still hanging? (LA Times, BFYA, Stonewall)

Subjects: Art; Chinese Americans; Cupertino, California

Khorram, Adib.

Darius the Great Is Not Okay. 2018. 9780525552963. **J** **S**

Darius is so-called Fractional Persian: his mother is from Iran, but his father is the "Teutonic Ubermensch Steven Kellner." Darius's grandfather in Iran is not doing well, and the whole family goes to spend an extended spring break there. Darius struggles with his disapproving father, his own clinical depression, and the fact that his little sister Laleh speaks much better Farsi than he does. But once in Iran, Darius begins to find out more about his family and himself. He also meets Sohrab, the boy next door, who helps Darius feel like a "True Persian" for the first time. (Morris Award, BFYA, Rainbow)

Subjects: Depression; Grandparents; Iran; LGBTQIA+; Persian Americans

Quintero, Isabel.

Gabi, a Girl in Pieces. 2014. 981935955948. **J** **S**

Gabi's life is somewhat messy, and she chronicles her senior year in a journal. Gabi's dad is a meth addict; her mom worries that Gabi is becoming "too white"; her best friend Cindy is about to become a statistic: Hispanic Teen Mom #3,789,258; her other best friend Sebastian has just come out as gay, which was far from a surprise to Gabi but which caused his parents to kick him out of the house. Through poetry and food and friends, Gabi finds a way to express herself as a whole person, both Mexican and American. (Morris Award, Bloomer, BFYA)

Subjects: Family; Friends; Latinx; LGBTQIA+; Mexican Americans; Pregnancy; Rape

Sánchez, Erika.

I Am Not Your Perfect Mexican Daughter. 2015. 9781524700485. **J** **S**

Julia knows what she wants: She wants to write. She wants to leave Chicago, go away to college, and major in English. What she doesn't want is to stay at home, get work in an office somewhere, and be the "perfect Mexican daughter." But when her older sister Olga is killed in a traffic accident, Julia is the only one left to fulfill her mother's dreams. Julia doesn't understand her mother's life, and Ama doesn't seem to understand that Julia is grieving too but processing her grief in a very different way. When Julia discovers that Olga may have had a secret life that neither she nor Ama knew about, she is compelled to find out more. After an attempt at self-harm lands Julia in the hospital, she is sent to Mexico for a month, where she learns a lot about her parents and their struggles and begins to come to terms with who she is. (NBA Finalist, BFYA)

Subjects: Chicago; Depression; Grief; Mexican Americans; Mexico; Sisters

Stone, Nic.

Dear Martin. 2017. 9781101939499. **J S**

African American seventeen-year-old Justyce McAllister goes to a mostly white prep school and is college bound. But when he is arrested (by a white cop) while helping a friend, he begins to examine his life and where he fits in the intersection between his black neighborhood and his white school. The third-person narrative is interspersed with Justyce's journal, in which he writes letters to Dr. Martin Luther King Jr. as a way to explore his thoughts about race and society.

Subjects: African Americans; #BlackLivesMatter; Boarding Schools; Letters; Police Brutality; Racism

Thomas, Angie.

The Hate U Give. 2017. 9780062498533. **J S**

Starr knows how to code-switch. At home she's Garden Heights Starr, living in a poor black neighborhood where her parents grew up. At school she's another Starr, one of the few black kids in a mostly white suburban school, changing the way she talks. But one night she is at a party in Garden Heights and meets up with a childhood friend, Khalil. Violence erupts at the party, so Khalil takes Starr home, but on their way he is pulled over and, when he reaches for a hairbrush, is shot and killed by a white police officer. As the only witness, Starr is suddenly thrust into the spotlight of a case that quickly becomes not just local but national news. She finds herself trying to decide what, if anything, to say, as well as how—or whether—to continue to live these two different lives. (Printz Honor, BFYA, Morris Award, NBA Finalist, LA Times Finalist, Walden Award, Film)

Subjects: #BlackLivesMatter; Family; Gun Violence; Police Brutality

Yang, Kelly.

Front Desk. 2019. 9781338157796. **M**

Mia Tang and her parents are recent immigrants from China, having arrived in the early 1990s. After some effort, they obtain a job managing a motel, where Mia often runs the front desk because her English is better than that of her parents and because they are busy cleaning rooms. The motel's owner, Mr. Yao, is also Chinese, but he is cruel and exploitative. Mia, who wants to be a writer, faces bullying and racism at school, where the only other Chinese American is Mr. Yao's son. But with determination and hard work, the family manages to make a living, as well as help other immigrant families.

Subjects: California; Chinese Americans; Immigration; Motels; Racism

Yoon, David.

Frankly in Love. 2019. 9781984812209. **J S**

Frank Li's Korean immigrant parents want Frank and his sister to stay close to their Korean roots. When Frank's older sister dated—and then married—a black man, they disowned her. Now Frank wants to date a white girl but doesn't want to deal with the backlash. So he makes a deal with Joy, one of the girls in their Korean American social group, who is in a similar situation: the two of them will pretend to date in order to appease their parents, but it will only be a cover for their real dates. The only problem is that Frank starts to realize that he likes Joy a whole lot better than the girl he thought he wanted to date.

Subjects: Dating; Immigrants; Korean Americans; Southern California

Yoon, Nicola.

The Sun Is Also a Star. 2016. 9780553496680. **J** **S**

Natasha is a scientist at heart, but today she is trying to keep from being deported to Jamaica. She has lived in New York almost her whole life, albeit without proper documentation. Daniel is a child of South Korean immigrants; his parents want him to become a doctor, but he knows he's really a poet. Somehow they end up spending most of the day together, moving around New York City, falling in love while each learns about the other's—as well as his or her own—ethnic background. (Printz Honor, BFYA, TTT, CSK Steptoe, Walden Finalist)

Subjects: Deportation; Jamaican Americans; Korean Americans; New York; Poetry

Gender and Sexual Identity

What does it mean to be a boy? A girl? What if you are attracted to the opposite sex, the same sex, both, or neither? What if you have both male and female body parts? Who one is and whom one is attracted to are a huge part of teen identity. The books in this section deal with teens who explore those issues. Some are proactively exploring because of its importance in their lives. Others have the exploration thrust upon them, like Kristin in *None of the Above*, who learns in her senior year of high school that she is intersex—that is, although she appears to be a girl, she has male chromosomes.

The teens in these stories are dealing with who they are, finding their own identity in the context of gender and sex. Other stories about LGBTQIA+ teens can be found in Chapter 3, Romance, and in the index.

Brown, Jaye Robin.

Georgia Peaches and Other Forbidden Fruit. 2016. 9780062270986. **S**

When Joanna (Jo) moves with her preacher father and his new wife from Atlanta to rural Georgia, she reluctantly agrees to stay in the closet so as not to upset the new in-laws. Jo has always been out and proud and in fact hopes ultimately to work with other queer Christian teens. What she doesn't anticipate is falling for a girl at her new school, someone who is just beginning to acknowledge her own sexuality. Dealing with her faith, her sexuality, family pressures, and school all mean it's a complicated year for Jo. (Rainbow)

Subjects: Evangelical Christians; Faith; LGBTQIA+; Georgia

Deaver, Mason.

I Wish You All the Best. 2019. 9781338306125. **S**

Ben is starting over in a new town and a new school. Ben came out to their parents as nonbinary, and their parents kicked them out. So Ben is living with their older sister and her husband—a sister Ben hasn't seen in 10 years and a brother-in-law Ben has never met. Ben isn't quite ready to come out to the whole world yet, so they are dealing with meeting new people who unintentionally misgender them. Still, the alternative seems worse. But a good therapist, a caring sister and brother-in-law, an online nonbinary buddy, and some wonderful new friends all help Ben come to terms with who they are. And one of those new friends, Nathan, may turn out to be more than just a friend to Ben.

Subjects: Art; LGBTQIA+; Nonbinary; North Carolina; Parents; Siblings

Girard, M.-E.

Girl Mans Up. 2016. 9780062404176. **S**

Pen doesn't really fit any of the stereotypes about gender. She dresses mostly "like a boy," to the displeasure of her Portuguese immigrant parents, but she doesn't want to be "that girl" either. As she struggles with finding her identity, she also must deal with mockery, with bullying, and maybe even with falling in love. (Morris Finalist, Bloomer, BFYA, Rainbow, Lambda)

Subjects: Bullying; LGBTQIA+; Nonbinary; Portuguese Americans

Gregorio, I. W.

None of the Above. 2015. 9780062335319. **J** **S**

What do you do when you don't fit in? What do you do when you don't fully belong to a certain category? Kristin is a teenager when she goes to the doctor and finds out that she is intersex. She was born with typical male (XY) chromosomes and internal testes—instead of ovaries and a uterus. But on the outside she appears typically female. What makes a real woman? What if the biggest difference between boys and girls is how people treat them, like what color parents think their children should wear, what kinds of activities they sign up their kids for in kindergarten. How do you live when everyone thinks life is a multiple-choice question—male or female—and you're none of the above? (Lambda)

Subjects: Intersex; LGBTQIA+

King, A. S.

Ask the Passengers. 2012. 9780316194686. **J** **S**

Astrid Jones lives in small town called Unity Valley, a small town in Pennsylvania that lives up to its name by valuing conformity. Astrid has never been crazy about living there, but now that she's been secretly dating a girl, she finds life there even worse. On top of that, her family has really fallen to pieces. Her dad doesn't work much and is stoned most of the time, and her sister and mom seem to have their own exclusive clique. So Astrid spends a lot of her free time lying on a picnic table staring up at the sky. Whenever she sees a plane, she sends all of her love up to it. She and her girlfriend Dee have been going out for a while, and Dee is pushing for a lot more sex than Astrid is ready to give. Dee wants Astrid to come out so that they can date more publicly, but Astrid isn't even really sure how to describe her sexuality. She knows she cares for Dee and wants to date her, but, she says, "I'm questioning the strict definitions and boxes of all *sexualities* and why we care so much about other people's intimate business." (LA Times, Walden)

Subjects: Coming Out; Families; LGBTQIA+; Pennsylvania; Small Towns

Konigsberg, Bill.

Openly Straight. 2013. 9780545509893. **J S**

Rafe is tired of being the model gay kid in his super progressive school and town in Colorado. So when he transfers to a boarding school in Massachusetts for his junior year, he decides not to mention his sexuality and to let everyone assume he is straight. It works for a while, but eventually Rafe learns that people are always going to make assumptions about you, and hiding his real self is much more exhausting and difficult than he had imagined it would be. (BFYA, Rainbow)

Subjects: Boarding Schools; Boulder, Colorado; Massachusetts; Coming Out; LGBTQIA+

Levithan, David.

Two Boys Kissing. 2013. 9780307931900. **J S**

After their friend Tariq is the victim of a hate crime, friends and ex-boyfriends Harry and Craig decide to make a statement by breaking the Guinness World Record for kissing—32 hours. Their story and the stories of their friends are narrated by a sort of Greek chorus of gay men who died of AIDS in the 1980s and 1990s and who express their hopes and fears for the current generation. The story is about the anxiety of falling in and out of love, about loving and hating your family and friends, and about wanting to be honest about who you are but being afraid of what might happen. (Stonewall, Lambda, NBA)

Subjects: Guinness Book of World Records; Kissing; LGBTQIA+

Saenz, Benjamin Alire.

Aristotle and Dante Discover the Secrets of the Universe. 2012. 9781442408920. **J S**

Ari says, "The problem with my lie was that it was someone else's idea." He is a good kid but a bit of a loner, and he definitely has culturally based ideas of what it means to be a man. His dad is a Vietnam vet who never talks about his horrific experiences during the war. His sisters are much older and have moved away. No one talks about Ari's older brother, who is in prison, and Ari can barely remember him. And then one summer Ari meets Dante, who is in many ways his opposite—effusive, emotional, and detached from his Mexican heritage. Dante teaches Ari to swim, and a friendship is born that changes both boys' lives. (Printz Honor, BFYA, Stonewall)

Subjects: El Paso, Texas; Friendship; LGBTQIA+; Mexican Americans

Faith

Faith plays a major role in the lives of many teens. Sometimes the faith in which a teen has been raised becomes constricting; at other times teens without faith find it. In still other situations, teens are looking for ways to live with and express their faith while still living in the largely secular society that is America today. Like novels in which the characters find their identity through, or despite, their ethnicity, race, or sexual identity, the characters in these novels are trying to figure out what makes them who they are in terms of their faith.

Abdel-Fatteh, Randa.

Does My Head Look Big in This? 2007. 9780049919470. **J** **S**

Amal, a typical eighth-grader, attends a private school in Melbourne. She decides to start wearing the hijab full-time, which makes it pretty obvious that she is the only Muslim in her school. She has a couple of Islamic girlfriends, but they attend a different high school. Her two best friends at school also see themselves as outsiders: Eileen is Japanese Australian, and Simone thinks she is fat. Two very attractive boys start hanging around with the girls. Like Hassan in John Green's *An Abundance of Katherines*, Amal finds she can stay true to her faith and still be a real contemporary teen.

Subjects: Australia; Hijab; Muslims

Bliss, Bryan.

No Parking at the End Times. 2015. 9780062275417. **S**

Abigail, her twin brother Aaron, and their parents are living in a van on the streets of San Francisco. They were meant to be gone by now, taken up in the Rapture. Abigail's father has followed Brother John from North Carolina to the West Coast because the world was supposed to end at midnight on New Year's Eve. But now it's weeks later, and they're still here. Abigail is torn between relying on the judgment of her parents—who still trust the guidance of Brother John—or following Aaron's call to strike out on their own in order to survive.

Subjects: Dysfunctional Families; Evangelical Christianity; Homelessness; Rapture; San Francisco; Twins

Chayil, Elishes.

Hush. 2010. 9780802720887. **S**

Gittel is a 17-year-old Chassidic Jew, preparing to be married to a man her parents have chosen for her. She is very much a part of the very close, indeed closed culture of her little part of Brooklyn. However, she cannot forget the suicide of her friend Devory, when the girls were 10 years old. She knows that Devory had been subjected to sexual abuse from a man in the community, and Gittel finds it harder and harder to reconcile that with her faith and culture. She knows that speaking out will make *her* a target in the community, possibly even make it impossible for her to marry and have a good life. (Morris Finalist, BFYA)

Subjects: Brooklyn; Chassidic Jews; Orthodox Judaism; Sexual Abuse

Hautman, Pete.

Godless. 2004. 9781416908166. **S**

Hulking Jason ("J") Bock, agnostic and leaning toward atheism, comes up with the idea of starting his own religion that worships a 10-legged god, the town's water tower. The followers include Magda, a girl from his Catholic Church; Henry, a remarkably intelligent and well-read bully who knows how to get to the top of the tower; Dan, the Lutheran minister's son, who is more or less a nonentity; and Shim, his best friend, who seems to be descending into schizophrenia as he writes the holy book of the Chutengodians. (BBYA, NBA)

Subjects: Agnostics; Atheists; Mental Illness; Religion

Henry, Katie.

Heretics Anonymous. 2018. 9780062698872. 🄹 🅂

Michael, although he identifies as an atheist, ends up attending a conservative Catholic school when his family moves to a new town. He makes friends with a group that call themselves Heretics Anonymous: a gay Jew, a Korean American Unitarian Universalist who may be on the spectrum, a Celtic Reconstructionist Polytheist, and a rebellious but devout Catholic Latina (she thinks it would be great if she could be a priest). Despite their differences, these misfits agree that something should be done about some of the school's hypocrisies. These bright, questioning, hilarious teenagers sometimes go too far, but in the process they learn a lot about one another and about tolerance and kindness.

Subjects: Atheists; Catholic Church; Catholic Schools; Jews; LGBTQIA+; Pagans

Jarzab, Anna.

The Opposite of Hallelujah. 2012. 9780385738361. 🅂

Caro pretty much has the perfect life. She gets good grades (especially in science and math), she has good friends, she has a cute boyfriend, and her parents are great. She also has a much older sister, Hannah, but Hannah hasn't lived at home since Caro was eight, and she hasn't even seen Hannah since she was 12. At that point, she started telling people at school that Hannah was dead, since it seemed the easiest explanation—because, well, Hannah joined a convent. You'd think the phrase "contemplative nun" would mean something to kids who'd been attending Catholic school their entire lives, but it really didn't. . . . To them, nuns were practically prehistoric, and it didn't make any sense that Caro's then 23-year-old sister—tall, thin, and blond as Barbie–was working on her fourth year at the Sisters of Grace convent in Middleton, Indiana. And, frankly, the whole convent thing was always a bit of a mystery to Caro and to her parents anyway, all of whom were basically Christmas and Easter Catholics. But now Hannah is coming home. She has left the convent, but she isn't talking about it. How is Caro's family supposed to incorporate a whole new adult into their lives—especially when all Hannah wants to do is stay in her room, reading or sleeping?

Subjects: Catholic Church; Catholic School; Nuns; Religion; Sisters

Mafi, Tahereh.

A Very Large Expanse of Sea. 2018. 9780062866561. 🄹 🅂

Shirin is Muslim. Her family is originally from Iran, and she wears the hijab, although in all other respects she is a normal American teenager. The story takes place just a year after 9/11, and Shirin is starting yet another new school—necessarily because her father's job causes the family to move a lot. Shirin has gotten used to holding herself apart from other kids. Now, however, she has joined a breakdancing group with her brother and some of his friends, and she is starting to come out of her shell. Then she meets Ocean James, a popular (and decidedly non-Muslim) boy at school, who further manages to chip away at her defenses. Ocean is sweet but not at all aware of the extent of his white privilege, and Shirin needs to move cautiously in her relationship with him, especially in the light of reactions from the rest of their classmates. Shirin must learn how to integrate her faith into a hostile American society. (NBA)

Subjects: Breakdancing; First Love; Hijab; Muslims; Prejudice

Mathieu, Jennifer.

Devoted. 2015. 9781596439115. **J** **S**

Rachel's family is part of a conservative and patriarchal Christian sect. She helps to homeschool her younger siblings and prepares herself to be a good wife and mother someday. But she loves to read, and she's intelligent and thoughtful, and she finds it hard to reconcile some of the dictates of her father with her own common sense. One day she reads the blog of Lauren, a young woman who had been banished from the community, and that opens up even more questions. Rachel is devoted to God and loves her family, but she struggles to reconcile her strict, conservative Christian upbringing with the modern secular world.

Subjects: Christian Life; Homeschooling; Quiverfull; Texas

Sanchez, Alex.

The God Box. 2007. 9781416908999. **S**

How can Paul reconcile his deeply felt Christianity with his attraction to other boys?

Subjects: Christian Life; Latinx; LGBTQIA+

Passions

The teenage years are a time when young people latch onto passions that they often carry forward for the rest of their lives. The novels in this section deal with protagonists in relation to activities that often consume them. Many involve the arts, but activism, sports, and even games provide strong themes that set these books apart.

Art, Poetry, Writing

Many teens feel great passion for art of all kinds, wanting to create representations, no matter how abstract, of their visions of life, love, and angst.

Anderson, Laurie Halse, Illustrated by Emily Carroll.

Speak: The Graphic Novel. 2018. 9780374300289. **J** **S**

Anderson's classic novel is now in graphic novel format. The black-and-white illustrations are a perfect companion to the story of Melinda's freshman year in high school, where she is a pariah because she called the police at an end-of-summer party. But through art, she is finally able to speak out about the boy who raped her at that party. (Bloomer, GGN)

Subjects: Art; Graphic Novels; High School; #MeToo; Rape

Crowley, Cath.

Graffiti Moon. 2012. 9780375869532. **J** **S**

Senior year is over, and Lucy has the perfect way to celebrate: Tonight, she's going to find Shadow, the mysterious graffiti artist whose work appears all over the city. He's out there somewhere—spraying color, spraying birds and blue sky on the night—and Lucy knows a guy who paints like Shadow is someone she could fall for. Really fall for. Instead, Lucy's stuck at a party with Ed, the guy she's managed to avoid since the most awkward date of her life. But when Ed tells her he knows where to find Shadow, they're suddenly on an all-night search around the city. And what Lucy can't see is the one thing that's right before her eyes. (BFYA)

Subjects: Australia; Graffiti; High School Graduation; Street Art

Nelson, Jandy.

I'll Give You the Sun. 2014. 9780803734968. **S**

Jude and Noah are twins. Noah tells the story of before, when they were inseparable. Jude tells the story of now, when the two barely speak to one another. Family secrets, painting, sculpture, ghosts, first love, grief—all are entwined in this beautiful story about two passionate people. (Printz Award, BFYA, Stonewall)

Subjects: Art; Grief; LGBTQIA+; Magical Realism; Painting; Sculpture; Twins

Rowell, Rainbow.

Fangirl. 2013. 9781250030955. **S**

Cath and Wren are identical twins, and until recently they did absolutely everything together. Now they're off to university, and Wren has decided she doesn't want to be one-half of a pair any more—she wants to dance, meet boys, go to parties, and let loose. It's not so easy for Cath. She would rather bury herself in the fanfiction she writes, where there's romance far more intense than anything she's experienced in real life. Now Cath has to decide whether she's ready to open her heart to new people and new experiences, and she's realizing that there's more to learn about love than she ever thought possible. (BFYA)

Subjects: College; Fanfiction; Nebraska; Twins

Music

Music plays an important role in the lives of teens. It often defines their generation, and they often use the music they are passionate about to define themselves—whether that means making music, studying music, or listening to music. It is becoming quite common to find playlists included in teen novels, featuring songs that reflect the theme or events of the book. Look under "playlists" in the index for more books that contain these.

Albertalli, Becky.

Leah on the Offbeat. 2018. 9780062643803. **S**

In this companion book to *Simon vs. the Homo Sapiens Agenda*, it's spring of senior year, and everyone is thinking about college, the prom, and all the what-comes-nexts. But Leah isn't entirely sure what she wants to do. She's a drummer in an all-girl rock band. She's bisexual but only out to her mom, despite seriously crushing on her friend Abby. As tensions run high and friendships shift and change, Leah relies on her music to keep herself going.

Subjects: Atlanta; Body Positivity; Drummers; Friends; High School; LGBTQIA+; Music

Cohn, Rachel, and David Levithan.

Nick and Nora's Infinite Playlist. 2006. 980375846144. **S**

The story of a single night told in alternating chapters by Nick and Norah, who meet at a Manhattan club, and fall in love as they go from club to club listening to different bands. (BBYA)

Subjects: Music; New York; Playlists; Punk Rock; Romance

Going, K. L.

Fat Kid Rules the World. 2003. 9780142402085. **J** **S**

When a skinny homeless kid saves him from throwing himself in front of a train, 17-year-old Troy, obese and lonely, finds a new identity as a drummer for Curt's band, Rage/Tectonic. (BBYA, Printz Honor)

Subjects: Music; New York; Obesity; Punk Rock; Suicide

Krovatin, Christopher.

Heavy Metal and You. 2005. 9780439743990. **S**

Sam Markus loves heavy metal music and life on the edge at his expensive prep school, but things change when he starts going out with "straight-edge" Melissa. (BBYA)

Subjects: Heavy Metal Music; Prep Schools; Rock Music

Rowell, Rainbow.

Eleanor and Park. 2013. 9781250012579. **J** **S**

In 1980s Omaha, Eleanor and Park meet on the school bus. They are both outsiders: Eleanor because she's new, she's overweight, and she dresses "funny"; Park because he's a geeky Korean American kid with a strange love for indie rock. But gradually they form a friendship, bonded by music and comics. But even music isn't enough to improve Eleanor's unstable home life, with an abusive stepfather. Park tries to help, but there's only so much a 15-year-old can do, no matter how much he likes Eleanor. (BFYA, Printz Honor)

Subjects: 1980s; Abuse; Alternative Rock Music; Comics; Omaha

Rubens, Michael.

The Bad Decisions Playlist. 2016. 9780544096677. J S

Austin is a 16-year-old slacker. He can't even seem to finish the one thing he really wants to do: write songs. His mother has never told him anything about his father, so Austin is shocked when his dad shows up on the doorstep—and he's Shane Tyler, a famous rock musician and one of Austin's idols. Austin decides to spend time with his father, while keeping it a secret from his mother and her straightlaced fiancé. It's one in a series of bad decisions that Austin makes that summer.

Subjects: Divorce; Fathers and Sons; Rock Musicians

Sales, Leila.

This Song Will Save Your Life. 2013. 9780374351380. S

Nearly a year after a failed suicide attempt, 16-year-old Elise discovers that she has the passion and the talent to be a disc jockey. (BFYA)

Subjects: DJs; Music; Suicide

Thomas, Angie.

On the Come Up. 2019. 9780062498564. J S

Sixteen-year-old Brianna ("Bri") Jackson has one passion, one goal, one dream: to be a rap star. Bri's father was an up-and-coming rapper who was killed by a rival gang when Bri was 12. She lives with her mother, a former drug addict who is now clean and working minimum wage jobs, and with her brother, who has a college degree but works at a pizza place. She knows that if she can succeed in hip-hop, she can make a big difference in her family's life. After she is humiliated by a school security guard, she writes and records a rap that brings in all her frustrations, fears, and hopes, and it goes viral. Then Bri finds out that when you become popular, you also put yourself at the mercy of whatever the public decides about you. But Bri still knows this about herself: "You'll never silence me, and you'll never kill my dream. Just recognize when you say brilliant that you're also saying Bri."

Subjects: African Americans; Hip-Hop; Rappers

Zarr, Sara.

The Lucy Variations. 2013. 9780316205016. S

Lucy once had a promising career as a concert pianist, but after she walked out of a concert in Prague, all her family's attention is now on her younger brother Gus. When Gus gets a new piano teacher, Lucy begins to rebuild her relationship with music and with her family. (BFYA)

Subjects: Brothers and Sisters; Piano

Sports

Sports is a passion for many teens. Even in times of declining school budgets, sports are not cut because they are one of the incentives that keep many teens in school. Fortunately, an increasing number of books feature female athletes and a variety of sports.

Alexander, Kwame.

The Crossover Series. Ⓜ Ⓙ

The Crossover. **2014. 9780544935204.**

Twins Josh ("Filthy McNasty") and Jordan ("JB") Bell are stars on their middle school basketball team. They have always been close, but things are starting to change. JB is spending more time with a girl, and the twins' dad, a former pro basketball player who has always encouraged them, is struggling with health problems. The story is told in a variety of verse forms, from hip-hop style to free verse. Also available as a graphic novel. (BFYA, Coretta Scott King Honor)

Subjects: African Americans; Basketball; Fathers and Sons; Twins; Verse Novels

Rebound. **2015. 9780544868137.**

This prequel to *The Crossover* tells the story of Josh and JB's father, Chuck Bell. After his father dies, Chuck spends the summer with his grandparents, where he is exposed to the wonders of basketball and jazz.

Subjects: African Americans; Basketball; Grief; Jazz; Verse Novels

Booked. **2016. 9780544570986.**

Eighth-grader Nick lives and breathes soccer—at least until an emergency appendectomy takes him out of the big tournament. He claims to hate words, despite having a huge vocabulary, thanks to his linguistics professor father. But ultimately, as much as he loves soccer, it's words that help him defeat bullies and come to terms with his parents' divorce. (BFYA)

Subjects: African Americans; Bullying; Divorce; Middle School; Soccer; Verse Novels; Words

Backman, Frederick.

Beartown. **2017. 9781501160769.** Ⓞ

Beartown is a hockey town, and for the first time in years, they are about to compete in the national semifinals, something that could lead to funding from the big sponsors. And that in turn could help the town in a big way. They've got great young players, and all looks good. But then it changes in an instant when Maya, the daughter of the team's general manager, is raped by one of the team's star players. The whole town is thrown into conflict over what happened and whom to believe. And underlying it all is the question about what it will mean for the team and for the town's future.

Subjects: Hockey; #MeToo; Rape; Sweden

Feinstein, John.

The Prodigy. **2018. 9780374305956.** Ⓢ

Frank Baker is a teenage golf prodigy. His plan is to take one of the college scholarships on offer and play at college for at least a couple of years before turning pro. His dad, on the other hand, is eager for Frank to cash in and go pro right out of high school. When Frank reaches the finals of the U.S. Amateur Championship, he receives an invitation to participate in the Master's Tournament, and the stakes are raised.

Subjects: Fathers and Sons; Golf

Jamieson, Victoria.

Roller Girl. 2015. 9780525429678. **M** **J**

Astrid Vasquez, dubbed Ass-turd by her nemesis, Rachel, has been best friends with Nicole forever. During one of her mom's "Evenings of Cultural Enlightenment," the girls attend a roller derby match, and afterward Astrid's life changes in many ways. She wants to join the derby. She and Nicole are going to have so much fun at junior derby camp, it's going to be amazing—except that Nicole doesn't want to go. She plans to go to ballet camp instead . . . with Rachel. (Newbery Honor)

Subjects: Friendship; Graphic Novels; Middle School; Roller Derby

Klages, Ellen.

Out of Left Field. 2018. 9780425288597. **M** **J**

In 1957, girls aren't allowed in Little League, even when, like Katy, they're the best baseball player in town. When Katy is told that women simply don't play baseball, she sets out to prove them wrong and learns about the history of women's baseball. Recommend this book to fans of the movie *A League of Their Own.*

Subjects: All American Girls Professional Baseball League; Baseball; Female Athletes; Little League; Negro League Baseball; San Francisco Bay Area

Murdock, Catherine Gilbert.

Dairy Queen. **M** **J** **S**

DJ Schwenk, daughter of a dairy farmer, is one of her town's best athletes.

Subjects: Basketball; Farming; Female Athletes; Football; Wisconsin

Dairy Queen. 2006. 9780618863358.

DJ Schwenk has always played football with her brothers, so during one summer she ends up training the rival school's quarterback and decides to go out for football herself. (BBYA)

The Off Season. 2007. 9780618934935.

DJ's junior year starts out well. She is playing football, and Brian is now her boyfriend, but things start going wrong. When she injures her shoulder and can't play, she realizes Brian doesn't want to be seen with her, and then her older brother suffers a broken neck on the football field. (BBYA)

Front and Center. 2009. 9780618959822.

With football season behind her, DJ turns to basketball and thoughts of college as scouts pour into her town.

Reynolds, Jason.

Ghost. 2016. 9781481450157. **M** **J**

Castle "Ghost" Crenshaw has been running ever since his dad pulled a loaded gun on Ghost and his mom. Now he runs because he's good at it, and a track coach recognizes his talent. But can Ghost get his act together enough to succeed at a real sport like track? (BFYA)

Subjects: African Americans; Family Violence; Runners

Volponi, Paul.

Final Four. 2013. 9780670012640. **M** **J**

Four college hoops players meet in the semifinal of the NCAA tournament. Their struggles and dreams are told in flashbacks, journal entries, newspaper articles, TV interviews, and basketball play-by-play. (BFYA)

Subjects: African Americans; Basketball; NCAA Tournament

White, Ellen Emerson.

A Season of Daring Greatly. 2017. 9780062463234.

Jill is her high school baseball team's star pitcher, and now she is the first woman to be drafted by a major league baseball team. So instead of going off to Stanford for college, she's headed for a minor league season. Her rookie season is a challenge: media attention, heckling and hazing, and just the hard work of suddenly playing ball at a whole new level. But Jill is tall, strong, disciplined and has a 90-mph fastball, and she is determined to be more than just a temporary news item.

Subjects: Baseball; Minor League Baseball; Pittsburgh Pirates; Women in Sports

Theater and Dance

A passion for theater, dance, and other performance arts is another avocation that keeps teens motivated and in school.

Charaipotra, Sona, and Dhonielle Clayton.

Tiny Pretty Things. 2015. 9780062342393. **S**

Gigi, June, and Bette take turns narrating this tale of the cutthroat competition at the American Ballet Conservatory.

Subjects: Ballet; Competition; New York

Federle, Tim.

Better Nate Than Ever. **M** **J**

Nate dreams of starring in a Broadway show, but that's hard to do when you are only 13 and you live in Jankburg, Pennsylvania.

Subjects: LGBTQIA+; Musical Theater; New York; Pennsylvania

Better Nate Than Ever. 2013. 9781442446892.

When auditions are held in New York for *E.T.: The Musical* and Nate's parents happen to be away for the weekend, leaving him in the care of his older brother, Nate sees his chance to break free of his small town and launch a career in the big city. With the help of his best friend Libby, he embarks on a daring escape to New York, where a simple audition unravels into a night of unanticipated adventure. (BFYA, Stonewall, Lambda, Golden Kite)

Five, Six, Seven, Nate! 2014. 9781442446939.

Nate has made it to Broadway, although admittedly second understudy to the title character in *ET: The Musical* isn't exactly the role of a lifetime. But he's living in New York with his Aunt Heidi and learning the Broadway ropes, complete with snotty child actors, stage mothers, and cranky directors.

Nate Expectations. 2018. 9781481404129.

ET: The Musical has closed on Broadway, alas, and Nate is back in Jankburg, Pennsylvania, where he comes out as gay to his classmates and where he and his best friend Libby figure out how to put on a musical production of Charles Dickens' *Great Expectations.*

Flack, Sophie.

Bunheads. 2011. 9780316126540. **J** **S**

Nineteen-year-old Hannah has always wanted to be a ballerina, and ever since she was 14, she has been part of the corps of the Manhattan Ballet. She wants to become a soloist, but she is well aware that it means more of the same: never eating as much as she would like, endless rehearsals, rarely seeing her family, and basically no social life. Not to mention extreme competition with the very girls she lives and works with daily. Meeting two new young men causes Hannah to take a look at her life and decide what she really wants.

Subjects: Ballet; Competition; New York

Lockhart, E.

Dramarama. 2007. 9780786838158. **S**

Sayde and her best friend Douglas ("Demi") are musical theater fans. They can't wait to get of out Ohio and off to summer drama camp. Only once they get there, it seems that Demi has really hit his stride and found his people, while Sayde is perhaps not as good an actress as she always thought she was.

Subjects: Drama Camp; Friendship; Theater

Telgemeier, Raina.

Drama. 2012. 9780606267380. **M** **J**

Seventh-grader Callie loves musical theater but realizes she isn't much of an actor or singer. So she's thrilled to be on the set design crew of her middle school musical, *Moon over Mississippi.* She has big plans for the sets, even though the production has a very limited budget. Meanwhile, she has a crush on eighth-grader Greg, who prefers stuck-up Bonnie, the star of the musical, and Callie doesn't even realize that Greg's little brother is interested in her. Friends, theater, and middle-school drama abound in this graphic novel. (GGN, Stonewall)

Subjects: Drama; Middle School; Theater

Games

Bridge, poker, chess, video games—these are all activities that may take up a lot of a teen's time and mental energy. But those skills may also lead to the protagonist's growth. Books about computer and virtual reality games may also be found in Chapter 5, Speculative Fiction.

Dill, Julie.

Bluff. 2017. 9781944995058. **S**

Seventeen-year-old Chelsea does her best to keep herself and her single dad afloat by negotiating with creditors, shopping thriftily, and even borrowing money. But she discovers that her skill at poker has an even bigger payoff. She passes for 18 and starts playing at a Cherokee Nation casino. But life soon gets complicated, as she leads a double life and falls into a gambling addiction.

Subjects: Casinos; Gambling; Oklahoma; Poker

Klass, David.

Grandmaster. 2014. 9780374327712. **J** **S**

Daniel joins the school chess team, partly because he's not much of an athlete and he feels the need to join something. He is shocked when he is invited to a father–son chess tournament. But his teammates know something that Daniel doesn't know: His father was a grandmaster as a teenager.

Subjects: Chess; Fathers and Sons

Sachar, Louis.

Cardturner. 2010. 9780385736626. **J** **S**

Sixteen-year-old Alton is recruited to drive Trapp, his wealthy blind great-uncle, to his bridge club and to assist him during play. Alton is gradually seduced by the complexities of bridge and secretly begins to play on his own. (BFYA)

Subjects: Blind; Bridge; Cards; Uncles

Social and Political Activism

Books about activism reflect the times in which they are published. When the world is at peace and the economy is healthy, activism is less likely to play a major role in the lives of teens. War, politics, and the economy often spark activism, but so do issues like consumerism, conservation, and pollution.

Doctorow, Cory, and Jen Wang.

In Real Life. 2014. 9781596436589. **M** **J** **S**

Anda joins a massively multiplayer role-playing game called Coarsegold. At first she plays it just as a game, but soon she realizes that there is a disturbing underworld in Coarsegold. Anda meets Raymond, a poor kid from China, who collects in-game valuable objects for the purpose of selling them to other players (often in first world countries) for real money. When Anda realizes how Raymond is being exploited, she encourages him to stand up for himself. (GGN)

Subjects: Exploitation; Graphic Novels; Poverty; Role-playing Games

Kisner, Adrienne.

Dear Rachel Maddow. 2019. 9781250146021. **M** **J** **S**

Brynn Harper begins writing to MSNBC news anchor Rachel Maddow as a school assignment. Brynn has just broken up with her girlfriend, and she's not doing too well in school ever since the death of her brother. Her poor grades mean that she can no longer be on the school newspaper. In the course of writing to Rachel, she begins to be able to express some of her frustrations, including the fact that certain students in her school seem to be more equal than others. Brynn knows that Rachel would stand up to the injustice, so she is inspired to do the same.

Subjects: Epistolary Novels; E-mails; Grief; School Politics

Stamper, Phil.

The Gravity of Us. 2020. 9781547600144. **S**

Cal is a 17-year-old social media influencer. He has a half-million followers for his vlog and an upcoming internship with BuzzFeed. He shares news about what's going on around Brooklyn, and he has acquired quite a following for his posts on NASA's upcoming manned Mars mission, the Orpheus program. But his plans come to a screeching halt when his father is selected to be the 20th and final astronaut for the Orpheus program. The family must move immediately to Houston, and Cal's social media presence is severely curtailed by NASA's rules and by the fact that the whole project is being covered by a reality TV show called StarWatch. Once in Houston, though, Cal meets Leon, the son of another astronaut, and the two find themselves falling in love. At the same time, his journalistic instincts lead Cal to uncover secrets about StarWatch and Orpheus, and he has to figure out a way to expose the truth without hurting his father or Leon's mother.

Subjects: Astronauts; Houston; Mars Mission; Reality TV; Social Media

Cooking

With the advent of TV shows like *Iron Chef, Cupcake Wars, The Great British Bake-Off, Top Chef,* and *Chopped,* many teens are finding their passion in the kitchen. Teens who desire to become chefs are a new theme in YA literature. These books contain some of these teen cooks. See also: *Bloom* and *The Way You Make Me Feel* in Chapter 3 and *With the Fire on High* in this chapter, under "Teen Pregnancy and Parenting."

Alsaid, Adi.

North of Happy. 2017. 9780373212286. **S**

Carlos and his brother Felix were on the search for the perfect taco in Mexico City when Felix was killed by a stray bullet. Carlos can't stay in Mexico City any longer, so after graduation, he heads for Washington State's San Juan Islands and the restaurant of his favorite celebrity chef, Elise St. Croix. He gets a job washing dishes, but before long he is being trained by Chef Elise and also developing a relationship with the chef's daughter, Emma. Carlos's summer in the kitchen is punctuated by conversations with Felix's ghost. Each chapter begins with a recipe, from The Perfect Taco, to Thai Bruschetta, to Seaweed Salad, and more.

Subjects: Cooking; Ghosts; Grief; Latinx; Magical Realism; Restaurants; San Juan Islands

Fiore, Kelly.

Taste Test. **2013. 9780802728388.** **J** **S**

Nora has grown up in her dad's North Carolina barbecue restaurant. Now she has entered a reality TV show, *Taste Test*, in hopes of winning a $50,000 scholarship to a Paris culinary school. A celebrity chef, a burgeoning romance, and possible sabotage keep things hopping.

Subjects: Contests; Cooking; Reality TV; Recipes

Ockler, Sarah.

Bittersweet. **2012. 9781442430365.** **J** **S**

Avery was once an accomplished competitive skater. But after her parents' divorce and a move with her mother to a small upstate New York town, she focuses her energies on baking cupcakes to sell at her mom's diner. At least until she ends up helping out with coaching for the high school hockey team. Skating or baking?

Subjects: Baking; Cupcakes; Figure Skating; Ice Hockey; New York State

Strohm, Stephanie Kate.

Love à la Mode. **2018. 9781368019040.** **M** **J**

Rosie is a reliable daughter and older sister, but her real passion is baking. And when she gets accepted to a prestigious cooking school for teens—in Paris, yet!—of course, she wants to go. There she meets Henry, who grew up helping in his dad's Korean restaurant and who wants to be a chef. But the cooking school proves challenging for both of them. Relationships with their teacher and with superstar student Bodie Tal keep interfering in the romance that is sparking between Rosie and Henry.

Subjects: Baking; Cooking; Korean Americans; Paris; Romance

Williams, Kathryn.

Pizza, Love, and Other Stuff That Made Me Famous. **2012. 9780805092851.** **M** **J**

Sophie has always helped out in her family's Mediterranean-style restaurant in Washington, D.C., and she knows she wants to have her own restaurant someday. But the stakes are raised when she gets accepted to a reality TV show called *Teen Test Kitchen*.

Subjects: Chefs; Cooking; Napa, California

Coming of Age

To some extent, all teen fiction is about coming of age, since that is the primary function of the teen years in real life. Coming of age can involve tragedy, or it can be comic. These novels usually involve teens recognizing that it is time to take responsibility for their own life choices, figuring out who they are as individuals and how they want to live.

Davis, Jenny Fran.

Everything Must Go. 2017. 9781250119766. **S**

Flora Goldwasser goes to a ritzy Upper East Side high school. She is fashion obsessed, although the fashions in this case owe more to Jackie Kennedy than to anyone more modern. As "Miss Tulip," she writes a fashion blog. Life changes dramatically for Flora when she develops a crush on her history tutor, Elijah, and she learns that he is going to teach the following year at his alma mater, Quare, a very alternative boarding school in upstate New York. Flora gets herself accepted to Quare for the following year, but Elijah changes his plans. Flora stays at Quare. Although she finds it very odd at first, she begins to find a place for herself around people who aren't impressed with living lives centered around materialism and social acceptance of gender norms. The story is told in letters, blog posts, e-mails, and news stories.

Subjects: Alternative Schools; Boarding Schools; Epistolary Novels; Fashion; Feminism

Dessen, Sarah.

Along for the Ride. 2009. 9780670011940. **S**

Auden has always been a responsible kid—especially after her parents divorced. Now, the summer before college, she impulsively decides to spend the summer with her father and his new wife and baby in a North Carolina beach town. She's not sure exactly how to remake herself into a "normal" teenager, but some new friends help, and a fellow insomniac takes her on nighttime journeys around the town.

Subjects: Bicycles; Divorce; North Carolina; Stepfamilies; Summer Romance

Once and for All. 2017. 9780425290330. **S**

Louna's mom is a wedding planner, so Louna has very few, if any, illusions about weddings or romance. And she is certainly not interested in finding a new boyfriend, as she is still grieving over Ethan, who died in a school shooting. But as part of the latest wedding that Louna and her mom are working, she meets oh-so-charming Ambrose. She resists the growing attraction, but Ambrose is not easily discouraged.

Subjects: School Shootings; Summer Romance; Weddings

Goo, Maureen.

The Way You Make Me Feel. 2018. 9780374304089. **J** **S**

Clara loves pranks, but when one goes a little too far, she ends up in a fight with Rose. As a result, both girls are sentenced to work in Clara's father's Korean Brazilian food truck (the KoBra) for the summer. They become allies and friends as each gradually breaks open protective layers. A kind, handsome boy adds a sweet summer romance to the mix.

Subjects: Food Trucks; Humor; Korean Americans; Los Angeles; Romance; Summer Jobs

Green, John.

An Abundance of Katherines. 2006. 9780525476887. **S**

Colin has always been a little different from his peers: He has an IQ of 200, he has thousands of dollars from winning a game show for kids, he speaks a number of dead (and living) languages, and he has had exactly 19 girlfriends, all of whom have dumped him, and all of whom were named Katherine. When Katherine no. 19 breaks his heart just after graduation, Hassan, Colin's only friend, convinces him to go on a road trip to clear his mind and get over the Katherines. Eventually they find themselves in a tiny town in Tennessee, a town so rural that Hassan, an observant Muslim, feels that he should introduce himself by saying: "Hi, I'm Hassan. I'm not a terrorist." They meet a girl named Lindsey and decide to stay in Gunshot, Tennessee, for the summer. Now, while Hassan is beginning a relationship with his first girlfriend ever, Colin begins to develop the Theorem of Underlying Katherine Predictability, a mathematical theory to explain why he is always the dumpee and never the dumper in his entanglements with the Katherines. But his burgeoning relationship with Lindsay threatens to complicate the whole theory, while at the same time Lindsey is finding out a lot about her town, her mom, and who she really is. (Printz Honor, BBYA)

Subjects: Anagrams; Girlfriends; Muslims; Road Trips

Looking for Alaska. 2005. 9780525475064. **S**

Geeky 16-year-old Miles Halter, known as Pudge, leaves Florida for a boarding school in Alabama, where he finds other brilliant teens with whom he smokes, drinks, and plays pranks. When he falls "in lust" with Alaska, a troubled, beautiful, intelligent girl who lives down the hall, his life is bound to change. (Printz Award, BBYA)

Subjects: Alabama; Boarding Schools; Obituaries

Hautman, Pete.

Road Tripped. 2019. 9781534405905. **S**

Steven Gerald ("Stiggy") Gabriel is on the road. He just couldn't stay in Minnesota any longer, after his father's suicide, his mother's collapse, and his girlfriend's disappearance. He decides he's going to take his father's Mustang and follow the Mississippi River from its source in Minnesota to its mouth in New Orleans. Along the way, Stiggy has plenty of time to think, and he also meets up with some people who give him new things to think about.

Subjects: Breakups; Cars; Grief; Great River Road; Minnesota; Road Trips

Johnson, Maureen.

13 Little Blue Envelopes. 2005. 9780060541439. **J S**

Ginny's Aunt Peg died from a brain tumor—and Ginny never got to say good-bye. But then Ginny receives a blue envelope from Aunt Peg in the mail. It contains $1,000 in cash and the instructions to pick up a package of envelopes that start Ginny on a trip around Europe. The instructions are specific: no cell phones, no maps, and Ginny can open only one envelope at a time, after she's completed each task in the previous letter. The 13 little blue envelopes start Ginny on a voyage of discovery—both about the world and about herself. (BBYA)

Subjects: Art; Europe; Grief; Road Trips; Travel

Kade, Stacey.

Finding Felicity. 2018. 9781481464253. **S**

Caroline is an introvert and finds it hard to make friends. When her parents divorce and she and her mother move to Arizona, she finds it's easier to answer her mother's questions about her friends by just making things up. Because she is a fan of the old TV show *Felicity*, she uses characters and incidents from the show to people the stories she tells her mother. Her deception comes to light at graduation, and her mother insists that Caroline see a therapist over the summer, or she won't be allowed to go away to college. Caroline is sure that college will be her opportunity to have the real life she wants, so she cooperates, at least to some extent. Starting college is more of a challenge than she expects, but her therapy, some new friends, and, yes, even *Felicity*, help her succeed.

Subjects: College; Self-Esteem; Social Anxiety

Kaplan, Ariel.

We Regret to Inform You. 2018. 9781524773717. **S**

This is a smart, funny book that's also a bit of a mystery. Mischa is a senior at a ritzy prep school in Virginia. She's there on scholarship, and she's one of the school's top students: she's got the grades, the test scores, the extracurriculars, the whole package. So when everyone starts getting their college acceptances and Mischa gets only rejections, she's shocked. And when she gets rejected by even her "safety" school, she's dumbfounded—until she visits the college and finds out that the transcript they received bears no resemblance to her real transcript. Does someone have it in for Mischa, or is there something even more nefarious going on? (BFYA)

Subjects: College Admissions; Friends; Geeks; Humor; Prep Schools

Kennedy, Katie.

Learning to Swear in America. 2016. 9781619639096. **S**

Yuri is a 17-year-old genius—a Russian PhD physicist who has been sent to Pasadena to help a team of scientists at the Jet Propulsion Lab. There is an asteroid on a collision course with Earth, and Yuri and the others have to figure out how to stop it. Yuri has a good idea of how, but he has to convince the NASA scientists that he knows what he's talking about, even if he is just 17 and his research hasn't been published yet. Meanwhile, Yuri meets a girl who reminds him that besides being a prodigy, he's also a regular teenage boy. Can Yuri save the world and learn to swear in English?

Subjects: Asteroids; NASA; Russians; Science

LaCour, Nina.

We Are Okay. 2017. 9780525425892. **S**

In this very quiet but very lovely book, the reader meets Marin, who grew up in San Francisco with her Gramps, ever since her mother died when she was three years old. But Gramps died just before Marin left for college. Now it's Christmas break, and she is spending it alone in a dorm in upstate New York—that is, until her best friend from home shows up and helps Marin come to terms with her grief and the uncertainties in her life. (Printz Award, BFYA)

Subjects: College; Friends; Grandparents; Grief; New York

Lubar, David.

Character, Driven. 2016. 9780765316332. **S**

Eighteen-year-old narrator Cliff warns the reader that this story doesn't have a lot of plot: It is character driven. Cliff is a senior in high school who has never really had a girlfriend but who is taken with the new girl in school, Jillian. Unfortunately, he can't quite figure out a way to get her to notice him. Meanwhile, he works on his art, and he works two jobs to help out his family, since his father is unemployed, and his mother works part-time in a bakery. When he finally gets the nerve to talk to Jillian, he finds they actually have a lot in common and that they like each other. Cliff is funny, intelligent, caring, and also carrying a big secret, as he comes of age in this novel. (BFYA)

Subjects: Fathers and Sons; High School; Humor; Sex; Teenage Boys; Unreliable Narrator

Mackler, Carolyn.

The Earth, My Butt, and Other Big Round Things. (Rev. Ed.). 2018. 9781681197982. **S**

This is an updated edition of the 2003 Printz Honor novel. Fifteen-year-old Virginia doesn't feel she fits in her family. They are thin and athletic, and she's, well, not. Her parents are busy professionals; in fact, her mother is a noted psychologist who specializes in teenagers. Her older sister is off in the Peace Corps in Burkina Faso, her older brother is living it up at Columbia, her best friend has moved to Seattle, and Ginny is on her own, developing the "Fat Girl Code of Conduct" to help her navigate her relationship with Froggy Welsh. But when her brother is accused of rape, Ginny begins to come to the realization of her own worth and sees that not everyone else is as perfect as they look. (Printz Honor, BBYA)

Subjects: Body Image; Date Rape; Families; First Love; #MeToo; New York; Plus Size; Self Esteem

The Universe Is Expanding, and So Am I. 2018. 9781681195995. **S**

Five months after the events of *The Earth, My Butt, and Other Big Round Things*, Ginny Shreve has moved forward a lot in understanding herself and her family. But, of course, nothing stays the same, and things are thrown into upheaval when her brother Byron is arrested for the date rape that they all thought was in the past. Meanwhile, Ginny is not so sure about her relationship with Froggy, and she has also met a new guy who seems pretty wonderful.

Subjects: Body Image; Date Rape; #MeToo; New York

Marchetta, Melina.

The Piper's Son. 2011. 9780763647582. ⑤

Five years after the events of *Saving Francesca*, Marchetta takes up the story of Tom Mackee, one of Francesca's friends. Tom was going to be a musician, but things have fallen apart for him. His favorite uncle was killed in a terrorist attack, and Tom's method of coping has been to drink too much, take too many drugs, and have too many one-night-stands. He's estranged from pretty much everyone he ever loved, but his Aunt Georgie has taken him in. Georgie herself is going through some tough times, as she is dealing with an unexpected pregnancy by an ex-boyfriend she thought was out of her life. Both Tom and Georgie are very confused, very angry, and very, very sad. Together they find their ways back to being a family. (BFYA)

Subjects: Australia; Family; Friends; Music

Saving Francesca. 2004. 9730375829833. ⑤

Francesca is one of only a few girls at a previously all-boys' school. She's finding that making friends with the other girls isn't particularly easy, but neither is getting along with the boys, who don't really want the girls there. Plus, Francesca has to cope without her main support person—her mother, who is suffering from depression and can barely make it through each day, much less help Francesca find her place in school and the world. Francesca eventually does make friends, and readers who like her world might be interested in following up the story a few years later, in *The Piper's Son*.

Subjects: Australia; Depression; Prep School

Rabb, Margo.

Kissing in America. 2015. 9780062322371. ⑆ ⑤

Two years after her father's death in a plane crash, Eva is still mourning. Her practical, feminist mother, a women's studies professor, doesn't really approve of the fact that Eva immerses herself in romance novels. But it's Eva's escape. She and her father used to read and write poetry together, but she hasn't been able to do that since he died. She meets Will at school and is even able to talk to him about her grief, but the next thing she knows, Will is moving to California. Eva convinces her best friend Annie to apply to be on a game show, *The Smartest Girl in America*, and the two of them head off to California, ostensibly to be on the show but really to find Will. It turns out that a road trip and a best friend are just what Eva needs to start looking at her life in a whole new way. (Bloomer, BFYA)

Subjects: California; Friends; Grief; New York; Road Trips

Reynolds, Jason.

Long Way Down. 2018. 9781481438254. Ⓜ ⑆ ⑤

Fifteen-year-old Will learned The Rules from his brother Shawn: (1) No crying. (2) No snitching. (3) Revenge. And now that Shawn has been shot and killed, Will is on his way to take care of rule 3. Except on his way down in the elevator, someone gets on at each floor—but they're all people who can't really be there because they are all people that Will knows are dead. Each of them has something to tell Will. What happens during this short elevator ride helps Will figure out what kind of man he wants to be. (Printz Honor, Newbery Honor, BFYA, NBA, LA Times, Walden, Edgar)

Subjects: African Americans; Death; Family; Ghosts; Manhood; Race

Van Draanen, Wendelin.

Wild Bird. 2017. 9781101940457. **J** **S**

Fourteen-year-old Wren is roughly awakened at 3:47 in the morning and taken to a wilderness therapy camp in the Utah desert. Wren can't believe that her parents and her goody-goody sister could just stand there and let it happen, but now she has to face the consequences of her actions: drug use, shoplifting, vandalism, and other behaviors. She is even more shocked when she learns that the camp leaders (and other campers) expect her to build her own shelter, light her own fire, and cook her own meals. But over the course of the next eight weeks, Wren comes to appreciate her own strengths and abilities and those of her fellow campers, most of whom, she realizes, have had much worse lives than she has. (BFYA)

Subjects: Adventure Therapy; Utah; Wilderness Survival

Zusak, Markus.

I Am the Messenger. 2005. 9780375830990. **S**

Here's how Ed's day starts: face down on the floor of a bank, with an incompetent bank robber holding a gun on him. Here's how his day ends: Ed manages to stop the bank robber—with his own gun—and gets written up in the papers as a hero. And then he gets an envelope in the mail that contains a single playing card—an Ace of Diamonds—with three addresses written on it. Nothing else. No other instructions. Ed has no idea who sent it or what it's for. But he can't quite ignore it. He knows that at 19, he's just a slacker. But who knows? Maybe going to the addresses on the card will be the start of something big! (Printz Honor, BBYA)

Subjects: Australia; Cab Drivers; Heroes; Self-Esteem

Relationships

Teens are all about relationships—with those they are attracted to, those with whom they live, and those with whom they spend their time. Friendship is at its most intense during adolescence, and many teen novels deal with friendships evolving and changing during this turbulent time. Adolescence is also the time when teens evaluate what family means to them and whether the values of the family they grew up in are the values they want to carry on into adulthood. This can mean drawing away from the family or moving closer. During the teen years in particular, family can take on many shapes and forms.

Friends

Many teens feel that their primary relationships are with their peers, so it is no wonder that the theme of friendship is prevalent in novels for teens. These novels enable teens to see reflections of themselves and their friends, as well as other options for friendship that they may never have considered.

Chmakova, Svetlana.

Awkward. 2015. 9780316381321. **M** **J**

Peppi Torres is new at Berrybrook Middle School, where she can't quite seem to find her place. Now the art club that she belongs to is vying against the science club for a spot in the school fair. And one of the science club members is Jaime, a boy she knows she owes an apology to but can't quite bring herself to express. All the awkwardness of middle school is in the graphic novel, along with the joys of finding a diverse group of friends. (GGN)

Subjects: Art; Friends; Graphic Novels; Middle School; Science

Brave. 2017. 9780316363174. **M** **J**

Jensen Graham, one of the science club kids from *Awkward*, is obsessed with sunspots. He gets bullied because of that and because of his size. What he does not realize is how much he is being bullied until he is handed a survey by friends on the newspaper staff. After answering so many questions about bullying to the affirmative, he discovers this one: "What culture would *you* want to build? What would be the norm there? Which actions would help build this culture?" That is an epiphany for Jensen and also a catalyst for change at the school. (GGN)

Subjects: Bullying; Friends; Graphic Novels; Middle School

Crush. 2018. 9780316363235. **M** **J**

Jorge is known as The Sheriff at Berrybrook Middle School because he's a big guy, and he "encourages" bullies to leave their victims alone. Jorge has a crush on Jazmine, but he can't even seem to open his mouth whenever she's around. (GGN)

Subjects: Friends; Graphic Novels; Middle School

Doll, Jen.

Unclaimed Baggage. 2018. 9780374306069. **J** **S**

Unclaimed Baggage is a store in Alabama that sells the contents of baggage left at airports. Three teenagers—Nell, who has just moved there from Chicago; Doris, who stopped going to church and incurred the wrath of their conservative town; and Grant, a football hero who injured his girlfriend while driving drunk—work at the store and patch together a friendship over the course of a summer.

Subjects: Friendship; Lost Articles

Flinn, Alex.

Girls of July. 2019. 9780062447838. **S**

Spider spends the summers in an isolated cabin in the Adirondacks with her grandmother, Ruthie. This year, to make some money, she advertises for three girls to come and spend the month of July with them: mountain lakes, blackberries, stargazing, and no cell phone reception. The three who take up the offer are Britta, an outgoing actress; Meredith, a serious college-bound studier; and Kate, a southern debutante who is running from a family scandal. The four of them couldn't be more different. But somehow they grow to accept and like one another over the course of the month, which does indeed include the advertised amenities—plus a 50-year-old mystery, first love, and new responsibilities. Suggest to teens who enjoyed *The Sisterhood of the Traveling Pants*.

Subjects: Adirondacks; Friendship; Playlists; Theater

Halpern, Sue.

Summer Hours at the Robbers Library. 2018. 9780062678973. **S** **O**

Teenaged Sunny is sentenced to do community service at the Riverton (New Hampshire) Public Library. Her supervisor is Kit, who has come to Riverton escaping her past. The library is frequented by The Four—four older gentlemen from the town, as well as new arrival Rusty, who used to work on Wall Street. Over the course of a summer, secrets are revealed, friendships develop, and lives are changed.

Subjects: Community Service; Friends; Homeschooling; Libraries; New Hampshire; Summer

Hubbard, Jenny.

And We Stay. 2014. 9780385740579. **S**

Emily is sent to the Amherst School for Girls after her ex-boyfriend's suicide and her own abortion. Emily feels an affinity for another Amherst girl—Emily Dickinson—and as she begins to connect with new friends, her poetry reveals the story of how she got there. (BFYA, Printz Honor)

Subjects: Amherst, Massachusetts; Boarding Schools; Emily Dickinson; Poetry; Suicide

Johnston, E. K.

Exit, Pursued by a Bear. 2016. 9781101994580. **S**

Hermione is a confident, happy teenager, cocaptain of her school's award-winning cheerleading squad. The summer before grade 12, the whole squad goes to cheer camp, as they always do. But while they are there, Hermione is drugged and raped. Hermione is fortunate to have a strong support group—family, friends, doctors, police—who do absolutely everything right. And yet there is still plenty for Hermione to cope with, including the reactions of both friends and strangers who somehow want to make it Hermione's "fault." But Hermione refuses to be defined by this one incident in her life. (Bloomer)

Subjects: Abortion; Camp; Canada; Cheerleading; Date Rape; High School; #MeToo; PTSD

King, A. S.

Please Ignore Vera Dietz. 2010. 9780375865862. **J** **S**

Vera's longtime childhood friend Charlie is dead. She is hurt by his death, but her feelings are far from straightforward. Charlie could sometimes be a real pain, and their relationship was strained at times. But still she grieves.

And she tries to avoid the grief by working harder than ever—40 hours a week delivering pizzas, on top of her senior-year studies. As Vera copes with her grief and tries to find out exactly what happened the night Charlie died, she also struggles with the expectations of her father and her own desires to be more than what her small town expects her to be. (Printz Honor, BFYA)

Subjects: Grief; LGBTQIA+; Pizza Delivery; Small Towns

Longo, Jennifer.

Six Feet over It. 2014. 9780449818718. **M** **J**

Fourteen-year-old Leigh lives and works in a graveyard in Hangtown, California. She would have preferred to stay in the beach town of Mendocino, but her father bought the graveyard and moved the family. Leigh is still grieving the death of her best friend and still worrying about her sister Kai, whose leukemia is now, thankfully, in remission. But gradually she makes friends: the young Mexican groundskeeper, Dario; and Elanor, who works in her family's flower shop. Together, they manage to push through Leigh's reserve and help her rejoin the world of the living.

Subjects: Family; Friends; Graveyards; Grief

Schumacher, Julie.

The Unbearable Book Club for Unsinkable Girls. 2012. 9780385737739. **S**

Adrienne is stuck at home for the summer with a knee injury. Her single mom decides that the two of them should start a mother–daughter book club. The four girls who form the nucleus of the book club are all going into junior year AP English, so they have a ready-made book list. But the four of them are far from being friends—at least when the summer starts. (BFYA)

Subjects: Book Clubs; Friends; Summer

Tamaki, Mariko. Illustrated by Rosemary Valero-O'Connor.

Laura Dean Keeps Breaking Up with Me. 2019. 9781250312846. **J** **S**

In this graphic novel, Frederica is thrilled to be dating Laura Dean, the most popular girl in school. Only Laura Dean isn't really the greatest girlfriend. She keeps breaking up with Freddy, but Freddy keeps taking her back, always thinking that this time it will be different. Freddy tries to find out from others (an advice columnist, a seer, friends) what she is doing wrong in the relationship. In fact, she is so absorbed with Laura that she misses out on what is going on in her best friend Doodle's life. As Freddy pulls herself out of a toxic relationship and learns to appreciate herself, she also realizes what being a friend really means. (BFYA, GGN, Printz Honor, Rainbow)

Subjects: Friends; Graphic Novels; LGBTQIA+; Toxic Relationships

Whaley, John Corey.

Highly Illogical Behavior. 2017. 9780525428183. **S**

Sol is sixteen, anxious, and agoraphobic. He hasn't left the house in three years. His parents homeschool him, and he's happy with his books, his movies, and *Star*

Trek. Lisa is driven. She wants to get into a prestigious college psychology program, and she decides that the way to do it is to "fix" Sol and write up the case for her application. But Lisa comes to realize that Sol is much more than just a case study. The two develop a strong friendship, and Lisa even brings her boyfriend Clark into the mix, and Clark and Sol begin to develop their own relationship. It turns out that friends can sometimes help you do things you never thought you could do. (BFYA, Rainbow)

Subjects: Agoraphobia; Anxiety; LGBTQIA+; Psychology

Woodson, Jacqueline.

Harbor Me. 2018. 9780399252525. **M** **J**

Six students—Holly, Hayley, Amari, Tiago, Esteban, and Ashley—are pulled out of class and informed that every Friday at 2 p.m. they will be meeting together to talk—no teachers, no parents, just them. Over the course of the year, they share their stories and draw closer, helping one another through the trials of middle school and troubled families. (BFYA)

Subjects: Friendship; Immigration; Incarceration; Middle School

Families

Family is the basic relationship that everyone starts out with, but by the teen years it can mean many different things. Family can be constricting, but it can also be freeing. Family can mean supportive parents and siblings, or it can mean a toxic situation that the teen needs to escape from. These books include all kinds of families.

Allen, Sarah Addison.

First Frost. 2015. 9781250019837. **S** **O**

All of the Waverly women have a special kind of magic. Sydney does hair— and she can make your day (or week) better or worse because of the style. Her sister Claire takes after their grandmother Mary and makes food and candies from the edible flowers that grow in the yard—food that makes everyone feel better. Even distant cousin Evanelle has the ability to give people exactly what they need—whether they know it or not. Fifteen-year-old Bay, Sydney's daughter, has the gift of knowing what things (and people) belong together. So she knows that she is somehow meant to be in the life of 18-year-old Josh, a rich kid, soccer player, and basically high school royalty. At the beginning of the school year, she even writes Josh a note telling him so, but it only succeeds in making Bay more of a pariah in school than she already is. Meanwhile, Sydney wants a baby, Claire isn't sure that her candy-making business is the right thing, and a stranger arrives in town, a con man who has some sort of interest in the Waverlys. First frost is always a time of upheaval for the Waverly women, and as that day approaches (coinciding this year with Halloween), all of these issues come to a head in this delightful novel of magical realism that will appeal to fans of Alice Hoffman and Maggie Stiefvater's Raven Boys cycle.

Subjects: Magical Realism; Mothers and Daughters; Sisters

Benway, Robin.

Far from the Tree. 2017. 9780062330628. **J** **S**

As Grace struggles with having put her own daughter up for adoption, she goes searching for her own biological half-siblings. She finds two, both from the same mother: Maya and Joaquin. All three have had different experiences of being adopted. Grace grew up as a much loved only child. Joaquin, the eldest, has spent his entire life in foster homes and finds it hard to accept that his current foster parents really want to adopt him. Maya's adoptive parents had a biological child just a year after Maya was adopted, and Maya sometimes wonders if her sister is the preferred child. The three decide to meet, and they bond as they share their stories and come to understand their differences and their similarities. (BFYA)

Subjects: Adoption; Foster Care; Teen Pregnancy

Crossan, Sarah.

One. 2015. 9780062118752. **J** **S**

Tippi and Grace share so much—they are conjoined twins, joined at the waist: separate heads, hearts, arms, but only one set of legs. Grace tells their story in free verse, as they go to school, make friends, and must decide how to live out their lives.

Subjects: Conjoined Twins; Novels in Verse; Sisters

Dellaira, Ava.

In Search of Us. 2014. 9780374305314. **S**

Seventeen-year-old Angie has always believed that her father was dead. When she finds out that her mother lied about that, she sets off for California to find out for herself. In alternating chapters, Angie's mother, Marilyn, tells the story of herself at 17, pushed by her mother into an acting career and finding solace with her African American neighbor, James. Two seventeen-year-old girls, a generation apart, explore love and the meaning of family.

Subjects: Biracial; California; Single Parents

Dessen, Sarah.

The Rest of the Story. 2019. 9780062933621. **J** **S**

Emma's mother died when Emma was 10. She remembers the stories her mother used to tell her about the lake where she grew up and met Emma's father. Emma has vague memories of going to the lake when she was small, but she has had nothing to do with her mother's family for years. Now her father is getting remarried and going on a honeymoon, and her paternal grandmother is having her home remodeled. Emma's summer plans have fallen through, so she is going to the lake to spend the month with her maternal grandmother and a whole slew of cousins she doesn't really remember.

Subjects: Cousins; Family; Lakes; Motels; Summer

Flores-Scott, Patrick.

American Road Trip. 2018. 9781627797412. **S**

Teodoro ("T") Avila is more or less coasting. He'd much rather hang out with his best friend Caleb and play video games than study. Then one day he runs into Wendy, a girl he knew when they were kids. She wants to attend University of Washington, and suddenly, T is motivated to change his ways and try to get into the school too. He and Caleb agree to join a program for "underachievers with potential." He even gets a job so he can hire a tutor. But then T's brother Manny comes home from a tour in Iraq, suffering from PTSD. T is somewhat freaked out by Manny's outbursts, but then their sister Xochitl decides that what all of them need is a road trip— visiting family members and friends and eventually arriving in Hatch, New Mexico, where Manny, Teo, and Xochitl all find their way forward during a summer spent living with their Uncle Ed. (BFYA)

Subjects: California; College; Mexican American; New Mexico; PTSD; Road Trips

Hicks, Faith Erin.

Friends with Boys. 2012. 9781596435568. **J** **S**

Maggie has always been homeschooled, but now she is joining her older brothers in public school. To complicate matters, their mother has taken off, and Maggie doesn't have anyone to lean on during this big transition. That is, until the ghost of a sea captain's wife starts visiting her in her room at night. Her brothers do their best to help her, but they have their own problems, and Maggie is often left to fend for herself and find her own set of friends. But family comes through in the end, and Maggie's brother Daniel, in particular, helps her find her way. (GGN)

Subjects: Brothers and Sisters; Ghosts; Graphic Novels; High School; Homeschooling

Hinton, S. E.

The Outsiders. 1967. 9780670532575. **M** **J** **S**

This is a classic that still resonates today, about a group of teenage boys: the brothers Darry, Sodapop, and Ponyboy and their friends Dallas and Johnny. Darry is looking after his younger brothers after their parents died. All of them are so-called greasers, living in Oklahoma, and trying to find their way in a society that seems to dismiss them. The ways they care for one another and their struggles to make a life and a home for themselves make this a great book to recommend to fans of Markus Zusak's *Bridge of Clay.*

Subjects: Brothers; Friends; Gangs; Oklahoma

Jamieson, Victoria.

All's Faire in Middle School. 2017. 9780525429982. **M** **J**

Imogene ("Impy") has had an unusual childhood: She has always been homeschooled, and she spends several months of the year being part of the Florida Renaissance Faire, where her mother runs a shop and her father plays the bad guy in all the Faire's shows. But now she is going to school—middle school—and her job is to figure out how to negotiate middle school when your family is not exactly what most kids would call normal. (GGN)

Subjects: Family; Friends; Graphic Novels; Middle School; Renaissance Faires

Malone, Jen.

Changes in Latitudes. 2017. 9780062380173. **J** **S**

Cassie is thrown by her parents' divorce, especially after she overhears them fighting and comes to believe that her mother's infidelity caused the breakup. So she is less than thrilled when, after her father moves overseas for work, her mother announces that she, Cassie, and Cassie's brother Drew are going to sail a boat from Oregon to Mexico. They will be traveling in a sort of caravan with several other boats. Cassie resists everything about the trip, at least until she meets Jonah, a deckhand on one of the other boats.

Subjects: Divorce; Families; Mexico; Oregon; Sailing; San Francisco; Santa Cruz

Ruby, Laura.

Bone Gap. 2015. 9780062317605. **S**

When Finn was 15 years old, his widowed mother decided she was done parenting and took off to be with an orthodontist she met online. His brother Sean was just about to go off to college but instead got a job as a paramedic and stayed on to raise Finn. They were alone, eating from cans and making do, until a young woman named Roza came along. Finn found her hiding in the barn one morning, terrified and wearing one shoe. She was too scared to talk but took a key to the empty upstairs apartment when the brothers offered it. The three of them were just beginning to become a sort of family together when she disappeared. Finn was the only witness, but he cannot describe the face of the man who took Roza. Sean and the rest of the town believe Finn is just protecting Sean's feelings because another woman has abandoned them. But Roza is being held in a sort of netherworld, and she struggles to return to Finn and Sean. (Printz Award, BFYA)

Subjects: Brothers; Kidnapping; Magical Realism; Small Towns

Sheehan, Judy.

I Woke Up Dead at the Mall. 2016. 9780553512465. **M** **J**

One minute, Manhattan teen Sarah is at her father's wedding, wearing a hideous mango chiffon bridesmaid's dress. The next minute she's dead and at the Mall of America, in Minnesota (still in mango chiffon, unfortunately). She and a group of other New York teens all have to accomplish several things: attend their funerals, go back and relive one particular day, and find a way to move on to the afterlife. For Sarah, it means saving her father's life.

Subjects: Divorce; Ghosts; Humor; Mall of America; Murder

Voros, Ria.

The Center of the Universe. 2019. 9781525300387. **J** **S**

Grace is a shy 17-year-old who wants to be an astrophysicist. Her mother is the locally well-known TV anchor, GG Carter. Besides the normal mother–daughter conflict, Grace feels that GG favors her career over her family and resents her for that. Then GG disappears. In trying to find out what happened to her mother, Grace learns about herself, her mother, her grandmother, and more as she looks at the patterns of her life and of her mother's life.

Subjects: Astrophysics; Missing Persons; Mothers and Daughters

Younge-Ullman, Danielle.

Everything Beautiful Is Not Ruined. 2017. 9780425287590. **J S**

Ingrid has auditioned and been accepted for her senior year at Ayerton, a special music school in London. Her mother, a one-time opera singer who lost her voice, does not approve of Ingrid devoting her life to music. The loss of her voice and her career has thrown her into depression, and she is unwilling even to talk about music until Ingrid decides to take part in her school's production of *Wizard of Oz*. She grudgingly admits that Ingrid is good but still doesn't want her to focus her life on music. Her condition: Ingrid can go to Ayerton if she spends three weeks at Peak Wilderness, a summer camp in the wilds of northern Canada. The chapters alternate between the story of Ingrid's younger life and what led up to this summer and the story of what actually happens during those 21 days at Peak Wilderness. (BFYA)

Subjects: Family Secrets; Singing; Mothers and Daughters; Music; Wilderness Survival

Zusak, Markus.

Bridge of Clay. 2018. 9780385614290. **S O**

There are five Dunbar brothers. Matthew, the oldest, responsible one, narrates this tale. Next comes Rory, the fighter. Then Henry, the wheeler-dealer. Clay is the quiet one, the one Matthew calls "the best of us." And Tommy is the baby, the animal lover. They live on their own because their mother is dead and their father has left them. Then one day, their father shows up at their house and asks whether one of the boys will come and help him build a bridge. Clay, 16, decides to go. Matthew tells many stories here: the story of their father's youth and first marriage; the story of their mother Penelope's childhood in communist Poland, her escape to Australia with nothing much besides copies of *The Iliad* and *The Odyssey*; the story of their parents' meeting and their own childhoods; the story of their mother's death; the story of the bridge; and the story of Clay's friendship with a girl jockey named Carey Novac. There's also a mule named Achilles, a goldfish named Agamemnon, and a bird named Telemachus. It is a story about family and grief and history and the power of storytelling.

Subjects: Australia; Brothers; Death; Grief; Jockeys

Teen Pregnancy and Parenting

Even though the rate of teen pregnancy has declined, it is still a serious issue that teens face—and not just teen girls. The following stories focus on how the protagonist faces pregnancy, makes decisions about the future, and in some cases how he or she parents. The benchmark title for this topic is one of the most award-winning books in teen literature, Angela Johnson's *The First Part Last*.

Acevedo, Elizabeth.

With the Fire on High. 2019. 9780062662835. **J** **S**

Emoni Santiago, an Afro–Puerto Rican teen from Philadelphia, loves to cook, loves her *abuela*, and loves her toddler daughter Emma (whom she usually calls Babygirl). When she has an opportunity to take a special cooking class at school, she jumps at the chance, even though she doesn't think she'll be able to attend the culminating event: a week-long class trip to Spain. Taking Babygirl to daycare, sharing her (rather unwillingly) with Emma's father and his mother, helping 'Buela out around the house, and finding time to create unique culinary con-coctions, all while keeping up with schoolwork, make for a full life for Emoni. (BFYA)

Subjects: Cooking; Latinx; Multigenerational Families; Spain; Teen Parents

Johnson, Angela.

The First Part Last. 2003. 9780689849237. **M** **J** **S**

On Bobby's 16th birthday, his girlfriend Nia handed him a balloon and said, "Bobby, I've got something to tell you." Now Bobby is raising his daughter, Feather. And even though Bobby lives with his family, he knows the rules: "If she hollers, she is mine. If she needs to be changed, she is always mine. In the diction-ary next to 'sitter,' there is not a picture of Grandma. It's time to grow up. Too late, you're out of time. Be a grown-up."

Bobby loves Feather, but sometimes being a grown-up is harder than it looks, and Bobby has to figure it all out. (Printz Award, BBYA)

Subjects: Brooklyn; Graffiti; Street Art; Teen Fathers

Nolan, Han.

Pregnant Pause. 2011. 9780152065706. **J** **S**

Elly is pregnant at 16. Her missionary parents are going to Kenya, so Elly feels she has no other choice than to marry Liam, the baby's father, despite the fact that he drinks too much and plays around on her. She goes to work at her in-laws' "fat camp" where she hopes to be able to make a difference and also to figure out what she is going to do once the baby arrives.

Subjects: Camps; Maine; Marriage; Obesity; Teen Mothers

Schmidt, Gary D.

Orbiting Jupiter. 2015. 9780544462229. **M** **J** **S**

Jack's new foster brother is 14-year-old Joseph. Joseph has spent time in juvie for attacking a teacher, has spent his life dealing with an abusive father, and himself became a father at the age of 13. Living with Jack's family on a farm in Maine should be just the thing he needs, but he is obsessed with finding his daughter, Jupiter.

Subjects: Abuse; Foster Care; Maine; Teen Fathers

Zarr, Sara.

How to Save a Life. 2011. 9780316036054. **S**

Jill and her mother Robin are still struggling a year after the death of Jill's father. So Jill is astonished and definitely not happy when Robin announces that she is bringing 18-year-old Mandy to live with them. Mandy is seven months pregnant and lacking support of any kind. Robin wants to take care of Mandy and adopt her baby. With the story told in alternating voices from Jill and Mandy, the two young women struggle with their own demons and find it hard at first to find anything in common. (BFYA)

Subjects: Adoption; Grief; Teen Pregnancy

Fostering Arrangements

Stories about teens who live in homes not their own or with families to which they don't belong hold fascination for many teens. Check "foster care" in the index for more novels that feature this kind of arrangement. Some stories with this theme are horrifying; others are poignant and heartwarming.

Barthelmess, Nikki.

The Quiet You Carry. 2019. 9781635830286. **S**

Seventeen-year-old Victoria is locked out of her home and is now living in a crowded, chaotic foster home. She tries to cope with finishing high school, all the while worried about the 14-year-old stepsister who was left behind.

Subjects: Abuse; Foster Care Friends; Reno, Nevada; Stepfamilies

Crutcher, Chris.

Losers Bracket. 2018. 9780062220066. **S**

Annie Boots has a great foster family, but that doesn't mean that she doesn't want to see her birth mother and sister. In fact, Annie has figured out that, despite being an excellent multisport athlete, if she can manage to lose the first match and then move up the loser's bracket, there will be more opportunities for her mother and sister to show up at one of her games. Annie is especially concerned about her nephew Frankie, and when Frankie goes missing at one of Annie's swim meets, she feels that it must be her fault. Fortunately, despite the chaos, Annie is surrounded by people who genuinely care for her: foster parents who love her, even though they have high expectations of her; a case worker who knows the whole story; a therapist who can help Annie look at the big picture; a librarian who knows the power of stories; an insightful foster brother; and even her mother's boyfriend, a man who lives life without judgment. Annie is pulled between two worlds but refuses to give up on either of them.

Subjects: Basketball; Female Athletes; Foster Care; Librarians; Social Workers; Swimming

Dessen, Sarah.

Lock and Key. 2008. 9780670010882. **S**

Ruby lives alone in a squalid yellow house for a few months due to her alcoholic mother's abandonment. Even after her older sister and brother-in-law take her in, Ruby is desperate to maintain her independence. She is uncomfortable with suddenly living in her sister's super-posh community. Ruby must come to terms with her shared past with her sister and their complicated relationship with their sketchy mother. Life is complicated by the boy next door (with a secret) who helps her realize that the lines between family, loyalty, and what's right are not always clear or comfortable

Subjects: Abandonment; Mothers and Daughters; Sisters

Homelessness and Runaways

Stories dealing with the issues of homelessness and runaways can be grim and depressing but can also be life affirming. Protagonists in these novels may be orphans, but more often they have been abandoned or have left home to escape abuse or other toxic situations.

Ayarbe, Heidi.

Compromised. 2010. 9780061728518. **S**

Maya grew up on the streets with her con man father. When he lands in prison in Reno, she escapes foster care and heads for Idaho to find an aunt who supposedly lives there. Her trip is complicated by the addition of two other street kids.

Subjects: Homelessness; Idaho; Nevada; Runaways

Bohjalian, Chris.

Close Your Eyes, Hold Hands.

Sixteen-year-old Emily is a high school junior in Vermont, an Emily Dickinson fan, the only child of parents who also had no siblings, and a girl with a few friends (but not many) and some small impulse control issues. Then the nuclear plant, where her father is a lead engineer and her mother is the public relations officer, has a catastrophic meltdown. Not only were both her parents on-site and thus probably dead, but word soon leaks out that her father may have been responsible for the accident, due to his being drunk on the job. Emily, certain she will be hated by the thousands who are now evacuating their homes, slips away from her teachers and classmates and sets out on her own. Now Emily is an entirely different person: She is known as Abby; she lives in a drug dealer's apartment, or in various shelters, or in an igloo made of frozen bags of leaves; she earns quick money by "servicing" truckers at the truck stop or by stealing; she begins cutting herself. Then she meets nine-year-old Cameron, and although she never liked kids, she finds new purpose in taking care of him—until, that is, he becomes dangerously ill.

Subjects: Homelessness; Nuclear Disasters; Runaways; Vermont

Booth, Coe.

Tyrell. 2006. 9780439838795. **S**

> After Tyrell's father goes back to prison, Tyrell, his mom, and his brother become homeless. All the shelters are full, so they are sent to a disgusting, roach-infested hotel. When Tryell finds out his family won't be moved out of the crummy hotel because his mother has welfare fraud convictions, he decides he has to make enough money to move them into an apartment. Even though his mother wants him to take up drug dealing for money, Tyrell resists.
>
> **Subjects**: African Americans; Bronx; DJs; Drugs; Homelessness; Hotels

Cupala, Holly.

Don't Breathe a Word. 2011. 9780061766695. **S**

> Escaping her overprotective parents and manipulative, abusive boyfriend, Joy runs away and lives among the homeless teen population of Seattle's Capitol Hill.
>
> **Subjects**: Homelessness; Runaways; Seattle

Frost, Helen.

Keesha's House. 2003. 978037434043. **M** **J** **S**

> This verse novel tells the tales of several different teens whose messed-up lives take a turn for the better when they find respite at Keesha's House. Stephie is pregnant, Harris has been kicked out of home by parents who can't accept that he's gay, and Dontay has run away from his foster family after breaking some of their rules. (BBYA, Printz Honor)
>
> **Subjects**: Foster Care; Homelessness; LGBTQIA+; Pregnancy; Sestinas; Sonnets; Verse Novels

Quick, Matthew.

Sorta Like a Rock Star. 2010. 9780316043526. **J** **S**

> Despite living in an old school bus with her mother, Amber is relentlessly upbeat. But when her mother is killed, she slips into depression. The various people whom Amber has cheered over the years rally behind her to help her recover.
>
> **Subjects**: Depression; Homelessness; Murder; Optimism

Strasser, Todd.

Can't Get There from Here. 2004. 9780689841699. **J** **S**

> Living as part of a New York City tribe of homeless teens, Maybe receives help from a young librarian who has the same skin condition that she has. (BBYA)
>
> **Subjects:** Homelessness; Librarians; New York; Vitiligo

Yee, Paul.

Money Boy. 2010. 9781554980949. **S**

Ray's Chinese immigrant father disowns him when he finds that Ray has been looking at gay websites on his computer. Ray finds himself on the streets of Toronto, where he is beaten, robbed, and taken advantage of. He must decide whether to become a "money boy"—a teen male prostitute.

Subjects: Chinese Immigrants; LGBTQIA+; Homelessness; Toronto

Death, Disability, Disease

Death, disability, and disease are three of the most dramatic situations that can impact a teen's life, and these stories illuminate how teens may deal with these issues. These are the books to give to the teen reader who wants "a book that will make me cry."

Crowley, Cath.

Words in Deep Blue. 2017. 9781101937648. **S**

Henry and Rachel were once best friends, until Rachel's family moved away to the sea. Now Rachel is back, grieving the death of her brother and working in Howling Books, the store owned by Henry's parents. The store has a local tradition: the Letter Library, where people leave messages and underline special passages in books. Rachel once left a letter for Henry, but he never responded. Now that she's back, he has a girlfriend, and Rachel's grief has made her unwilling to open her heart. But somehow the books and the messages help them find their way back to each other.

Subjects: Australia; Bookstores; Grief; Love Letters

Dellaira, Ava.

Love Letters to the Dead. 2014. 9780374346676. **S**

The class assignment was to write a letter to a dead person. She only needed to write one letter. Instead she has a whole notebook full. First she wrote to Kurt Cobain, whom her sister May loved. He died young, just like May. Soon there are letters to Amy Winehouse, Amelia Earhart, Janis Joplin, and Heath Ledger, to name a few. She tells them about starting high school in the midst of a broken family: her divorced parents, her absent mother, and her dead sister, whom she worshiped.s. She even confronts what happened on the day May was supposed to be looking out for her.

Subjects: Death; Divorce; Epistolary Novels; Grief; Letters; Sisters

Forman, Gayle.

If I Stay. 2009. 9780525421030. **J S**

Mia, an exceptionally talented 17-year-old cellist, is waiting to hear if she has been accepted to Julliard. She's madly in love with her punk rocker boyfriend, who shares her passion for music, and is close to her wonderful parents and little brother. A family outing takes a strange turn when Mia finds herself outside the car, looking at her dead parents. Mia realizes she is outside her own body, as she is taken to a Portland hospital, where she tries to decide whether to go on with her parents or stay in this world. (BBYA)

Subjects: Accidents; Musicians; Oregon; Out of Body Experiences

Freitas, Donna.

The Survival Kit. 2011. 9780374399177. **S**

When Rose's mother dies of cancer, Rose loses all interest in her normal activities: cheerleading, her boyfriend Chris, school. On the day of her mother's funeral, Rose finds that her mother has left her a "survival kit": a box containing a variety of cryptic items, including an iPod, photos of peonies, a crystal heart. Although resistant at first, Rose gradually begins to sort through the survival kit items, determining how she can use them to move beyond her crippling grief.

Subjects: Cancer; Death; Grief

Friend, Natasha.

How We Roll. 2018. 9780374305666. **M** **J**

Quinn has alopecia, an autoimmune disorder that has caused her to lose all her hair. Her so-called friends back at her old school in eighth grade weren't very nice about it. Now her family has moved, and she is starting over in a high school across the country, where no one knows that she's wearing a wig. She just wants to be anonymous, which is hard when you also have a special needs brother. In her new school, she meets Nick, a former star football player who lost his legs in a car accident.

Subjects: Alopecia; Amputees; Autism Spectrum; Massachusetts; Prosthetics

Green, John.

The Fault in Our Stars. 2012. 9780142424179. **S**

Hazel Grace and Gus both have cancer, though Gus's is in remission. They meet in a teen cancer support group. Hazel resists falling for Gus because her cancer is terminal, and she doesn't want to be the cause of more suffering in his life. But they nevertheless form a close friendship, and Gus helps Hazel fulfill one of her deepest wishes: to travel to Amsterdam to meet the author of her favorite novel, with hopes of finding out what he thinks happened after the closing pages. Not to be read without a nearby box of tissues. (BFYA)

Subjects: Amputees; Amsterdam; Cancer

Turtles All the Way Down. 2017. 9780525555360. **J** **S**

Sixteen-year-old Aza suffers from anxiety and obsessive compulsive disorder. She and her friend Daisy decide to investigate the whereabouts of a missing man in order to get the cash reward. The man, a wanted criminal, happens to be the father of Aza's childhood friend, Davis. The mystery moves the plot, but the real story is Aza and her spiraling thoughts: "The thing about a spiral is, is you follow it forward, it never actually ends. It just keeps tightening, infinitely." (BFYA)

Subjects: Anxiety; Friends; Missing People; Obsessive Compulsive Disorder

Hepler, Heather.

We Were Beautiful. 2019. 9780310766438. **J S**

Mia's life changed a year ago when she was in a car accident that killed her sister and disfigured Mia's face. Now her family is falling apart: Her mother has left to join a convent, and her father is always on business trips. So Mia is going to spend the summer in New York with the grandmother she has never met. Her grandmother has arranged for Mia to have a job at a nearby diner, and Mia is rather overwhelmed to find herself taken in immediately by the loud, loving Brunelli family, who run the diner. Blue-haired Fig, in particular, latches onto Mia and gets her involved in an organization called Art Attack, and, through Fig, she meets Cooper, who has his own facial disfigurement. Fig, Cooper, and other friends Mia meets that summer, including her rather brusque grandmother, all help Mia come to terms with her grief and her guilt.

Subjects: Diners; Facial Disfigurement; Grandmothers; Grief; Guilt; New York

Holt, K. A.

From You to Me. 2018. 9781338193305. **M J**

In Amelia's middle school, on the first day of school, each eighth-grader is presented with a letter that he or she wrote in the sixth grade. But Amelia is instead presented with a letter written by her sister, Clara, who died just before the beginning of her own eighth-grade year. Amelia reads Clara's letter, with its list of things Clara wanted to do by eighth grade, and she decides to accomplish the list of items herself: try out for softball, host a party, come up with a stellar class prank, ask a boy to a dance. Helped by her best friend Taylor and a boy named Twitch, who had been a good friend of Clara's, Amelia grows throughout the year and begins to come to terms with her grief over Clara.

Subjects: Families; Grief; Pranks; Sisters

Plozza, Shivaun.

Tin Heart. 2018. 9781250312761. **S**

Marlowe, back at school after a heart transplant, just wants to be a normal girl. But normal is hard when you are known as the Dying Girl, your little brother is a Project Runway fan who dresses in self-designed costumes every day, your mother is a vegan activist, and you live in a natural food store that is next door to a butcher shop (and the butcher's son just happens to be super hot). Then there's the fact that Marlowe really wants to find the family of her heart donor, so she can thank them, but they apparently don't want to be found. But when Marlowe pushes her way into the life of the girl who may be the sister of her donor, she begins to realize that it isn't all about her; other people have feelings too.

Subjects: Australia; Grief; Heart Transplants; Vegans

Schneider, Robin.

Extraordinary Means. 2018. 9780062217165. **J** **S**

When Lane arrives at Latham House, he isn't at all sure what to expect. He, like the other residents, has a form of tuberculosis that has proved to be resistant to all forms of antibiotic. Lane expects that life is going to go on as usual—take his AP classes, practice for the SAT, prepare for college—but it turns out that it's hard to do all that when you're sick. Then he meets Sadie, Nick, Charlie, and Marina. Actually, he has already met Sadie—they went to the same summer camp when they were 13. But the group—the clique, really—stand out at Latham House. They're willing to take risks, to disobey rules, to act more like regular teenagers and less like sick kids. But they also learn that "the thing about trying to cheat death is that, in the end, you still lose."

Subjects: Boarding Schools; Death; Tuberculosis

Yoon, Nicola.

Everything, Everything. 2015. 9780553496642. **J** **S**

Maddy suffers from severe combined immunodeficiency disorder—she's basically allergic to everything. She never leaves her apartment and never sees anyone other than her doctor-mother and a nurse. When Olly moves in next door, they begin a secret relationship, first just online but eventually in real life. Maddy, in love for the first time, considers risking everything to be with Olly. (BFYA, Film)

Subjects: First Love; Immunodeficiency

Zappia, Francesca.

Made You Up. 2015. 9780062290106. **J** **S**

Alex is starting a new school at the beginning of senior year, following an unfortunate incident at her previous school. It's a particular challenge because Alex struggles with knowing what is real and what is not. She has paranoid schizophrenia, and she keeps things under control by using medication and obsessive "perimeter checks" and by taking pictures so that she can compare them with her memory later on. Even so, this school is strange, with its principal who seems to be obsessed with the gym's scoreboard and the blue-eyed valedictorian, Miles, who falls asleep during most classes and does pranks for money the rest of the time. Alex thinks that Miles may be the boy who helped her free the lobsters in the supermarket tank when they were seven, a boy—and an incident—that she thought until now were figments of her illness. Alex and Miles are drawn together, both of them struggling with their own demons but both of them needing something the other has to offer.

Subjects: Mental Illness; Paranoid Schizophrenia; Unreliable Narrator

Sarah's Picks

Acevedo, Elizabeth. *With the Fire on High.*

Crowley, Cath. *Graffiti Moon.*

Henry, Katie. *Heretics Anonymous.*

Jarzab, Anna. *The Opposite of Hallelujah.*

Johnston, E. K. *Exit, Pursued by a Bear.*

Rowell, Rainbow. *Fangirl.*

Chapter 2

Historical Fiction

Historical fiction tends to be among the more literary-leaning genres. The central appeal, typically, is a specific time period about which readers can learn and in which they can be immersed. Some time periods, like World War II and the Holocaust in particular, are much more common than others, like, say, 1950s Spain, which has a single title in this chapter, Ruta Sepetys's *The Fountains of Silence.*

When dealing with historical fiction, the question is always how to qualify what counts as "historical." If our measure for a quality definition is its parity with average readers' ideas of the same concept, then objective measures focusing on dates or years—for example, "A book can be historical fiction only if it takes place at least eighty years before the date of its composition"—are pointless.

A better tack is to think of historical fiction as being separated out from other genres by its focus on period details and generally as happening in a past that feels sufficiently unfamiliar. For many teen readers, a novel set in the early 1990s, a time with a significantly different technological and cultural landscape, will feel "historical." For those of us who lived through the 1990s, though, it may not feel that way.

Historical fiction almost always overlaps with another genre, typically realistic fiction, mystery, or romance, but historical horror and fantasy are also common. Due to this and the countless time periods and locations in which historical fiction can be set, the subject index will be an extremely useful tool when navigating this section.

North American Historical Fiction

The vast majority of titles set in North America take place in the United States, with a sliver of a minority occurring in Canada or Mexico, and they generally occur after European colonists arrived on the continent. The most recent title takes place in the early 1990s.

North American Fiction before 1900

The earliest settings in this section occur during the colonial era in the United States and present-day Canada. As is increasingly common for YA titles, many of the stories here address social issues with the commonest of those topics relating to race, gender, and labor.

Anderson, Laurie Halse.

Seeds of America. **M** **J** **S**

This trilogy is well researched and historically rich. It takes place during the Revolutionary War and is told from the perspective of two slaves, Isobel and Curzon. It cuts a different image of the meaning of America's fight for freedom than when, as is typical, it is told from the perspective of free, white characters.

Subjects: American Revolution; Slavery

Chains. 2008. 9781416905868.

> During the storied year of 1776, Isabel and her younger sister, Ruth, were purchased by a wealthy Loyalist family as slaves. After Ruth is sent away, Isabel is on her own in the household run by cruel masters. When an opportunity is presented for her to gain freedom and get her sister back by spying on her owners for the Revolutionaries, she seizes it. However, she soon learns that very few people are trustworthy and that those who are fighting for freedom from Britain aren't necessarily fighting for everyone's freedom. (NBA, BFYA)

Forge. 2010. 9781416961451.

> After Isabel and Curzon escaped, the spent some time together before Isabel left Curzon to look for Ruth. Curzon heads west and eventually joins the rebels' army. He fights through the harsh winter at Valley Forge, as alluded to by the title, but is eventually recaptured and enslaved alongside Isabel again. (BFYA)

Ashes. 2016. 9781416961475.

> Five years after Isobel and Ruth were sold to the Loyalist family and three years after Isabel and Curzon began searching for Ruth, they find her on a plantation just outside Charleston, South Carolina. Ruth doesn't have the reaction Isabel had hoped for, but she and Aberdeen, a fellow slave from the plantation, join Curzon and Isabel as they head north. (BFYA)

Anderson, M. T.

The Astonishing Life of Octavian Nothing, Traitor to the Nation. **S**

Octavian Nothing, dressed in fine clothes and a good powdered wig, is growing up in a household of scholars who use numbers rather than names. He and his mother, an accomplished princess from a far-off land, are the only ones in this house of scholars who are named rather than numbered. As the American colonists veer toward revolution, Octavian discovers that he and his mother are not members of the academy but rather slaves and study objects.

Subjects: 18th Century; African Americans; American Revolution; Communes; Scholars; Slavery

The Astonishing Life of Octavian Nothing, Traitor to the Nation: The Pox Party. 2006. 9780763624026.

> The first volume of Octavian's story tells about his childhood and coming-of-age as an experimental subject of study in a household of colonial philosophers. (BBYA, Printz Honor, NBA)

The Astonishing Life of Octavian Nothing, Traitor to the Nation: The Kingdom on the Waves. 2008. 9780763629502.

> The second volume details Octavian's life in British-occupied Boston when freedom is offered to slaves who take up the British cause. (BBYA)

Avi.

The Seer of Shadows. 2008. 9780060000158. **M**

> Horace, an apprentice photographer, discovers a ghost in a portrait he takes and with Pegg, a black servant girl, uncovers the truth behind the death of his client's daughter.
>
> **Subjects**: 1872; 19th Century; Ghosts; Photography; Seers

Bolden, Tonya.

Crossing Ebenezer Creek. 2017. 9781599903194. **J** **S**

> Those who are familiar with what happened at Ebenezer Creek as the Civil War neared its end will still be racked by the intensity of this story. After her plantation was liberated by Union soldiers, Mariah, her brother Zeke, and other former slaves followed behind the army as they traveled. Here she meets Caleb, a free black man, and the two instantly gravitate toward each other. This is the story of a tragedy and about characters who lived painful lives, and the reader is spared little of their pain. (BFYA)
>
> **Subjects**: Betrayal; Civil War; Ebenezer Creek; Emancipation; Georgia; Sexual Abuse

de la Cruz, Melissa.

Alex & Eliza. **J** **S**

> This well researched historical romance paints the portrait of one of America's earliest power couples: Alexander Hamilton and Eliza Schuyler. It's an excellent read for American history enthusiasts, fans of the *Hamilton* musical, and readers who want to read a realistic romance about an actual couple.
>
> **Subjects:** Founding Fathers; Hamilton, Alexander; New York City; Power Couples; Schuyler, Eliza

> *Alex & Eliza.* 2017. 9781524739621.
>
> > One of the founding families and among the most prominent members of society, the Schuylers throw an extravagant annual ball. This year, however, is anything but ordinary for Eliza, one of the three beautiful and charming Schuyler sisters, since it is the year she meets Alexander Hamilton.

> *Love & War.* 2018. 9781524739652.
>
> > Alex and Eliza have their young marriage tested on multiple fronts, not all of them directly related to the War for American Independence.

> *All for One.* 2019. 9780525515883.
>
> > This title, which sees Alex and Eliza doing well in New York City and adopting an orphan into the family, is the concluding entry in the trilogy.

Draper, Sharon.

Copper Sun. 2006. 9781416953487. **S**

Amari, a 15-year-old anticipating her wedding, witnesses the slaying of everyone in her African village except the strong young adults, who are taken captive as slaves. After surviving the horrifying middle passage, she is bought at auction as a gift for Clay Derby, the son of a plantation owner in South Carolina. Polly, born in Beaufort, Carolina Colony, is an indentured servant with 14 years to serve for her parents' debt. This harrowing tale is full of adventure as the two girls and the cook's young son, who had been used as alligator bait, escape and head south toward Spanish Florida. (Coretta Scott King Award)

Subjects: 18th Century; African Americans; Fort Mose, Florida; Indentured Servants; Middle Passage; Runaways; Slavery; South Carolina; St. Augustine, Florida

Kelly, Jacqueline.

Calpurnia Tate. **M**

Calpurnia Tate lives in Texas at the turn of the 20th century, a time and place in which females dealt with strict expectations. Unfortunately, for Calpurnia, these gender roles and her own interests don't always align.

Subjects: 1890s; Animals; Fentress, Texas; Gender Roles; Science

The Evolution of Calpurnia Tate. 2009. 9780312659301.

Calpurnia Tate, age 11 and three-quarters in 1899, lives in Fentress, Texas, with her immediate family, which includes six brothers; her grandfather, an avid naturalist who was an officer in the Civil War; and a few servants. Her love of reading and science is supported by her grandfather. This comforting slice-of-life tale, told in vignettes, illuminates family life, the role of girls, courting, and science a hundred years ago. (Newbery, BBYA, Bloomer)

Curious World of Calpurnia Tate. 2015. 9781250115027.

Calpurnia continues to experience both joys and heartbreak as she pursues her interests when and where she can while coming up against the harsh realities of a sexist social structure. She and her brother attempt to care for clandestine pets; she studies under the tutelage of Dr. Pritzker, a veterinarian; and she and her grandfather continue their exploration of science.

Lee, Stacey.

The Downstairs Girl. 2019. 9781524740955. **J S**

Jo Kuan, who is growing up beneath a newspaper office in 1890 Atlanta, has a secret: She is the author of a popular advice column. Exceedingly few among Atlanta's white population would expect a Chinese American teenager to be capable of writing the column. Moreover, if they found out about her, there would be unpleasant consequences to say the least.

Subjects: Advice Columns; Atlanta; Chinese Americans; Newspapers; Prejudice

Lester, Julius.

Day of Tears: A Novel in Dialogue. 2005. 9780786804900. **S**

The biggest slave auction in American history, told in dialogue from multiple viewpoints, gives insight into the lives of African American families torn apart, abolitionists trying to end slavery, slave owners, and others. (BBYA, Coretta Scott King Award)

Subjects: 19th Century; African Americans; Alternate Formats; Multiple Protagonists; Slavery

Miller, Sarah.

Miss Spitfire: Reaching Helen Keller. 2007. 9781416925422. **J S**

Annie Sullivan, Helen Keller's teacher, tells her own side of the story in this fictional biography of the troubled girl who became a prolific author and political activist. (BBYA)

Subjects: 19th Century; 20th Century; Biographical Fiction; Blind; Deaf; Handicaps; Keller, Helen; Sullivan, Annie; Teachers

Mosley, Walter.

47. 2005. 9780316110358. **J S**

47 is a young slave boy on a Georgia plantation in the 1830s. He is not allowed a name, only the number with which he was branded. His life changes when a mysterious 14-year-old runaway slave, Tall John, shows up and teaches him to read.

Subjects: 1830s; Education; Science Fiction; Slavery; Time Travel

Rinaldi, Ann.

Come Juneteenth. 2007. 9780152059477. **J S**

Betrayed by the family she loves, Sis Goose runs away from the Texas plantation where she has always lived after finding out from Union soldiers that she and the rest of the slaves had been freed two years earlier.

Subjects: 19th Century; Juneteenth; Sad Stories; Slavery; Texas

Or Give Me Death. 2003. 9780152166878. **J**

Patrick Henry's family has problems beyond those brought on by living in a country yearning for freedom. While he is out talking to the populace about the wrongs of British rule, at home his wife Sarah is going insane and endangering their children. The story is told by 16-year-old daughter Patsy and nine-year-old daughter Anne, who must deal with a mother locked in the cellar to keep the family safe.

Subjects: 18th Century; Biographical Fiction; Colonies; Mental Illness; Sisters

An Unlikely Friendship: A Novel of Mary Todd Lincoln and Elizabeth Keckley. 2007. 9780152055974. **M J**

Raised on an affluent Kentucky plantation, Mary Todd lived a privileged life despite having a harsh stepmother. Lizzy grew up as a slave, the daughter of a slave and her white master, and became an accomplished seamstress, ultimately buying her own freedom. When their paths cross, the two women who seemed so different become best friends.

Subjects: African Americans; Biographical Fiction; First Ladies; Keckley, Elizabeth; Lincoln, Mary Todd; Seamstresses; Slaves

20th-Century North America

A lot happened in the United States in the 20th century, including a handful of world-altering wars and significant social changes. America has mostly fought its wars abroad, though, so what life during wartime looked like for American citizens is significantly different from the experience of those living close to or directly in war zones. In terms of social change, the most obvious are those relating to labor, race, and gender; however, one of the things that makes this era feel the most unfamiliar is that communications technology seems so primitive.

Acosta, Daniel.

Iron River. 2018. 9781941026939. **J S**

Manuel ("Man-on-Fire") Moldonado Jr. is a redheaded Latino who lives, literally, on the other side of the tracks. The Pacific Railroad, also known as the iron river, separating Manuel's Mexican American neighborhood from the white neighborhood, serves as a hangout spot for Manuel and his three friends. One day, they find a dead hobo there, which is bad enough on its own. A racist cop, though, tries to pin the hobo's death on them.

Subjects: California; Pacific Railroad; Prejudice; San Gabriel

Andrews, Jan.

To See the Stars. 2019. 9781927917176. **J S**

Edie is a 14-year-old of meager means who takes the opportunities to work that come to her. She works in a factory and joins the labor reform movement. Through her eyes, readers see the before, during, and after of the tragic Triangle Shirtwaist Factory.

Subjects: Immigrants; Labor Issues; Triangle Shirtwaist Factory

Blume, Judy.

In the Unlikely Event. 2015. 9780525434771. **S**

In the early 1950s within a span of 58 winter days, three planes crashed in Elizabeth, New Jersey. This real, bizarre stretch of time is the inspiration for Blume's novel, which follows a number of characters focused on 15-year-old Miri and her household, which includes her mother, her grandmother, and her uncle. Everyone in town is impacted by the plane crashes one way or another.

Subjects: 1950s; Elizabeth, New Jersey; Plane Crashes

Blundell, Judy.

What I Saw and How I Lied. 2008. 9780439903462. **J** **S**

Fifteen-year-old Evie adores her glamorous mother, Bev, and her stepfather, Joe, who recently returned from World War II. When the family suddenly heads to Palm Beach, Florida, after Joe receives repeated phone calls from a former comrade in arms, they wind up in a hotel in the nearly deserted off-season town, where a wealthy, attractive couple called the Graysons befriends them. Soon Peter, a gorgeous 23-year-old who served in the war with Joe, turns up, and Evie falls hard for him. (NBA, BBYA)

Subjects: 1940s; Anti-Semitism; Murder Trials; Palm Beach, Florida; Veterans

Bolden, Tonya.

Saving Savannah. 2020. 9781681198040. **J** **S**

Taking place in Washington, D.C., in the early 1900s, this is the story of Savannah, a relatively privileged African American girl from a well-to-do family. Her journey is one that begins in comfort and wends its way into activism by way of a boy named Neil. It is a time of great social change, replete with competing ideologies, that would result in, among other things, the 19th Amendment and women's right to vote.

Subjects: Activism; Prejudice; Suffragists; Washington, D.C.

Brandon, James.

Ziggy, Stardust & Me. 2019. 9780525517641. **J** **S**

Jonathan, a gay teen in the early 1970s, is oppressed both personally by individuals and generally by the law. The story is hard to watch, but it's understandable that he tries to extirpate his homosexuality via painful conversion therapy. His story, however, is ultimately about the journey of self-acceptance.

Subjects: 1970s; Homophobia; LGBTQIA+; Missouri; Native Americans; Prejudice

Carlton, Susan Kaplan.

In the Neighborhood of True. 2019. 9781616208608. **J** **S**

Ruth's life is complicated. She lives in Atlanta with her mother and sister—they moved there following her father's death—and it's not just where her mother is from, it's the place where she once won the coveted title of Magnolia Queen. That legacy, though, is somewhat at odds with Ruth's current situation, where she is an outsider for her Jewish faith in a prejudiced town. After a romance develops between her and a boy, her life becomes even more difficult when that boy's brother bombs her synagogue.

Subjects: Atlanta; Hate Crimes; Jewish Diaspora; Prejudice; Terrorism

Crowder, Melanie.

Audacity. 2015. 9780147512499. **J** **S**

This novel is about the activist and leader of the shirtwaist strike, Clara Lemlich Shavelson. Clara immigrated to the United States with her family, escaping the violent anti-Semitism rampant in Russia. Clara is nothing if not fiercely determined to rise above her situation: Compelled to work in a factory instead of going to school, she finds a way to lead a union and effect meaningful change. (BFYA, Popular Paperbacks)

Subjects: Immigrants; Labor Unions

Devlin, Calla.

Tell Me Something Real. 2016. 9781481461153. **M** **J** **S**

The three Babcock sisters, each with her own personality, care for their mother while she receives experimental treatment for leukemia in Mexico, just across the border from their San Diego home, while their father is forced to work. As present as the fear of loss is, an act of betrayal is at the crux of this story. (Morris Finalist)

Subjects: 1970s; Betrayal; Grief; Illness; Mothers and Daughters; Siblings

Donnelly, Jennifer.

A Northern Light. 2007. 9780312360191. **S**

Mattie Gokey, who has a fascination with words and wants to go to college, takes a job at a resort in the Adirondacks in 1906, where she is on the scene for the murder that inspired Dreiser's *An American Tragedy*. (BBYA, Printz Honor)

Subjects: Adirondacks; Murder; Resorts; Word Play

Foxlee, Karen.

Lenny's Book of Everything. 2019. 9781524770129. **M** **J**

Crushing and beautiful, this is the story of Lenny and her brother Davey. Davey has gigantism caused by pituitary tumors and can't stop growing, which is preventing him—and Lenny—from living a "normal" life. They are granted a span of respite while they devour Burrel's *Build-It-At-Home Encyclopedia* as it is shipped to them book by book over the course of three years.

Subjects: 1970s; Bullying; Health Conditions; Ohio; Siblings; Special Needs

Hesse, Monica.

The War Outside. 2018. 9780316316699. **J** **S**

Upon the entry on the United States in World War II, two girls, Haruko and Margot, and their families, who are Japanese and German, respectively, are sent to an internment camp in Crystal City, Texas, by the United States government despite having done nothing wrong. The Japanese and German prisoners are kept in the same camp but tend to avoid each other. Haruko and Margot, however, strike up a friendship. As the tensions inside the camp are compounded by the times and events, the girls' relationship is tested. (BFYA)

Subjects: Crystal City, Texas; U.S. Internment Camps; Xenophobia

Hitchcock, Bonnie-Sue.

The Smell of Other People's Houses. 2016. 9780553497816. **M** **J** **S**

This is a realistic, heartfelt view into the trying lives of four poor teen-agers living in Birch Park, Alaska, a small fishing village, in the 1970s. Their stories weave in and out of one another's as they experience the ups and downs of very different—yet similar—lives. (Morris Finalist, Walden)

Subjects: Alaska; Native American; Poverty; Small Town

Kadohata, Cynthia.

Cracker! The Best Dog in Vietnam. 2007. 9781416906377. **M** **J**

Cracker, a German shepherd, is paired with Rick and sent to Vietnam to sniff for bombs. Together, they experience the war until they are both wounded and separated.

Subjects: Dogs; Vietnam War

Kira-Kira. 2004. 9780689856396. **M** **J**

In 1950s Georgia, Japanese American sisters, Katie and Lynn, are very close. Katie looks up to her older sister, Lynn, who guides her as their parents work long, grueling hours in a poultry plant. (Newbery)

Subjects: 1950s; Asian Americans; Cancer; Georgia; Sisters

Kalmar, Daphne.

A Stitch in Time. 2018. 9781250154989. **M**

After her Pops died and left her an orphan, Donut, an 11-year-old with a taxidermy hobby, has to contend with her wet blanket of an aunt, Aunt Agnes. Agnes has plans to move Donut from Vermont to Boston, which would mean losing her best friend, Tiny, in addition to all the other familiar things in her life. Donut decides to lay low in a cabin, hoping Aunt Agnes will simply give up.

Subjects: 1920s; Grief; Taxidermy; Vermont

Keenan, Sheila.

Dogs of War. 2013. 9780545128889. **M** **J** **S**

Based on true events, Keenan tells three stories of three dogs and their owners who fought in three different wars. Donnie and his dog Boots help the wounded in World War I; Loki, a sled dog, helps his handler in a tense search for a missing soldier in World War II; and, in the final story, a man who fought in the Vietnam War laments the treatment of military dogs, in particular one named Sheba. (GGN)

Subjects: Dogs; Graphic Novels; Short Stories; Vietnam War; World War I; World War II

Kiely, Brendan.

The Gospel of Winter. 2014. 9781442484894. **S**

Aidan is a 16-year-old in 2001 whose well-to-do parents leave a lot to be desired in many ways. Adrift, Aidan drinks and does drugs, but he also develops an ostensibly positive relationship with Father Greg. Father Greg's intentions, however, are sickeningly twisted. This title confronts sexual abuse in the Catholic Church head-on. (BFYA)

Subjects: Catholic Church; Connecticut; Drug Use; Friendship; Priests; Sexual Abuse

Larson, Kirby.

Hattie Big Sky. 2006. 9780385733137. **M J**

Yearning for a home of her own, 16-year-old Hattie leaves Iowa for Montana to take over her late uncle's homestead as war rages in Europe. (BBYA, Newbery)

Subjects: 20th Century; Homesteading; Montana; Orphans; World War I

Lee, Stacey.

Outrun the Moon. 2016. 9780147516916. **M J S**

Mercy Wong is the ambitious, capable 15-year-old daughter of a Chinatown launderer. Having gained her way into a prestigious school, she fabricates a new, loftier backstory to tell her classmates. Just after that lie is exposed for what it is, tragedy strikes: The historic earthquake of 1906 topples the city and throws lives into chaos. However, sometimes tragedy brings out the best in people. (BFYA)

Subjects: Chinese Americans; Earthquakes; Immigrants; Prejudice; San Francisco

Medina, Meg.

Burn Baby Burn. 2016. 9781536200270. **J S**

The year 1977 was an epically bad time to live in New York City: There was a blackout; there were arsons; and, to top it off, Son of Sam, a serial killer, was on the loose. High school senior Nora, however, has problems of her own: Her father is barely involved with her; her mother is almost entirely dependent on her; her brother, Hector, is a drug dealer who's seemingly growing more violent and abusive by the day. While coping with all these issues, she's still trying to graduate high school, work and save money, and navigate a new crush. The telling is raw, tense, and relatable. (BFYA)

Subjects: Family; Independence; New York City; Tense

Myers, Walter Dean.

Harlem Summer. 2007. 9780439368438. **J S**

Sixteen-year-old Mark Purvis gets on the wrong side of mobster Dutch Schultz during the blazingly hot Harlem summer of 1925 and ends up working for W.E.B. DuBois's magazine, *The Crisis*, a job that takes him into the path of many of the famous people of the Harlem Renaissance.

Subjects: 1920s; Celebrities; Harlem Renaissance; Mobsters; Musicians; New York; Writers

Nazemian, Abdi.

Like a Love Story. 2019. 9780062839367. **J** **S**

Living in New York City amid the AIDS epidemic, Art is an openly gay teen whose best friend, Judy, like him, is bullied by cruel classmates. Nevertheless, when Reza, a new boy from Toronto, transfers into the school, he and Judy date. When Reza and Art eventually get together, which is a much better fit, the impact it has on their relationship with Judy might not be what readers expect.

Subjects: AIDS Epidemic; LGBTQIA+; New York City

Patel, Sonia.

Rani Patel in Full Effect. 2016. 9781941026502. **S**

Rani is the daughter of Gujarati Indian immigrants living in Hawaii in the early 1990s. Suffering from the trauma of having been sexually abused by her father, witnessing the toxic relationship between her parents, and feeling like a social outsider leave her looking for a place to belong, which she finds in hip-hop and slam poetry. (Morris Finalist, Bloomer, BFYA)

Subjects: Hawaii; Hip-Hop; Immigrants; Incest; Sexual Abuse; Trauma

Pérez, Ashley Hope.

Out of Darkness. 2015. 9781467742023. **J** **S**

Naomi, a teenage Latina, and her two half siblings recently moved from bustling San Antonio to the town of New London, Texas. New London is largely an oil town, and racial tensions are high, subjecting Naomi to ample abuse. As she tries to navigate a complicated relationship with her father, take care of her younger siblings, go to school, and manage her feelings for a boy named Wash, the story, which is told from multiple perspectives, drives interminably forward toward the tragedy that opens the book: a school explosion that kills 300. (BFYA, Printz Honor)

Subjects: New London, Texas; Prejudice; School Tragedy

Perkins, Mitali.

You Bring the Distant Near. 2017. 9781250233868. **J** **S**

This is a story of family, culture, and change, told from the perspectives of three generations of women. Ranee is the mother of Sonia and Tara and the grandmother of Anna and Chantal. Ranee grows tremendously as a woman who held onto tradition at the cost of relationships to a grandmother who puts family first. Sonia and Tara, having been moved from Ghana to London and then from London to New York City, grow up in a culture different from their mother's. The youngest generation, Anna and Chantal, have an experience more immediately recognizable as that of the stereotypical American teenager. (BFYA)

Subjects: Family; Immigrants; Multiple Perspectives

Schlitz, Laura Amy.

The Hired Girl. 2015. 9780763694500. **M** **J**

This is the diary of Joan who, raised on the American dream by her mother but treated cruelly by her father, runs away from the family farm after her father crosses a line and burns her books. She flees to the big city of Baltimore and lies about her age, saying she is 18 when she is actually only 14. Getting a job working in the house of a wealthy family, she gets to know them and their other employee, while really getting to know what means to live among an entirely different kind of household from where she grew up. (BFYA)

Subjects: Abusive Parents; Catholicism; Diary; Orthodox Jews; Servants; World War II

Schmidt, Gary D.

Lizzie Bright and the Buckminster Boy. 2004. 9780618439294. **M** **J**

Turner, a preacher's kid, moves to Phippsburg, Maine, where he becomes an immediate outcast, but does find friendship with Lizzie Bright Griffin, an African American girl. The local leaders have decided their town would be a fine vacation destination if only they can rid the area of the "undesirables" who live on Malaga Island, which is Lizzie's home. (BBYA, Printz Honor, Newbery Honor)

Subjects: African Americans; Baseball; Churches; Eugenics; Minister's Children; Phippsburg, Maine

Okay for Now. 2011. 9780544022805. **M** **J**

After his abusive father mouths off to his boss and gets fired from his job, Doug Swieteck and his family move to the small town of Marysville, New York. In Marysville, Doug begins life as an outsider, often resorting to less than kind behavior when interacting with people. However, he has a good heart, and he slowly develops a few life-changing relationships. One is with a male librarian who patiently but persistently unlocks Doug's love of art. Another is with a cantankerous playwright. Set in the 1960s, Doug also has a brother who has gone off to fight in Vietnam and returns a substantially altered man. (BFYA, NBA)

Subjects: 1960s; Abusive Parents; Marysville, New York

The Wednesday Wars. 2007. 9780618724833. **M** **J**

As the only Presbyterian in his seventh-grade class in 1967, Holling Hoodhood must remain at school on Wednesday afternoons when his Jewish classmates attend Hebrew school and the Catholics attend catechism. On those days, his teacher makes him read Shakespeare. It proves to be an eventful year in Holling's life and in the world, with the Vietnam War looming large and the assassinations of Dr. Martin Luther King Jr. and Bobby Kennedy. (BBYA, Newbery Honor)

Subjects: 1960s; Long Island, New York; Shakespeare; Vietnam War

Sepetys, Ruta.

Out of the Easy. 2013. 9780399256929. **O**

Set in the 1950s in New Orleans, Josie, who is very nearly an adult, dreams of attending Smith College. However, her current situation is rough: The daughter of a prostitute with little to her name, she has the deck stacked against her. Things take a turn when she is thrown into a murder investigation and indebted to the mob—thanks to her mother. Moreover, she also has not one but two love interests: her clean-cut coworker and a bad boy biker. (BFYA)

Subjects: 1950s; New Orleans; Prostitution

Shabazz, Ilyasah.

X. 2015. 9780763690922. **J** **S**

This raw, unadulterated fictionalized biography of Malcolm X was written, in part, by one of his daughters. It tells the story of his tough childhood, including the suspicious death of his father and subsequent breakup of his family, ending with his time in prison as a young man. It is a true-to-life portrait of his experiences. (BFYA, Coretta Scott King)

Subjects: Abuse; Civil Rights; X, Malcolm

Shepherd, Gail.

The True History of Lyndie B. Hawkins. 2019. 9780525428459. **M** **J**

This slice of a not-so-comfortable life tells the story of Lyndie, an 11-year-old girl who lives in Tennessee. Her father is a veteran who served in Vietnam and struggles with alcoholism and other demons. When she and her father move in with her grandparents, she clashes with her grandmother and has other issues.

Subjects: 1980s; Alcoholism; Family; PTSD; Tennessee

Smith, Sherri L.

Flygirl. 2009. 9780399247095. **M** **J** **S**

Ida Mae Jones loves to fly. She flies her late father's crop duster in Slidell, Louisiana, and works as a maid to earn the money to go to Chicago to test for her pilot's license—because in the 1940s, no place in the South will award one to a Negro girl. When war breaks out, her beloved older brother quits medical school and enlists. With all resources going to the war effort, Ida Mae can no longer fly her father's plane, and she begins to pine for the sky. Then the WASP program in announced, a civilian corps of women who ferry planes and perform other flying tasks for the Army Air Force. Ida Mae applies, using her father's altered pilot's license and passing as white. (BBYA)

Subjects: African Americans; Pilots; World War II

Wolk, Lauren.

Wolf Hollow. 2016. 9780316260633. **M** **J**

Annabelle is an 11-year-old living in Wolf Hollow, a country town in Pennsylvania, in 1943. She and her family are something like friends with a rambling World War I veteran who always carries three guns with him. Annabelle's life takes a turn for the worse when the new girl in town, Betty, begins viciously bullying her. Then, when Betty goes missing and suspicions fall on Annabelle's veteran friend, she clings to the idea of his innocence.

Subjects: Bullying; Missing Persons; Pennsylvania; Veterans; World War II

Wynne-Jones, Tim.

The Emperor of Any Place. 2015. 9780763694425. **J** **S**

After Evan finds his father dead, his head resting on a book, neighbors insist he call the grandfather he never knew to come to Canada to help him sort things out. After a phone call from a stranger who tells Evan not to get involved in the mystery surrounding the book, he reads it and discovers an eerie story about an Okinawan soldier marooned on a heart-shaped island, a monstrous beast, ghostly children, ravenous ghouls, an American airman who has amputated his own hand, and a mystery involving his autocratic militaristic grandfather. (BFYA)

Subjects: Canada; Family; Grief; Supernatural; World War II

World Historical Fiction

YA historical fiction remains heavily focused on the West and Western history, with the overwhelming majority taking place in North America or Europe. While more characters from different cultures are being featured in YA historical fiction, it is still the case that an infinitesimal number of the popular books being published take place in other parts of the world.

World Historical Fiction before 1900

If a book is set outside of North America any time before 1900, it will be found here. These titles range from the ancient world, to the middle ages, to the Industrial Age.

Anstey, Cindy.

Deadly Curious. 2020. 9781250252272. **J** **S**

Sophia gets her chance to make her case for being the first women to join the Bow Street Runners, a revered crew of detectives, by taking on a case for a friend whose brother died under dubious circumstances.

Subjects: Detective; Family; London

Auxier, Jonathan.

Sweep: The Story of a Girl and Her Monsters. 2018. 9780735264359. **M** **J**

Nan Sparrow, who has a brutally difficult and extremely dangerous job as a chimney sweep in Victorian England, learned the trade from the paternal Sweep, who disappeared five years ago, leaving behind only his hat and a piece of coal. Her new boss, Wilkie Crudd, is nothing like Sweep, so when she is miraculously saved from a chimney fire, she awakes to find that the coal has turned into a golem—and that she has the chance to live a life of freedom. (Sydney Taylor Book Award)

Subjects: 19th Century; Child Labor; Golems; Jewish Folklore; Orphans; Victorian England

Avi.

Crispin. 🄼

In 14th-century England, orphaned Crispin finds he has a secret identity.

Subjects: 14th Century; England; Hidden Identity; Jugglers; Orphans

Crispin: The Cross of Lead. 2002. 9780786808281.

After his mother dies, the 13-year-old boy who has always just been called Asta's son discovers that he has a name, Crispin. When he goes to see the village priest to find out what the writing on his mother's lead cross says, he finds the man murdered. Lord Furnival's steward accuses Crispin of the crime and labels him a wolf's head—wanted, dead or alive. On the run, Crispin takes up with Bear, an itinerant juggler who helps him discover his true identity. (Newbery)

Crispin: At the Edge of the World. 2006. 9780786851522.

When Bear is wounded, he and Crispin find help from Old Aude, who protects Troth, a young girl with a cleft lip. The villagers rise up against them, but Crispin, Bear, and Troth flee to Brittany, where they encounter further danger.

Crispin: The End of Time. 2010. 9780061740831.

Crispin and Troth venture northwards to Iceland, as Bear would have wanted. Troth, however, stays behind at a convent they visit along the way. On his own, Crispin falls in with a traveling group of musicians, who prove to be liars and thieves.

The Traitors' Gate. 2007. 9780689853357. 🄼 🄹

When his father is arrested for selling secrets, 14-year-old John Huffman investigates in an attempt to prove his innocence.

Subjects: 19th Century; London

Berry, Julie.

The Passion of Dolssa. 2016. 9780451469922. 🄹 🅂

Under the conceit of being a document written by a monk in 1290, this is the story of Dolssa de Stigate, who was persecuted in the Inquisition for her heretical Christian mysticism. Unlike so many others, Dolssa managed to evade execution, thanks in large part to a matchmaker named Botille and her sisters. Although Dolssa is not a real historical figure, the time period is beautifully rendered, and the story itself is immersive. (BFYA, Printz Honor)

Subjects: Albigenses; Catholicism; France; Inquisition; Religion; Siblings

Gratz, Alan.

Samurai Shortstop. 2006. 9780803730755. 🄹 🅂

Sixteen-year-old Toyo Shimada lives in a challenging time as the Emperor has outlawed his family's Samurai traditions, and he is sent to a boarding school in Tokyo. (BBYA)

Subjects: 1890s; Baseball; Tokyo, Japan

Lawrence, Caroline.

The Roman Mysteries. 🅼

Flavia Gemina, a Roman sea captain's daughter, and her friends, Lupus, Jonathan, and Nubia, find and solve mysteries in several locations in the ancient world, including Ostia, North Africa, Pompeii, Rome, Greece, Turkey, and Egypt.

Subjects: Egypt; Friends; Greece; Mysteries; North Africa; Ostia; Pompeii; Rome; Turkey

The Thieves of Ostia. 2002. 9780761315827.

> Twelve-year-old Flavia finds three new friends, Lupus, Jonathan, and Nubia, when she sets out to solve the mystery of why dogs on their street have been slain.

The Secrets of Vesuvius. 2002. 9780761315834.

> When the four sleuths visit Flavia's uncle on a farm near Pompeii, they meet a blacksmith who may help them solve a riddle and find they must escape from the eruption of Mount Vesuvius.

The Pirates of Pompeii. 2003. 9781842550229.

> Living in a refugee camp following the volcanic eruption of Mount Vesuvius, the four sleuths take on a case involving missing children.

The Assassins of Rome. 2003. 9780761319405.

> Jonathan learns that his mother, who he thought had died in the siege of Jerusalem, may actually have been taken as a slave, when his uncle arrives on a mission to warn the emperor of an assassination plot.

The Dolphins of Laurentum. 2003. 9781842550243.

> After Flavia's father's ship is sunk and creditors come demanding their money, the foursome decide to retrieve the treasure from a sunken ship.

The Twelve Tasks of Flavia Gemina. 2004. 9781842550250.

> Flavia is unhappy when her father starts a relationship with a new woman in town and starts looking for a husband for Flavia.

The Enemies of Jupiter. 2005. 9781596430488.

> Flavia, Jonathan, Lupus, and Nubia are summoned to Rome by Emperor Titus to try to find the cause of a plague.

The Gladiators from Capua. 2005. 9781596430747.

> Flavia, Nubia, and Lupus wrangle an invitation to the opening of the Coliseum in the hope they will find their fears for Jonathan unfounded.

The Colossus of Rhodes. 2006. 9781596430822.

> As Lupus searches for his mother, the friends set out for Rhodes, home of one of the Seven Wonders of the World.

The Fugitive from Corinth. 2006. 9781842555156.

> The companions are off to Greece on a case involving their tutor and a stabbing.

The Sirens of Surrentum. 2006. 9781842555064.

> When the four friends visit a luxurious villa in Surrentum, they find themselves on the trail of a poisoner.

The Charioteer of Delphi. 2006. 9781596430853.

> A missing racehorse draws Nubia into a mystery while the companions are in Rome celebrating the Festival of Jupiter.

The Slave Girl from Jerusalem. 2007. 9781842555729.

> A slave girl is accused of a triple murder, and it is up to the four friends to get to the bottom of the mystery.

The Beggar of Volubilis. 2008. 9781842556047.

> The Emperor Titus sends the four companions on a quest that takes them across Northern Africa to find a gem called Nero's Eye.

The Scribes from Alexandria. 2008. 9781842556054.

> The four are shipwrecked near the coast of Alexandria.

The Prophet from Ephesus. 2009. 9781842556061.

> The gang flee from Titus while trying to solve a kidnapping case.

The Man from Pomegranate Street. 2009. 9781842556085.

> The foursome investigate the cause of Titus's suspicious death.

Lee, Mackenzie.

Montague Siblings. S

Strong voice, diverse characters, and raucous high jinks make this series about two siblings highly readable. The first book focuses more on the pleasure-loving brother, Monty, whereas the second focuses on the career-minded sister, Felicity.

Subjects: 18th Century; Drug Use; LGBTQIA+; Pirates; Prejudice; Siblings

The Gentleman's Guide to Vice and Virtue. 2017. 9780062382818.

> Monty, the 18-year-old hedonistic heir to a wealthy estate, travels across 1700s Europe with his little sister, Felicity, and his best friend and crush, Percy. Having promised to behave until they deliver Felicity safely at school, Monty wastes little time before getting wasted, screwing up the plan, and sending them on the run from a Duke. Full of sensual indulgence as well as social commentary, this is a highly entertaining story with substantial depth. (Stonewall, BFYA, Rainbow)

The Lady's Guide to Petticoats and Piracy. 2018. 9780062795328.

> Felicity, the focus of this sequel, fights for her goal of becoming a doctor against the prejudice and the mores of the times, while also discovering what can happen when one accepts the kindness of strangers. (Bloomer, BFYA, Rainbow)

Maniscalco, Kerri.

Stalking Jack the Ripper. J S

Audrey, a mixed-race teenage girl, Thomas, an intelligent and blunt teenage boy, and Audrey's uncle, a pioneering forensic scientist, investigate murders. Each book focuses on a different historically inspired killer. The science is realistic, and the descriptions of the autopsies can be vivid.

Subjects: 19th Century; Autopsies; Forensic Science; Mystery; Nobility

Stalking Jack the Ripper. 2016. 9780316273497.

Audrey Rose Wordsworth, daughter of the wealthy and important Lord Wordsworth, apprentices in her uncle's lab where, in the late 1800s, he carves up cadavers in the interest of forensic science. Being a woman, the teenage Aubrey isn't allowed to attend her uncle's lectures or be interested in science, so she lies and disguises herself when necessary to pursue her passion. She, her uncle, and the precocious Thomas investigate the murders of Jack the Ripper.

Hunting Prince Dracula. 2017. 9780316551663.

Audrey and Thomas plan to attend a top-tier forensics school in Romania, home to the infamous Vlad the Impaler, the inspiration for Dracula. While there, however, they investigate a series of linked murders. Oddly, some murders look as if they were committed by vampires, while others appear to have been killed for being suspected as vampires.

Escaping from Houdini. 2018. 9780316551700.

Audrey, her uncle, and Thomas set sail on a glitzy cruise ship for America. Opportunities abound aboard the ship for intimacy and entertainment, including a carnival, but when people start turning up dead, with a tarot card at the scene of each murder, they do what they do best and investigate the killings.

Capturing the Devil. 2019. 9780316485548.

Audrey and Thomas take on the White City Devil in the final book of this series.

McCullough, Joy.

Blood Water Paint. 2018. 9780735232112. **S**

This is the harrowing, true story of Artemisia Gentileschi, an Italian Baroque painter, who created beautiful art and gained recognition despite suffering greatly in a patriarchal society that routinely oppressed women. She was raped as a teenager and tortured at the trial while testifying against her assailant. Nevertheless, she persisted in part due to the stories of other strong women. (Bloomer, BFYA, Morris Finalist, NBA)

Subjects: 1600s; Artists; Rome; Sexual Violence; Verse

Meyer, Carolyn.

Duchessina: A Novel of Catherine de' Medici. 2007. 9780152055882. **S**

Orphaned as an infant, Catherine de' Medici, a wealthy heiress, grows up with relatives (including the pope) and in convents until, at the age of 14, she is married off to Henri II of France.

Subjects: 16th Century; Catherine, Queen of France; Florence, Italy; France; Henri II, King; Orphans

Meyer, L. A.

Bloody Jack. 🄹 🅂

As a 12-year-old orphan living on the streets of London after her family dies of the pestilence, Mary Faber looks for a way out by disguising herself as a boy and shipping out as a ship's boy on HMS *Dolphin*.

Subjects: Girls Dressed as Boys; Pirates; Sailing

Bloody Jack: Being an Account of the Curious Adventures of Mary "Jacky" Faber, Ship's Boy. 2002. 9780152167318.

> Jacky takes to life on the high seas, chasing pirates, acquiring the nickname "Bloody Jack" after killing a man and being taken captive by pirates. As she grows older, it becomes harder to hide the fact that she is a girl. Then she falls in love with Jaimy, a fellow sailor. (BBYA)

Curse of the Blue Tattoo: Being an Account of the Misadventures of Jacky Faber, Midshipman and Fine Lady. 2004. 9780152051150.

> Put off the *Dolphin* after it is discovered that she is a girl, Jacky Faber ends up at a proper Boston boarding school, where she, of course, finds trouble. Despite sending letters to Jaimy, she doesn't hear back from him. (BBYA)

> **Subjects**: Boarding Schools; Boston

Under the Jolly Roger: Being an Account of the Further Nautical Adventures of Jacky Faber. 2005. 9780152053451.

> Making her way back to England on a whaler, Jacky discovers Jaimy with another girl, then takes to the streets, where she is captured by a press gang and put on a British warship.

> **Subject**: Privateers

In the Belly of the Bloodhound: Being an Account of a Particularly Peculiar Adventure in the Life of Jacky Faber. 2006. 9780152055578.

> Back in Boston at the boarding school, Jacky and her classmates are kidnapped while on a boating excursion and shipped off to the slave markets of North Africa.

Mississippi Jack: Being an Account of the Further Waterborne Adventures of Jacky Faber, Midshipman, Fine Lady, and Lily of the West. 2007. 9780152060039.

> On her way back to Boston after her last adventure, Jacky is arrested by the British on piracy charges, but she escapes and heads for the American frontier.

> **Subjects**: Mississippi River; New Orleans; Riverboats

My Bonny Light Horseman: Being an Account of the Further Adventures of Jacky Faber, in Love and War. 2008. 9780152061876.

> Disguised again as a male, Jacky winds up in the French Army, fighting alongside Napoleon.

> **Subjects**: Dancer; Paris; Spies

Rapture of the Deep: Being an Account of the Further Adventures of Jacky Faber, Soldier, Sailor, Mermaid, Spy. 2009. 9780152065010.

> Kidnapped just before her wedding, Jacky is off to the Florida Keys to find a lost Spanish treasure and replenish the coffers of the British crown, depleted by the expenses of the Napoleonic War.

> **Subjects**: Diving; Exploration; Pirates; Treasure

The Wake of the Lorelei Lee: Being an Account of the Further Adventures of Jacky Faber, on Her Way to Botany Bay. 2010. 9780547327686.

> Having purchased a passenger ship, Jacky docks in London, only to be arrested and sentenced to be transported to Australia.

The Mark of the Golden Dragon: Being an Account of the Further Adventures of Jacky Faber, Jewel of the East, Vexation of the West, and Pearl of the South China Sea. 2011. 9780547517643.

> Jacky heads back to London, seeking to clear her name and Jaimy's. Jacky must use all her wiles in order to get there, meanwhile Jaimy is off trying to avenge her.

Viva Jacquelina! Being an Account of the Further Adventures of Jacky Faber, Over the Hills and Far Away. 2012. 9780544234390.

> Working for the British, Jacky is still looking for her betrothed. In the process, she becomes entangled in the Spanish Inquisition and has other exciting adventures and encounters.

> **Subjects**: Goya, Francisco; Spanish Inquisition

Boston Jacky: Being an Account of the Further Adventures of Jacky Faber, Taking Care of Business. 2013. 9780544439146.

> Arriving in Boston, Jacky upsets multiple parties including the Women's Temperance Union and has a surprising encounter with Jaimy.

> **Subjects**: Boston; Women's Temperance Movement

Wild Rover No More: Being the Last Recorded Account of the Life & Times of Jacky Faber. 2014. 9780544217775.

> The closing title in the series, Jacky meets a young Edgar Allen Poe, joins the circus, and is charged with treason.

Mitchell, Saundra, ed.

All Out: The No-Longer-Secret Stories of Queer Teens throughout the Ages. **2018. 9781335470454.**

> This collection, edited by Saundra Mitchell, features 17 stories by different authors. Diverse in era and locale, ranging from the 14th to the 20th centuries, these stories also feature an array of characters. LGBTQIA+ identity features include gay, lesbian, trans, and people on the ace spectrum. (BFYA)

> **Subjects**: LGBTQIA+; Short Stories

Spooner, Meagan.

Sherwood. 2019. 9780062422316. **J** **S**

Sitting somewhere between medieval historical fiction and folklore, Sherwood is an inventive, gender-swapped retelling of the story of Robin Hood. Robin of Locksley and Maid Marian were going to live happily ever after, then Robin was killed abroad. Now Marian dodges the (less than) romantic overtures of Guy of Gisborne while donning the late Robin's green cloak and fighting for a just society

Subjects: Feminist; Folklore; Grief; Medieval; Robin Hood

20th-Century World Historical Fiction

By no means is this subcategory limited to World War II titles, but they do make up the majority of titles. Again, the overwhelming majority are set in Europe; however, the themes vary widely, as do their appeal factors.

Alkaf, Hanna.

The Weight of Our Sky. 2019. 978153442608. **J** **S**

On May 13 1969, race riots exploded in Kuala Lumpur, the capital of Malaysia. Amid the chaos and violence, 16-year-old Melati, who is Malay and has OCD, is separated from her mother and taken in by a Chinese family, but she refuses to give up on finding her mother.

Subjects: Kuala Lumpur, Malaysia; Mental Illness; OCD

Avi.

The Button War. 2018. 9780763690533. **M** **J** **S**

Twelve-year-old Patryk's village in Poland had been occupied by the Russians up until the Germans bombed his school and drove the Russians out. While war is being waged by the adults, Jurek, the self-appointed King of Patryk's gaggle of friends, starts a childish game: Each of the friends will steal buttons from the soldiers, and whoever ends up with the most will become King. Things get dark, though, as Patryk's friends and fellow button hunters begin turning up dead.

Subjects: Friends; Poland; World War II

Barker, Michelle.

The House of One Thousand Eyes. 2018. 9781773210711. **S**

In the 1980s, while Germany was still split in two, East Germany was run by the Communist Party, whose iron fist was often the Stasi, the secret police. This is the world in which Lena, a 17-year-old, lost her parents, had a breakdown, was institutionalized, then moved in with her Auntie, who gets her a job as a janitor for the Stasi. The job, which is ostensibly a lucky break, is actually soul crushing as Lena is regularly sexually abused there. When the one bright light in her life, her author uncle whom she visits once a week, disappears, she does what she must to figure out what happened to him. (BFYA)

Subjects: East Germany; Grief; Mental Illness; Oppression; Rape; Sexual Abuse

Bennett, Jenn.

The Lady Rogue. 2019. 9781534431997. **O**

Seventeen-year-old Theo goes on a trip with her father, who is a widower and aficionado of antiques. Although her father hasn't been very present since the death of her mother, it's still odd that he disappears. It's also odd—if also a little bit welcome—to be told by Huck, a former lover interest, that her father went missing while looking for an artifact that belonged to the infamous Vlad the Impaler.

Subjects: Europe; Istanbul; Paranormal; Vlad the Impaler

Berry, Julie.

Lovely War. 2019. 9780451469939. **J S**

In 1942, Aphrodite and Ares meet for a tryst and are ensnared, literally, by Aphrodite's husband, Hephaestus, who puts them on trial. In her defense, Aphrodite recounts the intertwining stories of four people whose lives were shaped by World War I: James, who dreams of being an architect but who gets sent to the trenches instead; Hazel, a gifted pianist who supports the war as a nurse; Aubrey, a black musician of considerable talent in the U.S. Army; and Colette, another gifted musician whose life was obliterated by the war. (Walden Award)

Subjects: Epic; Greek Gods; Magical Realism; Racism

Boyne, John.

The Boy at the Top of the Mountain. 2016. 9781250115058. **J S**

Unfortunately timely, this is the portrait of a young boy's gradual transformation in the years leading up to the outbreak of World War II. Pierrot, a French orphan, is taken in by his German aunt who works at the Berghof, Hitler's alpine estate, and she promptly changes his name to its German counterpart, Pieter. Pieter is intoxicated by Hitler's attention and certitude, soaking up his ideology and becoming a different person.

Subjects: Berghof; Hitler, Adolf; Orphan

The Boy in the Striped Pajamas. 2006. 9780385751063. **J S**

When his father is appointed as commandant, nine-year-old Bruno is uprooted from his Berlin home and moves to the country, where he sees a huge wire fence and hundreds of people in striped pajamas. As he explores the perimeter, he meets Shmuel, a boy who shares his same birthday but who lives on the other side of the fence. (IRA YAC)

Subjects: Auschwitz; Concentration Camps; Germans; Holocaust; Jews; Poland; World War II

Bradley, Kimberly Brubaker.

The War That Saved My Life. Ⓜ Ⓙ
Set during World War II but mostly taking place in the countryside, this is the story of Ada, a young girl who has spent most of her life without comforts or anchoring.

Subjects: Abuse; Disabilities; England; Mothers and Daughters; World War II

The War That Saved My Life. 2015. 9780147510488.
Ada, a young girl with a disability, lives a wretched life under her mother's tyranny. When bombs start falling on London, Ada's mother sends Ada's brother away to safety, giving little thought to Ada. However, Ada accompanies her brother, and the two are spirited into the countryside where they are taken in by Susan, a woman who is loving in her own way. Ada has difficulty adapting to a parental figure so different from her mother, but with time she does and grows into a fuller person. (Schneider Family Book Award, Newbery Honor)

The War I Finally Won. 2017. 9780525429203.
Ada and Jamie continue their new life with Susan, with Ada recovering from surgery. The pressures of the war force the community closer together, and Ada must overcome the scars left by her past.

Crowder, Melanie.

An Uninterrupted View of the Sky. 2017. 9780399169007. Ⓙ Ⓢ
In Bolivia in 1999, 17-year-old Francisco's father is unjustly arrested in connection with a law created in response to the United States' foreign policy on drug production. The Bolivian prison experience is very different from the one in the United States. For instance, Francisco and his sister stay with their father in prison after their mother leaves them there. Moreover, amenities that are provided to prisoners by default in the States, like mattresses, must be bought. Amid such a trying situation, Francisco nevertheless does his best to take care of his sister, attend school, and be a teenager.

Subjects: Abandonment; Bolivia; Prison; War on Drugs

DeWoskin, Rachel.

Someday We Will Fly. 2019. 9780670014965. Ⓙ Ⓢ
During World War II, many Jewish people fled to Japanese-occupied Shanghai. Lillia, whose circus-performing family is from Poland, does just this with her father and sister. Unfortunately, her mother, Alenka, disappears before she is able to leave with them. Escaping is one thing, but carving out a home and existence is another. In order to make ends meet, Lillia dances at a gentleman's club, unbeknownst to her father. All the while, they hold out hope that Alenka will join them.

Subjects: Performers; Refugees; Shanghai

Ennis, Garth, Steve Epting, and Elizabeth Breitweiser.

Sara. 2019. 9781732748538. **J** **S**

It's year two of the siege of Leningrad, and the Russians are still fighting off the Germans. Among these fighters is Sara, a crack shot who contends with her own inner demons as well as with the madness that is the external world. Engrossing artwork complements the straightforward but captivating story of a woman at war in a complicated world.

Subjects: Graphic Novels; Leningrad; Snipers

Garretson, Dee.

All Is Fair. 2019. 9781250168696. **M** **J** **S**

In the waning year of World War I, an aristocratic teen, Lady Mina Tretheway, hungers to make a meaningful contribution to the war effort instead of merely attending to her noble duties. When she receives a coded message, she and two companions begin a fast-paced adventure that tests their intelligence as much as their courage and resolve.

Subjects: Aristocracy; Cryptography

Gratz, Alan.

Projekt 1065. 2016. 9780545880169. **M** **J** **S**

Britain taps Michael O'Shaunessey, a 12-year-old boy living in Berlin with his parents who are Irish ambassadors and British intelligence personnel, to gather intel on the Nazis. Michael does this by joining the Nazi Youth and becoming an exemplary member. The ruse pays off in short order when he learns that his classmate's father designs planes for the Nazis. Then the Nazis task him with killing someone. Just how far is Michael willing to go to gather lifesaving information?

Subjects: Berlin, Germany; Nazi Youth; Spies; World War II

Hartnett, Sonya.

The Silver Donkey. 2006. 9780763629373. **M**

Two young sisters, Marcelle and Coco, find a blinded World War I deserter starving in the woods near their home. They smuggle food to him, and he tells them stories about a little silver donkey.

Subjects: Deserters; Donkeys; France; Literary; World War I

Hesse, Monica.

Girl in the Blue Coat. 2016. 978-0316260633. **M** **J** **S**

Living in Nazi-occupied Amsterdam in 1943, 18-year-old Hanneke earns a living and helps support her family by sourcing elicit contraband like food, alcohol, and tobacco. She is stunned when a client asks her to find a missing Jewish girl who was last seen in a blue coat, but she takes the job. Her investigation is eye-opening and transformative in more ways than one. (BFYA, Edgar Award)

Subjects: Amsterdam, Holland; Missing Persons

Iturbe, Antonio.

The Librarian of Auschwitz. 2017. 9781627796187. **J** **S**

This book is based on the true story of Dita Kraus, who was a prisoner at Auschwitz and who was assigned to help at Block 31, a part of the camp where children were looked after. Unofficially, she is also given the responsibility of protecting one of the prisoners' greatest treasures: a collection of eight books. Alongside the narrative of Dita's experience at Auschwitz, readers also learn about her past in Prague and the stories of other prisoners. (BFYA)

Subjects: Auschwitz; Books; Concentration Camps; Holocaust; Librarians; World War II

Killeen, Matt.

Orphan Monster Spy. 2018. 9780451478733. **J** **S**

After her mother was killed while they were attempting to flee Germany, Sarah is taken in by a British spy who asks her to undertake a dangerous, duplicitous mission: infiltrate an elite boarding school and get close enough to the other girls to steal secret plans from their Nazi parents. It sounds like a tall order—and, to be sure, it is—but Sarah looks the part with her blonde hair and blue eyes and is a consummate actor. (BFYA)

Subjects: Boarding School; Spies

Morpurgo, Michael.

Private Peaceful. 2004. 9780439636483. **J** **S**

Tommo Peaceful goes off to World War I with his older brother Charlie, who has married Molly, Tommo's best friend. They leave behind their widowed mother and their developmentally disabled brother. Descriptive of life in the trenches and the unfair treatment of the soldiers at the hands of a sadistic sergeant, this story is told through flashbacks, as Tommo waits for dawn, checking the watch that belonged to Charlie. (BBYA)

Subjects: Brothers; Literary; Trench Warfare; World War I

War Horse. 2007. 9780439796637. **M**

This is a story about World War I as told from the viewpoint of Joey, an English farm horse who is sold to the army, then captured by the Germans. Joey always yearns for Albert, the boy on the farm who was too young to join up when Joey first went to war. Like Private Peaceful, this book delivers a powerful antiwar message.

Subjects: Animal Protagonist; England; France; Germany; Horses; World War I

Peet, Mal.

Tamar: A Novel of Espionage, Passion, and Betrayal. 2007. 9780763634889. **S**

Tamar was given her name by her grandfather, who worked with the Resistance in Holland during World War II. After he dies, Tamar finds information that leads her back to the story of her namesake. (BBYA)

Subjects: Holland; Literary; Resistance; World War II

Sepetys, Ruta.

Between Shades of Gray. 2011. 9780142420591. **M** **J** **S**

Two years after World War II begins, Lina, a 16-year-old Lithuanian girl, and her family are taken by Soviet authorities and shipped off to labor camps. Lina's creative spirit fights to survive by creating drawings with hidden meanings and passing them along, hoping that they will somehow reach her father, from whom she, her mother, and her brother were separated when they were captured. It is based on the stories of the author's relatives. (Morris Award)

Subjects: Artists; Labor Camps; Lithuania; Secret Codes; Survival

Salt to the Sea. 2016. 9780142423622. **J** **S**

In 1945 Eastern Europe, four teenage refugees from different countries flee the advancing Russian army, hoping to escape danger aboard a ship. Unbeknownst to them, they are headed for the *Wilhelm Gustloff*, which never made it to its destination—it sank, torpedoed by a Soviet submarine, killing over 9,000 of its passengers. (BFYA)

Subjects: Multiple Perspectives; Refugees; Shipwrecks

The Fountains of Silence. 2019. 9780399160318. **J** **S**

Taking place in Madrid, Spain, during General Francisco Franco's rule—1957 to be exact—the story of life after the Spanish War unfolds. Franco has recently reopened Spain to foreigners, who come for business and leisure. For some, like 18-year-old Daniel Matheson, this means vacationing to a special place: It's where his mother grew up, and it's a chance to take some stunning photographs. For others, like Ana and her family, it means work: She is one of the staff members at Daniel's hotel. However, beyond the glitz, there is a dark, oppressive government that values power over people.

Subjects: 1950s; Franco, Francisco; Madrid, Spain; Oppression; Photography

Sheth, Kashmire.

Keeping Corner. 2008. 9780786838592. **M** **J**

In 1918, 12-year-old Leela is widowed before she ever lives with her husband. Now she must shave her head and spend a year confined to a "keeping corner" in the house to mourn him. Meanwhile, India is changing, and Gandhi is working toward independence for the country. (BBYA)

Subjects: Child Brides; India; Widows

Smith, Roland.

Elephant Run. 2007. 9781423104025. **M**

When the London bombings demolish their apartment in World War II, Nick Freestone's mother sends him to live with his father in Burma, but then the Japanese invade, and his father is taken prisoner. Pressed into service for the Japanese, Nick and his new friend, Mya, escape on elephant back and set out to rescue their loved ones. (BBYA)

Subjects: Burma; Elephants; World War II

Stamper, Vesper.

What the Night Sings. 2018. 9781524700386. **J** **S**

> Gerta, a 16-year-old who was imprisoned in a concentration camp, survives and must somehow go back to normal life. Her love of music and talent with the viola help her find something resembling a normal life, but she is still unable to sing. Unlike many other books about the sufferings of the Holocaust, this title looks at the life of a survivor after being liberated from the camps. (BFYA, Golden Kite Award, Morris Finalist)
>
> **Subjects**: Bergen-Belsen Concentration Camp; Holocaust; Illustrated; Musicians

Venkatraman, Padma.

Climbing the Stairs. 2008. 9780399247460. **M** **J** **S**

> After her father suffers brain damage in a riot that is part of the independence movement, 15-year-old Vidya and her family must move in with conservative relatives in Bombay, who believe she should marry soon and not go to college. (BBYA)
>
> **Subjects**: 1940s; Independence; India; World War II

Wein, Elizabeth.

Code Name Verity. **J** **S**

> This series offers intense historical fiction about pilots, espionage, friendship, and more. The first book is an intense tale of being captured by the enemy and loyalty. The second book, *Rose Under Fire*, is a kind of sequel that follows a new character but that sees familiar characters return. Lastly, *The Pearl Thief* is a prequel, detailing a period in Julia's life before her capture.
>
> **Subjects:** Alternate Format; Friendship; Holocaust; Loyalty; Spies; World War II

Code Name Verity. 2012. 9781405258210.

> > Queenie, a spy, and Maddie, a pilot, both from the UK are over France when their plane goes down. Believing Maddie doomed, Queenie leaves her behind but is captured, imprisoned, tortured, and forced to write a confession. She slowly fills them in on what she knows about the British war effort while the stories of those around her—including her late friend Maddie—are also told. Full of twists and hooks, readers find this one hard to put down. (Printz Honor, Carnegie Medal)

Rose Under Fire. 2013. 9781423183099.

> > Told indirectly through diary entries by other means, this is the story of Rose Justice, a female pilot who ferries planes in Europe during World War II. Unfortunately, she is captured and sent to Ravensbrük, the infamous women's prison camp, where she suffers greatly, witnesses horrors of inhumanity, and befriends women who have been used for Nazi experiments. This novel can be read and enjoyed as a stand-alone. (BFYA)
> >
> > **Subject**: Ravensbrük

The Pearl Thief. 2017. 9781484717165.

> Julia, a 15-year-old Scottish aristocrat, is knocked unconscious while visiting her family's estate and awakes in the hospital with some memories missing. Although she was rescued by an itinerant people called "the Travellers," they are nevertheless suspected as her assailants, so strong are the prejudices against them. Julia befriends the Travellers and, eventually, works to solve the case of a scholar who was murdered. This companion novel and prequel to Code Name Verity stands on its own.
>
> **Subjects**: Memory Loss; Prejudice; Sexuality

Wild, Ailsa, et al.

The Invisible War: A World War I Tale of Two Scales. 2019. 9781541541559. **M** **J**

Using striking black-and-white illustrations, this graphic novel tells the story of Annie Barnaby, a nurse on the Western Front of World War I.

Subjects: Graphic Novel; Nurses

Wilson, Kip.

White Rose. 2019. 9781328594433. **J** **S**

The story is based on the real historical figure of Sophie Scholl, a nonviolent activist who was executed for her work opposing the Nazi's cruelty. It takes place across two timelines, one being about her life when she was young and the second being about her life following her arrest. White Rose is the name of the larger movement against the Nazis of which she is a member; she was not the only White Rose member to be captured and killed. This story is told in striking verse.

Subjects: Germany; Nonviolent Activism; Resistance; Verse; World War II

Yolen, Jane.

Mapping the Bones. 2018. 9780399257780. **M** **J** **S**

Loosely inspired by "Hansel and Gretel," this is the tale of Chaim and Gittel, 14-year-old twins who endure tragedy and suffering at the hands of the Nazis. In the beginning, they are living with their family in a Polish ghetto, but when they catch wind of an impending relocation, arrangements are made for them and two other children to escape. The escape fails, and the children are taken to a concentration camp. At the camp, the twins are prime subjects for the awful experiments of one of Dr. Mengele's protégés. (Golden Kite Award)

Subjects: Concentration Camps; Holocaust; Twins; World War II

Zusak, Markus.

The Book Thief. 2006. 9780375931000. **S**

The story of Liesel, a foster child living in Munich during World War II, is narrated by Death, who tells of Liesel's theft of books, her foster parents, and the Jewish man the family hides in their basement. (BBYA, Printz Honor, PP)

Subjects: Books; Death; Foster Children; Jews; Munich, Germany; World War II

Sam's Picks

Berry, Julie. *Lovely War.*

Ennis, Garth, Steve Epting, and Elizabeth Breitweiser. *Sara.*

Maniscalco, Kerri. *Stalking Jack the Ripper.*

Schmidt, Gary. *Okay for Now.*

Sepetys, Ruta. *The Fountains of Silence.*

Chapter 3

Romance

Teens are romantic creatures by nature. Many teens are involved in romantic relationships, and even if they are not, they may think about them, dream about them, and hope for them. Although the majority of teen novels have some element of romance, the novels in this chapter revolve around the romantic elements. This type of novel focuses on emotions, but unlike the traditional adult romance novel, it does not have to end with a "happily ever after." In fact, in these books the "ever after" is often ignored, since the book focuses more on starting a dating relationship. Historical romances can be found in Chapter 2, Historical Fiction. Other love stories can be found in Fantasy (Chapter 5, Speculative Fiction).

Contemporary Romance

These novels take place in the present day and focus on the relationships between the main characters.

Albright, Emily.

The Heir and the Spare. 2016. 9781440590108. **J** **S**

Evie's mother dies when she is six, but she leaves a stack of letters for Evie's father to give her to read, once each year on her birthday. On her 17th birthday, she receives an extra letter, postmarked London. This letter tells Evie that her mother has kept a secret and that now she is sending Evie on a series of quests. First task: Graduate from high school and get admitted to Oxford University, where the next letter will find her. Once at Oxford, she begins her mother's quest but also meets Prince Edmund, the second son of the King of England.

Subjects: Oxford, England; College; England; Letters; Mothers and Daughters; Royalty

Bennett, Jenn.

Serious Moonlight. 2019. 9781534425149. **S**

Birdie Lindbergh is a loner with a passion for mystery novels and movies. She was homeschooled by her grandmother on Bainbridge Island, and now basically the only people in her life are her grandfather, her "honorary aunt" Mona, and Miss Patty, who runs the Moonlight Diner in Seattle. Birdie is at the Moonlight after interviewing for a job at the Cascadia Hotel when she meets Daniel Aoki, a Japanese American magician, and surprises even herself by hooking up with him in his car—and then fleeing the scene. She is even more surprised when she turns up at the Cascadia for her new job and discovers that Daniel is a coworker. Daniel draws Birdie into a cautious friendship by suggesting that the two of them investigate whether a mysterious guest at the hotel is actually famed reclusive mystery writer Raymond Darke.

Subjects: Biracial; Dancers; Diners; Hearing Impaired; Hotels; Japanese Americans; Magicians; Mystery Writers; Narcolepsy; Seattle

Cross, Julie, and Mark Perini.

You before Anyone Else. 2016. 9781492604921. **S O**

What Finley really wants to do with her life is to reopen her mother's Connecticut dance studio, which closed after a car accident killed her mother and disabled her father. To earn money, she is modeling in New York, where she lives with several other models. At a shoot, she meets Eddie, who is just getting his start in modeling. He is hoping to earn some money quickly, while avoiding running into his wealthy parents, who think he is doing a summer course at Princeton, prior to starting college in the fall. Finley is hardworking and straightforward, and Eddie is charming and funny but clearly hiding something. The two manage to turn what was intended to be a one-night-stand into a genuine friendship. Eddie gradually reveals to Finley the depth and importance of his secret and the way it could change both of their lives. Plenty of high society, high fashion, high drama, and romance.

Subjects: Connecticut; Dance; Fashion; Modeling; New Adult; New York

Doktorski, Jennifer.

How My Summer Went up in Flames. 2013. 9781442459403. **S**

After Rosie's boyfriend Joey cheats on her, she sets his car on fire—but not entirely intentionally. She was burning her mementos from their relationship in his driveway, and his car sort of got in the way. But despite her anger, she still wants Joey back. Joey doesn't want her, though; he serves a temporary restraining order on her. To get her out of town and away from Joey, Rosie's parents send her on a road trip with her best friend Matty and his two friends, Spencer and Logan. Rosie isn't a bit excited to be traveling in a car with three nerds who constantly discuss *Star Wars*, but as time goes on, a small spark begins to kindle between Rosie and Logan.

Subjects: Friendship; New Jersey; Road Trips

Forman, Gayle.

Just One Day. 2013. 9780525425915. **S**

The summer after Allyson graduates from high school, she takes the "Teen Tours! Cultural Extravaganza" to Europe, along with her best friend, Melanie. Allyson is a good girl from Pennsylvania—she gets good grades, she doesn't drink, she does what is expected of her. So she even surprises herself when, on the tour's last day, she persuades Melanie to skip the scheduled performance of *Hamlet* by the Royal Shakespeare Company to go to the free outdoor "Guerrilla Will" production of *Twelfth Night*. There, she is completely smitten by the young man who plays Sebastian. Amazingly enough, the next day, she runs into "Sebastian," who, it turns out, is a 19-year-old Dutchman named Willem. One thing leads to another, and suddenly Allyson—whom Willem has decided to call Lulu because she looks like the silent film actress Louise Brooks—is headed for Paris with Willem for just one day. So "Lulu" and Willem spend the day—and night—in Paris, but in the morning, Willem is gone. Allyson is devastated because she thought she and Willem really had something, and she doesn't know why he left. What's more, she doesn't know how to get in touch with him—she never learned his last name—and he doesn't even know her real name, so he can't get in touch with her. Although it was just one day that she spent with Willem, it changed her whole life. (BFYA)

Subjects: College; London; New Adult; Paris; Shakespeare

Just One Year. 2013. 9780525425922. **S**

Willem and Lulu shared a magical day in Paris, but when Willem wakes up, he doesn't know where he is or what happened to him—just that he must find Lulu. This companion book to *Just One Day* tells the story from Willem's point of view and follows up with what happened to him in the year after that magical day in Paris.

Subjects: Amsterdam; Europe; Paris

Goo, Maureen.

Somewhere Only We Knew. 2019. 9780374310578. **J** **S**

Lucky is a California girl, but now she's a K-pop star, touring the world. Korean American Jack is the son of a businessman currently living in Hong Kong. His father wants him to go to college and join the business, but Jack's real love is photography, and he moonlights as a paparazzo, selling celebrity photos to a tabloid. Late one night after a show, Lucky, worn out and craving a hamburger, slips by her security people and eventually runs into Jack in the streets of Hong Kong. Once Jack realizes who she is, he comes up with a plan to stay with Lucky all night and sell the story and photos to his media connections. In alternating voices, Lucky and Jack describe their night together and their growing attraction to one another.

Subjects: Hong Kong; Korean Americans; K-pop; Photography

Hawkins, Rachel.

Royals. 2018. 9781524738235. **J** **S**

Daisy's older sister is engaged to the Crown Prince of Scotland, and suddenly Daisy is being hauled off to Scotland along with her sister to learn the ropes of royalty. All does not go well, especially when the prince's younger brother keeps trying to embroil Daisy in scandal. But Miles, the young courtier who has been assigned to Daisy, adds a bit of interest to the summer for Daisy. See also: *Her Royal Highness*, in the section "LGBTQIA+ Romance."

Subjects: Publicity; Royalty

"If Only . . ." Series. 🕡 🔳

These stand-alone titles are light, contemporary romances that focus on teenage girls who want what they can't have and fall for someone they shouldn't. Each novel presents a different what-if situation.

Baratz-Logsted, Lauren.

Red Girl, Blue Boy. 2015. 9781619635005.

> Katie's father is the Republican candidate for president; Drew's mother is the Democratic candidate. Katie and Drew meet on a morning talk show and find themselves drawn to one another. But campaign intrigue can't help but interfere with their relationship.

Subjects: Politics; Presidential Campaigns

Burkhart, Jessica.

Wild Hearts. 2015. 9781619632585.

> Brie's father is a land developer who constantly moves the family, depending on where his next project is meant to happen. This time it's Lost Spring, Wyoming. The problem is that the resort hotel that Brie's father wants to build is going to displace a population of wild mustangs, and the locals don't want that to happen. Brie meets Logan, the son of the man who is heading up the protests against Brie's father. In this Romeo-and-Juliet situation, Brie and Logan are going to have to find a way to stop the feud between their fathers if they ever hope to be together.

Subjects: Horses; Hotels; Real Estate Development; Wyoming

Finnegan, Amy.

Not in the Script. 2014. 9781619633971.

> Emma is used to the spotlight, having grown up as a child actor. Jake works as a model to earn money for his family. He isn't used to the paparazzi. Jake and Emma are costarring in a hot new TV show, along with Brett, a Hollywood hottie whom Emma has had a long-distance crush on. Once they're all working together, Emma realizes that, despite the fondest wishes of the paparazzi, it is actually Jake that she really has feelings for.

Subjects: Hollywood; Paparazzi; Tabloids; Television Shows

Hubbard, Mandy.

Everything But the Truth. 2015. 9781619636590.

> Holly's mother manages a retirement home for the wealthy on Mercer Island, near Seattle, and Holly helps out, delivering lunches and flirting with the old men. Then she meets Malik, the grandson of one of the wealthiest of the residents. He assumes that Holly is also visiting a wealthy grandparent, and Holly doesn't bother to correct him, since she assumes they'll never see one another again. But as they start to click and see one another more often, Holly finds it harder and harder to tell Malik the truth.

Subjects: Grandparents; Mothers and Daughters; Seattle; Social Classes

Hubbard, Mandy.

Fool Me Twice. 2014. 9781619632301.

Landon and Mackenzie spend summers working at the Serenity Ranch and Spa. The summer between junior and senior years, they were an item, until Landon dumped Mackenzie for another girl. Now, the summer after senior year, they're back at Serenity. Awkward. Then Landon bumps his head and gets amnesia—he thinks it's last summer and that he and Mackenzie are still together. Mack uses the situation as an opportunity for revenge—she'll let him fall for her all over again and then dump him, so he can see what it feels like. But can she do it?

Subjects: Amnesia; Horses; Summer Romance; Washington State

Rae, Kristin.

What You Always Wanted. 2016. 9781619638211.

Maddie Brooks is a theater nut, and she loves classic movies, especially ones with Gene Kelly. Her father's job has moved the family from Chicago to suburban Houston, and she focuses her energies on getting a part in a local production of *Crazy for You*. The big problem is that she doesn't know how to tap-dance. When she starts carpooling to school with her next-door neighbor, baseball star Jesse Morales, she doesn't expect anything to come of it, but when she learns that he is a former dancer, she enlists him to help her out.

Subjects: Baseball; Dance; Houston; Movies

Rae, Kristin.

Wish You Were Italian. 2014. 9781619632851.

Seventeen-year-old Pippa's parents send her to Italy for the summer to study art history. Instead, Pippa takes the money for the program and decides to see Italy on her own. She makes her own list of goals for the summer, including falling in love with an Italian boy. That certainly seems possible when she meets Bruno, but then there's Darren, an American archeology student, who keeps showing up at just the wrong (or right) moment.

Subjects: Florence; Italy

Stultz, Kelly Fiore.

Just Like the Movies. 2014. 9781619633544.

Marijke is pretty, popular, and athletic, and she's got a great boyfriend, except for the fact that she's not entirely sure that Tommy really cares about her. Lily is kind of a nerd who can never seem to get a boyfriend, even though she's had a crush on Joe for forever. After running into each other at a showing of *Titanic*, Lily and Marijke wonder why life can't be more like the movies. So they decide to set up some movie-like grand gestures and get Tommy and Joe to take them to the prom.

Subjects: Friendship; Love; Movies; Prom

Kenneally, Miranda.

The Hundred Oaks Series. J S

These are loosely connected romance novels, all of which take place at Hundred Oaks High School and most of which feature girl athletes. The series need not be read in order, but characters from the earlier novels often appear in later ones.

Catching Jordan. 2011. 9781402262272.

Jordan is the female quarterback and captain of the school's football team and is used to being just one of the guys. Then new kid Ty shows up to join the team, and suddenly Jordan is feeling challenged, both on the football field and in her heart.

Subjects: Football; Romance; Tennessee

Stealing Parker. 2012. 9781402271878.

When Parker's mother comes out as a lesbian, Parker is thrown for a loop. She quits softball and starts hopping from boy to boy in an effort to prove that she is straight. When she realizes how much she misses softball, she takes a job as an assistant manager on the boys' baseball team, which now has a new, handsome, 23-year-old coach.

Subjects: Baseball; LGBTQIA+; Mothers and Daughters; Tennessee

Things I Can't Forget. 2013. 9781402271908.

Kate is spending the summer working at a church camp. She is struggling with her own beliefs, especially since she recently helped her friend Emily get an abortion. While not everyone at the camp is as friendly as Kate would like, she's happy to see cocounselor Matt, the boy who gave her her first kiss back in junior high.

Subjects: Abortion; Camp; Summer Romance

Racing Savannah. 2013. 9781402284762.

Savannah's father is a horse trainer, and she would like to be a jockey someday. Helping him out at his job at Cedar Hill Farms, she meets Jack, the son of the owner.

Subjects: Horse Racing; Tennessee

Breathe, Annie, Breathe. 2014. 9781402284793.

Annie is training for the Country Music Marathon in Nashville, despite the fact that she doesn't much like running. But she's doing it in tribute to her boyfriend Kyle, who died before he could run in the marathon. Helping her along are new running friends, her coach, and, especially her coach's brother, Jeremiah.

Subjects: Grief; Marathons; Runners; Tennessee

Jesse's Girl. 2015. 9781402284823.

Maya loves music. She plays the guitar and is part of an 1980s music tribute band. Her school requires every senior to shadow a professional for a day, so when Maya put down, "I want to be a musician," she figured she would end up in the electronics section of WalMart. Instead, she finds herself shadowing Jesse Scott, the 18-year-old country music star who just happens to be her principal's nephew. Despite being from Tennessee, however, she is not a fan of country music. Jesse has enough girls hanging around him that he's not particularly happy with Maya's presence, either. But the two of them spend a day together, and both learn something about themselves and their dreams.

Subjects: Country Music; Nashville, Tennessee; Playlists

Defending Taylor. 2016. 9781492630081.

Taylor Lukens gets kicked out of her private school, where she was soccer team captain, valedictorian, and president of the debate team. She's also the daughter of a Tennessee senator. But she was found with drugs (Adderall), and she doesn't feel she can tell anyone that they belonged to her boyfriend. The only person at Hundred Oaks she might be able to trust is Ezra, her older brother's best friend.

Subjects: Female Athletes; Soccer; Tennessee

Coming Up for Air. 2017. 9781492630111.

Like many elite teen athletes, Maggie has very little time for a personal life. Everything is about swimming and Maggie's hope to qualify for the Olympics. Fortunately, her best friend Levi is also a swimmer, so at least they have each other. But when Maggie goes to Berkeley for a college visit and hangs out with rival Roxy, she begins to realize that, unlike Roxy, she has missed out on a lot of normal high school experiences. She figures she can remedy that at least partly by getting Levi to teach her how to make out with a guy.

Subjects: Best Friends; Friendship; Swimmers

Klein, Jen.

Hearts Made for Breaking. 2019. 9781524700089. **S**

Lark knows what she wants, and it isn't commitment. She finds cute boys who are jocks or scholars or both, she gets them to fall for her, then she does something so that they'll break up with her before things get too serious. Now her best friends, Cooper and Katie, decide that it is time for Lark to try something different, so they challenge her to pick a boy, different from her usual type, get to know him, and actually give the relationship a chance. She chooses Ardy, the new transfer student. Everyone says he's "undateable," and that's an interesting challenge in itself. But she finds herself becoming intrigued with him. He pushes her out of her comfort zone, and so, naturally, she makes mistakes. But she also finds that there's more than one way to fall in love and more than one way to break a heart.

Subjects: California; Falconry; High School

Lindner, April.

Love, Lucy. 2015. 9780316400695. **J S**

Lucy's parents want her to give up her dreams of being in the musical theater and study for a nice, practical major like business. She agrees to follow their advice after her father offers her a trip through Europe the summer after graduation as a sort of bribe. In Italy, she meets an American boy,

Jesse, who is wandering Europe playing music. The two have a summer fling, but she heads home for college, and Jesse stays in Europe. Once in college, Lucy decides to forget Jesse, and she also decides to major in business but also try out for the school's musical, Rent. When Jesse shows up unexpectedly, Lucy has some big decisions to make.

Subjects: College; Fathers and Daughters; Italy; Musical Theater; Summer Romance

Matson, Morgan.

Amy and Roger's Epic Detour. 2011. 9781416990666. **M** **J** **S**

Amy's mother has already moved from California to Connecticut to start a new job, Amy's twin brother is in rehab, and her father recently died in a car crash. She is the last one left, the house is about to be sold, and she has to get the family car from California to Connecticut. Amy doesn't want to drive across America or anywhere else. Enter Roger, a family friend's son who has to go visit his father in Philadelphia. Amy's mom has arranged for Roger to drive Amy across the country. Amy's mom has set the route, planned the stops, and booked the hotels. But . . . Both Amy and Roger have their own goals and plans for this trip, which truly becomes an epic detour. (BFYA)

Subjects: Grief; Playlists; Road Trips; Summer Romance

Menon, Sandhya.

From Twinkle, with Love. 2018. 9781481495400. **J** **S**

Twinkle wants to be a filmmaker, in the vein of her heroes: Sofia Coppola, Jane Campion, Nora Ephron, Mira Nair, Ava DuVernay, and other pioneering women. So when her classmate Sahil Roy approaches her and suggests that they make a film together for an upcoming festival, she agrees—and it doesn't hurt that Sahil's twin brother, Neil, is Twinkle's crush. Told in letters from Twinkle to her women filmmaker heroes, interspersed with texts between Sahil and his friends.

Subjects: Colorado; Desis; Epistolary Novels; Filmmaking; Indian Americans

There's Something About Sweetie. 2019. 9781534416789. **J** **S**

Ashish Patel is the younger brother of Rishi, from *When Dimple Met Rishi*. Rishi is the perfect Desi (Indian American) son, and Ashish loves him but resents him a little. Ashish doesn't date Desi girls, but when his latest girlfriend dumps him, and he can't seem to be his old flirtatious self, he succumbs to his parents' plea to let them set him up with an Indian girl. His mother decides on Sweetie Nair, but when she meets with Sweetie and her mother, Sweetie's mother refuses the match. Her mother tells Sweetie that she is the wrong girl for Ashish because, well, Sweetie is fat. Sweetie decides to take matters into her own hands because she knows that, while she may be fat, she's also an interesting, intelligent person, a good friend, and the fastest runner in her high school. Sweetie and Ashish's growing friendship is a delight, as they both set out to prove something to themselves and to their parents.

Subjects: California; Desis; Indian Americans; Matchmaking; Runners

When Dimple Met Rishi. 2017. 9781481478687. **J** **S**

Dimple wants to go to a summer program on web development at San Francisco State. She is shocked when her parents—traditional Indian parents who are intent on finding her the perfect Indian husband—agree. But when she gets to San Francisco, she finds out why: Rishi Patel is also attending the program, and he informs her that she is his future wife—all arranged by their respective parents! Dimple is determined not to like Rishi, but then they end up partnered on a big project, and gradually she learns that there's more to him than she initially thought. (BFYA, Bloomer)

Subjects: California; Cartoonists; Desis; Friends; Indian Americans; Matchmaking; San Francisco; Web Development

Smith, Jennifer E.

Field Notes on Love. 2019. 9780399559419. **J** **S**

Hugo is a sextuplet, and he's fine with being surrounded by his siblings. He's even fine with the fact that the six of them are minor celebrities in their hometown of Surrey, England. There are certainly perks—like the fact that a benefactor has provided scholarships for all six siblings to attend college—provided they all go to the same local college. But Hugo sometimes longs to break out on his own. So he and his girlfriend, Margaret Campbell, who is going to go to college in California, come up with a great plan: They'll fly to New York together, then take the train across the country, stopping in a few cities along the way. But then she breaks up with him and, as a parting gift, gives him the tickets for the trip. However, since she made all the reservations, they're all in her name, not to mention they're nonrefundable and nontransferable. But that's not going to stop Hugo, so he conducts a search for another Margaret Campbell to make the trip with. Mae Campbell (Margaret is her full name) is an aspiring filmmaker, but she has just been rejected by the University of Southern California's (USC) film school. When she sees Hugo's ad searching for another Margaret Campbell, she feels that this is the opportunity she has been looking for, something to stir up the creative juices and give her a chance to make a new film to use in convincing USC that they were wrong. The two meet at New York's Penn Station and head out on a weeklong trip of discovery that changes both of them.

Subjects: California; Chicago; Denver; England; Road Trips; Sextuplets; Trains

Hello, Goodbye, and Everything in Between. 2015. 9780316334426. **J** **S**

Aidan and Clare are high school sweethearts, but now they are headed to college on opposite sides of the country. On the night before they part, they take a nostalgic tour of their past, trying to decide whether to break up now or wait for the inevitable to happen once they're both in college.

Subjects: Chicago; College

The Statistical Probability of Love at First Sight. 2012. 9780316122382. **J** **S**

Seventeen-year-old Hadley would like to be anywhere but on a plane to England to attend her father's second marriage to a woman she's never met. That's all she can think about as she waits in the airport lounge, frustrated and relieved that she missed her flight and will have to wait for another one. It's all she can think about—until she meets Oliver. He takes the seat next to her on the trans-Atlantic flight, and with his British accent and witty banter, Hadley begins to wish the plane would stay in the air forever. But they go their own ways after the flight, not even exchanging phone numbers or e-mails. Will they ever see one another again? Will she be able to forgive her father and accept her stepmother? What is going to happen on this trip to England? And what is the statistical probability of love at first sight?

Subjects: Airplanes; Divorce; England; Stepmothers

This Is What Happy Looks Like. 2013. 9780316212816. **M** **J**

Because of a typo, Graham accidentally sends Ellie an e-mail about his pig, Wilbur. The two carry on a flirtatious conversation, which leads them to a deeper relationship. Little does Ellie know, Graham is actually a popular teenage actor, and he is coming to her small town in Maine to shoot his new movie. Ellie is intrigued to meet Graham in person, but she is wary of the paparazzi who naturally accompany him. She is protecting a family secret and doesn't want to be photographed with him or even let her mother know she is seeing him. But she can't deny the chemistry between them.

Subjects: Maine; Movie Stars; Online Dating

Strohmeyer, Sarah.

Prince in Disguise. 2017. 9781484768174. **J** **S**

Dylan's sister Dusty is a former Miss Tennessee and the winner on a reality TV show called *Prince in Disguise*. As Dusty's maid of honor, Dylan (and the rest of the family) are off to the Scottish Highlands for the filming of the reality TV wedding. There Dylan meets the groom's friend, Jamie, and while she actually sort of likes him, the last thing she wants is for her romance to play out on television.

Subjects: Scotland; Sisters; Royalty; Weddings

This Is My Brain on Boys. 2018. 9780062259622. **J** **S**

Addie Emerson sees love as a function of brain chemicals. In fact, she is working on an experiment that she hopes will win her the coveted Athenian Award, which will in turn enable her to get a full scholarship to Harvard. So during the summer between junior and senior years, she is back at her school, Academy 355, trying to prove that she can make any two people fall in love by putting them in the right situations. Her test subjects are Lauren, a beautiful, blond, athletic girl looking for extra credit, and two boys: Alex and Kris. Addie's plan is to make Lauren fall in love with Kris, using Alex as her control. The only problem is that Addie seems to be falling for Kris just a bit herself—even though she has no intention of dating, at least until after she gets her PhD. Helped—and sometimes hindered—by her lab partner Dex, her best friend Tess, and Tess's boyfriend Ed, Addie moves forward with her attempts to put Lauren and Kris in situations that will stimulate their brain adrenaline, dopamine, and amine synthesis, thus leading naturally to love. But Kris has plans of his own that don't include Lauren. And Addie may not be showing all of her cards, anyway. Screwball comedy meets neuroscience.

Subjects: Humor; Matchmaking; Science; Summer

Welch, Jenna Evans.

Love and Gelato. 2016. 9781481432542. **J** **S**

After Lina's mother dies, Lina moves to Tuscany to live with the father she has never met. One of the things Lina's mother left her is a journal detailing the years she herself spent in Tuscany when she was not much older than Lina. As Lina reads the diary, she begins to learn things she never knew about her mother, and she begins to piece together the answers to some mysteries. Meanwhile, a handsome neighbor, Ren, is determined that Lina should make the most of her time in Tuscany, and he makes it his job to show her around and get her to fall in love with Tuscany.

Subjects: Diaries; Fathers and Daughters; Florence; Grief; Mothers and Daughters; Secrets; Tuscany

Wen, Abigail Hing.

Loveboat, Taipei. 2020. 9780062957276. **J** **S**

Ohio teen Ever Wong gets a late acceptance to her dream school: the Dance Department at NYU's Tisch School of the Arts. Her parents, however, have other plans for her: attend Northwestern and become a doctor. But first, they have decided, she needs to learn something about her culture, so she is going to spend eight weeks in Taiwan at *Chien Tan*, studying Mandarin, an introduction to Chinese medicine, and calligraphy. Upon arrival in Taipei, Ever meets her roommate Sophie, who informs Ever that *Chien Tan* is also known as Loveboat, Taipei, a place where Chinese American teens meet up, hook up, and even ultimately find partners. So Ever decides that now is the time to break the Wong Family Rules, such as Dress Like a Nun, No Drinking, No Kissing Boys, Curfew at Ten, and more. Together, she and Sophie, along with Sophie's cousin the "Wonder Boy" Rick Woo and Rick's roommate Xavier, set out to have the best summer ever.

Subjects: Chinese Americans; Dance; Family; Summer Romance; Taipei

West, Kasie.

Fame, Fate, and the First Kiss. 2019. 9780062675798. **M** **J** **S**

Lacey is a high school senior and an actress. She just got her first big role, playing a zombie in a movie starring Grant James, the hottest young Hollywood star. Unfortunately, Lacey and Grant's chemistry on camera just isn't there, so she decides she needs to spend more time with him to get to know him better. Meanwhile, she still has to keep up with her homework, which isn't going well. So her dad hires a tutor, a senior named Donovan, to come to the set and help her out. Between Grant, Donovan, and the fact that someone seems to be trying to sabotage Lacey's role in the film, Lacey has a busy senior year.

Subjects: Hollywood; Los Angeles; Movies

On the Fence. 2014. 9780062235671. **M** **J** **S**

Charlotte (Charlie) is the only girl in her house, so she's pretty good at lots of so-called "boy" things. She would definitely rather play soccer than go shopping. But at 16, she starts working at a local boutique, filled with lots of so-called girl things, and she meets a guy who doesn't know anything about her tomboy past. Meanwhile, in the evenings, she meets her next-door neighbor and honorary brother Braden at the fence, where they sit back-to-back and tell each other everything. But Charlie isn't sure that she can really tell Braden everything—when that includes that fact that she's falling for him.

Subjects: Boy Next Door; Brothers; Sports

Chick Lit

Teen chick lit usually follows the stories of groups of friends, with the emphasis on romance, and even though these stories often touch on tougher issues, the tone is light. The support of friends is of major importance. One of the classics of YA chick lit is *The Sisterhood of the Traveling Pants* (2001), by Ann Brashares, and its sequels.

Han, Jenny.

Lara Jean Series. J S

The Korean American Song sisters (Lara Jean, Kitty, and Margot), daughters of a widowed father, have their ups and downs, but ultimately they are always there for one another. The three books are being made into movies by Netflix.

To All the Boys I've Loved Before. 2014. 9781442426702.

Sixteen-year-old Lara Jean has written to each of the five boys that she has loved, telling them exactly what she loves about them. The letters are stored in the hat box where she keeps her prized possessions. Writing them serves to set her free, to exorcise her feelings of unrequited love. But one day, two of the boys tell her that they have received her letters. One is her older sister's boyfriend, Josh, and the other is Peter K., whom she kissed in middle school. Both boys are actually rather flattered by the letters, but Lara Jean is horrified and embarrassed, especially because she still has feelings for Josh. She tells Josh that she doesn't really like him because she is actually dating Peter, and Peter agrees to go along with the ruse, since he has just broken up with his long-term girlfriend. Over the course of the fall semester, Lara Jean learns a lot about love—both romantic and familial—and friendship, and begins to come to terms with who she is apart from being one of the "Song girls" (three Korean American sisters who have been interdependent since the death of their mother). (Film)

Subjects: Biracial Teens; Korean Americans; Letters; Sisters

P.S. I Still Love You. 2015. 9781442426733.

Now that Lara Jean and Peter are actually dating, everything should be perfect. But then John McClaren, Lara Jean's middle school crush and one of the boys she wrote to in *To All the Boys I've Loved Before*, moves back to town, complicating Lara Jean's feelings.

Subjects: Biracial Teens; Dating; Friendship; Korean Americans; Sisters

Always and Forever, Lara Jean. 2017. 9781481430487.

Lara Jean and Peter's relationship is finally on an even keel—at least until Lara Jean's college acceptance letters arrive, and she and Peter have to decide how they're going to manage a long-distance relationship. Meanwhile, Lara Jean's dad is getting remarried, while all the usual senior year stuff is going on. As always, the Song sisters help Lara Jean figure out her life.

Subjects: Biracial Teens; College; Korean Americans; Sisters

Keplinger, Kody.

The D.U.F.F.: Designated Ugly Fat Friend. 2010. 9780316084239. **J** **S**

Bianca knows very well that her two best friends are beautiful, but that doesn't mean she likes it when high school womanizer Wesley refers to her as a Duff (designated ugly fat friend). But despite Wesley's ulterior motives (getting closer to Bianca's friends), Bianca finds herself drawn to him. He makes a particularly good distraction from the disaster that is her home life. But is it a real relationship or just sex?

Subjects: Body Image; Divorce; Family Problems; Sex

Murphy, Julie.

Dumplin'. 2015. 9780062931306. **J** **S**

Willowdean ("Will") knows who she is: a Texan, a cashier at Harpy's Burgers & Dogs, a Dolly Parton fan, and a fat girl. She knows that she is *not* who her mom, who calls her Dumplin,wants her to be: thin and fashion-obsessed. Will's mom is a former Miss Teen Blue Bonnet and now runs the local beauty pageant. After Will falls for a hunky prep school coworker and then loses him in a fit of insecurity, she decides to put herself out there and sign up for the Miss Teen Blue Bonnet Pageant. Her mother isn't thrilled with her decision, and neither is her best friend, but Will forges ahead, gathering other misfit pageant contestants and a drag queen or two as a support group and proving to herself, at least, that she can be in a beauty contest and still be who she really is. Now a Netflix movie. (Bloomer, BFYA, Film)

Subjects: Beauty Pageants; Body Image; Dolly Parton; Drag Queens; Friends; Mothers and Daughters; Texas

3

Perkins, Stephanie.

Anna and the French Kiss. 2010. 9780525423270. **J** **S**

Anna resents being sent to a boarding school in Paris; she'd rather be at home in Atlanta with her best friend, younger brother, and Mom, not to mention the boy she is sure is about to become her boyfriend. Instead, her pushy father (too much money, not enough class) sends her away. But, well, it's Paris, and over the course of the year, Anna grows to know and love the city (and its many small movie theaters) and to learn French. But the real heart of the story is her friendship with a small group of classmates, in particular with Etienne St. Clair. Of course, there are obstacles, but love will find a way. (BFYA)

Subjects: Boarding School; Movies; Paris

Isla and the Happily Ever After. 2014. 9780525425632. **J** **S**

Going back to the Paris boarding school of *Anna and the French Kiss*, this book is centered around Josh, who was the best friend of St. Clair (Anna's boyfriend). Isla has a French mother who is an alumna of the school and two sisters who attend as well. She's been in love with Josh for a long time and is thrilled that they are finally getting together. Obstacles include

Josh's apparent desire to get himself kicked out of school and worries about what the new relationship might do to Isla's best friend, a boy on the autism spectrum.

Subjects: Autism Spectrum; Barcelona; Boarding Schools; New York; Paris

Lola and the Boy Next Door. 2011. 9780525423287. **J** **S**

Lola is a budding costume designer who lives with her two dads in San Francisco. She is also a friend of Anna and St. Clair from *Anna and the French Kiss*, who show up frequently in this book with advice and counsel. Lola's new next-door neighbors are actually old next-door neighbors, Cricket Bell and his sister Calliope. The family has moved a lot because Calliope is a figure skater, so they go where her career takes them. Lola has never gotten along well with Calliope, but she always liked Cricket—until he moved away and broke her heart. Now he's back, and Lola is interested again; it's just that there's her rock singer boyfriend standing in the way. (BFYA)

Subjects: Boy Next Door; Costumes; Fashion; Gay Dads; Inventors; San Francisco

Strohmeyer, Sarah.

How Zoe Made Her Dreams (Mostly) Come True. 2013. 9780062187451. **J** **S**

Zoe and her cousin and best friend Jess are excited to get an internship at Fairyland, a princess-themed amusement park. However, they are less than thrilled with the roles they are assigned: Jess as Little Red Riding Hood and Zoe as a lady-in-waiting (i.e., personal slave) to the demanding Queen. Everyone knows that each year one of the interns will win a $25,000 "Dream and Do" grant, and that kind of money would make a big difference to both girls. On the other hand, all the other interns are vying for the grant, and most of them are pretty ruthless. When Zoe meets a very charming prince, she must decide what is more important: love or money.

Subjects: Amusement Parks; Cousins; Friends; Summer; Summer Romance

Smart Girls Get What They Want. 2012. 9780061953408. **S**

Gigi, Bea, and Neerja are best friends, and they have the same goals: to do well in school and get into Ivy League colleges. But when they realize that they are on their way to becoming high school nobodies in the process, they decide to make some changes. Drama club, the ski team, and student government all play a part, as do boys, of course.

Subjects: Best Friends; High School

LGBTQIA+ Romance

In previous editions of this book, stories about LGBTQIA+ teens mostly focused on the hardships of being queer in a straight world. Now, fortunately, there are more books that feature queer teens having the same sorts of romantic coming-of-age as straight teens do. These books are increasingly popular with teens of all sexualities. See also: some of the titles in Chapter 1, "Gender and Sexual Identity," and look for LGBTQIA+ in the index.

Albertalli, Becky.

Simon vs. the Homo Sapiens Agenda. 2016. 9780062348678. **J** **S**

Simon Spier is 16 and in love. Sure, he has never met the mysterious "Blue" in person, but he's falling hard and fast over their e-mail love letters. There's only one problem: Simon is gay, and he hasn't told anyone else. Coming out might look easy in the movies, but it's another matter in real life. That all changes when a classmate catches a look at his e-mail and his secret online romance. Now Simon is being blackmailed: He must help set Martin up with Simon's new friend Abby, or Martin will reveal his big secret on the school's unofficial and gossip-fueled Tumblr—the very same Tumblr where Simon encountered Blue in the first place. It's not just Simon's neck on the line. Blue is confusing and flirtatious but, above all, secretive. All Simon knows about him is that they go to the same school, so how would Blue feel if his secret leaked out because Simon decided he wouldn't play matchmaker? It's up to Simon to navigate Martin's demands without compromising himself, Blue, or his friends. (NBA, Morris Award, Lambda)

Subjects: High School; LGBTQIA+; Romance; Social Media

Albertalli, Becky, and Adam Silvera.

What If It's Us. 2018. 9780062795250. **J** **S**

This summer romance is told in two voices: Arthur is a white, Jewish, Broadway-obsessed Georgia boy who is in New York for a summer internship. Ben is a Puerto Rican, a Catholic, and a native New Yorker who is attending summer school. They meet in a post office, fail to exchange numbers, but eventually manage to get together, for a series of not-so-successful "first" dates. As the summer draws to a close, they must decide whether they are meant to be boyfriends or friends.

Subjects: ADHD; Broadway; LGBTQIA+; New York; Summer Romance; Theater

Callender, Kacen.

This Is Kind of an Epic Love Story. 2018. 9780062820228. **S**

Seattle teens Nate and Flo were once a couple, but now they are just friends. Nate advises Flo about her new relationship with Lydia, and Flo encourages Nate to find someone new in his life. But Nate, a movie buff, has decided that he doesn't believe in happy endings. When Flo sees the new kid at school, she suggests that maybe he's the one for Nate. But Nate hasn't told her that the new kid is actually Oliver James Hernandéz, Nate's former best friend, who has now moved back to town. Nate still carries some guilt over the way his friendship with Ollie ended, so he isn't at all sure that this particular relationship could ever have a happy ending.

Subjects: Biracial; Friends; Hearing Impaired; LGBTQIA+; Mothers and Sons; Seattle

Dugan, Jennifer.

Hot Dog Girl. 2019. 9780525516255. **J** **S**

Elouise ("Lou") Parker has big plans for the summer. She has always spent her summers at the Magic Castle Playland amusement park, and now she's old enough to work there—although, admittedly, wearing a hot dog costume wasn't her first job choice. But, still, her best friend Seeley is also working there, as is her crush, Nick (and Nick's girlfriend, Jessa). The park's owner has announced that this will be its last season, and Lou hopes to change that decision, but meanwhile she's also occupied with winning over Nick, with a far-fetched plan to "fake-date" Seeley, so they can double date with Nick and Jessa. But as the summer goes on, Lou begins to realize that it's actually Seeley that she has feelings for.

Subjects: Amusement Parks; LGBTQIA+; New England; Summer

Hawkins, Rachel.

Her Royal Highness. 2019. 9781524738266. **J** **S**

Texan Millie Quint loves all things Scottish and has just suffered a heartbreak at home, so when she wins a full scholarship to the remote Gregorstoun [boarding] School, in the Scottish Highlands, it is a dream come true. For Princess Flora, on the other hand, Gregorstoun is a penance for bad behavior, and she arrives determined to find a way to be thrown out. When the two girls discover they are roommates, sparks fly, first in negative ways and then romantically.

Subjects: Boarding Schools; LGBTQIA+; Princesses; Roommates; Royalty; Scotland

Lauren, Christina.

Autoboyography. 2017. 9781481481687. **S**

As a "half-Jewish queer kid in a straight and Mormon town," Tanner stays in the closet after moving from Palo Alto, California, to Provo, Utah. That is, until he meets Sebastian, the Brigham Young University student who is serving as a teaching assistant in Tanner's novel-writing seminar. Sebastian, son of a Mormon bishop, responds to Tanner's flirting, but he isn't exactly ready to be out. (Lambda)

Subjects: Latter Day Saints; LGBTQIA+; Mormons; Novel Writing; Provo, Utah

Levithan, David.

Boy Meets Boy. 2003. 9780375832994. **J** **S**

When this book was first published in 2003, it was regarded as an almost impossible version of the world, in which the gay kids are out and accepted; the homecoming drag queen, Infinite Darlene, is also captain of the football team; the quiz bowl team are the school's top "athletes"; and the gay–straight alliance exists to turn the straight kids into better dancers. Okay, well, maybe some of that is still a bit far-fetched, but share this book with teens who like a lighthearted LGBTQIA+ romance, in which being gay is not the problem, but first love is. Paul, a high school sophomore, falls for Noah, loses him, and tries to win him back. (BBYA)

Subjects: Drag Queens; First Love; Humor; LGBTQIA+; Quiz Bowl

Panetta, Kevin. Illustrated by Savanna Ganucheau.

Bloom. 2019. 9781250196910. **S**

In this graphic novel, Aristotle ("Ari") Kyrkos knows what he wants to do after graduation, and it isn't working in his family's bakery. He wants to move to Baltimore with his friends and make music. But he promises his father he won't leave him in the lurch, so he first hires someone to help out at the bakery: Hector Galea, a culinary school student who has taken a leave of absence to sort out his grandmother's estate. Hector makes a real difference in the bakery, and Ari finds himself not so eager to leave after all. The romance between Hector and Ari builds gradually, and both young men learn something about friendship and growing up.

Subjects: Bakeries; Baltimore; Graphic Novels; LGBTQIA+; Mid-Atlantic Coast; Playlists; Summer Romance

Safi, Aminah Mae.

Tell Me How You Really Feel. 2019. 9781250299482. **S**

Sana and Rachel are very, very different. Sana is South Asian/Persian American, Muslim, and an overachiever: straight As, cheerleader, headed for Princeton. Rachel is Jewish Mexican, lives with her single dad, attends high school on scholarship, and wants to go to NYU—if only she can finish making her audition movie. The two girls don't get along, ever since freshman year when Sana asked Rachel out, and Rachel thought it was a prank. But now, after a literal head-to-head collision, they are forced to work together to complete Rachel's film. Over the course of their senior year, they reveal themselves to one another and find themselves falling in love.

Subjects: Biracial; Cheerleading; Jews; LGBTQIA+; Mexican Americans; Movies; South Asians

Spalding, Amy.

The Summer of Jordi Pérez (and the Best Burger in Los Angeles). 2018. 9781510727663. **J S**

Abby gets a coveted summer internship at her all-time favorite boutique on the strength of her blog, *+style*, which focuses on plus-size fashion. She has hopes that the internship will lead to an actual job in the fall. But when she turns up for the first day of the internship, there is another intern, Jordi Pérez, a girl Abby knows vaguely from school. The two of them are going to be sharing the intern duties, but there's still going to be only one job in the fall. Abby is frustrated that her social media skills aren't being put to full use, while Jordi's photography skills are. And then there's the complication that Abby is definitely falling for Jordi, and apparently vice versa, and everyone knows you shouldn't have a relationship with a work colleague. Meanwhile, Abby is unexpectedly falling into friendship with the lacrosse-playing Jax, best friend of her best friend's boyfriend, and Jax and Abby are traveling all over Los Angeles rating burgers for his dad's new restaurant app. Summer romance, summer job, summer fun! (BFYA, Rainbow)

Subjects: Body Positivity; Fashion; First Love; Hamburgers; Latinx; LGBTQIA+; Los Angeles; Photography; Social Media

Stone, Nic.

Odd One Out. 2018. 9781101939536. **S**

Courtney Aloysius Cooper IV ("Coop") and his next-door neighbor Jupiter ("Jupe") are best friends. Although Coop knows that Jupe is a lesbian, he has been in love with her for almost as long as he can remember. Enter Rae Chin, the new girl in school, who becomes friends with Coop and Jupe and who is sexually attracted to both of them.

Subjects: African Americans; Biracial Teens; Latinx; LGBTQIA+

Collections of Romance Short Stories

Let It Snow: Three Holiday Romances. 2008. 9780142412145. **J S**

These are three interconnected holiday love stories by John Green, Maureen Johnson, and Lauren Myracle.

Subjects: Christmas; Short Stories; Winter

Meet Cute: Some People Are Destined to Meet. 2018. 9781328759870. **J S**

Fourteen popular YA authors, including Sara Shepard (*Pretty Little Liars*), Nina LaCour (*We Are Okay*), Julie Murphy (*Dumplin'*), and Dhonielle Clayton (*The Belles*), contribute short stories to this collection about first meetings. The stories range from contemporary realism to the fantastical, and the settings and characters are diverse, including straight, LGBTQIA+, and multiple ethnicities.

Subjects: Romance; Short Stories

My True Love Gave to Me: Twelve Holiday Stories. 2014. 9781250059307. **J S**

Edited by Stephanie Perkins (*Anna and the French Kiss*), this winter holiday–themed collection includes stories by Holly Black, David Levithan, Gayle Forman, Rainbow Rowell, Laini Taylor, Matt de la Peña, Jenny Han, and others.

Subjects: Christmas; Romance; Short Stories; Winter

Summer Days and Summer Nights: Twelve Love Stories. 2016. 9781250079121. **J S**

Edited by Stephanie Perkins (*Anna and the French Kiss*), this collection of short stories featuring summer romance includes stories by Cassandra Clare, Tim Federle, Francesca Lia Block, Libba Bray, Leigh Bardugo, and others. The stories cover the gamut: fantasy, time loops, realistic, funny, as well as a diversity of love relationships (boy–boy, boy–girl, girl–girl).

Subjects: Short Stories; Summer Romance

Three Sides of a Heart: Stories About Love Triangles. 2017. 9780062424471. **J S**

This collection, edited by Natalie C. Parker, contains stories written by Rae Carson, Brandy Colbert, EK Johnston, Julie Murphy, Garth Nix, Veronica Roth, Sabaa Tahir, and others. The stories cover all genres.

Subject: Short Stories

Sarah's Picks

Forman, Gayle. *Just One Day.*

Matson, Morgan. *Amy & Roger's Epic Detour.*

Menon, Sandhya. *There's Something About Sweetie.*

Smith, Jennifer E. *The Statistical Probability of Love at First Sight.*

Spalding, Amy. *The Summer of Jordi Pérez (and the Best Burger in Los Angeles).*

Chapter **4**

Adrenaline

Adrenaline is a combination genre that includes a host of subgenres, all of which are intended to get the mind and heart racing. Books that we call page-turners often fall into one of these subgenres: mystery, suspense, thrillers, action-adventure, war, espionage and terrorism, or survival. Generally these books involve some element of danger, and plot twists are common. Teens who like these genres may also enjoy science fiction and paranormal books.

Mystery

Mysteries are defined as stories that hinge on detection. A crime has been committed or is suspected, and a character investigates. In adult mysteries, the investigator is often a professional but sometimes an amateur investigator. Because teenagers are too young to be actual detectives, the teen protagonist of a YA mystery is usually someone who has some sort of stake in solving the mystery. In adult mysteries, it is almost always a murder; in YA mysteries, it can be any number of things.

Mysteries with historical settings engage readers looking for the thrills inherent in a mystery as well as those who like to read about bygone times and cultures. Bear in mind that "historical" for teens means anything that happened before they were born. Readers who are interested in mysteries that take place in the past can also find them in Chapter 2, "Historical Fiction."

Contemporary Mysteries

Abrahams, Peter.

The Echo Falls Mysteries. **M** **J**

Thirteen-year-old Ingrid Levin-Hill, the daughter of the chief of police of the small town Echo Falls, Connecticut, finds herself involved in various mysteries.

Subjects: Connecticut; Small Towns

Down the Rabbit Hole. 2005. 9780060737016.

Busy with her role as Alice in the local performance of *Alice in Wonderland* and short on time, 13-year-old Ingrid Levin-Hill becomes lost while running to soccer practice. A woman helps her on her way, but when Ingrid finds out that the woman was murdered that same day, she begins investigating on her own.

Behind the Curtain. 2006. 9780060737061.

While investigating her football-playing brother's sudden increase in muscle, which she suspects is due to steroids, eighth-grade sleuth Ingrid is kidnapped, escapes from the trunk where she was stashed, and starts looking for her kidnapper.

Into the Dark. 2008. 9780060737085.

Ninth-grader Ingrid finds a dead body on her grandfather's land. When he becomes the prime suspect, she must use her sleuthing prowess to clear his name.

Cavallaro, Brittany.

The Charlotte Holmes Mysteries. **J** **S**

Charlotte Holmes is a descendant of the great Sherlock Holmes. At boarding school in Connecticut, she meets James ("Jamie") Watson, who is a descendant of Dr. John Watson. Together the two investigate mysteries in much the same way as their famous ancestors. Fans of the *Sherlock* and *Elementary* television series will enjoy this take on the famous stories.

Subjects: Boarding School; Connecticut; Sherlock Holmes

A Study in Charlotte. 2016. 9780062398901.

A fellow student who is a date rapist is murdered, and Jamie is one of the suspects.

The Last of August. 2017. 9780062398949.

Charlotte and Jamie go to England for winter break, but when Charlotte's Uncle Leander disappears, they head off to Berlin on the trail of an art forgery ring.

Subjects: Art Forgery; Berlin; Sussex, England

The Case for Jamie. 2018. 9780062398970.

A year after the events of *The Last of August,* Jamie is back at school, but Charlotte is still on the run after the events of the previous book. The two of them haven't spoken, but somehow they are being pulled back together.

A Question of Holmes. 2019. 9780062840226.

Charlotte and Jamie are back together, this time at a summer theater program in Oxford, England, where they get involved in investigating a cold case.

Subjects: Oxford, England; Theater

Coben, Harlan.

The Mickey Bolitar Series. **M** **J** **S**

Myron Bolitar is a recurring character in Coben's mysteries and thrillers for adults. Mickey is Myron's teenage nephew, who moves in with him after his father

(Myron's brother) dies, and his mother goes to rehab. He's not thrilled about his new high school, but fortunately Mickey makes friends with Ema and Spoon, who help him with his investigations.

Subject: New Jersey

Shelter. 2011. 9780142422038.

Mickey looks into the disappearance of his girlfriend Ashley. Meanwhile, a crazy neighborhood lady tells him that his father is not really dead.

Subject: Missing Girls

Seconds Away. 2012. 9780399256516.

Mickey's friend Rachel is injured, and her mother murdered. Mickey and his friends investigate the Abeona Shelter and its connection with his father.

Found. 2014. 9781409124511.

Ema's (possibly fictitious) online boyfriend has vanished, and Mickey helps her look for him, while continuing to learn more about his father's death.

Dowd, Siobhan.

The London Eye Mystery. 2008. 9780375849763. **M**

Ted and Kat see their cousin Salin get on the London Eye, an enclosed Ferris wheel–like sightseeing attraction on the banks of the Thames, but when the ride is over, Salin is gone. Twelve-year-old Ted, who thinks differently and may be on the autism spectrum, uses his skills to solve the mystery ahead of the police. (BBYA)

Subjects: Baseball; Brothers and Sisters; Cousins; London; Missing Persons

Fredericks, Mariah.

The Girl in the Park. 2012. 9780375868436. **S**

Rain's best friend Wendy turns up dead in the park after a party with other kids from their prep school. Rain knows that Wendy was considered a wild girl, but Rain feels compelled to find out what happened and speak up for Wendy.

Subjects: Murder; Prep Schools

Green, John.

Paper Towns. 2008. 9780525478188. **S**

When they were kids, Margo Roth Spiegelman was Q's best friend. Now a month before high school graduation, Margo has disappeared after taking Q on a night of pranks involving a dead fish and a depilatory. Worried that Margo may have committed suicide, Q and his friends start tracking her down, using clues she has left behind. (BBYA, Edgar Award)

Subjects: Maps; Missing Persons; Pranks

Jackson, Tiffany.

Monday's Not Coming. 2018. 9780062422699. **J** **S**

Claudia and Monday are best friends. That's why Claudia is worried that Monday hasn't answered any of the letters she wrote to her all summer, while Claudia was in the South visiting her grandmother. And then Monday doesn't show up on the first day of school. No one seems concerned except Claudia. But Claudia can't let it go. She keeps pushing, trying to find out what happened to Monday, even if it means finding out things she'd rather not know. (BFYA)

Subjects: Abuse; Missing Girls; Washington, D.C.

Jarzab, Anna.

All Unquiet Things. 2010. 9780385738354. **S**

A year after the murder of his ex-girlfriend Carly, Neily begins to believe that perhaps the wrong person has been sent to prison. After the murder, Carly's uncle, the father of her best friend/cousin Audrey, was convicted. Neily and Audrey are both outcasts now at Brighton Day School, Neily because some think he killed Carly and Audrey because her father was convicted of the crime. They join forces to find out who shot Carly and why.

Subjects: California; High School; Murder

Johnson, Maureen.

The Truly Devious Mysteries. **M** **J** **S**

Stevie Bell wants to be a detective. She has immersed herself in stories of true crime, in details of forensic science, and in information about how to tail, interrogate, and investigate. Now she hopes to put her theoretical knowledge into practice because she has been accepted as a student at Ellingham Academy, a unique boarding school in the wilderness of Vermont, where only the most creative, bright, and inventive are admitted.

Subjects: Boarding Schools; Cold Cases; Forensics; Vermont

Truly Devious. 2018. 9780062338051.

Stevie has a particular reason for wanting to be at Ellingham: Shortly after the school opened in 1936, the founder's wife was murdered, and his daughter went missing. The crimes have never been solved, but Stevie is convinced that, being on site, she will be able to find out what really happened. But when one of her classmates turns up dead, the stakes get dramatically higher. (BFYA)

The Vanishing Stair. 2019. 9780062338082.

Stevie's parents have pulled her out of Ellingham after the events of the first book, but a surprising ally enables her to return. There she continues to delve into both the mystery of the past, using the contents of an old tea tin she found in the attic, and the mystery of the present—the death that occurred in the first book.

The Hand on the Wall. 2020. 9780062338112.

In the series finale, Stevie pulls together all the threads of mysteries past and present—to her own peril.

Marney, Ellie.

The Every Series.

In this Australian homage to the Sherlock Holmes stories, the protagonists are Rachel Watts and James Mycroft, both of whom are teenagers in grief. Watts is mourning the life her family had in the country before moving to a busy Melbourne suburb; Mycroft's parents were both killed in a car accident that he alone survived.

Subjects: Forensics; London, England; Melbourne, Victoria, Australia; Sherlock Holmes

Every Breath. 2013. 9781770497726.

Mycroft and Watts discover the body of a homeless man, Dave, outside the zoo where Mycroft's aunt works. As they investigate the murder, they also find themselves drawing closer together.

Subjects: Forensics; Homelessness; Murder

Every Word. 2014. 9781770497757.

Watts follows Mycroft to London, where he is investigating a car crash that is suspiciously like the one that killed his parents. The theft of a Shakespeare first folio and the death of a rare books conservator are all somehow mixed up in the mystery of Mycroft's parents' death, and Watts wants to help.

Subjects: Forensics; London; Oxford; Rare Books; Shakespeare

Every Move. 2015. 9781743318539.

Watts is suffering from PTSD, in the form of serious nightmares, after the events of the previous book. The introduction of a new character, Harris Derwent, complicates Watts and Mycroft's relationship, but meanwhile Mycroft is still on the trail of his parents' killer.

Subject: PTSD

McNamee, Graham.

Defender. 2016. 9780553498950. **J S**

Tyne ("Tiny") is a 6-foot 3-inch basketball player who lives with her family in an aging apartment complex in Toronto, where her dad is the superintendent. Tyne does odd jobs around the building to help her dad. One day, while investigating a crack in the basement wall, she finds the body of a dead teenage girl. Horrified, she hurries to tell her dad, but he comes back and tells her that there was nothing there—it must have been a reaction to the pain medication Tyne has been taking for her injured knee. She trusts and loves her dad, but she is sure he is hiding something—why? With the help of her boyfriend Stick, she begins to investigate, uncovering family and neighborhood secrets in the process.

Subjects: Basketball; Missing Girls; Murder; Toronto

Petty, Heather.

The Lock and Mori Mysteries. Ⓜ Ⓙ Ⓢ

In this take on the Sherlock Holmes mysteries, Sherlock ("Lock") and James Moriarty ("Mori") are high school students in present-day London. Mori is the daughter of a London police detective, who is grieving, alcoholic, and abusive to Mori and her younger brothers after the death of his wife.

Subjects: Abuse; Families; Friendship; London; Sherlock Holmes

Lock and Mori. 2015. 9781481423038.

> Mori and Lock meet in Regent's Park after the death of the father of one of their schoolmates and agree to investigate the murder, sharing information with each other. But as Mori begins to realize that her mother's past is tied up with this present-day murder, she pulls away from Lock and begins keeping her own secrets.

Mind Games. 2017. 9781481423069.

> Despite having solved the Regent's Park murders, Mori now finds that the police suspect that she herself may have been involved.

Final Fall. 2017. 9781481423090.

> Mori vows vengeance on those who have harmed her, forcing her ever further away from Lock.

Shepard, Sara.

The Amateurs. 2016. 9781484742273. Ⓢ

Five years after the death of her sister, Aerin posts a query to an online forum that helps solve cold cases. Four teens respond to Aerin's call for help and set out to solve the case.

Subjects: Cold Cases; Murder

Summers, Courtney.

Sadie. 2018. 9781250105714. Ⓢ

Nineteen-year-old Sadie is in search of a man named Keith, her mother's former boyfriend. Keith abused Sadie as a child, and Sadie is convinced that he killed her sister Mattie. Carrying a switchblade knife that once belonged to Keith, Sadie crisscrosses Colorado in search of a man who clearly doesn't want to be found. But when Sadie's car is found abandoned on the side of the road, she herself is a missing girl. A radio host named West McCray sets out in search of Sadie. The novel is told in alternating voices: One voice is Sadie's own, as the reader follows her progress in hunting Keith; the other is West's, as he narrates a true crime podcast about his search for Sadie. As the tension builds, the two versions of the story collide. (Edgar Award)

Subjects: Abuse; Colorado; Missing Girls; Podcasts

Thomas, Kara.

The Cheerleaders. 2018. 9781524718329. **S**

Monica's sister Jennifer is one of five cheerleaders who died five years ago, all within a few weeks of one another. Monica is now 16, and she discovers a stack of letters and Jen's cell phone in the desk of her stepfather, a police officer. Monica begins to explore the events of five years ago, finding that the story she had been told has some gaping holes. Monica's story is told in alternating chapters with the events of Jen's life leading up to her death. (BFYA)

Subjects: Cheerleaders; Family; High School; Murder

Tromly, Stephanie.

Trouble Is a Friend of Mine. 2016. 9780525428404. **S**

Expecting to be bored in upstate New York after moving there from Brooklyn, 16-year-old Zoe instead finds herself involved in a serious of madcap adventures with Philip Digby, who involves Zoe in helping him investigate a local kidnapping.

Subjects: Humor; Missing Girls; New York State

Historical Mysteries

Bradley, Alan.

The Flavia de Luce Mysteries. **S** **O**

In these mysteries set in the 1950s, Flavia de Luce is a precocious 11-year-old amateur sleuth, future chemist, and poison enthusiast. She lives with her widowed father and two older sisters at Buckshaw—a decaying English countryside mansion.

Subjects: Chemistry; England; Poisons

The Sweetness at the Bottom of the Pie. 2009. 9780385342308.

Flavia finds a dead bird on the doorstep, with a postage stamp pinned to its beak.

The Weed That Strings the Hangman's Bag. 2010. 9780385342315.

Flavia investigates the death of a famous puppeteer.

A Red Herring without Mustard. 2011. 9780385342322.

Flavia is kept more than busy investigating a gypsy fortuneteller who has been beaten, two bodies, a smuggling ring, a missing painting, and a secret religion.

I Am Half-Sick of Shadows. 2011. 9780385344012.

A film crew arrives at Buckshaw to shoot a movie with famous actress Phyllis Wyvern. When a snowstorm strands half the village at Buckshaw, Flavia has plenty of suspects for the murder of Wyvern—found dead with a strip of celluloid film around her neck.

Speaking from among the Bones. 2013. 9780385344036.

> The opening of the tomb of St. Tancred at the village church reveals—what else?—a dead body for Flavia to investigate—and it isn't St. Tancred.

The Dead in Their Vaulted Arches. 2014. 9780385344050.

> A stranger is pushed under a train just after passing a cryptic message to Flavia.

As Chimney Sweepers Come to Dust. 2015. 9780345539939.

> Flavia is sent to Canada to boarding school, and naturally she immediately discovers a body in her dorm room chimney.

Thrice the Brinded Cat Hath Mew'd. 2016. 9781409149507.

> Back from Canada, Flavia finds the dead body of a local wood-carver. The only witness to the death appears to be a cat.

The Grave's a Fine and Private Place. 2018. 9781409172888.

> On a boating trip with her sisters, Flavia puts her hand into the water and catches not a fish but a human head.

The Golden Tresses of the Dead. 2019. 9780345540027.

> Flavia's sister is getting married, and a severed finger turns up in the wedding cake.

Bray, Libba.

The Diviners Series. ⬛

In 1926, Evie O'Neill is sent to live with her uncle in New York City. She soon finds herself helping him solve a series of grisly murders with ties to the occult. Since she herself has psychic abilities, this is a perfect match.

Subjects: New York; Prohibition Era; Psychic Abilities; Serial Killers

The Diviners. 2012. 9780316126113. ⬛

> Evie is convinced that the perpetrator of a series of murders is a man who was hanged for murder 50 years ago. (BFYA)

Lair of Dreams. 2015. 9780316126045. ⬛

> Now the star of her own radio program, Evie, the "Sweetheart Seer," investigates a sleeping sickness that has struck New York. (Rainbow)

Before the Devil Breaks You. 2017. 9780316126069. ⬛

> The staff and residents of an insane asylum are terrorized by malevolent ghosts.

The King of Crows. 2020. 9780316126090. ⬛

> The Diviners square off against the King of Crows.

Donnelly, Jennifer.

A Northern Light. 2012. 9780152053109. ⬛

In 1906, Mattie Gokey wants to go to college and become a writer, but she is spending the summer working at a hotel in the Adirondacks. The murder of a young female guest is the catalyst that helps Mattie decide the course of her future. (Printz Honor, BBYA)

Subjects: Adirondacks; Hotels; Murder; Resorts; Word Play

These Shallow Graves. **2015. 9780385737654. S**

In the 1890s, Jo Monfort is called home from boarding school due to her father's death. Everyone assumes it was suicide, but Jo doesn't believe it. Enlisting the help of a young reporter, Eddie Gallagher, Jo sets out to find out who murdered her father. (BFYA, Bloomer)

Subjects: Fathers and Daughters; Murder; New York; Reporters

Haines, Kathryn Miller.

The Girl Is Murder. **2011. 9781596436091. J S**

Fifteen-year-old Iris's father was wounded at Pearl Harbor, and now, in 1942, he is working as a detective in Manhattan. When one of his cases involves the disappearance of one of her classmates, Iris can't resist doing some investigating on her own.

Subjects: Fathers and Daughters; Missing Girls; New York

The Girl Is Trouble. **2012. 9781596436107. J S**

After her success in *The Girl Is Murder*, Iris is allowed to help in more of her father's cases. But when she finds that he is investigating her mother's supposed suicide as a possible murder, Iris isn't sure how much she wants to help. Meanwhile, her school's Jewish Student Federation wants her to find out who has been leaving anti-Semitic notes in lockers.

Subjects: Anti-Semitism; Fathers and Daughters; New York; Suicide

Owens, Delia.

Where the Crawdads Sing. **2018. 9780735219113. O**

Kya Clark is known as the Marsh Girl—she has been living on her own in the swamps of North Carolina since she was a kid. When Chase, the local football hero and town golden boy, is murdered in the swamp, in 1969, 19-year-old Kya is immediately suspected. But why would she murder Chase, and how could she have done it?

Subjects: Natural History; North Carolina; Murder; Survival

Sepetys, Ruta.

Out of the Easy. **2013. 9780147508430. S**

Seventeen-year-old Josie Moraine lives on her own in 1950s New Orleans, working in a bookstore and dreaming of going away to Smith College. Her mother is a prostitute, and Josie tries to have little to do with her, but when a mysterious death leads her mother to skip town, a local crime boss comes after Josie to repay her mother's debt. With the help of some friends, Josie has to find out what is going on and take charge of her own destiny.

Subjects: Mob; Mothers and Daughters; Murder; New Orleans; Prostitutes

Silvey, Craig.

Jasper Jones. 2011. 9781742372624. ⓙ Ⓢ

In the middle of the night, Jasper knocks on Charlie's window and asks for help. The help turns out to be disposing of the body of Laura, found hanging from a tree. Unless Charlie helps him, Jasper will be blamed for the murder. Charlie is a bookish, quiet kid, and Jasper is the local outcast—a mixed-race boy who lives on his own in the outback. Together they're an unusual pair in their small-minded small town, where racism abounds. But together they explore the mystery of Laura's death.

Subjects: Australia; Coming-of-Age; Racism; Small Towns; Vietnamese Australians

Springer, Nancy.

Enola Holmes Mysteries. Ⓜ ⓙ

Enola, age 14, is the much younger sister of Sherlock and Mycroft Holmes, but the mystery-solving gene runs strong throughout this family.

Subjects: 1880s; London

The Case of the Missing Marquess. 2006. 9780399243042.

When her mother goes missing, Enola heads off to London searching for her. Along the way, she uncovers the case of a kidnapped marquess, a case she solves using her deductive skills.

The Case of the Left-Handed Lady. 2007. 9780142411902.

On the run from her older brothers, who want to send her to a boarding school, Enola, utilizing disguises, sets up shop in London as a perditorian, a finder of the lost.

The Case of the Bizarre Bouquets. 2008. 9780399245183.

When Dr. Watson goes missing, Enola finds clues in the flowers sent to his wife.

The Case of the Peculiar Pink Fan. 2008. 9780399247804.

Enola's friend Lady Cecily, from *The Case of the Left-Handed Lady*, needs help and leaves Enola a clue in the form of a pink fan.

The Case of the Cryptic Crinoline. 2009. 9780399247811.

Florence Nightingale helps Enola solve the disappearance of Mrs. Tupper, her landlady and a Crimean War widow.

The Case of the Gypsy Goodbye. 2010. 9780399252365.

In the conclusion to the series, Enola investigates the disappearance of a society woman named Lady Blanchefleur. Meanwhile, she comes to terms with her two older brothers.

Winspear, Jacqueline.

Maisie Dobbs. 2003. 9781616954079. Ⓞ

Maisie Dobbs goes to work as a housemaid at the age of 14. Her love of books draws the attention of the lady of the house, who arranges for Maisie to be educated and ultimately to go to Cambridge. World War I breaks out while Maisie is at university, and she leaves to become a nurse. After the war, she completes her education and sets up shop as a private investigator. (Alex Award).

Subjects: England; Private Investigators; World War I

Suspense

Like mysteries, YA suspense novels may or may not involve a death. The common feature is some kind of crime or suspected crime and an element of not knowing what will or did happen. Actual investigation into the crime may or may not be an element. In many cases, the suspense comes from the psychological tension and uncertainty. The protagonist is often in some kind of peril. These stories are often dark.

Anthony, Jessica, and Rodrigo Corral.

Chopsticks. 2012. 9781595144355. **J** **S**

Presented not in text, but in scrapbook format, this is part mystery, part love story, part psychological thriller. Glory is a teen piano prodigy whose descent into mental illness has led her to play "Chopsticks" obsessively. Is her romance with Francisco real or part of her mental illness? Photos, text messages, and other clues are all part of a bigger puzzle.

Subjects: Mental Illness; Piano Players; Scrapbook

Cook, Eileen.

You Owe Me a Murder. 2019. 9781328519023. **S**

In a take on the *Strangers on a Train* plot, Kim is on her way to London with a class trip when she meets Nicki. She pours her woes out to Nicki, mainly that her ex-boyfriend and his new girlfriend are also on the trip. Nicki sympathizes and even jokingly suggests that they make a list of all the reasons Nicki should murder Kim's ex-boyfriend and Kim should murder Nicki's alcoholic mother. Kim doesn't expect to see Nicki again once they get off the plane, but first Kim's ex falls (or is pushed?) in front of a train, and then Nicki starts showing up around town, reminding Kim that she owes Nicki a murder.

Subjects: Blackmail; London; Murder; Unreliable Narrator

Cribbs, Gia.

The Disappearance of Sloane Sullivan. 2018. 9781335015372. **J** **S**

Sloane Sullivan is on her 19th name, 19th home, 19th school. She has gotten really good at blending in, noticing when things aren't quite right, and making only surface-level friends. She's also gotten quite good at figuring out escape routes. Ever since she and her father witnessed a murder, when she was 12, she's been on the run from a U.S. Marshal. Now, just weeks before she's going to graduate from high school and go off to college, everything changes, and suddenly nothing is the way she thought it was.

Subjects: Friends; Kidnapping; Romance; Survival; Witness Protection

Heath, Jack.

Money Run. 2013. 9780545512664. **M** **J**

Ash and Benjamin are thieves: Ash does the actual stealing, while Benjamin supports her from the background via computer. Now they are attempting to rob billionaire businessman Hammond Buckland, which would be challenging enough in itself but which gets even more complicated when an assassin named Michael Peachey shows up. Ash finds herself caught in the middle, both trying to accomplish her original job and figuring out what Peachey has in mind, and why. Full of chase scenes, techno gadgets, ingenious plans, and witty repartee.

Subjects: Assassins; Gadgets; Thieves

Henry, April.

The Girl I Used to Be. 2016. 9781627793322. **S**

Olivia is a 17-year-old emancipated minor who was once known as Ariel Benson. When she was three, her mother was killed, presumably by her father, and Ariel was left outside a Walmart. Now she opens the door to two police detectives, who inform her that her father is no longer a suspect in her mother's killing—because it now appears that he, too, was killed on the same day as her mother. That means that it must have been her parents' killer who took her away from the scene of the crime that day. Curiosity moves Olivia to go to Medford, Oregon, where she and her parents had lived, to see what she can find out. While keeping her identity a secret, she begins to meet the people who were her parents' neighbors and friends—including Duncan, a boy she used to play with as a child. Together, Olivia and Duncan start to unravel the mystery of what happened on that day in the woods 14 years ago. (Edgar Award)

Subjects: Assumed Identity; Murder; Oregon

The Girl Who Was Supposed to Die. 2013. 9781250044372. **J** **S**

Cady comes to with the taste of blood in her mouth and the fingernails of her pinkie and ring fingers missing. She can hear two men discussing the need to get rid of her. She is going to die, but she doesn't know why. Using skills she didn't even know she had, she manages to escape and go on the run. When she reaches a local police station, they tell her that she has escaped from an inpatient mental health program for teens. On the run again, with the help of Ty, a boy she meets during a McDonald's stop, Cady tries to stay alive, figure out who she really is, and stop a biological weapons scheme along the way. Fast-paced suspense.

Subjects: Amnesia; Biological Warfare; Identity Theft; Oregon

Run, Hide, Fight Back. 2019. 9781627795890. **M** **J** **S**

When a group of ski-masked men start shooting up a Portland mall, Miranda follows the rules she learned in an active shooter drill at school: first run; then, if you can't get away, hide; finally, and only if necessary, fight back. Miranda finds herself hiding in the storeroom of a clothing store with four other teens; meanwhile, she knows that her childhood friend, Parker, is somewhere else in the mall with his seven-year-old sister. Told mainly from Miranda and Parker's points of view, this is a tense thriller that explores what people will do when placed in extreme peril.

Subjects: Active Shooter; Portland, Oregon; Shopping Malls

King, Stephen.

Mr. Mercedes. 2014. 9781476754451. **O**

In this combination detective story and psychological thriller, "Mr. Mercedes" is the press's nickname for a guy who drove a Mercedes into a crowd waiting outside a job fair in an unnamed Midwestern city, killing eight and wounding dozens. He was never caught, but one day a year or so later, he sends a taunting letter to the now retired detective, Bill Hodges, who once was in charge of the case. Hodges, who has been contemplating suicide, finds a new lease on life in tracking down Mr. Mercedes, with the help of his 17-year-old neighbor and friend, Jerome Robinson. The action moves between Hodges's point of view and that of Mr. Mercedes, Brady Hartsfield, who is feeling the need to commit more murder and mayhem.

Subjects: Detectives; Serial Killers; Suspense

Kuehn, Stephanie.

Charm and Strange. 2012. 9781250021946. **S**

Quarks, which come in "flavors" (up, down, top, bottom, charm, strange) contain (as Kuehn reminds us) "particles of matter and antimatter, and where the two touch exists this constant stream of creation and annihilation." It's a metaphor for the life of Win, who is now in boarding school in Vermont but who was once a 10-year-old tennis phenom known as Drew. Win is angry, damaged, and not in touch with his family, and in the past, Drew had his issues but at least had an intact family, so clearly something is wrong. The tension builds, showing the damage that can be done by toxic or detached parents but also showing the resilience of teenagers. This one is part psychological thriller, part coming-of-age story, a bit of a mystery, a story about family and friendship. (Morris Award)

Subjects: Boarding Schools; Coming of Age; Family; Friendship; Quarks; Tennis; Unreliable Narrator

Complicit. 2014. 9781250044594. **S**

Jamie's older sister Cate is about to be released from juvenile detention, and Jamie is terrified but also intrigued. Cate's conviction was the result of her violent, risky behavior after the murder of their mother, an event that left Jamie highly medicated and struggling with memory loss. Now, Jamie is desperate to know about his past and what really happened to their mother—desperate enough to confront both his volatile sister and his own dark, tattered memories. (BFYA)

Subjects: Amnesia; Brothers and Sisters; California; Cataplexy; Mental Illness

Lockhart, E.

Genuine Fraud. 2017. 9780385744775. **S**

Who is Jule? She changes clothes, hair, accent, and backstory as necessary. Who is Imogen? Jule's best friend? Maybe. Jule's and Imogen's lives cross and twist until it's hard to know who is telling the truth and who is living a lie. (LA Times)

Subjects: False Identity; London; Martha's Vineyard; Mexico; Murder; New York; Psychological Suspense; Unreliable Narrator

We Were Liars. 2014. 9780385741262. **S**

Cady's extended family spends every summer on their private island near Martha's Vineyard. Cady and her cousins love their time there. But something happens during Cady's 15th summer, and by her 17th summer, she's still trying to put all the pieces together. (BFYA)

Subjects: Cape Cod; Cousins; Islands; Trauma; Unreliable Narrator

Lyga, Barry.

I Hunt Killers. 2012. 9780316125840. **S**

Jazz is the son of a serial killer, and, due to his upbringing, he worries that he may have evil proclivities himself. Now there appears to be a new serial killer at work in town, and Jazz is trying to help the police, even though he can't help wondering if he is really the right person for this job.

Subjects: Black Humor; Forensics; Serial Killers

McCoy, Mary.

I, Claudia. 2018. 9781541530676. **S**

Imperial Day Academy is an expensive prep school in Los Angeles, guided by two student organizations: the Student Senate and the Honor Council. Students must sign an honor pledge, and the Honor Council is the sole body to determine infractions. Claudia has no intention of getting involved in school politics, but events pull her in. Parallels to ancient Rome abound in this suspenseful novel about ambition, integrity, manipulation, and morality. (Printz Honor, BFYA)

Subjects: California; Classics Retold; Los Angeles; Prep Schools; School Politics; Unreliable Narrator

McCreight, Kimberly.

Reconstructing Amelia. 2013. 9780062224360. **O**

Even the closest parents and children keep secrets from one another. Kate is a high-powered litigation attorney in Manhattan. She lives in Park Slope, Brooklyn, with her 15-year-old daughter Amelia, who attends the prestigious Grace Hall School. Kate is called to the school to pick up Amelia, who has been found cheating, but by the time she arrives, Amelia is lying dead on the ground, presumably having jumped from the school's roof. The police and the school are eager to call it a suicide and move on, but Kate isn't ready to believe it yet, especially after she receives an anonymous text that says "Amelia didn't jump." The story is told in alternating voices, both Kate's and Amelia's, as well as with text messages, Facebook posts, and blog posts. The tension ratchets up as it becomes clear that Amelia was involved with a secret club at Grace Hall and that she was receiving anonymous texts of her own. Meanwhile, she was also falling in love for the first time, trying to maintain her loyalty to her oldest friend, and developing a relationship with a new friend. Kate struggles to reconstruct the last weeks of Amelia's life, and her efforts reveal that Amelia was searching for her own answers about Kate's past. **Readalike**: *The Night Olivia Fell*

Subjects: Brooklyn; Bullying; Cheating; Mothers and Daughters; Prep Schools; Suicide

McDonald, Christina.

The Night Olivia Fell. 2019. 9781501184000. **O**

Olivia has fallen off a bridge. She is brain dead, but because she is pregnant, she is being kept on life support. Her mother, Abi, doesn't believe it was an accident, and she begins to investigate what was going on in Olivia's life. Told with flashbacks from Olivia's point of view.

Readalike: *Reconstructing Amelia*

Subjects: Coma; Mothers and Daughters; Pregnant Teens

McNamee, Graham.

Acceleration. 2003. 9780307975959. **J S**

Seventeen-year-old Duncan works at the Lost and Found of the Toronto Traffic Authority. He finds the journal of a would-be serial killer. When the police don't seem interested, Duncan and two of his friends investigate, hoping to track him down before he strikes.

Subjects: Serial Killers; Toronto

Mejia, Mindy.

Everything You Want Me to Be. 2017. 9781501123429. **O**

Eighteen-year-old Hattie has it made. Good family, good grades, good job, nice boyfriend, a lead role in the school play, and plans to head off to New York after graduation. So when she is found murdered one Saturday in April of her senior year, no one can understand why. Her father's best friend, Del, is the county sheriff in their southern Minnesota town, and, as the sheriff investigates the murder, it soon becomes clear that Hattie was not everything that she appeared to be on the surface. Facts about Hattie's life and relationships are revealed bit by bit in this story told from three points of view: Hattie's, Del's, and that of Hattie's English teacher, Peter.

Subjects: Minnesota; Murder; Small Towns; Teenage Girls

Rosenfield, Kat.

Amelia Anne Is Dead and Gone. 2012. 9780525423898. **S**

The day after graduation, Amelia Anne's body is found brutally murdered on the side of the road. Becca is spending her last summer at home before college, and she has a painful desire to get as far away as possible from her stultifying hometown, while at the same time she fears losing something important. Short chapters that tell the story of Amelia Anne's life are alternated with the story of Becca's summer. And as Becca learns what happened to Amelia Anne, the reader can see the parallel struggles of the two young women. (Edgar Finalist)

Subjects: Dating Violence; Murder; Small Towns

Sedgwick, Marcus.

Revolver. 2009. 9781842551868. **M** **J** **S**

Sig is alone in a remote cabin in the Arctic Circle with the dead body of his father when a man shows up demanding the gold that he says Sig's father owes him. (Printz Honor, BFYA)

Subjects: Arctic Circle; Fathers; Revenge

Smith, Sherri L.

Pasadena. 2016. 9781101996256. **S**

In this noir tale, Jude has just arrived on the Jersey shore to visit her cousins and perhaps reconcile with her father when she gets a call from her friend Joey that sends her right back home to Pasadena. Her friend Maggie Kim has been found dead in her swimming pool. Over the next few days, leading up to Maggie's funeral, Jude grapples with some major questions: Did Maggie commit suicide? Was she murdered? Was it an accident? And what does it mean when the person you thought was your best friend clearly was keeping secrets from you? As Jude talks with Joey and with their other friends, she realizes that Maggie had a lot of people who thought they were her "best friend," but none of them really knew the complete Maggie. As Jude spends a steamy California summer learning about the secrets that everyone keeps, she begins to come to grips with the meaning of death and friendship, of love and grief, of forgiveness and endurance.

Subjects: Death; Friends; Grief; Pasadena, California

Stampler, Helen Redisch.

How to Disappear. 2016. 9781481443937. **J** **S**

Jack's father was a hitman, and his brother has the same shady associates, but Jack has always tried to stay on the straight and narrow. Now, however, his brother has summoned him to prison and told him in no uncertain terms that he needs to find a girl who has disappeared—a girl who has murdered one of his associates—and to murder her—or else both Jack's brother and their mother may be in danger. Nicolette is the girl Jack is chasing. Or wait a minute—is her name Cat? Or Bean? Or Kelly? Or Kaylie? She is definitely running from something, although perhaps not what Jack thinks she's running from. As Jack and Nicolette get closer to each other, they both need to figure out how to disappear.

Subjects: False Identity; Psychological Suspense

Stork, Francisco X.

Disappeared. 2017. 9780545944472. **S**

Sara Zapata and her brother Emiliano live in Ciudad Juarez, Mexico. Sara works for a newspaper, and when her best friend, Linda, joins the ever growing ranks of missing girls, Sara uses her column to bring attention to their plight. While the families of the missing girls are appreciative, the criminal underworld retaliates against her with death threats. Meanwhile Emiliano, still in high school, has a crush on a rich girl. In order to make money, he agrees to use his small business of selling local art as a way to smuggle drugs. Eventually, both Sara and Emiliano realize that the only way out is to head across the border (illegally) to join their father in the United States. (BFYA)

Subjects: Brothers and Sisters; Desert; Immigration; Latinx; Mexico; Missing Girls; Reporters

Suma, Nova Ren.

17 & Gone. 2013. 9780525423409. **S**

Shortly before her 17th birthday, Lauren begins to see the spirits of first one but soon dozens of 17-year-old girls who have gone missing and are assumed runaways; she is particularly obsessed with the first girl she encounters, who Lauren is sure did not run away but was kidnapped. As her obsession with "her girls" grows, she grows increasingly distant from friends and family. Do her visions mean that the girls have all died? That they are somehow able to cry out to Lauren to save them? Or do they mean that Lauren is in the grip of a diseased mind?

Subjects: Ghosts; Mental Illness; Murder

Werlin, Nancy.

And Then There Were Four. 2017. 9780803740723. **J S**

Five students at the prestigious Rockland Academy are summoned for a meeting of the Leaders Club in an empty campus building. Once they are all together, the ceiling falls in and injures the students. Although they all manage to escape the destruction, they begin to realize that something sinister is going on—in fact, it seems like their parents want them dead.

Subjects: Conspiracy Theories; Diabetes; Dysfunctional Families; Friendship; Huntington's Disease

Rules of Survival. 2006. 9780142410714. **J S**

Matt tries to protect his sisters from their dangerously deranged mother over the course of three years, as he ages from 13 to 16. When his mother kidnaps one of his sisters, Matt finds out just how far he is willing to go to protect her. (NBA, BBYA)

Subjects: Brothers and Sisters; Child Abuse; Kidnapping

4

Adventure/Thrillers

Action-adventure books, or thrillers, might be described as the type of book that would make a good movie. The pacing is fast and furious, and the plots are often outlandish. The protagonists are larger than life; sometimes they are even criminals. A strong dose of suspension of disbelief may be required when the protagonist is a teenager who is getting into all sorts of unrealistic predicaments. Humor is often an element as well.

Action-Adventure

Benway, Robin.

Also Known As. 2013. 9780802733900. **J** **S**

Maggie is the daughter of international spies. Her own particular specialties are lockpicking and safecracking. But she's also a teenage girl, so when the organization needs someone to infiltrate a New York high school and befriend a boy named Jesse, Maggie is the logical choice. Since she has never attended school before, she must learn to navigate cliques, classes, and other high school realities, all while trying to fulfill her mission.

Subjects: New York; Romance; Spies

Carter, Ally.

The Heist Society Series. **M** **J** **S**

Katrina Bishop comes from a long line of art thieves and con artists. She thinks she's out of the family business once she has scammed her way into a top boarding school, but once a cat burglar, always a cat burglar!

Heist Society. 2010. 9781423116394.

Kat's father is the prime suspect when five paintings are stolen from a mobster. She and her friends have to figure out a way to steal back the paintings and clear her father's name.

Subjects: Art Theft; Austria; France; Italy; London; New York; Poland

Uncommon Criminals. 2011. 9781423147954.

Kat and her crew are approached by an elderly woman who wants them to steal the Cleopatra Emerald, a supposedly cursed gemstone. But has Kat herself fallen victim to a con?

Perfect Scoundrels. 2013. 9781423166009.

Kat's boyfriend Hale unexpectedly inherits his grandmother's billion-dollar corporation, and he realizes that there's no place for Kat and their old heists in his new position. But Kat isn't ready to give him up, especially after she learns that the will might have been altered in an elaborate con to steal the company's fortune.

Carter, Ally.

Not If I Save You First. 2018. 9781338134148. **M** **J** **S**

Maddie and Logan used to be best friends, back when they were 10 and her dad was a Secret Service agent for his dad, the president. But after an incident at the White House in which her father was injured, he and Maddie moved to Alaska. And despite all the letters she sent Logan, she never heard back. Six years later, Logan has made one too many social media mistakes for his parents' comfort, so they send him to spend some time completely off-line—with Maddie and her dad in Alaska. Unfortunately, Logan has hardly begun to settle in when Russian terrorists arrive to kidnap him. Suddenly all the wilderness survival skills Maddie has been learning for the past six years come into play. And even though she's mad at Logan for ignoring her for six years, he isn't going to die if she can do anything about it.

Subjects: Alaska; Secret Service; Survival; Terrorists; Wilderness

Fama, Elizabeth.

Plus One. 2014. 9780374360078. **S**

In this alternative version of history, after the flu pandemic of 1918, everyone was divided into "day" people (Rays) and "night" people (Smudges), and there are severe penalties for being out after curfew. The division has persisted to the present day. It's all supposed to be equal, but it turns out that over the years the Rays have accumulated a few more privileges than the Smudges. So when Sol (a Smudge) decides to "borrow" her newborn Ray niece from the hospital nursery so that her dying grandfather can see his new great-granddaughter, things don't go well. And when she falls for a guy who is a Ray, things are even more confused. Suddenly, Sol is on the run, relying on help from a whole bunch of unlikely characters.

Subjects: Alternate History; Chicago; First Love; Resistance Movements

Survival Stories

The common thread in survival stories is teens fighting for their lives, whether the danger comes from weather, wilderness, natural disaster, or predator. The protagonists in these stories are characterized by perseverance and ingenuity, especially in the face of fear and peril.

Bray, Libba.

Beauty Queens. 2012. 9780439895972. **M J S**

The plane carrying the participants in the Miss Teen Dream Pageant has crashed, killing most of those onboard, including all the adults. The surviving contestants will have to, well, survive on a delightful tropical island using their own wits, ingenuity, beauty products, and pageant-approved talents. (LA Times)

Subjects: Beauty Pageants; Corporate Espionage; Desert Islands; Humor; Plane Crash

Hannah, Kristin.

The Great Alone. 2018. 9780312577230. **O**

In 1978, Leni and her parents go to Alaska to make a new start in life. Her father has recently returned from Vietnam, after being a POW for six years. His PTSD means that he isn't great at holding down a job and is tormented by nightmares and prone to drinking. But an Army buddy has left him some land in Alaska, so the family goes there, with the intention to homestead. They are woefully unprepared for life in the wilderness and appropriately frightened by the number of people who warn them that they need to spend all summer preserving or storing food, or they'll never make it through the winter. Physical survival turns out not to be Leni's greatest concern, though, as the isolation and endless dark of the winter exacerbate her dad's mental illness and his proclivities toward violence.

Subjects: Alaska; Homesteading; PTSD

Johnston, Tim.

Descent. 2015. 9781616203047. **O**

A Wisconsin family is on vacation in Colorado so that 18-year-old Caitlin can spend some time running at altitude before she goes off to join the track team at college. On the first morning, she goes out to run, accompanied by her 15-year-old brother on a bicycle, and the next thing the parents know, the sheriff is calling them to say that Sean has been hit by a truck and is in the hospital and that Caitlin is nowhere to be found. This is a story of nearly unbearable psychological suspense, family drama, and survival, painful at times but ultimately life-affirming.

Subjects: Colorado; Families; Kidnapping; Runners; Torture

Kells, Claire.

Girl Underwater. 2015. 9780525954934. **S O**

A competitive swimmer from Stanford is on her way back home to Boston for Thanksgiving. Her plane crashes in the Rockies, and there are only five survivors: Avery, her fellow swimmer Colin, and three little boys, aged three, four, and six. The story is told in alternating chapters between the events of the crash and the postrescue aftermath. Avery has always been a swimmer, but now she's a girl underwater.

Subjects: Boston; Colorado; Plane Crash; PTSD; Stanford; Survival; Swimmers

Kephart, Beth.

This Is the Story of You. 2016. 9781452142845. **J S**

Seventeen-year-old Mira lives on a barrier island off the Jersey shore. Storms are a way of life, but on this occasion, a superstorm cuts off the island, and Mira is alone. Her single mom had taken her brother to the mainland for treatment, and now Mira has no way to contact her. As the storm rages and the sea floods their home, Mira has to figure out on her own what to save and how to survive. Complicating matters is a strange girl who is lurking around Mira's house and who has apparently been going through her things.

Subjects: Hurricanes; Islands; New Jersey; Storms; Survival

Kuehn, Stephanie.

When I Am Through with You. 2017. 9781101994733. **S**

Ben is a high school senior who is awaiting trial for murder. It's his girlfriend Rosie who died. But actually, seven students and a teacher went into the California wilderness on a weekend camping trip, and only three walked back out. What happened?

Subjects: California; Camping; Murder

Lake, Nick.

Hostage Three. 2013. 9781619631236. **S**

Amy is still grieving her mother's death by suicide, but her father is remarried and is forcing Amy to go on a round-the-world cruise on his yacht with him and her new stepmother. Somali pirates hijack the yacht in the Gulf of Aden, and Amy finds herself finding common ground with Farouz, the hijackers' translator.

Subjects: Grief; Pirates; Somalia; Yachts

In Darkness. 2012. 9781408819975. **S**

In 1791, the slave Toussaint L'Ouverture turned his dreams of creating an independent, free black state into reality when he led the Haitian revolution. In 2010, a catastrophic earthquake hits Haiti, killing over 200,000 people. Buried in darkness beneath the rubble of one of the buildings is a 15-year-old boy named Shorty. In the dark, Shorty cannot be sure whether he is awake or dreaming; he is driven to the brink of insanity by his thirst and the heat. The only way he survives is to retreat inside his mind and recall his childhood, his mother, his sister, and his hero—Toussaint L'Ouverture.

And somehow, the two of them—Shorty and Toussaint—find that on the other side of darkness is light. (Printz Award, BFYA)

Subjects: Earthquakes; Family; Haiti

Marshall, Kate Allie.

I Am Still Alive. 2018. 9780425290989. **M** **J** **S**

Jess hasn't seen her father for years. He couldn't ever quite live in civilization. But when her mother dies in a car crash and Jess herself is injured, she goes to Alaska to live with him. But it turns out that he lives quite a bit more remotely than Jess had ever imagined. And when the secrets of his past catch up with him, he is killed, their cabin is burned to the ground, and Jess is left on her own (with an adorable dog) to survive. She makes plenty of mistakes but manages to keep herself alive until her father's killers return.

Subjects: Alaska; Canada; Dogs; Fathers and Daughters; Survival; Terrorists

McCaughrean, Catherine.

White Darkness. 2007. 9780060890353. **S**

When her deranged Uncle Victor takes her along on his quest to make it to the South Pole, 14-year-old Sym fights for survival on the ice. Sym's life-saving mentor is the voice of Captain Laurence Titus Oates, of Robert Scott's ill-fated historical expedition. (Printz Award, BBYA)

Subjects: Antarctica; Bereavement; Grief; South Pole

Park, Kathy.

Notes from My Captivity. 2018. 9780062394026. **M** **J** **S**

Adrienne is off on the adventure of a lifetime: She's going to Russia with her stepdad, an anthropologist who is on the track of a family who disappeared into the Siberian wilderness 30 years ago and who are rumored still to be living somewhere out there. Adrienne doesn't really believe they exist, but she wants to be a journalist, and she hopes that her stepfather's search will make a great story, even if (especially if) he's wrong. But within days of arriving in Russia, things start to go wrong, and Adrienne finds herself the captive of the very family she didn't believe existed.

Subjects: Magical Realism; Russia; Siberia

Scarrow, Kristine.

The Gamer's Guide to Getting the Girl. **2019. 9781459744769.** 🟥 🟦

Zach and his friend Cooper are in the game store in the mall when the biggest storm in history hits. They are stranded at the mall, along with a handful of other people, until the storm passes and help can arrive. Zach really wants to get close to the girl he just met, Samara, but instead he finds himself helping to organize food, medical care, and security for everyone in the mall.

Subjects: Gaming; Malls; Saskatchewan, Canada; Storms

Storm, Jo.

Snowhook. **2019. 9781459743021.** 🟥 🟦 🟦

Hannah doesn't really like spending time at her family's "camp" in the northern reaches of Ontario; she'd rather be home in Toronto. But when her father is called away, and she and her mother and sister are snowed in, Hannah must use the skills she has learned. She has accidentally broken her mother's vital insulin vials, the phone lines are down, and she sees no option but to hook up the dogs to the dogsled and go to a neighboring cabin for help. But the weather is only one of the obstacles in her way as she struggles to fulfill her mission.

Subjects: Blizzards; Canada; Dogsleds; Snow; Wilderness Survival

Weir, Andy.

The Martian. **2012. 9780804139021.** 🟥

Six days into what should have been the greatest adventure of astronaut Mark Watney's life, everything has gone wrong. Now he's stranded on Mars, with no way to communicate with anyone. His crewmates are on the spacecraft, relatively close, but they (and everyone on Earth) think he's dead. He's in basically a tent (the Hab) that is designed to last for 31 days, and it's going to be at least four years before anyone else comes to Mars. If the oxygenator breaks down, he'll suffocate. If the water reclaimer breaks down, he'll die of thirst. If the Hab breaches, he'll explode. And if none of those things happen, he'll run out of food. But Mark is determined to survive. (Alex Award)

Subjects: Astronauts; Botany; Mars; Survival

Espionage and Terrorism

Teenage spies dealing with terrorist threats may seem like a preposterous proposition, but they make for a popular subgenre of the adventure novel. The Alex Rider series by Anthony Horowitz was at the forefront of this trend when *Stormbreaker* was first published in 2001, and the story continues to be popular, now in graphic novel format. Most of the books in this section feature teens who are recruited to be spies, but some also feature protagonists who have run afoul of terrorists or intelligence agencies.

Barter, Catherine.

Troublemakers. 2017. 9781512475494. **J** **S**

Fifteen-year-old Alena lives in London with her half brother Danny and his boyfriend Nick. Their mother died when Alena was three and Danny was 22. But Alena is getting curious, and Danny never wants to talk about their mother. Meanwhile, someone is leaving bombs randomly in supermarkets, making everyone nervous. As Alena starts to probe into her mother's life, she runs up against resistance from Danny. At the same time, Danny's new job with a law-and-order politician has caused problems with his and Nick's relationship. Well drawn characters and the gradual revealing of old secrets are the heart of this story that centers around the real meaning of family.

Subjects: Family; London; Terrorism

Carter, Ally.

The Gallagher Girls Series. **M** **J** **S**

The Gallagher Academy for Exceptional Young Women isn't exactly what it appears to be. Instead of math and reading, English and horseback riding, the girls who attend this school take courses in Covert Operations, Ancient Languages, Countries of the World, Culture and Assimilation, and Protection and Enforcement. The Gallagher Academy is, in a word, a school for spies. Cammie Morgan is a second-generation Gallagher girl. Her mother is the Academy's headmistress, and her father is also a spy but missing, presumed dead. Along with her friends, Macey, Bex, and Liz, Cammie has her own set of adventures.

Subjects: Adventure; Boarding Schools; Double Agents; Humor; Spies

I'd Tell You I Love You, But Then I'd Have to Kill You. 2006. 9781423100034.

Cammie is really looking forward to the new school year, but before she knows it, things are getting out of control. Her new CoveOps teacher seems to know all about Cammie's missing-and-presumed-dead father. Then she meets a boy in town, Josh, who finally sees her—really sees her—as no one else ever has. And now Cammie is balancing on a dangerous ledge—knowing that no one beyond the gates of The Gallagher Academy can ever know who she truly is and wanting nothing more than to spill all of her secrets to Josh.

Cross My Heart and Hope to Spy. 2007. 9781423100058.

The Gallagher Academy is hosting a boys' spy school, but security breaches abound, and Cammie and the girls have to stop the leaks.

Don't Judge a Girl by Her Cover. 2009. 9781423100058.

Someone is after Gallagher Girl Macey. Macey's dad is on the campaign trail, running for vice president of the United States, and Cammie, Bex, and Liz join them as Macey's personal security team.

Only the Good Spy Young. 2010. 9781423128205.

The Circle, an organization of double agents, has been trying to track down and kidnap Cammie. Now Cammie learns that someone she trusted is actually part of the Circle and may have been responsible for her father's death.

Out of Sight, Out of Time. 2012. 9781423147947.

Cammie leaves the Gallagher Academy to protect her family and friends, but the next thing she knows, she's in a convent in the Alps, with no memory of the past few months.

United We Spy. 2013. 9781423165996.

In the final book of the series, Cammie and her friends must track down the members of the Circle and stop them from implementing their evil plan.

Greenland, Shannon.

T-Minus. 2019. 9781640636644. M J

Sophie is the daughter of the (female) president of the United States. She is woken in the middle of the night by a call from her father, asking if she knows where her brother is. This is followed immediately by the arrival of her Secret Service detail, urging her to dress quickly and leave the house because a domestic terrorist group has put a hit out on her mother. The family members are to be separated for safety, but the last thing her father tells her before she leaves is, "Do not trust anyone. Your mother thinks this is coming from someone on the inside." But Sophie knows whom she can trust: the other members of the Teen Intelligence Agency, a training group for children of CIA workers. So over the course of just a little over 24 hours, Sophie and her friends attempt to follow all the trails and save Sophie's family before time runs out.

Subjects: Domestic Terrorism; President of the United States; Secret Service; Teen Spies; Washington, D.C.

Horowitz, Anthony.

Alex Rider Series. M J S

Alex Rider goes from 14-year-old schoolboy to superspy after his guardian is killed under mysterious circumstances, and he is forced to join the secret spy organization MI6. Alex is a sort of teenage James Bond, battling to stop megalomaniacs who are set on world domination. This series has been so successful that it has been adapted to film and graphic novel formats.

Subjects: Espionage; Gadgets

Stormbreaker. 2001. 9780399236204.

In his first mission Alex, age 14, after discovering that his uncle was a secret agent, takes on the job himself and must stop a diabolical scheme targeting Britain's schoolchildren with free computers that are programmed to unleash a horror that will kill an entire generation. (Film)

Point Blank. 2002. 9780399236211.

Alex is sent off to the French Alps to find out what is happening in an exclusive boarding school, where bad boy sons of the wealthy are sent and become surprisingly docile.

Skeleton Key. 2003. 9780399237775.

Whisked away from Wimbledon, Alex ends up in Cuba, where he must stop a general, armed with a nuclear weapon, who wants to reinstate the Soviet Union.

Eagle Strike. 2003. 9780399239793.

A vacation with his girlfriend's family in the south of France ends when Alex spots an assassin, has to survive a real-life computer game, and has to stop an insane rock star who is willing to annihilate anyone in his quest to rid the world of drugs. (BBYA)

Scorpia. 2006. 9780399241512.

While trying to decide whether his father was operating on the side of good or evil, Alex infiltrates Scorpia, a secret organization that is planning to destroy the relationship between Britain and the United States by killing off all 12- and 13-year-old British children.

Ark Angel. 2007. 9780399241529.

Recuperating from a gunshot wound, Alex stymies the kidnaping of a fellow patient, the son of a wealthy hotelier targeted by ecoterrorists who want to stop him from building a luxury hotel in space.

Snakehead. 2007. 9780399241611.

After crash-landing off the coast of Australia, Alex is recruited to help stop a band of smugglers, while still trying to uncover his parents' secrets.

Crocodile Tears. 2009. 9780399250569.

Alex is up against a con artist who wants to create a disaster of epic proportions, using genetically modified corn to deliver a virus, in order to profit from the resulting charity.

Scorpia Rising. 2011. 9780399250576.

Once again, Alex must face off against Scorpia, this time in the Middle East.

Russian Roulette: The Story of an Assassin. 2013. 9780399254413.

The back story of Yassen Gregorovich, the Russian assassin who has been Alex's archenemy.

Never Say Die. 2017. 9781524739300.

Alex relocates to San Francisco after the death of his mentor but soon finds himself traveling the world in an attempt to take down Scorpia once and for all.

Nightshade. 2020. 9780593115312.

Alex heads to Gibraltar to tackle a new criminal organization: Nightshade.

Rogers, Meghan.

Crossing the Line. 2018. 9780399176173. **J** **S**

Jocelyn was kidnapped by a North Korea spy agency (KATO) as a child, held with the help of an addicting drug, and trained to be a spy. When KATO sends her to the United States to infiltrate the group her parents once worked for, Jocelyn sees an opportunity for freedom—and to shut down KATO. But Jocelyn doesn't exactly get a warm welcome—especially not from the agent known as Scorpion, whom she has faced off with in the field more than once. With barely anyone on her side, Jocelyn has to finish what she started—and uncover new and unsettling information in the process.

Subjects: Double Agents; Espionage; North Korea; Terrorism

Walden, Mark.

H.I.V.E. Series. **M** **J**

Because of his inherent evil genius proclivities, 13-year-old orphan Otto Malpense is kidnapped and taken to a secret academy, where super villains are trained with the goal of world domination. He befriends Wing Fanchu, a martial arts expert; Laura Brand, an electronics expert; and Shelby Trinity, a talented jewel thief, all of whom have been brought to H.I.V.E. because of their potential as villains.

H.I.V.E.: Higher Institute of Villainous Education. 2007. 9781416935711.

Otto, Wing, Laura, and Shelby become friends when they are all abducted and taken to a secret school that has the objective of turning them into the next generation of super villains. They are all either the offspring of noted villains or orphans with the abilities to be master criminals. The academy is hidden in a volcano from which escape seems unlikely, but the four friends are willing to give escape a try.

Subjects: Islands; Schools; Volcanoes

The Overlord Protocol. 2008. 9781416935735.

When word comes that Wing's father has been killed, Otto, now 14, accompanies him to Japan for the funeral, but along the way they are attacked by ninjas who seem impervious to injury. During their escape, Otto and Wing uncover a plot by a nefarious villain who is set on annihilating H.I.V.E. using an evil artificial intelligence.

Subjects: Artificial Intelligence; Japan; Ninjas

Escape Velocity. 2011. 9781442421851.

After Dr. Nero, the head of H.I.V.E., is captured by H.O.P.E. (Hostile Operative Prosecution Executive), Otto and his friends have to rescue Dr. Nero if they ever want H.I.V.E. to return to normal.

Subjects: Artificial Intelligence; Criminals; Schools

Dreadnought. 2011. 9781442421868.

Otto is on his way to the Arctic for a hardcore training exercise. While onboard the *Dreadnought*, a high-tech airborne defense platform, they are ambushed by a renegade faction called the Disciples, and two of Otto's friends are kidnapped. Otto has to save his friends and figure out who the real enemies are.

Subject: Kidnapping

Rogue. 2011. 9781442421875.

Otto has been missing since the events of *Dreadnought*, and he is suspected of being responsible for a series of attacks on the world's villainous forces. Dr. Nero issues a capture-or-kill order for Otto, but Raven and Wing try to find him before the assassins do.

Subjects: Amazon Rainforest; Artificial Intelligence; Assassins

Zero Hour. 2012. 9781442421882.

Overlord, the evil artificial intelligence, is reborn and is moving from host body to host body in search of Otto. Dr. Nero activates Zero Hour in attempt to stop Overlord.

Subject: Artificial Intelligence

Aftershock. 2014. 9781442494671.

Otto and his companions are headed to Siberia to take part in a survival exercise called The Hunt. But there's a traitor among them. And, indeed, a civil war may be emerging among villain-kind.

Subjects: Siberia; Survival; Traitors

Deadlock. 2015. 9781442494701.

Otto and Raven must rescue their friends from the clutches of the Disciples.

Subjects: Criminals; Survival

Wein, Elizabeth.

Code Name Verity. **2012. 9781423152880.**

France. 1943. Verity, a British spy, has been captured by the Nazis. "I AM A COWARD," she explains. She has given the Nazis the wireless codes they wanted. She is now writing out her confession, explaining how and why she ended up in Ormaie in Nazi-occupied France, why she has the identity papers of Maddie Brodart, and why she is telling the truth and telling the Nazis every little thing. How much time has Verity bought for herself? A handful of days to write her confession and, after that, what?

Subjects: France; Pilots; Spies; World War II

Sarah's Picks

Donnelly, Jennifer. *A Northern Light*.

Fama, Elizabeth. *Plus One*.

Johnson, Maureen. *Truly Devious.*

Kells, Claire. *Girl Underwater.*

McNamee, Graham. *Acceleration.*

Summers, Courtney. *Sadie.*

Chapter 5

Speculative Fiction

By and large, speculative fiction, or SF as it is commonly called, is differentiated from other genres by treating the unreal as real. It encompasses a handful of genres including horror, paranormal, science fiction, and fantasy. While many readers are entrenched in only one of these—for instance, some science fiction readers want nothing to do with magic—it's not uncommon for a fan of one of these genres to be a fan of the others as well.

As librarians and booksellers who have "genrefied" collections know, many titles that fall under the SF umbrella don't fit neatly into one of its primary subgenres. For instance, *Contagion* and *Pitch Dark* are two books that are equal parts science fiction and horror. Moreover, a great part of horror is, at root, fantasy that simply explores some of the darker reaches of the world.

Paranormal and Horror

Horror is legion, containing everything from books that will creep up on you in your sleep to ones that are meant to strum heartstrings to others that are gross, revolting, and distressing. Given that a good deal of horror's enjoyment comes from how it preys on our anxieties, much of its effect is subjective and can be difficult to quantify for readers. It's best to remind readers that it is perfectly fine to read within their comfort zone, and, provided they are reading for pleasure, they can stop reading at any time for any reason.

Twilight is still a YA mainstay, but vampire and werewolf romances are losing some of their traction with the YA audience. Nevertheless, many a reader still wants a story with some solid fangs and fur in it. While horror has seen an increase in LGBTQIA+ representation, it hasn't seen the same general increase in diversity that other genres have.

For many readers, this is their absolute favorite genre across all media. Indeed, once horror gets its hooks into someone, it usually keeps them there. This is also a wonderful genre for reluctant readers and people who haven't become regular readers. Part of the reason for this is that, once a scary story begins, readers often feel a compulsion to reach the closure of resolution promised by the end of the story.

It should be noted that many grown-ups are much more concerned about age appropriateness when it comes to horror than other genres. It's best not to promise anything in terms of content; after all, what is considered "mature" is contingent on one's life experiences. But, then again, adding "read at your own risk" into a book talk can seriously increase its appeal.

Occult

The occult deals with one of our greatest fears: the unknown. These titles tend toward the scary.

Arden, Katherine.

Small Spaces. 2019. 9780525515043. **M J**

Ollie, a sixth-grade girl, turns to reading in order to cope with a difficult loss. When she sees a woman about to destroy an antique book, she rescues it and reads its creepy tale about a "smiling man" who makes steep bargains with people. Then she goes on a fateful field trip to a farm that has an eerie connection to the book. On their way home from the farm, the bus is stranded, and Ollie and two friends flee into the woods, heeding cryptic advice given by the bus driver and her mother's broken watch. All kinds of paranormal beings show up, including animate scarecrows, ghosts, and more.

Subject: Grief

Black, Holly.

Doll Bones. 2013. 9781416963998. **M J**

Three 12-year-old friends, Zach, Poppy, and Alice like to play a role-playing game together in which they go on exhilarating imaginary adventures. One day, though, Zach says he won't be playing anymore, a result of his father throwing away his "dolls." Poppy, however, calls for one last quest: They must bury the bone china doll, who was the Queen in their game because, according to Poppy, it is made out of the bones of a murdered girl. Eerie atmosphere and expert storytelling create a tense elegy to childhood that can be read on a deeper level or just enjoyed for the intense adventure that it is. (Mythopoeic)

Subjects: Dolls; Friends; Role-Playing Games

Carroll, Emily.

Through the Woods. 2014. 9781442465961. **M J S**

This collection of five creepy stories, which are perfectly complemented by Carroll's illustrations, has the feel of classic fairy tales and ghost stories. It's perfect for reading aloud or by oneself; just be prepared to feel unsettled. There is minimal blood. (GGN)

Subjects: Graphic Novel; Short Stories

Herman, Christine Lynn.

The Devouring Gray. 2019. 9781368024969. **S**

The Gray, located in Four Paths, New York, is a strange dimensional prison that holds a terrifying monster. Some denizens of the town have been custodians of the prison for generations, and they are aided in their duty by special powers. Forming the crux of the story are our teens' inherited responsibilities to the Gray and their battle to contain the monster within. This is similar in many ways to the TV series *Riverdale* and *Teen Wolf.*

Subjects: LGBTQIA+; Monsters

Horowitz, Anthony.

The Gatekeepers. M J

Foster child Matt Freeman, age 14, discovers that devil worshipers are trying to bring back evil beings who had been banished long ago by five children and that he may have the unique talents to stop them as one of five Gatekeepers who have been prophesied.

Subjects: Adventure; England; Portals; Witchcraft

Raven's Gate. 2005. 9780439679954.

> Fourteen-year-old Matt is sent to live with old Mrs. Deverill in the small village of Lesser Malling as punishment for a crime he did not commit. There he discovers sinister forces at work and finds out that he may be intended to be a blood sacrifice to open Raven's Gate, a portal to evil.

Evil Star. 2006. 9780439679961.

> Matt travels to Peru with journalist Richard, because a second gate to evil may be on the verge of opening. There he meets Pedro, another Gatekeeper.

> **Subject**: Peru

Nightrise. 2007. 9780439680011.

> Orphaned identical twins, Jamie and Scott, have a psychic bond that becomes essential to their survival after Scott is kidnapped by the evil Nightrise Corporation, and Jamie must travel back into the past.

> **Subjects**: Native Americans; Time Travel; Twins

Necropolis. 2009. 9780439680035.

> Puddles turn to blood in Necropolis, the onetime city of Hong Kong, where Matt, Richard, Jamie, and Scott go to find Scarlett, the fifth Gatekeeper and the only female in their quintet.

> **Subjects**: Adoption; China; Hong Kong; Indonesians

Oblivion. 2012. 9780439680042.

> Although the five Gatekeepers made it out of Hong Kong, they are far from being out of trouble. The King of the Old Ones is readying for an epic battle—in fact, the final battle, which will happen in bleak Oblivion.

Kraus, Daniel.

Rotters. 2011. 9780385738583. S

After his mother dies, Joey moves from Chicago to Iowa to live with Harnett, the father he's never met. Harnett is a rough character, the town pariah, and a lousy father. When Joey discovers that Harnett earns his living as a grave robber, it makes a lot of sense. It's also interesting, and Joey starts to tag along with his father, getting more and more involved in the dark world of pillaging graveyards. The fear factor comes from the visceral descriptions and creepy atmosphere.

Subjects: Fathers and Sons; Graves; Grief; Iowa

Kurtagich, Dawn.

Teeth in the Mist. 2019. 9780316478472. **S**

Three different stories in three different time periods come together to tell the dark, atmospheric tale of a Faustian deal and its fallout. There are two primary storylines: one set in the present day in which Zoey and a friend explore the ruins of Mill House, and one set in 1851 in which Roan, a 17-year-old, moves into Mill House as a ward. The final timeline is set in 1583 and explores the origins of Mill House.

Subjects: Faust; Gothic; Multiple Perspectives; Wales

McGuire, Seanan, and Rovina Cai.

Down among the Sticks and Bones. 2017. 9780765392039. **S**

This is the second entry in McGuire's Wayward Children series, but it can be read as a stand-alone. Eleanor West's Home for Wayward Children is a sanctuary for children who, having traveled to and returned from other worlds, need a special kind of environment. Jacqueline "Jack" and Jillian "Jill" are twin sisters who enter the world of the Moors by traveling down a magical staircase. Although at first the Moors seems like an enlightening, if dark escape in which the sisters can be different versions of themselves—Jack apprentices a resurrectionist while Jill stays with a powerful vampire—they discover that trouble can find you anywhere. (Alex Award)

Subjects: Magic; Parallel Worlds; Twins

Ostow, Micol.

Amity. 2014. 9781606841563. **S**

Ostow's adaption of *The Amityville Horror* (1977) for a teen audience happens on two timelines: Connor's and Gwen's, both of whom live in the haunted Amity house. Connor's storyline takes place 10 years before Gwen's, which unfolds in the present. Connor is plagued by horrific nightmares, while the house plays tricks on the family, doing its best to usher them into madness. It does the same to Gwen and her family, although her main concern is for her brother, Luke, who seems especially susceptible to the house's power. An excellent recommendation for fans of Netflix's *Haunting of Hill House*.

Subjects: Family; New England; Occult; Siblings

Whedon, Joss, Jordie Bellaire, Dan Mora, and Raul Angulo.

Buffy the Vampire Slayer: Vol. 1: High School Is Hell. 2019. 9781684153572. **J** **S**

Buffy, a high school student whose avocation is killing vampires and other evil beings, has trouble keeping a low profile in Sunnydale. Fortunately, she has two best friends, Xander and Willow, who have her back and will help keep her secret. Together they take on ancient vampires and hunt down a mysterious dealer of magical artifacts. This volume strikes a balance between being scary, humorous, action packed, and dramatic in turns, all while being entertaining for longtime Buffy fans and a great entry point for those new to the franchise.

Subjects: Friends; Graphic Novel; Urban Fantasy

White, Kiersten.

Slayer. 2019. 9781534404953. **S**

A modern entry in the beloved Buffyverse, this title follows Nina, who grew up with her twin sister, Artemis, in the Watcher Academy, where Watchers, those who guide Slayers, are reared. Although Nina leans more toward mending than rending and studies to be a healer, her destiny makes other demands of her: After Buffy sets off a calamitous event, Nina is chosen to be not just any Slayer but the very last Slayer, of whom much is expected.

Subjects: Buffy the Vampire Slayer; Twins; Urban Fantasy

Ghosts

Ghost stories can be scary, but by no means do they have to be.

Auxier, Jonathan.

The Night Gardener. 2014. 9781419715310. **M** **J**

Molly and Kip, sister and brother, older and younger respectively, emigrated from Ireland to England after their parents died, a tragic event Molly has kept concealed from Kip. For better or worse, they find work as servants at the Windsor estate, where grows a storied tree that supposedly works dark magic on people. The tree isn't the only creepy thing on the grounds; a spirit, The Night Gardener, also haunts it. Scary, plot driven, and with well developed characters, this is an enchanting read.

Subjects: Disabilities; England; Historical; Orphans; Siblings

Avi.

The Seer of Shadows. 2008. 9780060000158. **M** **J**

When science-minded apprentice photographer Horace Carpetine develops his first professional portrait, it includes the image of a ghost. In 1872 New York City, Horace teams up with a servant, who works for the family of the ghost, to discover what actually happened to the young socialite.

Subjects: 19th Century; Historical Fiction; New York; Photography

Berquist, Emma.

Missing, Presumed Dead. 2019. 9780062642813. **S**

Lexi is gifted—or cursed—with a special ability: Whenever she touches someone, she instantly knows how they will die. One night, Lexi bumps

5

into a girl, Jane, outside a nightclub and foresees a brutal death for her. Having already learned that she can't prevent the events she sees in her visions, Lexi doesn't try to save Jane. So, after Jane is killed, her ghost comes after Lexi and compels her to help catch her killer.

Subjects: Mystery; Thriller

Bérubé, Amelinda.

The Dark beneath the Ice. 2018. 9781492657071. **J** **S**

As Marianne's normal life begins to crumble—her parents get divorced, her mother is hospitalized, Marianne no longer dances—reality begins to slip away from her too. She's losing time, hearing strange things, and just doesn't feel like herself. She turns to Ron, the daughter of a psychic, for help, and the two, suspecting supernatural causes, attempt to free Marianne from a force that seems to be compelling her to drown herself. Full of emotion, chilling, and spooky, this is a robust page-turner that's more than just a ghost story.

Subjects: LGBTQIA+; Mental Illness

Blake, Kendare.

Anna. **S**

Theseus Cassio ("Cas") Lowood travels the country hunting and "killing" ghosts with his late father's athame, a kind of ceremonial knife.

Subjects: Ghost Hunters; Gory; Psychics

Anna Dressed in Blood. 2011. 9780765328656.

Cas's newest quarry Anna, the ghost of high school girl who was killed decades ago, is like nothing he's faced before. She is angry, murderous, powerful, and somehow friendly. The eventful plot speeds along and has elements of humor and romance alongside the horror.

Girl of Nightmares. 2012. 9780765328663.

Former rolling stone, Cas, hasn't moved on from Anna, and, in this volume, he fights to rescue his beloved from Hell.

Chupeco, Rin.

The Girl from the Well. **S**

This creepy series will appeal to fans of the Ring. In fact, Okiku, Tark's ghostly companion, is based on the same story that Ring is based on.

Subjects: Japanese Folklore; Okiku; Tattoos

The Girl from the Well. 2014. 9781402292187.

In a story narrated by Okiku, a vengeful ghost who delivers murderers' comeuppance, this creepy story opens with her doing just that: gruesomely killing a killer. For the past 300 years, little has changed for her: she identifies murderers by the ghosts of their victims who cling to their backs, then executes them. However, there's something special about Tark, a teenage boy, his strange, moving tattoos, and the dangerous spirit that seems to haunt him. Okiku tries to help him, and he wants to help himself, sending him on a journey to Japan, his mother's homeland, where he learns about the supernatural and maybe a chance to have the spirit exorcised.

The Suffering. 2015. 9781492629849.

Tark, who narrates this follow-up volume, teams up to take down evildoers who are alive or . . . otherwise. When Kagura, an exorcist and friend from Japan, goes missing in Aokigahara, also known as Japan's "suicide forest," the duo go after her. They are both tested—along with the audience—with questions of justice and what is right.

Gaiman, Neil.

Graveyard Book. 2008. 9780060530921. **M** **J** **S**

Nobody ("Bod") Owens, a precocious toddler, wanders away from his house and into a mostly abandoned cemetery just as an assassin breaks in and slays his parents and older sister. The ghostly residents of the cemetery take him under their wing. A living child being raised by ghosts presents some logistical problems, which are solved by a vampire guardian who is neither alive nor dead and can obtain food for Bod. As Bod grows up, he learns many of the ghostly skills, such as fading and scaring, and human skills, such as reading, and finds a living friend whose family figures him for an imaginary companion. As an adolescent, he learns that the assassin who killed his original family is still seeking him and that he must save himself. (Hugo, Newbery, BBYA)

Subjects: Family; Orphans

Hahn, Mary Downing.

Took. 2015. 9780544551534. **M** **J**

A small town in West Virginia is full of poverty, hauntings, and rumors. A witch, who calls the town home, takes a young girl to be her servant every 50 years. When Daniel's family hit upon hard times and move to this small town, he doesn't quite buy in to all the spooky stories. Then his sister, Erica, goes missing—just like how another girl went missing 50 years before—and Daniel must get her back.

Subjects: Alternative Format; Siblings

Levithan, David.

Marly's Ghost. 2005. 9780142409121. **M** **J**

Mourning the death by cancer of his girlfriend Marly, 16-year-old Ben experiences *A Christmas Carol* type of experience when Marly's ghost visits him, followed by the spirits of Valentine's Day past, present, and future.

Subjects: Death; Valentine's Day

Monahan, Hillary.

Bloody Mary. **J** **S**

The launch point for this series is the urban legend of Bloody Mary, a ghost who can supposedly be summoned to appear in a mirror by chanting her name. Bloody Mary is a terrifying figure who nonetheless is explored and given a fleshed-out backstory. This is a good fit for readers who like the movie *The Ring* or Rin Chupeco's <u>The Girl from the Well</u> series.

Subjects: Summoning; Urban Legends

MARY: The Summoning. 2014. 9781423185192.

A group of teenage girls, just like countless teens before them, try to summon Bloody Mary at the behest of their leader, Jess, who claims to know just how to do it. They succeed, and Mary appears in the mirror as if behind a window. Not satisfied with having done it once, Jess convinces them to do it again. This time, however, the result is truly terrifying: Mary escapes the mirror and begins to haunt them, appearing in shiny surfaces and tailing the narrator, Shauna.

MARY: Unleashed. 2015. 9781423185390.

The gang must band together to discover Mary's true story and solve her murder in order to lay her to rest. Having happened over a century ago in a place beset by obstacles, the task is anything but easy. For the reader, though, it is a rewarding journey that fills in more of Mary's backstory.

Reynolds, Jason.

Long Way Down. 2018. 9781481438261. **J S**

A ghost story more in the vein of *A Christmas Carol* than *Sixth Sense*, the events transpire during a single elevator ride taken by 15-year-old Will as he contemplates exacting revenge upon the person he believes killed Shawn, Will's brother, two days earlier. While on the elevator, Will is visited by a host of ghosts who all have something to say. The question looming over this title is whether Will will kill his brother's killer. (Printz Honor, Newbery Honor, BFYA, NBA, LA Times, Walden, Edgar)

Subjects: Guns; Masculinity; Revenge; Siblings; Verse

Winters, Cat.

In the Shadow of Blackbirds. 2013. 9781419710230.

In San Diego in 1918, during World War I, Mary Shelly Black, a 16-year-old, lives a life beset by death. While the war sucks up young men and kills them abroad, the Spanish Influence pandemic poses a more immediate, local threat. With so many loved ones dead, seances and spiritual photographs that capture the images of ghosts (examples of which are reproduced in the text) become a common means of coping with loss. For Mary, these parlor tricks become a reality when a near death experience gives her the ability to commune with the dead.

Subjects: 1910s; Grief; San Diego, California; Spanish Influenza; World War I

Monsters

What is a monster? Far from being a class of creature, "monster" is just a relationship descriptor like "husband" or "priest." A monster is something shrouded in the unknown that is also a threat. It's common for monster stories to be indictments of humanity, but, to be sure, monsters can also be just monsters.

Alameda, Courtney.

Pitch Dark. 2018. 9781250294579. **S**

This horror–science fiction hybrid takes place in space 400 years after the Pitch Dark sect hijacked ships full of resources meant to help humans survive beyond Earth's end. When both a Pitch Dark crew and a ship of settlers find a resource-filled ship, the *John Muir*, a struggle breaks out. Two teens, Tuck, who was hibernating aboard the *John Muir*, and Lana, who was aboard the settlers' ship, bump into each other and pair up to survive both political strife and the alien monsters who use sound to kill.

Subjects: Aliens; Sounds; Space

Bérubé, Amelinda. Illustrated by Danielle McNaughton.

Here There Are Monsters. 2019. 9781492671015. **S**

When her parents move Skye and her younger sister, Deirdre, across the country, Skye takes it as an opportunity to reinvent herself, and she thrives socially. Her sister Deirdre, however, becomes socially withdrawn, spending her time in the woods behind their remote house, creating a fantasy world and building sculptures out of sticks and animal bones. Then Deirdre goes missing, and no one can find her. Skye, however, gets a creepy invitation to track her sister down one night when something strange comes scratching at her window. This story can be unsettling as much for its horror elements as for the toxic relationships it depicts.

Subjects: Missing People; Sisters

Brallier, Max, and Douglas Holgate.

The Last Kids on Earth. 2015. 9780425292112. **M** **J**

This chapter book/graphic novel mash-up focuses on Jack Sullivan, a 13-year-old foster kid and survivor of the monster apocalypse. Hunkered down in his customized tree house, Jack manages to survive through ingenuity and a sense of humor. Eventually, he meets up with two former classmates, and together the trio set off to rescue another friend. This horror story is more about laughs and gross-outs than terror.

Subjects: Foster Kids; Funny; Graphic Novel Hybrid; Gross; Orphan; Postapocalyptic; Survival

Emezi, Akwaeke.

Pet. 2019. 9780525647072. **J** **S**

Pan's Labyrinth meets *The Hate U Give* in this story about real and metaphorical monsters. Jam is a trans teen living in Lucille, a supposedly socially enlightened town. When she accidentally bleeds on one of her mother's paintings, she brings forth a freaky monster whom she names and with whom she fights the dark things other people would rather ignore.

Subjects: LGBTQIA+; Race

5

Fama, Elizabeth.

Monstrous Beauty. 2012. 9781250034250. **S**

The storytelling alternates between the perspectives of Syrenka, a mermaid living in 1872, and 17-year-old Hester who's living in 2002. Hester, whose mother died giving birth to her and who fears a similar fate should she ever have kids, has resigned herself to a childless future. Syrenka, who fell in love with a human man and traded being a mermaid for the chance to be with him, has a rather morbid romance and is a sympathetic if monstrous character. As Hester discovers, she and Syrenka are connected in a dark way relating to a murder-suicide. (BFYA)

Subjects: 19th Century; Mermaids; Murder-Suicide; New England

Poblocki, Dan.

The Haunting of Gabriel Ashe. 2013. 9780545402712. **J** **S**

Gabe and his mother move into his grandma's house in a new town after their house burns down. An outsider in a new place, Gabe strikes up a friendship with Seth, who lives nearby. Together they play a make-believe game in which they are Robber Princes hunting down a baby-eating beast called The Hunter. Unbeknownst to Gabe, Seth is an outsider at school. When he finds this out, he does his best to distance himself from Seth, and Seth does not take it well. That, however, is the least of Gabe's concerns when he starts being stalked by a shadowy figure, and events from their make-believe game start to happen in real life. (BBYA)

Subjects: Friendship; Imagination; Loneliness; New Kid

Shepherd, Megan.

<u>Madman's Daughter Trilogy.</u> **S**

Shepherd tells three classics-inspired stories, choosing Juliet, a teenage girl from one of H. G. Wells's novels, to be the heroine instead of a side character. Each book is highly readable and balances horror and science fiction with a dose of romance.

Subjects: Dr. Jekyll and Mr. Hyde; Frankenstein; H. G. Wells; Historical; Mary Shelley; Medical Horror; Retold Classics

The Madman's Daughter. 2013. 9780062128034.

This is a retelling of H. G. Wells's *The Island of Dr. Moreau* from the perspective of Dr. Moreau's teenage daughter, Juliet. Juliet and her mother are left behind to fend for themselves when Dr. Moreau flees London for reasons tied to his experiments. Once Juliet's situation deteriorates to the point that she no longer has a choice, she makes the journey to the island where her father is living, picking up a couple of handsome male companions along the way. Her father has been continuing his experiments on the island, which involve combining humans and animals, forcing Juliet to contend with uncomfortable questions. (BFYA)

Her Dark Curiosity. 2014. 9780062128065.

Juliet makes it off her father's island and back to London where she has secured a guardian and work for herself. She isn't the only person to have made the trip to London, though. Edward Prince, one of her love interests, is also in London, and he is killing people while wrestling with the Dr. Jekyll persona he can't control. What's more, Juliet's medicine is starting to fail, and she must figure out a solution.

A Cold Legacy. 2015. 9780062128096.

Taking inspiration from Mary Shelley's Frankenstein, the final install-ment in the trilogy sees Juliet flee London for Scotland and the aegis provided by Elizabeth von Stein, who has developed an uncannily effective form of medicine. Juliet learns more about her family history and her role in the present, while she also tries to figure out just how like her father she is and what that might or might not mean.

White, Kiersten.

The Dark Descent of Elizabeth Frankenstein. 2018. 9780525577966. **S**

Elizabeth Lavenza will one day become Elizabeth Frankenstein after mar-rying Victor Frankenstein. She is not a prominent character in Shelley's Frankenstein, but in this retelling of the story, she is the main character. Living in a time period unkind to women, she depends on Victor for her existence. This means protecting him even when she'd rather not. Victor's experiments are gruesome and chilling, but she has little sway. However, she consistently displays strength which she is eventually able to harness. (BFYA)

Subjects: Historical; Mary Shelley; Medical Horror; Retold Classics

Winters, Cat.

The Raven's Tale. 2019. 9781419733628. **J S**

Young Edgar Allen Poe develops into the famous writer of legend with the help of Lenore, his muse. In this dark biographical fantasy, muses are real, frightening creatures who depend on their artist and, for the most part, cannot be seen by others.

Subjects: Muses; Poe, Edgar Allan; Slaves

Vampires, Werewolves, and Shapeshifters

All of these beings are variations on the human form and typically are able to "pass" for human. These stories aren't as popular as they once were, but that just means saying "vampires and werewolves" isn't going to immediately sell someone on a book.

Beatty, Robert.

Serafina. **M J**

A dark historical horror series, Serafina is set at the end of the 19th century in Asheville, North Carolina, in a real place, the Biltmore, which was owned by a real family, the Vanderbilts. From there, however, its closeness to reality is severed. Borrowing from regional folklore, Serafina tells the story of a spe-cial girl who longs for companionship and self-knowledge. In order to gain those things, though, sacrifices must be made, risks taken, and evils bested.

Subjects: 1900s; Cats; Folklore; Historical; North Carolina

5

Serafina and the Black Cloak. 2015. 9781484711873.

> Serafina lives a furtive life in the Vanderbilts' massive Biltmore estate. She lives in the basement with the paternal custodian, and she does her best to both catch rats and remain unknown to the proprietors. While sneaking around, though, she witnesses a horrific deed as a man devours a young girl with his black cape. Striking up an unlikely partnership with Braeden, one the Vanderbilts, she and he investigate the man with the black cloak. The intense journey also reveals Serafina's hidden past.

Serafina and the Twisted Staff. 2016. 9781484778067.

> Serafina's heroics endeared her in the Vanderbilts' hearts and earned her a legitimate spot at the Biltmore as Chief Rat Catcher. Finally aware of her nature as a catamount, she also develops a relationship with her mother. As comfortable as she is, it doesn't stay that way for long. When a powerful threat enters the woods, and curious strangers arrive at the estate, Serafina fights to defend her new life and the people in it.

Serafina and the Splintered Heart. 2017. 9781484778050.

> Paranormal custodian of the Biltmore, Serafina fends off a threat related to extreme weather.

Serafina and the Seven Stars. 2019. 9781368007597.

> Serafina moves out of the basements and finds herself out of sorts.

Black, Holly.

The Coldest Girl in Coldtown. **2013. 9780316213097.** S

> Coldtown is a modern city-prison that keeps vampires and their humans separate from the rest of the population. While anyone can enter Coldtown, one may only leave by presenting a special token. After a gruesome surprise, Tana, who has done her best to avoid all things vampire after she lost her mother to vampirism, hatches a plan to travel to Coldtown with her ex-boyfriend and a mysterious vampire, then enter Coldtown and, somehow, escape. (BFYA)

> **Subjects**: Dystopia; Social Media

Cast, P. C., and Kristin Cast.

House of Night. S

> In a world where seemingly random teenagers suddenly show signs that they are turning into vampyres, they must immediately move into one of the boarding schools, called House of Night, for any hope to survive. The time of change is dangerous and lengthy, sometimes resulting in death.

> **Subjects**: Boarding Schools; Cherokees; Goddess Worship; Grandmothers; Tattoos; Tulsa, Oklahoma; Zombies

Marked. 2007. 9780312360252.

> Sixteen-year-old Zoey Redbird, who hates her stepfather and the way her mother now always sides with him, is marked as a vampyre, and she must get to the House of Night soon or die. Her mentor is Neferet the High Priestess, who leads ceremonies in honor of the Goddess Nyx. Strangely enough, Zoey's faint moon mark has filled in like those on the brows of adult vampyres. She

feels the rituals of the school with an intensity unknown to her peers, and she now seems to be acquiring vampyre talents and proclivities way ahead of schedule. Of course, she will be tested, and she will have to rely on her friends and her own ethical compass if she is to survive.

Betrayed. 2007. 9780312360283.

Zoey has been gifted with great powers by the vampyre goddess Nyx. Now as the Leader of the Dark Daughters, it is her responsibility to use those gifts wisely. When ordinary teens from her life before she was Marked are murdered, Zoey begins to fear that someone from the House of Night is responsible.

Chosen. 2008. 9780312360306.

With three potential boyfriends, Zoey's life just keeps getting more complicated. Her friend and former roommate, Stevie Rae, is now undead, and other vampyres start turning up dead. Could Zoey's horrible stepfather or his church have something to do with it?

Untamed. 2008. 9780312379834.

One week after the events in Chosen, Zoey suddenly finds she is a total outsider. Neferet's plans, including war on humans in retribution for the vampyre deaths, spell a future of death and destruction.

Hunted. 2009. 9780312379827.

Taking refuge in the hidden Prohibition era tunnels under Omaha that Stevie Rae and the Red Fledglings have cleaned up may not keep Zoey and her friends safe from Neferet and her gorgeous, immortal consort, Kalona, a fallen angel who hides immense evil.

Tempted. 2009. 9780312567484.

In training as a High Priestess, Zoey begins to suspect Stevie Rae of hiding something involved with the dark force that is spreading out from under the Tulsa depot. Meanwhile, the number of guys in Zoey's life is up to three again, and maybe even more, as she finds herself attracted to Kalona, whom she loved in a previous life.

Burned. 2010. 9780312606169.

Zoey's heart is shattered, and she doesn't want to leave the Otherworld. Stark may be the only one who can bring her back, but he may have to die to do it. Stevie Rae is facing major problems with the Red Fledglings, and the horrible seer, Aphrodite, is now speaking with Nyx's own voice.

Awakened. 2011. 9780312650247.

Zoey's relationship with handsome Stark heats up while she lives on the Isle of Skye and is groomed to become queen. Stevie Rae and Rephaim also get a lot closer. Meanwhile, Neferet, having been exonerated and restored to power in Tulsa, is as determined as ever to bring Zoey and her life crashing down.

Destined. 2011. 9781905654871.

Having left the Isle of Skye and returned to Tulsa, a more powerful Zoey prepares to face off with the series' long-standing baddie, Neferet.

Rephaim has been granted human form and is finally free of Kalona, allowing the relationship between Rephaim and Stevie Rae to progress—that is, if everything goes according to plan.

Hidden. 2012. 9780312594428.

Neferet has finally been exposed to the Vampyre High Council. While that means Zoey and friends will finally have their support, it also means that Neferet has even less to lose.

Revealed. 2013. 9781250061409.

Zoey and the House of Night continue to be plagued by Neferet. The main event that kicks off this title is the death of an influential mortal on the House of Night campus.

Redeemed. 2014. 9781250055439.

In this final title in the series, readers can look forward to the long-anticipated showdown between good and evil, between Neferet and Zoey.

Mead, Richelle.

Vampire Academy. ◻J ◻S

Moroi, living vampires, and dhampirs, Guardians who are offspring of humans and Moroi with a combination of strong traits from both, survive against attacks by Strigoi, dead vampires with great powers and no morals. This story is set mostly in an exclusive and remote Montana boarding school for Moroi and dhampir teens.

Subjects: Dhampirs; Moroi; Strigoi

Vampire Academy. 2007. 9781594141743.

Rose is the dhampir Guardian of her best friend Lissa, a Moroi vampire princess. When the two of them are returned to St. Vladimir's Academy after running away, Rose must continue her training so she can continue to protect Lissa from the evil undead vampires called the Strigoi.

Frostbite. 2008. 9781595141750.

Under attack by the Strigoi, the Moroi and dhampirs decide that a remote Moroi ski resort is just the place to relax in safety for the holidays. Torn between her attraction for Dimitri, who is seven years older and her tutor, and Mason, who is an appropriate love interest and who is head over heels in love with her, Rose gets confused, and she acts badly when her estranged mother shows up.

Shadow Kiss. 2008. 9781595141972.

It is springtime at the Academy, but the Moroi are on edge due to the Strigoi threat. Rose, who is feeling strange after killing Strigoi, is conflicted by her attraction to Dimitri and her responsibility to Lissa.

Blood Promise. 2009. 9781595141989.

An attack has left many Moroi dead, and a fate far worse faces those abducted by the Strigoi. Rose had made a promise to Dimitri, and now that he has been taken to Siberia by the Strigoi, she must abandon Lissa and follow Dimitri's wishes.

Spirit Bound. 2010. 9781595142504.

>Back at St. Vladimir's and ready for graduation, Rose finds that she is being stalked after her failure in Siberia and that graduation may not be a new beginning after all.

Last Sacrifice. 2010. 9781595143068.

>Wrongfully imprisoned for a crime she didn't commit (murdering the queen), Rose faces execution. While her friends try to free her, Lissa seeks the Moroi's support for becoming the next monarch. This is the final entry in the series.

Meyer, Stephenie.

Twilight. **S**

What's a girl to do? When Bella moves to Forks, Washington, she meets two very attractive boys: Edward, a gorgeous white vampire, and Jacob, a gorgeous Native American werewolf. The best-selling *Twilight* series, like *Harry Potter*, has had a huge impact not only on teen readers but on adult readers as well. It has become an icon of popular culture, with Bella and Edward becoming recognizable names. While it has steadily been declining in popularity, it is still a touchstone title that most readers will know and about which they will likely have strong opinions even if they've never read it.

Subjects: Romance; Werewolves

Twilight. 2005. 9780316015844.

>When her mother remarries, 17-year-old Bella leaves the sunshine of Phoenix for the omnipresent rain and gloom of the Olympic peninsula where her dad lives. In her new school, she is forced to sit next to Edward, a gorgeous member of the elusive and standoffish Cullen family, who acts as though he hates Bella. When he uses preternatural speed to save Bella's life in the school parking lot, she discovers that they have a mutual fascination with each other (BBYA, Film)

New Moon. 2006. 9780316160193.

>After Edward and the rest of the vampire Cullen family leave Forks, Washington, upon realizing how very tempting 17-year-old Bella's blood is, Bella sinks into depression. To soothe her loneliness, she starts hanging out with Jacob but soon uncovers his secret and finds a hidden link to Edward that manifests when she is in danger. (Film)

Eclipse. 2007. 9780316160209.

>Bella is looking forward to graduation, when vampire Edward will marry her and she can become a vampire, which does not sit well with werewolf Jacob. As a string of murders torments the city of Seattle, Edward and Jacob vie for Bella's love. (Film)

Breaking Dawn. 2008. 9780316067928.

>Bella and Edward finally marry. The sexual consummation of their union results in an unforeseen circumstance, which delays her turning into a vampire until after a special delivery. The culmination of the *Twilight* saga brings big changes to all and wraps up diverse plot threads.

5

Schrieve, Hal.

Out of Salem. 2019. 9781609809010. **S**

Fourteen-year-old Z is a genderqueer witch-turned-zombie who was recently orphaned after their family died in a car crash that they "survived." Fortunately, Z finds a new family in a welcoming bookstore owner who takes them him. Z also finds a group of friends kind of like them: Aysel, a gay werewolf, and Tommy, a shapeshifter. The town of Salem, which is already unkind to monsters, becomes much more hostile when an apparent murder is blamed on a werewolf, ratcheting up tensions.

Subjects: 1990s; LGBTQIA+; Prejudice; Salem, Oregon

Shan, Darren.

Cirque du Freak. **M** **J**

Darren Shan's adventures with vampires and other denizens of the weird start when he and his friend Steve, both age 12, visit a very unusual freak show called Cirque de Freak. The <u>Cirque du Freak</u> series is also available in a manga graphic novel format.

Subjects: Circuses; Friends

Cirque du Freak: A Living Nightmare. 2001. 9780316605106.

After Darren sneaks out to go to Cirque du Freak, a bizarre traveling freak show, with his friend Steve, he ends up becoming a half-vampire. (Film: *The Vampire's Assistant*)

The Vampire's Assistant. 2001. 9780316606844.

Darren, having unwillingly joined Cirque du Freak, a traveling freak show, as Mr. Crepsley's assistant, becomes roommates with Evra, the snake boy. Even though he has been turned into a vampire, he refuses human blood, which makes him weaker and weaker. (Film)

Tunnels of Blood. 2002. 9780316606080.

Even though Darren, Evra, and Mr. Crepsley have left the Cirque du Freak, horrifying events won't leave them alone. After they move to the city, corpses completely drained of blood start turning up, and Darren and Evra begin an investigation. (Film: *The Vampire's Assistant*)

Vampire Mountain. 2002. 9780316605427.

Six years after the events in *Tunnels of Blood,* Darren accompanies Mr. Crepsley on a torturous trek to Vampire Mountain, where Darren meets the Vampire Princes and Generals and learns vampiric history.

Trials of Death. 2003. 9780316603959.

Inside Vampire Mountain, Darren is coming to terms with his vampire nature. While trying to complete five deadly, dangerous trials, Darren uncovers a diabolical plot.

The Vampire Prince. 2003. 9780316602747.

Even though he is sentenced to death, Darren, who was thrown out of Vampire Mountain after failing his "trials of death" and subsequently nursed back to health by a pack of wolves, journeys to the center of Vampire Mountain. He is attempting to stop the annihilation of the vampire clan by the evil vampaneze.

Hunters of the Dusk. 2004. 9780316602112.

Vampire Prince Darren Shan is one of three hunters who must try to stop the Vampaneze Lord, who has now created a new vampire hybrid, called Vampets, that could help the vampaneze wipe out the vampires.

Allies of the Night. 2004. 9780316155700.

Now in his thirties, Darren, who still looks like he is 15 years old, goes to Mr. Crepsley's hometown, where he is hunting vampaneze at night, and corpses drained of blood have been turning up. Darren is forced to go to high school when caught by truancy officer.

Killers of the Dawn. 2005. 9780316156264.

Darren and his allies are on the run, having escaped from a police station, pursued by a mob of humans and the vampaneze. Darren and company face the Lord of the Vampaneze in an underground confrontation.

The Lake of Souls. 2005. 9780316156264.

Darren and Harkat encounter fantasy game–like dangers on their quest to reach the Lake of Souls, in a slight detour on their mission to destroy the Lord of the Vampaneze and end the war between the vampires and vampaneze.

Lord of the Shadows. 2006. 9780316156288.

Now Darren knows the true identity of the Lord of the Vampaneze and that, to end the deadly war, one of them will have to become the Lord of the Shadows. Traveling again with the Cirque du Freak, Darren revisits his old hometown, where the whole mess started.

Sons of Destiny. 2006. 9780316156295.

"Dead if he loses. Damned if he wins." In the climax of the series, Darren Shan faces his onetime friend and longtime nemesis, Steve Leopard, in a deadly fight that will decide the fate of the vampires.

Slade, Arthur.

Amber Fang: Hunted. **2019. 9781459822696. J S**

Amber is an ethical vampire. Really. She meticulously researches each of her "meals" before devouring them, ensuring that they are murderers or the like who deserve to be eaten. All that research takes time, though, so when she is offered an opportunity to become an assassin whose marks are guaranteed to be dastardly evildoers, she gives it a shot. It's not quite the piece of cake it was supposed to be.

Subject: Vampires

Smallwood, Greg, Megan Smallwood, and Jack Morelli.

Vampironica. 2019. 9781682558331. S

Veronica, as a vampire, fights tooth and nail against an evil vampire who is trying to enslave the residents of Riverdale by turning them. This title is serious yet campy enough to be more entertaining than terror inducing. It also shows a very different version of the Riverdale world than is presented in the TV series, which could be used to pique fans' curiosity if only they know the show.

Subjects: Archiverse; Graphic Novels

Turrisi, Kim.

Carmilla. 2019. 9781525301308. S

Based on a popular web series, Carmilla is a vampire college story. Laura Hollis, the main character, is a lesbian first-year student. She is paired up with an amazing roommate, Betty, who mysteriously disappears one night. The university quickly replaces Betty with Carmilla, a much more difficult roommate who is, nonetheless, very attractive. Laura looks into Betty's disappearance, develops some crushes, realizes the university might be hiding something nefarious, and discovers that Carmilla is, in fact, a vampire.

Subjects: LGBTQIA+; Vampires; Web Series

Westerfeld, Scott.

Peeps. J S

Vampirism with a scientific background gives a unique twist to the duology. Peeps, people who are parasite positive and who are infected by the exchange of bodily fluids, find all that they loved anathema. However, some who are infected do not turn into ravening monsters who live with an entourage of rats but become carriers who can easily infect others. A secret city agency keeps tabs on the Peeps and enlists the carriers to hunt down the infected who have become vampires.

Subjects: Apocalypse; New York; Parasites; Rats; Science Fiction

Peeps. 2005. 9781595140319.

Cal, a college freshman living in New York, is parasite positive, a carrier for vampirism caused by a parasite-vectored infection, and must hunt for the girls he has kissed and unknowingly infected. The factual information about parasites that starts alternating chapters is chilling. (BBYA, TTT)

The Last Days. 2006. 9781595140623.

Five teen band members try to stave off an apocalypse that will engulf New York, as the parasite-infected vampires mutate and grow in numbers and giant worms break through the streets to consume people.

Zombies

Zombies are the undead or infected. Most of them have a taste for brains and are fixated on mindless consumption of the living. These stories can be campy, creepy, stomach turning, or all three depending on the author. However, one thing that just about all have in common is that they toy with notions of humanity and moral ambiguities.

Bacigalupi, Paolo.

Zombie Baseball Beatdown. 2013. 9780316220798. **M** **J** **S**

Three friends, Rabi, Miguel, and Joe, stumble upon the makings of a zombie apocalypse at a local meatpacking plant in Iowa. As they dig deeper, they begin to suspect a connection between the factory farming industry in their town and the monsters that are being made of normal people and cows. However, they discover that it might be even harder to fight corporations and industries than it is to fight zombies. This title offers social commentary while still being a funny and exciting adventure mystery.

Subjects: Big Business; Factory Farms; Funny; Undocumented Immigrants; Immigrant Experience; Prejudice

Bick, Ilsa J.

Ashes. **O**

As chance would have it, 17-year-old Alex is by herself when a series of electromagnetic pulses change the world forever by rendering most technology useless, killing most people, and turning others into zombie-esque abominations.

Subjects: Brain Tumors; Postapocalypse; Survival

Ashes. 2011. 9781606843857.

Alex isn't the only human with her senses about herself: She teams up with a young girl and a soldier. Together, they do what they must to survive, which can get gory but doesn't always involve threats that are as obvious as starving zombies.

Shadow. 2012. 9781606844458.

The next gory installation in this trilogy sees Alex kidnapped and Tom searching for her, while Peter and Chris face troubles of their own.

Monsters. 2013. 9781606845448.

Alex returns to rule as she and Tom do their best to carve out some kind of future for themselves and humanity. This hefty book also sees the return of a host of characters.

Ireland, Justina.

Dread Nation. 2018. 9780062570604. **J** **S**

In this alternate history, the American Civil War ended when the undead began to rise. Slavery may have been abolished, but white society still treats Native and Negro children with contempt, forcing them to attend combat schools and fight the undead for them. Jane McKeene, the biracial daughter of a wealthy white woman, is training to be an Attendant, a refined bodyguard for white women, at a prestigious school in Baltimore. When she looks into strange events surrounding the disappearance of a local family, she stumbles across a high-reaching conspiracy that reveals other humans, not the undead, to be the real monsters.

Subjects: Civil War; Slavery

5

Shan, Darren.

Zom-B. J S

This series of slim volumes from the author of the Cirque du Freak series has all the trappings of a quality zombie series: body horror, conspiracy, suspense, apocalyptic cityscapes, and compelling characters. The main character also struggles with more than just the undead: B's father is a prominent racist who abuses his family, and B has inherited some of his less savory opinions despite finding them distasteful.

Subjects: Body Horror; Prejudice; Racism; Torture

Zom-B. 2012. 9780316214407.

As news reports of zombies in Ireland begin to gain prominence, many believe it's just a hoax and go on with their daily lives. B, a racist, preteen bully with a miserable family life, is one of the deniers. While B isn't an especially admirable character, she certainly is compelling, often reflecting on her own beliefs and actions and always wanting to do better. Of course, B finds it hard to focus on self-improvement, though, while being chased through school by zombie hordes.

Zom-B Underground. 2013. 9780316214124.

Having been infected in the last book, B wakes up to find herself transformed and trapped in a lab. She's both human and zombie while also being neither: She is sentient, rational, and has emotions, but she can't blink or sleep, and her teeth won't stop growing. Other teens in the same state as her are also stuck in the lab, being ogled by scientists and forced to fight and "kill" full-on zombies.

Zom-B City. 2013. 9780316214360.

Having escaped the underground laboratory by the skin of her teeth, B sets out for London. The city has, unsurprisingly, changed significantly—just like B, who is coming to terms with her metamorphosis. With so few revitalized, B is a minority and must fear both the zombies who want to eat her and the zombie hunters who might not recognize her humanity.

Zom-B Angels. 2013. 9780316214148.

Strange clues found around the city start to give B some direction and lead her to a collective of people like B, known as The Angels, who are fighting to maintain humanity in the face of the mushrooming undead. The origin of the zombies becomes clearer, and B has to make some tough decisions as she continues to grow as a character.

Zom-B Baby. 2013. 9780316214209.

So far, B has stayed with The Angels, but, finally deciding where she stands on Dr. Oystein's mission, she decides to go back into the city on her own. Timothy, from the first book, makes an appearance, and he has an undead baby.

Zom-B Gladiator. 2014. 9780316214070.

B is captured and, as the title suggests, is forced to fight against other undead for the entertainment of wealthy people who have escaped the worst of the apocalypse by staying at sea.

Zom-B Mission. 2014. 9780316214285.

> Having returned to The Angels, B and other Angels are sent on a mission to find survivors in London and bring them to the safe haven of New Kirkland. It's anything but simple, both physically and morally.

Zom-B Clans. 2014. 9780316214292.

> The Ku Klux Klan, while attacking New Kirkland, capture Vinyl and hold him hostage. This title also sees the return of Dan-Dan.

Zom-B Family. 2014. 9780316214346.

> In this entry, which is heavy on torture and body horror, B, having been betrayed, is taken by Dan-Dan and his racist crew, which counts B's father among its members.

Zom-B Bride. 2015. 9780316214223.

> Saved, as it were, from Dan-Dan by the demented Mr. Dowling and his babies, B is taken into Mr. Dowling's fetid lair. Readers are let in on a lot of secrets in this book, including Mr. Dowling's grand plans, which include marrying B.

Zom-B Fugitive. 2015. 9780316214094.

> B flees Mr. Dowling's lair with what could be the key to triumph for Dr. Oystein and the living.

Zom-B Goddess. 2015. 9780316338455.

> The last book is the series finale in which B and Dr. Oystein have the chance to triumph in their own ways.

Tynion IV, James, and Eryk Donovan.

Memetic. **2015. 9781608867431.** **S**

A meme that makes nearly everyone who sees it experience bliss goes viral, literally. As it spreads across the globe, people become obsessed with it. What begins as an innocent—if weird—phenomenon turns into an international crisis when people who have seen the meme become violent and zombie-like. (GLAAD)

Subjects: Graphic Novel; LGBTQIA+; Memes

Witchcraft

Witches don't have to be women, even though they still typically are in contemporary popular fiction. The most common element among witches is that they are "others" with arcane knowledge or power.

Delaney, Joseph.

The Wardstone Chronicles. **M** **J**

Thomas Ward, the 12-year-old seventh son of a seventh son, apprentices with the Spook, Mr. Gregory, in order to become a spook himself, a job he's not sure he wants. Spooks use knowledge and other means in order to contain and extirpate supernatural threats like witches, bogarts, and ghasts.

The tone is spooky, and while the action is certainly a highlight, the series is not without its share of drama and intrigue.

Subject: Apprentices

Revenge of the Witch. 2004. 9780060766207.

Trusting Tom is misled by Alice, a girl around his own age, to feed Mother Malkin, a powerful witch whom the Spook had imprisoned, until she is strong enough to escape. Tom and the Spook must find a way to either contain her again or kill her. Alice, who is from a family of witches and is related to Mother Malkin, may or may not still be capable of redemption. (BBYA)

Curse of the Bane. 2005. 9780060766238.

Just as Tom is starting to make some progress as a spook, he and the Spook are forced to confront the Bane, an intensely powerful and malevolent being who kills its victims by smashing them like pancakes. Despite the events in the first book, Tom and Alice continue to be friends.

Night of the Soul Stealer. 2007. 9780060766269.

Tom and the Spook go to the Spook's winter home, where Tom discovers witches in pits in the cellar—one of whom was the Spook's sweetheart—and Morgan, a corrupt necromancer who once was the Spook's apprentice himself. Morgan, the primary nemesis, holds Tom's Father's spirit hostage, forcing Tom to play along with his dark designs.

Attack of the Fiend. 2007. 9780060891299.

Three witch clans who are typically at one another's throats have united under the common cause of summoning the Devil. One of the clans, the Malkins, have also taken the mysterious chests that Tom inherited from his mother. Moreover, one of Tom's brothers and the rest of his family have also been taken. Tom and the Spook face grisly threats, but they don't do it alone this time.

Wrath of the Bloodeye. 2008. 9780061344619.

The Spook sends Tom to his friend and fellow spook, Bill Arkwright, for some intense training. Under Bill's guidance, Tom tries to take down a water witch known as the Bloodeye.

Clash of the Demons. 2008. 9780061344640.

As always, the dangers in this book threaten to eclipse any other danger Tom has faced before: There is a possibility that the Devil, who is yet to be beaten, may join forces with a wildly strong being, the Ordeen. To win the day, Tom will have to team up with some of his former enemies, who, to his distaste, have become some of his mam's new friends.

Rise of the Huntress. 2010. 9780061715129.

With their home having been overtaken by soldiers in their absence, Tom, the Spook, and Alice flee to the island of Mona, where they aren't exactly welcomed with open arms. While on Mona, they also face a familiar foe, Bony Lizzie.

Rage of the Fallen. 2011. 9780062027580.

Dangers continue to escalate, forcing Tom, the Spook, and Alice to journey to Ireland. One of the many troubles that complicate things for the trio is that

Tom had been cursed to be plagued by a powerful goddess, Morrigan, should he ever step foot on Irish soil.

I Am Grimalkin. 2011. 9781782952541.

Switching up the formula, the narrator for this title is Grimalkin, the witch assassin who has allied herself with Tom in order to topple the Fiend. Readers are treated to a fresh perspective, a new story, and more information about this longtime side character.

The Spook's Blood. 2012. 9781782952558.

As the Spook tries to rebuild his library, he and Tom travel to a town where, supposedly, a woman has a trove of tomes for sale. All is not well there, though, and the imminent battle between Tom and Fiend begins to heat up. In this title, Tom's main threat is one of the Fiend's powerful minions—perhaps the strongest creature Tom has had to face yet.

Slither. 2012. 9780062192356.

A father's callous deal with a monster called Slither—if the Slither will save both of his daughters, then it can have one of them—contributes to Grimalkin and Tom's goal of ending the Fiend once and for all.

I Am Alice. 2013. 9780061715150.

Alice descends into a dark and demonic realm in order secure the weapon needed to slay the Fiend. As with *I am Grimalkin*, readers are treated to a new narrator, Tom's longtime companion, Alice.

The Spook's Revenge. 2013. 9781849414708.

The final book in the series delivers on the epic battle with the Fiend it's been setting up. It is also full of twists and surprises, including deaths and betrayals.

Higgins, F. E.

The Bone Magician. 2008. 9780312659448. **M** **J**

Pin Carpue, an undertaker's assistant, works to exonerate his father who has been accused of being a serial killer by figuring out who the real killer is. His investigation leads him to a magician who claims proficiency in necromantic arts.

Subject: Death

Lanagan, Margo.

The Brides of Rollrock Island. 2012. 9780375873362. **S**

Ostracized because of her looks, Misskaella discovers a different kind of power she has instead of beauty: She can create selkies, people who are conjured out of seals. The selkies she creates are beautiful women that the men on her island will pay dearly for. Nevertheless, despite attaining this power and its attendant wealth and influence, her life is still empty, and the selkies, who can turn back into seals if they have their sealskin, are no happier either. (BFYA)

Subjects: Selkies; Shapeshifters

Talley, Robin.

As I Descended. 2016. 9780062409232. **S**

If Maria and Lily, a closeted lesbian couple, are going to stay together after high school and attend Stanford together, Maria needs to win the Cawdor Kinsgley Prize. However, Delilah Dufrey, the most popular girl at school, is currently in line to receive it. Hating Delilah and motivated to usurp her, Maria and Lily summon help from spirits that haunt their school. The combination of paranormal aid and insidious ambition set the stage for a tragic outcome in this retelling of *Macbeth.* (Rainbow)

Subjects: LGBTQIA+; Macbeth; Retold Classics; Shakespeare; Virginia

Unexplained Phenomena

These titles are about mysterious unknowns, with many of them playing out like investigations or *X-Files* episodes.

Bowman, Erin.

Contagion. **M** **J** **S**

An effective blend of horror, science fiction, and thriller, the Contagion duology is fast-paced and creepy with deft world building and minimal graphic content. It is a solid recommendation for fans of the classic horror movie, *The Thing,* the scarier episodes of *The X-Files,* or the *Resident Evil* franchise.

Subjects: Isolation; Plagues; Science Fiction

Contagion. 2018. 9780062574145.

Althea and Nova, two teen girls in the employ of massive, multibillion-dollar conglomerate Hevetz, are part of a small crew dispatched to investigate the mysterious disappearance of the crew of Achlys, a remote planet. On Achlys, they discover a lot of corpses and a devastating infection. (Edgar)

Immunity. 2019. 9780062574176.

The political intrigue gets kicked up a notch when the surviving crew members are imprisoned by their "rescuers." Now they must find a way to confront dark forces who hope to weaponize the contagion against their political opponents.

Ireland, Justina.

Scream Site. 2018. 9781630781025. **J** **S**

Sabrina Sebastian is a 14-year-old aspiring journalist who wants to report on a truly big story. She sets her sights on debunking Scream Site, a burgeoning website where people post scary videos. There are even rumors of people who have gone missing in association with Scream Site. As she digs into the story, she starts uncovering unsettling truths. Then, when her sister goes missing after posting a video to the site, Sabrina's investigation has real stakes as it may be the only way to save her sister.

Subjects: Internet Culture; Journalism; Missing Person

Legrand, Claire.

Sawkill Girls. 2018. 9780062696601. **S**

The remote island of Sawkill Rock is, in many ways, a paradise, but that paradise has a dark secret: girls have been going missing for years, and, while people tell stories about an evil force that is taking them, nobody has done anything to stop it. Enter three girls: Marion, the new girl in town; Zoey, the sheriff's daughter; and Val, the one who's linked to the evil. Together, the three girls take on the darkness that others would rather ignore or even benefit from. (BFYA)

Subject: LGBTQIA+

Liggett, Kim.

The Unfortunates. 2018. 9780765381019. **J S**

After his wealthy, connected father helps him avoid jail time for an accident, Grant Franklin Tavish V is racked with guilt and plans to kill himself while on a solo caving trip. While on the trip, however, he and four other teens are trapped inside the cave by an avalanche. On the one hand, this is actually a good thing for Grant, who is able to connect with the other teens and grow as an individual; on the other hand, they are trapped in a cave, and Grant is pretty sure something is hunting them.

Subjects: Caves; Guilt; Privilege

Oppel, Kenneth.

The Nest. 2015. 9781481432337. **M J S**

Theodore, Steve's new baby brother, has a rare and complicated congenital disorder. It's a very difficult and stressful situation for the family. However, after being stung by a weird wasp, Steve is able to speak to their queen, an angelic sort of being. She promises Steve that she can help him and that she is there for him. She even promises to "fix" Theodore. As time goes on, though, Steve gets a better idea of what she means by "fix." It becomes more and more apparent that she is not a benevolent being with his best interests in mind. Eerie and emotionally powerful, this horror novel deals with complex issues like the difficulty of changing family composition.

Subjects: Mental Illness; New Family Member; Wasps

Priest, Cherie, and Tara O'Connor.

The Agony House. 2018. 9781338582178. **J S**

Denise, her mother, and her stepfather move into a rundown Victorian house in New Orleans with plans of fixing it up and turning it into a bed and breakfast. The house, however, isn't just old . . . it's odd. Things fall, and there are weird smells and unexplainable shadows. Then things begin to get dangerous and can't be attributed to mere coincidence: The house is haunted. Denise finds a manuscript for a graphic novel in the attic that appears to be the key to the hauntings, and excerpts from the graphic novel appear in the book in a seamless blend of formats.

Subjects: Alternate Formats; Gentrification; Graphic Novels; New Orleans

Ritter, William.

Jackaby. 🄹 🅂

This series, a sort of Sherlockian *X-Files* set in the late 19th century, combines horror and clever mysteries. Abigail Rook assists R. F. Jackaby, who can see what others cannot, as he investigates unexplainable phenomena in New England.

Subjects: Historical; Mystery; New England

Jackaby. 2014. 9781616205461.
> Abigail and R. F. Jackaby investigate a paranormal serial killer. (BFYA)

Beastly Bones. 2015. 9781616203542.
> Abigail and R. F. Jackaby investigate a mysterious and deadly beast that is somehow related to missing dinosaur bones. (BFYA)

Ghostly Echoes. 2016. 9781616205799.
> The duo is hired to solve the case of Jenny Cavanaugh's murder . . . by Jenny Cavanaugh's own ghost.

The Dire King. 2017. 9781616207625.
> This time, the duo is set against a twisted king who is attempting to unite our world with the Otherworld.

Stewart, Martin.

Sacrifice Box. 2018. 9780425289532. 🄹 🅂
> In the early 1980s, five friends, all of them in middle school, stumble upon a stone box. They decide to each leave an item in the box to commemorate their friendship, and they make a pact that they will never return to the box alone, open the box at night, or remove any of the items. Five years later, none of them are friends, and strange things begin to happen, like items from the box showing up in odd places.

Subjects: Body Horror; Pacts

Stroud, Jonathan.

Lockwood & Co. 🄼 🄹

As a result of The Happening, an inexplicable event whereby the dead began to return to the world of the living, agencies have sprung up that work to dispel these phenomena. Three kids, Anthony, George, and Lucy, are the proprietors of one such company, Lockwood & Co., which operates in London. It may seem odd that adults aren't the ones taking these issues to task in such a dangerous line of work; however, in this world, younger individuals with psychic gifts are the most able to sense and investigate the causes of such disturbances. This spooky mystery series is as enjoyable for its macabre elements as for its characters and their dynamics.

Subjects: Historical; London; Mysteries; Special Abilities

The Screaming Staircase. 2013. 9781423186922.
> Lockwood & Co. investigates happenings at Combe Carey Hall, an imposing mansion with the reputation of being very haunted. In fact, events there have already claimed the lives of others who investigated it. While it is widely

known that there are ghosts and paranormal actors in the world, this particular haunting might have more to it than just that.

The Whispering Skull. 2014. 9781423194620.

Lockwood & Co. is enlisted to track down a mysterious and coveted artifact called the bone-glass, a mirror whose image induces insanity. Lucy, having developed the ability to commune with a spirit connected to a skull inside a jar, helps guide the team; however, the spirit may or may not be wholly trustworthy. In this adventure, the gangs see all different sides of London from the posh to derelict, getting into and out of tricky situations.

The Hollow Boy. 2015. 9781484711897.

When Lucy, whose abilities continue to grow, for better or worse, returns to the agency, she discovers that a new member, Holly, has joined the team, leaving Lucy unsure about her role. This feeds into an even bigger problem: A haunting happening occurs that is so big that part of London has to be evacuated. As the gang look into the case, they began to unravel a deeply human conspiracy.

The Creeping Shadow. 2016. 9781484711903.

Lockwood calls upon Lucy, who has struck out on her own, to help her former employer with a case that involves the ghost of a cannibal. When things spin out of control, as they usually do for Lockwood & Co., they face imminent danger but also learn more about the shocking truth behind the specters plaguing London.

The Empty Grave. 2017. 9781484790069.

In the final entry in the series, Lockwood & Co. accidentally release a dangerous spirit and take on a vengeful spirit as a client. The mystery behind the spirits is finally revealed in this satisfying wrap-up.

Verano, M.

Diary of a Haunting. ◻J

This chilling series revolves around online diaries.

Subjects: Alternate Formats; Blogs; Diary; Gothic; Social Media

Diary of a Haunting. 2015. 9781481430685.

This is the online diary that Paige kept. After her parents divorced, she and her brother were whisked away from LA to Idaho to live in a creepy old house full of spiders. Weird things happen in the house, and Paige keeps track of them and her discoveries. Slowly the chilling history of the haunting is revealed.

Possession. 2016. 9781481464420.

Like the first book, this the online diary kept by a teenage girl and edited by Verano. Laetitia, a black teen, normally blogs about beauty; however, after a mysterious (read: occult) illness sets upon her, her posts become darker. The symptoms include violent visions and burning skin, but physicians dismiss her. With the medical community unable to help, Laetitia and her family turn to more spiritual remedies.

Book of Shadows. 2017. 9781481492034.

> The third book is connected to the first two books by the narrator and conceit of being told via an online diary. When Mel finds the perfect book to use as a diary; she takes it home and wants to write in it. The book proves to be too intimidating to be used as a mere journal, though, so she and her Wiccan friends write spells in it instead. Then the book starts writing its own spells, which actually work but at a cost.

Superheroes

Most superheroes do not belong under the Horror heading, but they can be considered paranormal, since, after all, their powers are often just that. When including the whole of the body of comics and graphic novels, this is a massive category. However, since graphic novels and comics are not the primary focus of this book, they make up a decently sized subgenre. In recent years, the Big Two, DC and Marvel, have tapped quite a few big-name authors to pen superhero novels.

Bardugo, Leigh.

Wonder Woman: Warbringer. 9780399549731. **S**

> Diana, Amazon Princess, is the only young person on Themyscira, an island otherwise populated by immortal adult women warriors, and she is eager to prove that she isn't just a kid. When she seizes an opportunity to play the hero and rescues Alia, an outsider, things don't work out quite how she hoped. Alia is a 17-year-old warbringer, which means that, no matter where she is, chaos is likely to erupt among the people around her. She is also the harbinger of a comic cataclysm. Diana must venture into the unfamiliar human world in order to save to it.

Subjects: DC Comics; Prophecies

Detective Comics: 80 Years of Batman. 2019. 9781401285388. **M** **J** **S**

> A selected omnibus of Batman comics spanning 80 years' worth of material, providing a panoramic view of the iconic hero's evolution over the decades.

Subjects: DC Comics; Graphic Novels

Lu, Marie.

Batman: Nightwalker. **S**

> Bruce Wayne is a pre-Batman high schooler who takes on baddies but gets apprehended and sentenced to community service in the process. His punishment takes him to Arkham Asylum. Having recently received his substantial inheritance, Bruce is determined to do what it takes to protect Gotham against a dastardly gang.

Subjects: Arkham Asylum; DC Comics; Gotham City

Maas, Sarah J.

Catwoman: Soulstealer. 2018. 9780399549694. **J** **S**

> Catwoman, whose real name is Selina Kyle, is a classic Batman villain. But in this story she is humanized as an older teen, who is an adept criminal but who doesn't commit crime for herself but rather to take care of her half-sister, Maggie, who has

cystic fibrosis. Other franchise favorites like Harley Quinn and Poison Ivy also make appearances.

Subjects: Cystic Fibrosis; DC Comics; Gotham City

Meyer, Marissa.

Renegades. **J** **S**

After a period of time called the Age of Anarchy, order has been restored to society, largely due to the efforts of the Renegades, an association of super-heroes similar to the Justice League or the Avengers.

Subjects: Resistance; Revenge; Secret Identities; Super Villains

Renegades. 2017. 9781250044662.

Sixteen-year-old Nova, who has sleep-related powers, blames the Renegades for failing to save her family from being killed. Currently, she lives with her uncle, who leads an anti-Renegades group of under-ground villains. As part of their plan to take the Renegades down, she infiltrates the group, posing as a member.

Archenemies. 2018. 9781250078308.

Adrian and Nova, in many ways mirror images of each other, continue to dance around their mutual feelings. They continue to struggle between doing what they feel is right and doing what is expected of them. Matters get more complicated with the development of a weapon that can permanently eliminate someone's powers.

Reynolds, Jason.

Miles Morales. 2017. 9781484788509. **J** **S**

Miles Morales, a teenager who is half black and half Puerto Rican, is a significantly different Spider-Man compared to the franchise's mainstay, Peter Parker. Miles's life is complicated, not just because relationships and school are tough but also because he has to protect the city from a gang of racist criminals. Fans of the movie *Enter the Spiderverse* will find a familiar but new story here.

Subjects: Marvel Comics; Prejudice; Racism

Sanderson, Brandon.

Reckoners Trilogy. **M** **J** **S**

This is a dark and realistic look at what happens when people develop superpowers. Epics, as such people are called, have taken over different regions of the world, ruling over cities with terrible powers like the ability to block out the sun or absolute invulnerability. The world of the Reckoners offers a fresh combination of Superhero and Dystopian fiction.

Subjects: Dystopia; Grief; Revolution; Super Villains

Steelheart. 2013. 9780385743570.

David, a teenager whose father was killed by an Epic, doesn't have powers, but that doesn't mean he's powerless. He intends to join up with the Reckoners, a guerilla group of Epic assassinators who fight to make the world a better place. (BFYA)

Firefight. 2015. 9780385743594.

After an epic victory—and a devastating betrayal—David risks going to New York City, which is controlled by Regalia, on his hunt for answers.

Calamity. 2016. 9780385743617.

Bringing a close to the series, David confronts an Epic who was—and still could be—a dear friend.

Sam's Picks

Black, Holly. *Doll Bones*.

Blake, Kendare. *Anna*.

Ireland, Justina. *Dread Nation*.

Smallwood, Greg, Megan Smallwood, and Jack Morelli. *Vampironica*.

Tynion IV, James and Eryk Donovan. *Memetic*.

Science Fiction

Science fiction is a big what-if?, where authors and readers get to explore imaginative ideas like potential futures, alternate presents, and distant worlds. All of these stories, though, use the real world as their ultimate reference point, permitting for a great degree of social commentary. For instance, it's easy to read *The Hunger Games* and find oneself asking questions about human nature related to such disparate yet connected phenomena as reality television, human brutality, and our thirst for justice.

Enjoyment of science fiction, however, doesn't have to be so cerebral. In fact, all of the titles listed here can be read and enjoyed simply for being good stories whether or not the reader engages or even picks up on the questions at play, for example, about ethical science and personhood being plumbed in Scott Westerfield's UnWound series.

There is little difference between fantasy and science fiction. After all, science is simply a method used for better understanding, in a certain way, things around us. If magic were real, it wouldn't break physics. It would simply mean we need to revisit our original hypotheses and adjust our theories. Likewise, the so-called black boxes of science fiction—the unexplained bits that let the stories work, like what allows a ship to travel at the speed of light—are as imaginary and baseless as a transportation spell.

The important thing to remember, though, is that it doesn't matter if we can deconstruct science fiction and fantasy into a single genre. What matters is what readers think and the language the storytelling uses. Indeed, what science fiction means for one reader may be totally different from what it means to another. For this reason, it's important to progress through the thematic elements of subgenres in the readers' advisory interaction instead of using subgenre names as a crutch or assuming that your understanding of the meaning of a genre is identical to theirs.

Action Adventure

These are "fast" books, driven by pulse-pounding plots, taut with suspense, and exploding with action. The titles here are a good fit for fans of action movies and readers in search of a book that will suck them in and have them fanning through the pages.

Doctorow, Cory.

Little Brother. **J** **S**

This is a high-stakes thrill ride with a tech-savvy hacker in the driver's seat. Nevertheless, much of the action happens IRL, in real life.

Subjects: Espionage; Freedoms; Hackers; San Francisco; Surveillance

Little Brother. 2008. 9780765319852.

"Those who would give up Essential Liberty to purchase a little Temporary Safety, deserve neither Liberty nor Safety" (Benjamin Franklin). Marcus Yallow and three of his friends skip out of school to participate in a game. In a horrible case of being in the wrong place at the wrong time, they witness the San Francisco Bay Bridge being blown up, perhaps by terrorists. When the quartet tries to go to ground in a BART station, the press of the crowd proves deadly, and Marcus's friend, Darryl, is stabbed. Up on the street, trying to flag down help to get Darryl to a hospital, the four are picked up as suspected terrorists by the Department of Homeland Security and taken to a secret prison, where Marcus is tortured and interrogated. Days later, he is allowed to go home but threatened with retribution if he reveals that he has been imprisoned and tortured. An accomplished hacker, Marcus figures out a way to fight back. (BBYA)

Homeland. 2013. 9780765333698.

When California suffers a significant economic downturn, Marcus is in the fortunate position of being recruited for a job running a politician's website. Then, Masha, now Marcus's friend, hands him a massive trove of sensitive information, which gets her nicked by the same people who tortured Marcus. Now his dilemma is to decide whether and how to release the information without ruining his life or compromising his employer.

Kaufman, Amie, and Jay Kristoff.

Aurora Rising. 2019. 9781524720964. **J** **S**

This is the first title in a new, pulse-pounding series from the creative duo behind The Illuminae Files. When the same overachieving ethos that drove Tyler ("Ty") Jones to graduate at the top of his class from the Aurora Academy also compels him to rescue a girl adrift in space who's been cryo-sleeping for hundreds of years, he misses his chance to participate in the Draft and ends up with a ragtag group of misfits. Their first mission takes an unexpected turn when they discover Auri, the girl Ty saved, hiding on their ship, on the run from the Global Intelligence Agency. Nothing less than the galaxy depends on her fate.

Subjects: Alternate Perspectives; Heist

5

Landers, Melissa.

Starflight Duology. **J** **S**

A delightful YA homage to the influential cult classic TV series, *Firefly*, this duology features star-crossed lovers, a rad female mechanic, fugitive royalty, and more. While the same characters appear in each book, each book features different main characters. They can be read in any order or as stand-alones.

Subjects: Fugitives; Pirates; Royalty; Siblings

Starflight. 2016. 9781484747865.

Solara Brooks is a crack mechanic and felon; in fact, she has tattoos across her knuckles that testify to her crimes. Her number one goal is to get off Earth and find work. However, being short on means, her only way of doing that is by indenturing herself to her stuck-up rich classmate, Doran, who is a detestable scion—and love interest. As Doran and Solara complete the rivals-to-lovers trope, they are taken aboard a transport craft operated by a ragtag crew of lovable misfits and outsiders.

Starfall. 2017. 9781484750254.

Switching leads from Solara and Doran to the plight of Princess Cassia, this title follows her and her trusty companion, Kane, as they flee ruthless bounty hunters and try to set things right on their home planet.

Lee, Yoon Ha.

Dragon Pearl. 2019. 9781368014748. **M** **J**

Thirteen-year-old Min, who hails from a family of shapeshifting fox spirits, is on the hunt for answers about her brother, who apparently left his post in order to hunt for the legendary Dragon Pearl. This all takes place in an intergalactic setting complete with laser battle and other hallmarks of the science fiction genre.

Subjects: Foxes; Siblings; Space Opera

McCarthy, Cori, and Amy Rose Capetta.

Once & Future. 2019. 9780316449274. **S**

Welcome to an interstellar future brought to you by—and controlled by—the Mercer Corporation. Ari, a queer 17-year-old girl, on the run from Mercer, crash-lands on Old Earth, finds a sword in a tree, and pulls it out. That sword is none other than Excalibur, the extraction of which begins the age-old Arthurian cycle anew. While Ari's primary goal is to defeat Mercer and free her mothers from their captivity, if she can unify humanity in the process, she will also free the world from the Arthurian cycle's eternal return.

Subjects: Arthurian; LGBTQIA+; Revolution

The Illuminae Files. **M** **J** **S**

This highly innovative series uses a nontraditional narrative style to tell its story. Memos, instant messages, transcripts, and other miscellany are used instead of straightforward prose. This could come off as gimmicky, but the assorted media complement the adventure so well, and the adventure itself is so gripping, that readers quickly find themselves absorbed.

Subjects: Alternate Formats; Space Opera

Illuminae. 2015. 9780553499117.

> Just after Kady and Ezra break up, all hell breaks loose. The mining colony where they live is attacked by BeiTech, using all manner of weapons. In the ensuing maelstrom, they both narrowly manage to escape, though each ends up on a different ship. The ships are being chased down, and the passengers on one are succumbing to a violent, behaviorally disruptive virus. (BFYA)

Gemina. 2016. 9780553499155.

> Aboard the *Heimdall*, the ship and beacon of safety that the survivors in the last book desperately wanted to reach, Hanna, the daughter of the commander, and Nik, a gang member, team up to stave off a hostile BeiTech takeover. BeiTech, it seems, will stop at nothing to ensure there are no witnesses to their heinous crimes.

Obsidio. 2018. 9780553499193.

> Back on the planet Kerenza IV, survivors are holding their breath waiting for reinforcements—if the people still alive from the first two books can be called that—to help them fight off BeiTech.

Nix, Garth.

A Confusion of Princes. **2012. 9780060096960.** **J** **S**

Nineteen-year-old Khemri is a prince, which isn't all that special considering there are literally millions of princes in the Empire. Nevertheless, this doesn't dissuade him from confidently believing that he will one day rule. When an inconvenient love takes hold of his heart, however, he slowly begins to transform into a new person, and part and parcel of this transformation is intense action and adventure. (BFYA)

Subjects: Princes; Space Opera

Reeve, Philip.

Railhead. **S**

The future world imagined by Reeve is breathtaking. Countless worlds are connected via interstellar sentient trains that communicate with one another by singing and that interface with humans via AI. Corporate interests largely control things, and there is a history of AI Guardians who used to control things but no longer exert such sway. Myriad otherworldly beings populate this far-flung universe.

Subjects: Aliens; Thieves; Trains; Space Opera

Railhead. 2016. 9781630790509.

> Zen Starling is a "railhead," a sort of foamer of the future, who keeps his head low and commits petty thefts in order to keep his family afloat. When he is approached by an odd man named Raven, who recruits him to work for a group of rebels, Zen accepts, and his life becomes a series of high-stakes gambits. Raven hopes for Zen to steal a powerful artifact called the Pyxis. (BFYA)

5

Black Light Express. 2017. 9781630790974.

> After being hoodwinked, Zen and the android Nova have fled through a new K-gate into an unknown world. Threnody would like to pursue Zen and take him to task for ruining her family, but, threatened by a coup, she flees aboard the likable *Ghost Wolf,* motivated by her own dangers.

Station Zero. 2019. 9781684460533.

> Threnody, Zen, and Nova contend with the changes wrought by the Great Network. Zen goes on the hunt to be reunited with Nova.

Sanderson, Brandon.

Skyward. 🄹 🅂

The humans living on the planet of Detritus have been under siege for ages. Their society lives underground and does their best to stay hidden, since the alien Krell will bomb anything that looks too conspicuous. Fighter pilots are the humans' main defense against the Krell.

Subjects: Aliens; Pilots; Underground Cities

Skyward. 2018. 9780399555770.

> Ostracized because of her father's cowardice, Spensa is determined to become a pilot just as he was, no matter the obstacles she must overcome or the sacrifices she must make to do so. With a true love for all things flight related, in her spare time, she repairs and rebuilds a ship she found. Fortunately, this means she's still able to help defend her people from the destructive Krell who oppress them.

Starsight. 2019. 9780399555817.

> Having uncovered part of the truth about her father, Spensa still wonders about how much she doesn't know.

Scalzi, John.

Redshirts: A Novel with Three Codas. **2012. 9780765334794.** 🅂

> The title of this novel is a reference to a common trope on *Star Trek*: The red shirts worn by characters meant that they would die in that episode. A starship crew-member investigates the mysterious disappearances of his fellow mates. (Hugo)

Subjects: Aliens; Funny; Metafiction

Skrutskie, Emily.

Hullmetal Girls. **2018. 9781524770198.** 🅂

> Scela are cyborgs, whose purpose is to protect the flotilla of ships, called The Fleet, where people live. When Aisha Un-Haad's brother falls ill, she volunteers to be made into a Scela in order to pay for treatment. Key Tanaka, however, had little reason—at least that she can remember—to become a Scela.

Subjects: Cyborgs; Plagues

Walden, Tillie.

On a Sunbeam. 2018. 9781250178138. **M** **J** **S**

This is a female-forward (all the characters are either female or nonbinary) and racially diverse exploration of friendship, love, and family in a freshly imagined sci-fi world. The narrative is split between two timelines: the present, in which Mia is a member of a crew that repairs abandoned space structures, and five years prior, when Mia was a student at a boarding school and fell in love with her classmate, Grace. (Hugo)

Subjects: Graphic Novels; LGBTQIA+

Bioengineering

Human bodies are troublesome things, and we've been tinkering with them for ages, piercing them, scarring them, dyeing them, contorting them, and so on. These titles take the idea of tinkering with bodies—or other biological organisms—taking them to wild places, exploring our comfort zones and potential repercussions.

Dayton, Arwen Elys.

Stronger, Faster, More Beautiful. 2018. 9780525580966. **S**

Six short stories combine to tell a larger tale of the glories and horrors of the human spirit and the desire for self-improvement. In this future, there are nearly no bounds to what science will let humans change about themselves: why not get stronger, faster, smarter, or more beautiful if you have the means? As the stories progress, Dayton shows how ugly beauty can be and just how imperfect perfection is.

Subjects: Body Modification; Self-image

Kincaid, S. J.

The Diabolic. **J** **S**

In the future when bioengineering has developed to the point of being able to pinpoint tasks for specific organism, a special kind of beings has been created, called diabolics. Diabolics are humanoids created for the sole purpose of protecting a particular individual; beyond that single goal, they aren't supposed to be able to do anything else, which includes think or feel for themselves.

Subjects: Albinism; Bodyguards; Drug Use; Romance

The Diabolic. 2016. 9781481472685.

Nemesis was created to be the diabolic for Sidonia. So, when Sidonia is called upon to attend the Emperor's perilous court, Nemesis poses as Sidonia and goes in her place. Of course, impersonating a human requires thinking and acting like one. Nemesis begins to become more and more humanlike, even feeling that most human of emotions, love. (BFYA)

5

The Empress. 2017. 9781534409927.

> Nemesis and her love, Tyrus, the newly minted Emperor, fight for knowledge, their love, and humanity.

The Nemesis. 2020. 9781534409958.

> Rumors abound in the Empire that Nemesis is not truly gone, but will be coming back to take on the now despotic Emperor Tyrus.

Oliver, Lauren.

Replica. S

A unique reading experience, each of the books in this duology are so-called flip books, each effectively containing two novels. Transitioning from one half of the book to the other requires literally flipping the book lest the text be upside down.

Subjects: Clones; Identity

Replica. 2016. 9780062394170.

> Lyra is a clone, one of thousands engineered at Haven, a secretive lab and compound. Gemma is a "real" girl, who has been raised by well-to-do parents and whose father has a hand in Haven. When Haven is bombed and Lyra escapes, she and Gemma team up to get to the bottom of the mysteries surrounding Lyra's former home.

Ringer. 2017. 9780062394194.

> They've had to swallow some unpalatable truths about themselves and the worlds they thought they knew, but Lyra and Gemma's stories aren't over yet. Lyra and Caelum search for people who might be able to cure Lyra of her disease, and Gemma's old life has been thoroughly tainted by her new knowledge.

Patterson, James.

Maximum Ride. J S

A group of six children, ages six to 14, escape from the bioengineering lab where they were created from a mixture of human and bird DNA, which enables them to fly. A popular and well made manga-style graphic novel series has also been made based on this series.

Subjects: Ecology; Espionage; Flying; Mad Scientists

Maximum Ride: The Angel Experiment. 2005. 9780316067959.

> Maximum Ride ("Max"), a 14-year-old flying girl, leads the "flock" on a quest across the country to rescue Angel, the youngest of the flying children, who has been taken back to the "School" by Erasers, a bioengineered combination of human and wolf. (Film)

Maximum Ride: School's Out—Forever. 2006. 9780316067966.

> A flying fight with Erasers leaves Fang so gravely injured that the Flock must take him to a hospital, which makes their existence known to the FBI. Taken in by an FBI agent, the six flying children enjoy a normal life—for a short time.

Maximum Ride: Saving the World and Other Extreme Sports. 2007. 9780316154277.

> The Flock face various enemies, and their travels take them to Germany and Venice Beach. Some of the mad scientists who created them are planning genocide for the world.

The Final Warning. 2008. 9780316002868.

> While on a mission to Antarctica in an attempt to stop global warming, the Flock encounter the plans hatched by the scientist who created them to auction them off.

Max. 2009. 9780316002899.

> Flying exhibitions to publicize an environmental group prove dangerous to Max and the flock. They also must stop an evil businessman who has been dumping radioactive waste into the ocean.

Fang. 2010. 9780316036191.

> In Africa for a photoshoot, Max and the Flock meet Dr. Gunther-Hagen, who is obsessed with them and tries to match Max up with Dylan, a bird kid, only eight months old, who has been aged to be the perfect mate. Meanwhile, Max is fearful for Fang because Angel has predicted his death.

Angel. 2011. 9780446545242.

> Max, whether or not she wants to, begins to fall for Dylan. Matters of the heart, though, pale in comparison to the dangerous cult bent on global genocide.

Nevermore. 2012. 9780316101844.

> Max has officially developed feelings for both Dylan and Fang, so when Fang returns, the two boys duke it out. Meanwhile, the fate of the world has never been in greater peril.

Maximum Ride Forever. 2015. 9780316207508.

> Almost a sequel of sorts to the rest of the series (the previous book was originally intended to be the last entry), this title picks up with Max living in a postapocalyptic world.

Pearson, Mary E.

The Jenna Fox Chronicles. 🄹 🅂

At this time, science has advanced to a point where human bodies can be created from scratch and consciousnesses can even be restored to bodies.

Subjects: Biomedical; California; Charter Schools; Comas; Near Future

The Adoration of Jenna Fox. 2008. 9780312594411.

> When 17-year-old Jenna Fox awakens from a coma with amnesia, she is told that she has been in a terrible accident. She is living in California with her mother and grandmother while her father commutes to Boston. As she convalesces, she watches video discs of her life. It seems her parents recorded almost her entire life, but some of the things she sees there make her question what is going on. Her grandmother, who

loved her in the vids, seems to hate her now. She had close friends but now nobody visits, calls, or writes. Then she meets a neighbor and discovers that her family had only recently moved to California. Why would a family move a daughter who was in a coma away from the great hospitals in a city where her father still works? When Jenna starts attending a small charter school, she becomes friends with a girl crippled by a biomedical disaster, which has turned her into an activist. (BBYA)

The Fox Inheritance. 2011. 9781250010322.

It turns out that Jenna's friends, Locke and Kara, who also had their bodies devastated by the car accident of the previous book, had their consciousnesses stored on a hard drive. Approximately two and half centuries after Jenna woke up, Locke and Kara have their minds reincorporated. Now they have minds and memories from a distant past living in a changed world: It's almost like they took a time machine into the future.

Fox Forever. 2013. 9781250010322.

Locke returns to Boston with a debt owed to the Network. While paying it off, he falls in love with Raine, whose father is a dangerous man.

Scalzi, John.

Zoe's Tale. 2008. 9780765316981. **S**

Told from the viewpoint of a teenage girl, this adventurous tale takes Zoe, who has had a very event-filled life, to a new world with her adoptive parents, who are to lead the colony. En route something goes wrong, and they end up orbiting the wrong planet but must make do. Because they are the targets of a conclave of spacefaring races that want to regulate human colonization, they must eschew all technology that could possibly emit a signal and give away their location.

Subjects: Adult Books for Teens; Immortality; Space Colonies

Silvera, Adam.

More Happy Than Not. 2015. 9781616955601. **S**

Aaron Soto, a 16-year-old boy with a girlfriend living in the Bronx, has had a more difficult life than many: His father committed suicide; Arron attempted suicide and was left with an ironic smiley face scar as a memento; he is poor; and he has developed feelings for a straight boy named Thomas. The unrequited love might not be so bad if it weren't for the toxic homophobia prevalent among his so-called friends. Aaron, sensibly, wants to fix his life, and it seems like the local Leteo Institute might just have the answer: They can erase painful memories. They may even be able to erase his gayness. (BFYA, Lambda)

Subjects: LGBTQIA+; Homophobia; Memory; Mental Health; Suicide

Suvada, Emily.

Mortal Coil. **S**

What if eating people infected with the Hydra virus was the only way to protect yourself from that virus? What if that virus made people explode? Such is the plight of this world that bioengineering has made utterly pedestrian.

Subjects: Hackers; Plagues; Survival

This Mortal Coil. 2017. 9781481496339.

> Catarina lives in a futuristic world where manipulating DNA is a pedestrian affair and where the Hydra virus is ravaging the population. Her father was kidnapped by a powerful corporation to develop a cure, so she's had to use her wits and supreme hacking skills to get by.

This Cruel Design. 2018. 9781481496360.

> Catarina continues to learn about herself and her past as she and Cole, having coupled up, hunt down a person they think has wreaked havoc on humanity. What's more, the Hydra virus has returned.

A Vicious Cure. Expected 2020. 9781534440944.

> Cat faces off against a new, formidable foe, and the fate of humanity hangs in the balance.

Thomas, Leah.

Because You'll Never Meet Me. 2015. 9781681190211. **S**

> Ollie, a 14-year-old boy who lives a socially isolated life in Michigan and is allergic to electricity, and Moritz, a 16-year-old without eyes who can "see" via superecholocation (listening to how the sound of clicking his tongue interacts with his environment), become unlikely pen pals and friends. Since Moritz also has a pacemaker, the two could never meet in person, and the story is told through alternating letters. (Morris Finalist)

> **Subjects**: Alternate Formats; Disabilities; Friendship; Letters

Virtual Reality

Hallucinations and the distance between perception and reality have been captivating human imaginations since, well, probably since consciousness first manifested. The idea of alternate worlds being just as real as this one gained traction in popular culture with the widespread success of the *Matrix*, which was actually based on Plato's allegory of the cave and an idea that had been floating around in science fiction literature since the 1950s. These stories take place in and across artificial realities, which include video games.

Ahmadi, Arvin.

Girl Gone Viral. 2019. 9780425289907. **J S**

> In the not so distant future, where many of our tech dreams of tomorrow like electric cars and ubiquitous drones have come true, a 17-year-old coder named Opal is driven to discover the truth about her father's mysterious disappearance. Most chalk it up to suicide, but she knows better, and, moreover, she knows who would know best: the elusive tech billionaire, Howie Mendelsohn, who was the last person to see her father before he vanished or died. Getting to Howie is a challenge, though, so when a virtual reality competition hosted by his company offers the winner an opportunity to meet him, Opal knows what she has to do: whatever it

takes to win. Driven by a noble goal, she nonetheless engages in shady behavior. Then again, who wouldn't break a rule or two to find out what happened to their family?

Subjects: Billionaires; Competitions; Hackers; Missing Person

Cline, Ernest.

Ready Player One. 2011. 9780307887443. **S**

Eighteen-year-old Wade Watts lives a fairly undesirable life in a trailer park in the year 2045, a life that he escapes via OASIS, a free-to-play MMORPG (massively multiplayer online role-playing game), a digital world that is much more exciting than everyday life. OASIS was designed by a billionaire who, now deceased, has left his estate and fortune to whoever can crack the 1980s pop culture–laden puzzles he designed in the game. So begins Wade's life-changing quest. (Alex Award)

Subjects: 1980s Pop Culture; Adult Books for Teens; Puzzles; Video Games

Kawahara, Reki.

Sword Art Online 1: Aincrad. 2014. 9780316371247. **J S**

This is the first book in a sprawling franchise that includes multiple series, manga, anime, and video games. The basic premise is that a teenage beta tester for the game, *Sword Art Online*, a VRMMORPG, or virtual reality massively multiplayer online role-playing game, gets trapped inside the game world along with all of the other players by the creator. None of them can leave until they beat the final boss, and, in the real world, no one can remove the haptic suits they wear to play the game without killing themselves. If players die in the game, they die in real life. This is a wildly popular franchise, and, for many, it may be their entrée into the science fiction genre.

Subjects: Anime; Light Novels; Manga; Video Games

Lu, Marie.

Warcross. **J S**

Warcross is a massively popular simulated reality game, and it's also how 18-year-old Emika Chen makes her living. While not quite the same as Ready Player One or Sword Art Online, it will appeal to fans of either, as well as those who like action-packed speculative fiction.

Subjects: Bounty Hunters; Hackers; Japan; Simulated Reality

Warcross. 2017. 9780399547973.

Emika Chen doesn't make money, as one might expect, by winning; instead, she makes it by hunting bounty's on hackers. One day she gets greedy and tries to hack into the game to steal an especially valuable item, when something goes wrong. She is exposed to the world as a hacker and summoned to the game's headquarters by its young creator. Far from getting in trouble, though, she is actually recruited to catch a protean hacker named Zero. (BFYA)

Wildcard. 2018. 9780399547997.

> Emika's life was never clear-cut; it's both murky and demands action. Having grown close to Hideo only to be betrayed by him, Emika finds Zero's cause much more sympathetic. Working with Zero, who happens to be Hideo's long-lost brother, also gives her a chance to learn more about him. Fortunately, the lenses she uses also subvert the algorithm Hideo is using to control other players.

Alternate Worlds and Parallel Worlds

Ahmed, Samira.

Internment. 2019. 9780316522694. **J** **S**

> In an alternate modern America (set in the aftermath of the 2016 election), this timely title imagines a country in which Islamophobia has not only gained widespread support but has led to the creation of internment camps for Muslim Americans. Layla, a teenager who has been sent to one of the camps along with her family, fights against this treatment alongside a cast of allies. This is a story of fascism and the dangers of complacency as well as hope, resistance, and solidarity.
>
> **Subjects**: Islamophobia; Muslims; Resistance; Xenophobia

Allison, John, Christine Larsen, and Sarah Stern.

By Night. 2019. 9781684152827. **J** **S**

> Jane, who has a background in hard science, works a tedious job at a lab. Out of the blue, her old friend Heather comes to town and goads her into exploring an abandoned factory. While exploring the office of the factory's former owner, who disappeared mysteriously, they discover a strange projector that lets them travel to another dimension. This might just be the disruptive break from reality Jane needed in order to make her dream of producing a documentary come true; after all, she now has a pretty amazing subject she could film.
>
> **Subjects**: Friends; Graphic Novel; Humor

Brown, Peter.

Wild Robot. **M**

> The story of ROZZUM unit ("Roz") 7134, the intelligent "crate wrecked" robot, is all about appreciating one's surroundings, living with compassion, and building relationships. Roz still faces danger, but she is not the sort of AI creation typical of most science fiction.
>
> **Subjects**: Illustrations; Robots

The Wild Robot. 2016. 9780316381994.

> A storm throws Roz's life off course before it really begins, washing the crate in which she is being transported ashore a human free island. Unpackaged by otters, Roz, unfit for island life but well suited to learning, observes how the island works and adapts. When she adopts a

5

gosling, her need for help brings her closer to the community. This idyllic life is eventually threated by external forces, and Roz may be the island's best hope for survival.

The Wild Robot Escapes. 2018. 9780316382045.

Having been painfully separated from her home and gosling and taken back to the factory, Roz awakes on a new assignment: she has been acquired by Mr. Shareef in order to help out on his farm. Fortunately, Roz still has her memories and can still speak to animals. Nevertheless, she craves what she had lost, and she hatches a plan to return home to the island.

Gaiman, Neil.

InterWorld. 2007. 9780061238963. **M**

Fourteen-year-old Joey Harker is a Walker, someone who can travel between all the parallel realities. He finds himself in several worlds as he works against two forces who are fighting for global domination.

Hernandez, Carlos.

Sal & Gabi Break the Universe. 2019. 9781368022828. **M J**

Being the new kid in school is tough, especially if you're like Sal Vidón and none of your teachers know how to handle someone with Type I diabetes. Life can also be complicated if, like Vidón, you can rip holes in spacetime, pulling objects from one dimension into another. For instance, imagine how awkward it is when he accidentally pulls a copy of his deceased mother into the kitchen where he, his dad, and his stepmom live. Fortunately, though, he may also have just the unlikely skill needed to save mover and shaker Gabi's brother. Or it could destroy the world—but where's the excitement if that's not a risk?

Subjects: Alternate Dimension; Cuba; Grief; Latinx; Type I Diabetes

Pon, Cindy.

Want. **J S**

If you've seen the pictures of smog-enshrouded cities like Los Angeles and Shang-hai, it won't be too hard to imagine yourself in Pon's near-future Taipei, where the pollution problem has grown so bad as to be fatal.

Subjects: Class Struggle; Pollution; Revolution; Spies

Want. 2017. 9781481489225.

Jin Corp is thriving amid the smog-choked city by producing pricey suits that can protect people from the toxic pollution they live in. They are so pricey, in fact, that only the rich can afford them, bifurcating society into those who have them and can be healthy and those whom the pollution will kill. Jason Zhou is a teenage orphan who isn't even close to being able to afford the luxury of a suit, and he's far from the only one in that situation. In fact, there is a movement brewing against Jin Corp, and Jason joins it. He goes undercover as one of the wealthy youths in order to infiltrate Jin Corp in order to get the intel needed to topple it.

Ruse. 2019. 9781534419926.

> Jason straddles a divide between the girl he loves, who is the daughter of the loathsome billionaire Jin, and the comrades with whom he bombed Jin's business. When Lingyi's friend is killed by Jin, she and her girlfriend seek retribution and Jason's aid in exacting it.

Stead, Rebecca.

First Light. 2007. 9780375840173. **M**

> Thea, a 14-year-old girl from a civilization that is built under the ice of Greenland, comes topside and meets Peter, the 12-year-old son of a glaciologist and a geneticist who are there studying global warming.

Subjects: Global Warming; Greenland; Utopias

Weir, Andy.

The Martian. 2014. 9780553418026. **O**

> After their vehicle is wrecked by a windstorm, Mark Watney, the only survivor, is stranded on Mars by himself. Not only is he alone on the planet, but he is essentially alone in the universe since the wreck damaged his suit and made it appear, to those on Earth, that he had died. Now he has to survive on Mars long enough to figure out how to communicate with people on Earth and come up with a way to get off the planet. Fortunately, he's a super nerdy astrobiologist whose knowledge and snarky humor may just be enough to sustain him. (Alex Award)

Subjects: Astronauts; Mars; Stranded; Survival

Steampunk

Fantastical Victorian technology at its finest, Steampunk imagines what the world would be like with more gears and less silicon. Robots, top hats, goggles, blimps, and gismos are all hallmarks of the subgenre. It has waned in popularity in recent years, but there are still fans out there.

Condie, Ally.

The Last Voyage of Poe Blythe. 2019. 9780525426455. **J** **S**

> Poe is an orphan in an apocalyptic world, which might not be so bad if Call, the only person who's ever really mattered to her, hadn't been killed by raiders. Carried along by a passionate vendetta against the raiders, Poe develops a deadly armor for dredges, massive ships that dredge for gold. Her convictions are challenged, though, when she is put in charge of her own dredge and sets out on a journey of her own.

Subjects: Engineer; Orphan

5

Hartley, A. J.

Alternative Detective. 🅙 🆂

Seventeen-year-old Anglet is a steeplejack, someone who scrambles around on the tops of buildings and towers doing repair work, living in the city of Bar-Selehm, which is essentially 19th-century South Africa. Harley's immersive world building includes an ethnically diverse city with complex race relations.

Subjects: 19th Century; Mysteries; South Africa

Steeplejack. 2016. 9780765383433.

Anglet's apprentice appears to have been murdered, and she is furtively hired to find out what happened to him. It turns out that the murder is connected to the high-profile theft of a precious jewel that served as a central beacon for the city and that both are part of an even larger scheme. (BFYA)

Firebrand. 2017. 9780765388124.

Anglet, who is now a sort of hybrid of private investigator and government agent working for Josiah Willinghouse, is called upon to infiltrate the hobnobbing elite at one of their clubs in order to discover what happened to stolen plans for a secret weapon.

Guardian. 2018. 9780765388155.

Josiah is accused of orchestrating the assassination of the prime minister, and Anglet sets out to prove his innocence and get to the bottom of what really happened.

Oppel, Kenneth.

Airborn Adventures. 🅙 🆂

In an alternate world where Edwardian mores are the norm, an element called Hydrium, a lighter-than-air gas, was discovered, leading to a world where air travel is the norm and great airships sail the sky.

Subjects: Exploration; Flight; Pirates; Scientific

Airborn. 2004. 9780060531829.

Teenage cabin boy Matt Cruse on the airship *Aurora* and wealthy passenger Kate de Vries find adventure as they track an unknown species, survive a shipwreck, and flee from pirates. (BBYA, Printz Honor)

Skybreaker. 2005. 9780060532291.

Matt, now attending the Airship Academy, is on his two-week training tour on a dilapidated and poorly captained freighter. He barely escapes death when the airship escapes disaster and ends up far above where it should be flying, and he catches sight of a fabled lost ship. (BBYA)

Starclimber. 2009. 9780060850879.

Matt and Kate are chosen to be members of the first crew of Astralnauts, who travel into outerspace aboard the Starclimber, Kate as a biologist and Matt as a crewmember.

Westerfeld, Scott.

Leviathan Trilogy. **M** **J** **S**

Mechanical monstrosities, living airships, towering Tesla coils, and other steampunk trappings are brought to life amid a reimagining of the events leading up to World War I.

Subjects: Alternate History; Bioengineering; Machines; World War I

Leviathan. 2009. 9781416971733.

Alek, the son of Archduke Ferdinand, is awakened in the middle of the night by two trusted advisers to go out in one of the armored walking war machines. It is the night his parents were assassinated, starting the Great War. Deryn Sharp, a girl from Glasgow, loves to fly, so she has assumed a male identity and the name Dylan and enlisted in the Air Service. The major division in the world is between the Clankers and the Darwinists: those who build complex, powerful machines and those who tweak DNA to engineer fantastical beasts. (BBYA)

Behemoth. 2010. 9781416971764.

As the plot continues to hurtle toward the outbreak of war on a global scale, Alek and Deryn find themselves in the thick of it all. After the *Leviathan* is damaged by a German attack, the two end up in Istanbul, which, like their friendship, is beset by questions of loyalty.

Goliath. 2011. 9781416971788.

Inventor of a purportedly devastating war machine, Nikola Tesla comes aboard the *Leviathan*. While battles about and there is no shortage of suspense, one of the main developments is that Alek finally learns that Dylan is actually Deryn.

Time Travel

Who hasn't imagined what it would be like to travel forward or backward in time? Readers of this subgenre may be interested in either the eras visited, the theoretical issues, or purely the adventure itself.

Falkner, Brian.

The Tomorrow Code. 2008. 9780375843655. **J** **S**

Tane and Rebecca have been best friends forever. Rebecca, at 14, is an outstanding scholar in math and science. Tane, a talented artist who thinks outside the box, is the son of a famous Maori artist. One night when Tane and Rebecca are watching the stars, they start discussing time travel and how, even though it may be impossible, communication between different times may work. They decide to build a receiver in case anyone from the future is trying to communicate with them, and soon they discover hidden messages being transmitted to them. Ultimately, they discover that they themselves, at some time in the future, are sending the messages warning of a peril that could destroy the world.

Subjects: Apocalyptic; Environmental; New Zealand

Paulsen, Gary.

The Time Hackers. 2005. 9780553487886. **M** **J**

Twelve-year-old Dorso Clayman, after finding many different dead things, including a cadaver that disappeared within seconds, and his pal Frank set out on a quest through time to find out who has been pranking them.

Subjects: Computers; Future; Gold; Pranks

Stead, Rebecca.

When You Reach Me. 2009. 9780375850868.

Miranda, a city kid who lives in Manhattan in the 1970s, is an average middle schooler obsessed with *A Wrinkle in Time.* Then her life starts slowly turning upside down. Her best friend is assaulted by a stranger and abruptly stops being her friend; an odd homeless man appears; and, strangest of all, she begins finding notes that someone from the future appears to be sending her. (BBYA, Newbery)

Subjects: 1970s; Manhattan; Single Mother

Aliens

Almost always depicted as more technologically advanced than humans, aliens tend to be sentient beings from elsewhere in outer space. They're out there.

Anderson, M. T.

Landscape with Invisible Hand. 2017. 9780763687892. **S**

Alien tech has made Earth awful for most people but not in the way one might expect. The vuvv haven't turned weapons on humans, instead they have simply given Earthlings technology that removes the need for most forms of labor, creating a bloated, asymmetric economy with big-time winners and then everybody else. Teenage couple Adam and Chloe strike gold when they begin broadcasting themselves going on 1950s–style dates for the vuvv's enjoyment.

Subjects: Economic Inequality; Entertainment; Painting

Hutchinson, Shaun David.

We Are the Ants. 2016. 9781481449649. **J** **S**

Aliens have given Henry, who is deeply depressed over his boyfriend's suicide, the power to save all of humanity or let the world end. This title may be more about feelings of grief, abandonment, and self-loathing, but it still retains the trappings of a classic abduction story. (BFYA, Rainbow)

Subjects: Abductions; Bullying; LGBTQIA+; Mental Health; Suicide

Lee, Fonda.

Exo. **M** **J**

About a century ago, aliens, called zhree, made contact with Earth. Since then, they have colonized the planet. Not altogether evil but definitely not good, the zhree let humans live on Earth still, just under their rule. The SecPac is the security force charged with managing other humans. In this world, some humans get "hardened," giving them a kind of malleable exoskeleton.

Subjects: Colonization; Intrigue; Oppression

Exo. 2017. 9780545933438.

> Donovan Reyes is the 17-year-old, whose father is Prime Liaison to the zhree overlords, is the son of one of the most powerful people in West America. He has also been upgraded with an exoskeleton and works for SecPac. His ostensibly straightforward life is upended when he is kidnapped by a group of human rebels and held hostage. (BFYA, Norton)

Cross Fire. 2018. 9781338139099.

> As the zhree transition off and away from Earth, Donovan gets caught up in the middle of its aftermath, which includes new aliens as potential rulers.

Meyer, Marissa.

Lunar Chronicles. 🄹 🅂

This series, which has become something of a YA staple since *Cinder* was published in 2012, tells the story of a distant future where the moon has been colonized, and the Lunar people have developed to a point that they are no longer quite human. Cinder, who knows less about herself than she thinks, is a special cyborg living on Earth, subjected to the extreme prejudice against cyborgs. Each book in the series is spun after a well-known fairy tale. In order, the influences are *Cinderella, Little Red Riding Hood, Rapunzel*, and *Snow White*.

Subjects: Cyber Punk; Cyborgs; Fairy Tales; Retold Classics

Cinder. 2012. 9781250007209.

> Cinder, a teenage cyborg, is the best mechanic in New Beijing and is solicited for a sensitive robot repair by the incognito, charming prince. Her evil stepmother, though, could care less about her. As the city is consumed by a strange plague, the government is offering to pay families who "volunteer" their cyborgs for dangerous medical experiments. Cinder's evil stepmother, of course, signs Cinder up. Cinder, though, is far more special them anyone had realized. (BFYA)

Scarlet. 2013. 9781250007216.

> Cider now knows that she is really the long lost Lunar Princess, which makes her a threat to the Lunar Queen. After escaping prison, she goes on the lam, eventually teaming up with Scarlet, the Little Red Riding Hood figure whose grandmother has gone missing, and Wolf, who may know something about the grandmother's whereabouts.

Cress. 2014. 9781250007223.

> In this Rapunzel-alike, Cress is a superlative hacker who is trapped in a satellite—instead of a tower—by the wicked Queen Levana. Cinder and the gang search for Cress and try to stop Kai's self-sacrificing political marriage to the Queen.

5

Winter. 2015. 9781250007230.

> The Snow White stand-in, Winter, the unfortunate stepdaughter of Queen Levana, may be just the key Cinder and her friends need to overthrow the Lunar monarch once and for all.

Meyer, Stephenie.

The Host. 2008. 9780316068048. **S**

When an alien race invades Earth and takes up residence in the bodies of humans, teenager Melanie avoids capture along with her younger brother but is eventually implanted with the consciousness of Wanderer. As the two vie for control of Melanie's body, something unprecedented happens. (BBYA)

Subjects: Adult Books for Teens; Invasions; Love Triangles

Smith, Ronald L.

The Owls Have Come to Take Us Away. 2019. 9781328841605.

Having filled his head with all sorts of theories about aliens, 12-year-old Simon isn't sure what to believe about them. Then he has a bizarre experience involving a bright light and an owl. Afterward, his memory is jumbled, but the event left a mark on him, literally. His parents don't think he was really abducted, but Simon is worried not just that he was but also about what he learned from the aliens.

Subjects: Alien Abductions; Memory

Utopia/Dystopia

Another term for this subgenre would be "social science fiction," since it primarily explores humanity as played out in societies with special parameters. These stories make social commentary easy, if not compulsory, and they are still popular with teens even years after *Hunger Games,* one of the most successful series in this or any genre, peaked in popularity.

Collins, Suzanne.

<u>Hunger Games.</u> **J S**

Sometime in the not-too-distant future, North America has been divided into 12 districts plus the Capitol. Each year, a boy and a girl are chosen from each of the districts to compete in a *Survivor*-like reality TV show (the book is based loosely on the tributes sent to the Minotaur in Greek Mythology). The winner is the one who survives when all the others are dead. It's kind of like *Fortnite* in real life.

Subjects: Battle Royale; Dystopia; Reality TV Shows

The Hunger Games. 2008. 9780439023528.

> Sixteen-year-old Katness lives in District 12, the poorest district in Panem. When her younger sister is chosen in a lottery to be the girl contestant from their district, Katniss volunteers to take her place, certain that it is a death sentence. Peeta, the boy who is chosen, has always been in love with Katniss, but now, in order to win, one of them will have to kill the other along with the other 22 contestants. (BBYA, Film)

Catching Fire. 2009. 9780439023498.

> The Capitol was not thrilled with what Katniss and Peeta did in the previous year's game. Now that it is time for the quarter Quell, the 75th playing of the Hunger Games, previous winners are required to compete again. With rumors of rebellion brewing, the Capitol sets out to squash it. (BBYA, Film)

Mockingjay. 2010. 9780439023511.

> The mockingjay, the bird that is on a pin worn by Katniss, becomes the symbol of a rebellion that takes Panem over the edge into war. (Film)

Dimaline, Cherie.

The Marrow Thieves. **2017. 9781770864863. J S**

> The world has lost the ability to dream, with a crucial exception being Native Americans. For some reason, their bone marrow can return dreams to those who have lost them, but the process of harvesting the marrow is painful, deadly, and forced. A group of teens from different Tribal Nations have banded together and are on the run north through an Earth devastated by climate change, fleeing from the Recruiters, government agents who capture Native Americans and force them into "schools" for harvesting. (BFYA)

> **Subjects**: Apocalyptic; Climate Change; Dreams; Native Americans

Donne, Alexa.

Brightly Burning. **2018. 9781328604385. M J**

> In this retelling of *Jane Eyre*, humans have fled Earth for life among the stars when it froze over and became inhospitable. Stella, an orphan and engineer eking out a meager existence about the lowly *Stalwart*, leaps at the chance to take a new job as a teacher aboard the luxurious *Rochester*. She is blown away by the amenities and all-around cushiness of her new lifestyle, and she is also taken with the captain of the ship, Hugo. However, something dark seems to be lurking beneath the glittering surface of the *Rochester*—some even say it's haunted.

> **Subjects**: Gothic; Jane Eyre; Retold Classics; Romance

Ducie, Joe.

The Rig. **2015. 9780544936744. J S**

> A 15-year-old English boy is sentenced to five years on the Rig, a floating maximum-security prison on an old oil rig. A tracker is affixed to his wrist that tracks his every movement, as well as the debt he owes the company that runs the rig. His transgression was merely stealing life-saving medicine for his mother, but he had already escaped from three other facilities. Something strange is happening deep under the sea under the Rig.

> **Subject**: Prisons

5

Edwards, Janet.

Earth Girl. J S

In the distant future, human technology has advanced tremendously, giving humans the freedom to travel and live among the stars. Some humans, however, aren't so lucky. These are the Handicaps, humans whose immune systems are suited only for Earth and so are forced to live there.

Subjects: Archaeology; Disability; Distant Future

Earth Girl. 2013. 9780007443499.

> Labeled a Handicapped, or a "throwback," Jarra was born with an immune system that can't handle traveling by portal and living among the planets like other people. Left on Earth by her parents, Jarra is cared for by the state, but her existence and self-conception are deeply marred by the prejudices against her and the other Handicaps. In order to prove to the "norms" (and herself) that she is just as good as they are, she applies to an archaeology program attended by off-world students that has a satellite program in New York City.

Earth Star. 2014. 9781616148973.

> A testament to how successful Jarra was in proving herself highly capable, she and Fian are charged with helping ensure the safety of people on Earth while a large, floating, alien sphere is investigated.

Earth Flight. 2015. 9780007443512.

> Jarra discovers a powerful artifact while on a dig. She also finds herself in a pickle: She may be the only one who can save humanity, but she must travel beyond Earth in order to do so.

Ness, Patrick.

Chaos Walking. J S

In a world where an infection called the Noise has made the thoughts of men and animals audible and pervasive, women have disappeared and boys become men at age 13.

Subjects: Dictators; Dogs; Single-Sex Societies

The Knife of Never Letting Go. 2009. 9780763639310.

> Todd Hewitt is almost 13, the age a boy becomes a man, on a planet devastated by a war with aliens that infected all the survivors with something called Noise, causing their thoughts to be broadcast. Other effects included animals being infected, causing them to talk and broadcast noise, and the end of women on the planet. In the swamp, looking for apples for one of his guardians with his talking dog, Manchee, Todd finds an area free of Noise and discovers a girl, Viola, who is the sole survivor of a small scouting ship crash. Things seem to be going from bad to worse in Prentisstown, leading to Todd's guardians sending him away, out on his own with a precious knife. As Todd, Viola, and Manchee flee toward Have, danger dogs every running step they take. (BBYA)

The Ask and the Answer. 2009. 9780763644901.

> Todd and Viola finally reach Have, only to find that Mayor Prentiss has arrived before them and set himself up as president. Separated, they find themselves on opposing sides of an epic conflict.

Monsters of Men. 2010. 9780763647513.

> As three armies converge on Prentisstown, Viola and Todd find themselves facing enormous moral decisions.

Shusterman, Neal.

Arc of a Scythe. 🇯 🇸

A few decades from now, in 2042, humans have conquered death and have become, truly, postmortal. In fact, killing oneself or "splatting" has become a pastime for some, since they will simply be revived. Of course, the Earth can't sustain a continually reproducing, immortal species. So a special task force of Scythes has been created to handle the population problem. Scythes are tasked with selectively killing people, and the people they kill don't come back to life.

Subjects: Corruption; Death; Government Agencies; Mortality

Scythe. 2016. 9781442472433.

> Two teens, Citra and Rowan, are chosen to be apprentices to Honorable Scythe Faraday, which involves rigorous mental and physical training in preparation for "gleaning" (killing) people. Scythes occupy a unique place in society as the sole dealers of death and—in addition to their families—the only people with no chance of an untimely death whatsoever. So being chosen for the apprenticeship is a mixed bag, but as the stakes are indelibly raised and as some Scythes, who perhaps revel in their power too much, begin transgressing norms, Citra and Rowan find their lives growing increasingly complicated. (BFYA, Printz Honor)

Thunderhead. 2018. 9781442472464.

> As Rowan, a failed Scythe, clandestinely reaps reapers, killing corrupt Scythes, Scythe Anastasia, formerly known as Citra, gleans under the guidance of Scythe Marie Curie. A new main character also comes into its own: The Thunderhead. The sentient, nearly omniscient AI cloud doesn't just run the world, it is also self-reflective and rational. One of the big questions raised here is whether or not the Thunderhead is capable or willing to break its own rules.

The Toll. 2019. 9781481497060.

> Citra and Rowan are still on the run, and the Thunderhead will communicate with only one person.

Unwind Dystology. 🇸

America's second civil war, The Heartland War, ended with "The Bill of Life," which states "that human life may not be touched from the moment of conception until a child reaches 13." However, between the ages of 13 and 18, a parent may choose to retroactively "abort" a child. Unwinds have all their parts harvested to live on in others.

Subjects: Exploitation; Runaways

Unwind. 2007. 9781416912040.

> Connor is in enough fights that his parents decide to have him unwound. Orphaned Risa doesn't have any exceptional talent that will keep the state home where she was raised from having her unwound to make room for more abandoned babies. Lev, the 10th child in a religious family who was raised as a tithe, is to be sacrificed when he hits 13. The adventures of these three teens, as they attempt to change their fates, make for a riveting, thought-provoking page-turner. (BBYA)

UnWholly. 2012. 9781442423671.

> The practice of unwinding has been challenged on a large scale by Connor, Lev, and Risa, but that doesn't mean things are going to simply change—at least not for the better. In this, the second entry of the series, we are introduced to Cam, a teenage boy made entirely out of unwound parts, which makes him a sort of Frankensteinian ship of Theseus, both existing and not existing at the same time. Cam, existential conflicts and all, joins up with the trio.

UnSouled. 2013. 9781442423701.

> Characters and side stories abound as the gang continue their quest to stop the practice of unwinding. Their quest, though, is anything but straightforward or easygoing.

UnDivided. 2014. 9781481409766.

> The gang competes with other groups who have their own solutions for the current state of affairs. For instance, Proactive Citizenry wants to stop unwinding by replacing it while creating more people like Cam, and a group of other teens want fire and violence to settle things.

Westerfeld, Scott.

Uglies Series. M J S

In a future where beauty rules, beautiful young adults live in a party-filled paradise, while old people are hidden away, and younger kids, Uglies, wait for the time they will receive the plastic surgery and body sculpting that will transform them into Pretties.

Subjects: Beauty; Rebellion

Uglies. 2005. 9780689865381.

> Fifteen-year-old Tally Youngblood is looking forward to her 16th birthday, when she will be remade, becoming beautiful, and move to the New Pretty Town, where the Pretties party. But just before her birthday, she is forced to spy on a friend who has run away rather than having the invasive extreme makeover, by infiltrating a renegade group hidden in "The Smoke." (BBYA)

Pretties. 2005. 9780689865398.

> Sixteen-year-old Tally, now an empty-headed Pretty, discovers a note and a stash of pills that she had left for herself before her surgery, which will cure the hidden effects of the Pretty treatment.

Specials. 2006. 9781416947950.

> Turned into a Special, a Pretty with enhanced physical abilities, Tally is part of a team that is out to eliminate the renegades plotting revolution in New Smoke.

Extras. 2007. 9781416951179.

> Even though *Extras* is billed as the fourth in the <u>Uglies</u> series, it stands alone. It is the story of Aya, a kicker, which is sort of like a modern-day influencer, who films stories with Moggle, her highly modified AI self-propelled camera, in an effort to improve her face rank in a county far from Pretty Town and New Smoke. When she finds the Shy Girls, a group of thrill seekers who surf the tops of the maglev trains, she joins them, hoping to find a story to kick that will ignite movement in her face rank, but instead she finds a story that is much, much bigger than she ever imagined. The fame-based economy is fascinating, as is the Japanese-like future culture.

Postapocalyptic

Stories of survival at heart, postapocalyptic titles take place during or after a cataclysmic event that destroys the infrastructure of the world as we know it.

Bacigalupi, Paolo.

Ship Breaker. 2010. 9780316056212. **M** **J** **S**

> Nailer, a teen living with his abusive father in a shack on the Gulf Coast, is part of a crew that lives off salvage redeemed from wrecked tankers. Climate change has increased the frequency of hurricanes and tornadoes. Nailer's job is to crawl through the ductwork of wrecks, salvaging copper wire and anything else that can be sold for food. He stakes each claim with a crew mark that matches the tattoo on his face. People who betray their crews are stripped of their crew tattoos, leaving them scarred and outcast. After a hurricane, he finds a wrecked clipper, a pleasure craft belonging to people of inconceivable wealth, but aboard is one survivor still clinging to life. If she were dead, salvaging the ship would make his fortune. (Printz, NBA, BBYA)

Subjects: Abuse; Scavenging

DuPrau, Jeanne.

<u>Books of Ember</u>. **M**

> This series deals with descendants of the inhabitants of a city that went underground and forgot about the directions to emerge once it was safe again.

Subjects: Refugees; Underground Cities

The Prophet of Yonwood. 2006. 9780375875267.

> Two hundred years before the time depicted in *The City of Ember*, 11-year-old Nickie goes to the homestead of her late great-grandfather in Yonwood, North Carolina. With the world on the brink of war, there are conflicting prophecies of fiery doom.

5

The City of Ember. 2003. 9780385736282.

As 12-year-olds, Doon and Lina experience Assignment Day, on which they are told what their jobs will be in the failing City of Ember. When they discover a fragment of instructions left by the founders, they come to the realization they must help the residents evacuate to the surface before it is too late.

The People of Sparks. 2004. 9780375828249.

The 400 residents of Ember are led out by Lina and Doon, finding a refuge in the town of Sparks at the edge of the wasteland that had been left by the Disaster that destroyed so much of the world.

The Diamond of Darkhold. 2008. 9780375855719.

With resources scarce in Sparks, Lina and Doon return to Ember, looking for something they believe will help the blended community after finding mention of it in the few remaining pages of a book.

Grant, Michael.

Gone. J S

Suddenly, in one instant, all adults and teens over 14 disappear and a barrier manifests, keeping the kids from leaving an approximately 20-square-mile radius surrounding Perdido Beach, California. Soon some of the kids begin experiencing mutations and gaining unusual powers, but they are not all that is mutating. Deep under the ground, a dark presence has started changing.

Subjects: Bullies; Mutations; Nuclear Power; Paranormal Abilities

Gone. 2008. 9780061448768.

Sam, who is weeks away from his 14th birthday, assumes a leadership role as the kids left behind in Perdido Beach try to figure out what has happened and how to survive. He leaps into a heroic role when he tries to rescue a little girl from a house fire. When all the adults and older teens disappear, driverless cars continue moving until they crash, stoves continue burning until turned off, and all matter of disasters happen. Along with Sam, Astrid, a brainy girl and his secret crush; Edilio, a Mexican immigrant with practical skills; and Mary, a girl who puts her own issues on a back burner, try to create order and safety in town as bullies try to take control. A little girl who can start fires, Lana, who almost dies in a car accident, finds healing powers, and a gang of troubled, rich kids from a private academy led by Caine, who has strong destructive powers, create and sometimes solve more problems.

Hunger. 2009. 9780061449079.

The kids have been living in the FAYZ for long enough to have eaten all the snack foods while the fresh foods rotted. Now hunger is rampant. More kids are developing paranormal powers, and a rift is growing between some of the kids with them and some of those without. Petey continues with his cryptic remarks, and Sam is going crazy trying to keep the community of Perdido Beach functioning. Along with some revelations about the nature of the changes in the world, new questions pop up. Action readers will love the shoot-outs at the nuclear power plant and the harrowing chase across the desert with the fuel rod.

Lies. 2010. 9780061449109.

Life in the FAYZ goes from bad to worse, as those with new paranormal powers and those without them face off, and the dead begin to return.

Plague. 2011. 9780061449147.

The Freaks and the Normals trying to survive in the FAYZ face the threat of dwindling water, as well as two horrific plagues: one a flu-like illness, the other swarms of flesh-eating bugs.

Fear. 2012. 9780061449178.

Things have only grown darker for the unfortunate souls in the FAYZ. Pete has been reborn, body horror abounds, and a dark mark spreads across the dome, threating to blot out the sun.

Light. 2013. 9780061449208.

As the title hints, the dome has become transparent, allowing people in the normal world—like parents and reporters—to see and communicate with those trapped inside. The gaiaphage's threat is larger than ever.

Monster. 2017. 9780062467850.

Even though the dome is in the past, the alien virus isn't through with humanity. Meteorites crash to Earth that carry the virus, mutating humans and granting them powers. Shade Darby, a teen, is determined to reach one of the crash sites first.

Villain. 2018. 9780062467874.

Humans granted superpowers by the alien virus rally together to take on the Charmer, a potent foe bent on destruction.

Patneaude, David.

Epitaph Road. 2010. 9781606840559. **J** **S**

The Elijah plague that killed 80 percent of all male humans brought the new government to the conclusion that the world was better off with fewer men, so the number of men allowed in the population has been strictly regulated. Those who excel on their tests are allowed interesting careers and the opportunity to reproduce. Kellen is preparing for his tests in a large Seattle house where he lives with his mother, aunt, and several housemates. Charlie Kellen's father, one of the few survivors of the plague, lives on his boat in a remote area. When Sunday and Tia come to visit from Nebraska, the three teens uncover a danger that they decide warrants warning Charlie about and are thrust into a high-speed conspiracy thriller that will keep readers turning pages.

Subjects: Gender; Plagues

Pfeffer, Susan Beth.

Last Survivors/Moon Crash/Life as We Knew It. **M** **J**

This postapocalyptic story starts when an asteroid hits the moon, shoving it out of its orbit. This causes tsunamis, volcanoes, and widespread death.

Subjects: Asteroids; Climate Change; Famine; Latinx; Moon; New York; Pennsylvania; Siblings; Survival

5

Life as We Knew It. 2006. 9780152058265.

> Typical 16-year-old Miranda chronicles her life in a diary that changes drastically after a meteor knocks the moon into a different orbit and plunges the Earth into a catastrophic disaster. (BBYA)

The Dead and the Gone. 2008. 9780152063115.

> In New York City, Alex Morales, a Puerto Rican American high school junior, ends up in charge of his family after they lose contact with his father, who is in Puerto Rico for a funeral, and with his mother, who works in a hospital in Queens. It is up to Alex to protect and care for his two younger sisters, Briana, 14, who is deeply religious, and Julie, 12, who has always been kind of a brat. This novel is horrifyingly real, and though Alex and his sisters are heroic, they are heroic in ordinary ways, as they slowly waste away due to starvation and cold.

The World We Live In. 2010. 9780547248042.

> Miranda and Alex meet a year after the apocalyptic collision of a meteor into the moon caused catastrophic changes to the world. The world is a cold, gray, dismal place with volcanic ash obscuring the sun, crops unable to grow, and food supplies growing always sparser. Miranda's family does find cause to celebrate when Matt returns from a fishing trip with a wife, and Miranda's dad, stepmother, and baby sibling show up with Alex and Julie.

The Shade of the Moon. 2013. 9780547813370.

> Miranda's little brother, Jon, takes center stage in the fourth installment in the series, which takes a look at society's bleak new normal.

Reeve, Philip.

Hungry City Chronicles. ▣ ▣

> In the far future, when most of the natural resources of the world have been consumed, traction cities rumble along on huge tracks, looking for other communities to consume for the resources their residents need. *Fever Crumb* (9780545207195, 2010) is the first in a prequel series set hundreds of years prior to the events in the Hungry City Chronicles.

Subjects: Anchorage; Assassins; London

Mortal Engines. 2003. 9780060082093.

> The Traction City, London, after long sulking in what was once the island of Britain, has headed for the former continent of Europe, its engineers planning a daring venture. Third Class Apprentice Tom Natsworthy meets his guild's chief, saves him from an assassin, and gives chase, only to be flung down a waste chute by the Head Historia. Tom and the failed assassin, Hester Shaw, then set out to follow the tracks of London and fall into many adventures, including uncovering a device that was used in the six-hour war, which brought down civilization as we know it. (BBYA)

Predator's Gold. 2004. 9780060721961.

> Tom and Hester, along with Pennyroyal, a famous explorer, are in an airship when they are forced to take refuge on the traction city Anchorage. They meet 16-year-old ruler Freya, who, after hearing Pennyroyal's stories, decides

to move her city to America, where she thinks she will find verdant fields instead of a dead continent. (BBYA)

Infernal Engines. 2005. 9780060826376.

Tom and Hester live in Anchorage with their 15-year-old daughter, Wren, who yearns for adventure. Unfortunately, it comes to her when she is kidnapped and her parents come to the rescue. (BBYA)

A Darkling Plain. 2007. 9780060890551.

Tom and Wren find a new London rising from the ashes as united Traction Cities fight the Green Storm's efforts to establish settlements that can start farming and won't roam looking for smaller communities to devour.

Smith, Andrew.

Grasshopper Jungle. **2014.** 9780525426035. **S**

Austin and his best friend, Robby, live ordinary lives in Iowa until they accidentally bring about the apocalypse via giant, hungry, and rapidly reproducing praying mantises. Austin narrates the story in an open, informal voice, describing not just the B-movie apocalypse but also his complicated attraction to both his girlfriend, Shann, and Robby. (Printz Honor)

Subjects: Friendship; Insects; Iowa; LGBTQIA+

Sam's Picks

Allison, John, Christine Larsen, and Sarah Stern. *By Night.*

Landers, Melissa. Starflight Duology.

Shusterman, Neal. Arc of a Scythe.

Walden, Tillie. *On a Sunbeam.*

Weir, Andy. *The Martian.*

Fantasy

Fantasy is a dominant force in YA publishing. Although, given the disparate variety of stories that fall under its heading and the immense popularity that Harry Potter and Percy Jackson have enjoyed, that shouldn't be much of a surprise. Fantasy is, most fundamentally, wonder-based fiction, both in terms of its appeal and inspiration.

More so than any of its cousins, namely horror, paranormal, and science fiction, speculative fiction is permitting of nearly anything. Someone can have the power to fly or bring drawings to life for no other reason than that the author says so. Consequently, it makes sense that readers who enjoy fantasy will also typically be open to books from other genres so long as they are seen as wonder filled. Additionally, they are used to reading long books and series.

It's by no means unique to fantasy, but in recent years the most noticeable trend has been an increase in stories that are non-Western and/or that do not feature a straight, white, cis male as the protagonist. For instance, Rick Riordan's eponymous publishing imprint, Rick Riordan Presents, is specifically dedicated to publishing underrepresented voices.

Epic

Epic fantasy, also known as high fantasy, is probably the most stereotypical kind of fantasy, featuring vast worlds, large characters, and plenty of quests. Although these tend to be longer books or series, an epic can certainly be a single book.

Adeyemi, Tomi.

Legacy of Orïsa. J S

Not only does this story, which takes its inspiration from West Africa, feel fresh, it also tells a sweeping epic about friendship, loyalty, family, love, and country. The movie rights were snapped up with no time to spare, and readers can most likely look forward to a saga of films in the future.

Subjects: Royalty; Siblings; Tigers; West Africa

Children of Blood and Bone. 2018. 9781250170972.

When magic disappeared from the world, King Saran, ruler of Orïsa, seized the chance to eradicate the maji, the people who could use magic. Among those killed was Zélie's mother. At 16, Zélie, who was too young at the time to be killed, encounters Amari, King Saran's daughter, who has a special scroll that unlocks Zélie's powers. Zélie, Amari, and Zélie's brother set off on a quest to restore magic to the world. (BFYA, Hugo, Morris Finalist, Nebula)

Children of Virtue and Vengeance. 2019. 9781250170996.

Nobody predicted the extent to which the world would be suffused with magic after Zélie completed the ceremony. Now the maji must be united in order to take on a ruthless enemy that has magic themselves.

Bardugo, Leigh.

Grisha Trilogy. S

This is where the Grishaverse and the story of Ravka begin. Deep world building with strong Russian and Slavic influences sets the backdrop for this gritty fantasy series, which has maintained much of its popularity since the first book came out in 2012.

Subject: Orphans

Shadow and Bone. 2012. 9781250027436.

Alina and Mal are best friends who grew up together as orphans. Now they have both joined the army, with Alina and Mal being given different assignments. When Alina's magical abilities manifest—something she had always been able to hide before—she is sent to hone her powers since they could be the key to defeating the Shadow Fold. (BFYA)

Siege and Storm. 2013. 9781250044433.

Alina, who is the Sun Summoner, and Mal were captured by the Darkling and put on a boat whose captain, Sturmhond, ends up giving them a window to escape once again. Back in Ravka, they must figure out what to do next and how to thwart the Darkling.

Ruin and Rising. 2014. 9781250063168.

Alina decides that, if she is going to defeat the Darkling, she must find the final amplifier in order to unlock the full potential of her powers.

King of Scars. 2019. 9781250142283. **S**

This is the first of a duology set in Bardugo's Grishaverse, though one need not have read any other titles to enjoy it. In the wake Ravka's civil war, its leader, Nikolai Lantsov, must balance delicate affairs both among his own people and with other nations while struggling with a serious personal issue, a terrible curse that compels him to transform into a monster. While issues simmer at home, he and Zoya Nazyalensky set off to find a cure. It has action, developed characters, and plenty of intrigue.

Subjects: Grishaverse; Politics; Royalty

Blake, Kendare.

Three Dark Crowns. **S**

The tone for this monarchy is set by its ruthless method of succession: triplets are separated at birth, then must kill one another until only one remains.

Subjects: Dark; Royalty; Sisters; Triplets

Three Dark Crowns. 2016. 9780062385444.

The island of Finnebrin has a unique monarchy: every queen births triplets, three daughters with different powers, who are separated and raised by different families. Once they come of age, they simply kill one another until one remains and is crowned queen. It would appear that one of the triplets in this generation's set has a clear advantage, but things don't always turn out how one expects.

One Dark Throne. 2017. 9780062686145.

The deadly competition for the throne continues to intensify as the sisters develop into more developed characters.

Two Dark Reigns. 2018. 9780062385468.

Having secured the throne, Katherine's rule is quickly threatened by rebellion. Arsinoe and Mirabella, who fled the island for the mainland, struggle to find a new normal and are subjected to visions of a Blue Queen who wants them to return home.

Five Dark Fates. 2019. 9780062686176.

The final entry in the series does its best to wrap up everything that began in the first three books.

5

Carson, Rae.

Fire and Thorns. **J** **S**

Carson's series makes use of many tropes common to the fantasy genre, but it is done well and it's not without its own unique touches. For instance, Godstones, the magical jewels borne in the navels of the chosen, help give the world its own flavor.

Subjects: Medieval; Princesses; Self-Image

The Girl of Fire and Thorns. 2011. 9780062026507.

Sixteen-year-old Elisa is a princess with little control over her own life. In fact, she is wed to a chump of a prince with no say in the matter. She is also self-conscious and eats in order to cope with feelings of inadequacies. As Elisa, who bears a Godstone in her navel, gets farther away from her kingdom, though, she becomes more of her own person. When she is kidnapped and taken through a desert to the borderlands, she must be self-reliant to save herself. (BFYA)

The Crown of Embers. 2012. 9780062026538.

Elisa and her newfound friends set off in search of answers about the power of the frustratingly opaque Godstone, which seems to be the key to her future and that of her country.

The Bitter Kingdom. 2013. 9780062026545.

In the final volume of the series, Elisa tracks down Hector, evades capture, and gains insight into her enemies' plans. It's an action-packed and satisfying conclusion to her adventure.

Cashore, Kristin.

Graceling. **J** **S**

Cashore's startlingly good debut novel *Graceling*, a finalist for the first Morris Award, is only slightly connected to her second book, *Fire*; however, the third book, *Bitterblue*, which could be read as a stand-alone, ties the series together. The books are set in a world where some individuals have unusual powers and abilities, indicated by anomalies of color: either two different-colored eyes or amazingly beautiful and unusual hair and skin color.

Subject: Royalty

Graceling. 2008. 9780152063962.

Gracelings are identified by their two different-colored eyes. Once they are discovered, the king takes them into his services so he can use whatever unusual talent they manifest. Katsa, niece of the king, has what appears to be the grace of killing, so she is forced to serve as her uncle's assassin. Hating what she has to do, Katsa starts up an underground movement to save any people she can, which is how she meets Prince Po, who has one eye of silver and one of gold. (BBYA, Mythopoeic, Morris Finalist)

Fire. 2009. 9780575085114.

In Dells, monsters are supernaturally gorgeous animals who have intensely colored hair, feathers, fur, or scales, as well as the ability to control the thoughts and actions of humans. Years before the events in *Graceling* and far away in Dells, Fire, beautiful beyond belief with her fiery hair, is the only living human monster. As war approaches, strangers with minds unreadably fogged put Fire in peril. (BBYA)

Bitterblue. 2012. 9780142426012.

After King Leck was assassinated by Katsa, his daughter, Bitterblue, succeeded him and assumed the throne of Monsea. Bitterblue takes her role as the leader of her people seriously, so she sneaks out at night in order to get a better feel for who they are. While doing so, she makes friendships and begins uncovering truths that challenge her view of her country. If she is to become the ruler she wants to be, she will have to undo much of her father's legacy. However, before she can do that, she must first discover all that he did. There are also external threats to her rule and country that further complicate an already complicated job.

Duncan, Emily A.

Wicked Saints. **2019. 9781250195661.** 🇯 🇸

Told from two perspectives, *Wicked Saints* delves into a dark world full of revenge, gods, magic, and teenagers. A holy war takes center stage and drives the plot forward, with the main characters being from opposing sides. The magic system includes blood magic, which requires actual bloodletting to work. This is the first in a planned series.

Subjects: Blood Magic; Dark Fantasy; Multiple Perspectives

Flanagan, John.

Ranger's Apprentice. 🇲 🇯 🇸

This sprawling story of a battle between good and evil features courageous and loyal teens and plenty of action-filled combat. It focuses on the life of Will Treaty, who in the first book is apprenticed to the Ranger Corps.

Subject: Action-Adventure

The Ruins of Gorlan. 2005. 9780399244544.

Fifteen-year-old Will, a ward of the castle, hopes to be chosen for Battleschool, but instead, because of his small stature, he is apprenticed to Ranger.

The Burning Bridge. 2006. 9780399244551.

Will, a 15-year-old ranger's apprentice, and Horace, a Battleschool apprentice, are traveling along the frontier when they find a partially built bridge and uncover Morgarath's covert plans for an invasion of Araluen.

The Icebound Land. 2007. 9780399244568.

When Will and Evanlyn, the incognito identity of Princess Cassandra, are captured by Skandians to be sold as slaves, Ranger, Halt, and Horace head to the frozen north in an attempt to rescue them.

5

The Battle for Skandia. 2008. 9780399244575.

> Will and Evanlyn escape from slavery, but before he and his friends can make it home, Halt discovers that the Temujai, who are attacking Skandia, also have designs on Aruluen. So they join forces to stop them.

Sorcerer in the North. 2008. 9780399250323.

> Will, no longer an apprentice, now an adult responsible for a fief on his own, is called away on a secret mission by his mentor, Halt.

Siege of Macindaw. 2009. 9780399250330.

> Arulen is in danger from a rogue knight who makes an alliance with the Scotti and holds Alyss, Will's love interest, captive in a tower. Will and Horace, along with a force of Skandians, moves to retake Macindaw Castle and restore it to its rightful owner.

Erak's Ransom. 2010. 9780399252051.

> Will and company face desert storms and warring tribesmen when they go to rescue Erak, a high-ranking Skandian. This story takes place chronologically between *The Battle for Skandia* and *Sorcerer in the North*.

Kings of Clonmel. 2010. 9780399252068.

> A religious cult, fomenting dissent, has thrown Hibernia into turmoil, so Halt, Will, and Horace set out for Clonmel to try to restore order.

Halt's Peril. 2010. 9780399252075.

> When Will and his friends are ambushed by the Outsiders, Halt is poisoned. The only way to get the antidote is to find a certain sorcerer.

The Emperor of Nihon-Ja. 2010. 9781741664485.

> After the good ruler of Nihon-Ja is overthrown, Horace, Will, and friends seek to restore him to power.

The Lost Stories. 2010. 9780399256189.

> This is a collection of nine new stories all about the main characters from the series.

Gidwitz, Adam.

The Inquisitor's Tale, Or, The Three Magical Children and Their Holy Dog. 2016. 9780142427378. 🄼 🄹 🅂

> Taking inspiration from *Canterbury Tales*, the narrative is comprised of 10 different stories about three special kids and their dog as told by various people to the Inquisitor who is on their trail. The three kids, Jeanne, William, and Jacob, who can, respectively, prognosticate, use immense strength, and magically heal, travel with a dog who came back from the dead, argue, and form an inspiring friendship. (Mythopoeic, Newbery)

Subjects: Inquisition; France; Middle Ages; Multiple Perspectives; Religion

Hartman, Rachel.

Seraphina. 🇯 🇸

Humans and dragons aren't exactly friendly with each other, but they have been able enjoy the last 40 years war free due to a pact they made in which humans will stay out of the dragons' territory and dragons will enter human territory only when they have taken their human forms (the dragons are shapeshifters). If there were a definitive YA fantasy dragon canon, this would be in it.

Subjects: Dragons; Intrigue; Musicians

Seraphina. 2013. 9780375866227.

Because of the tension and animosity between the two species, Seraphina, a talented musician who is half-human and half-dragon, must hide her heritage lest she become a target. Yet, whether people know what she is or not, she must still face nightly "grotesques," which are like waking dreams of memories that aren't her own. Things really get stirred up, though, when the prince of the humans is found dead, apparently decapitated by a dragon. (BFYA, Morris Award)

Shadow Scale: A Companion to Seraphina. 2015. 9780375866241.

While a civil war rages among the dragons, Seraphina sets out upon the unenviable task of locating and recruiting other human-dragon hybrids like herself. One of these hybrids, moreover, has a nasty ability that lets her get inside people's minds, and she isn't exactly Seraphina's ally.

He, Joan.

Descendant of the Crane. 2019. 9780807515518. 🇯 🇸

After her father, the king, dies suddenly and suspiciously, Princess Hesina becomes the leader of her nation, a place where magic is forbidden. She and a companion begin to investigate her father's death, suspecting it to be murder.

Subjects: Asian Influence; Mystery; Royalty

Johnston, E. K.

The Afterward. 2019. 9780735231894. 🇯 🇸

Apprentice Knight Kalanthe and Olsa Rhetsdaughter were part of a successful, monumentally important quest in which the Old God was defeated. Their lives, however, are anything but simple in the aftermath of their feat, and the quest, it turns out, isn't completely over. The adventuring group is primarily female, and the characters represent a variety of sexualities and ethnicities.

Subjects: Fame; Knights; LGBTQIA+; Royalty

5

Kaaberbøl, Lene.

Shamer Chronicles. [M]

Shamers can make people tell the truth, so they are often called in to solve crimes. Dina has inherited her mother's Shamer abilities. This series is getting re-released in 2019.

Subjects: Deception; Dragons; Dungeons; Murder; Politics; Truth

Shamer's Daughter. 2004. 9780805081114.

> Late one night, Dina's mother leaves for Dunark Castle to help solve a crime. The next day, when her mother has not returned, a stranger on a tall horse tells her that her mother needs her in Dunark. Entering the castle complex through a hidden gate, she is taken through an odiferous pit filled with dragons. Drakan has brought her to the castle because her mother is adamant that Nico, the ruler's son, who was found covered in blood next to the bodies of his father, pregnant stepmother, and toddler brother, is innocent of their murders. Drakan, usurper to the throne, in an attempt to make Dina's mother accuse Nico, locks Dina in Nico's cell for the night.

Shamer's Signet. 2005. 9780805082173.

> Told in alternating voices by Dina, now age 11, and her brother Davin. They are now living in the Highlands with their mother, a shamer, because the evil Drakon destroyed their former home. Drakon's cousin, Valdracu, assumes the identity of a clan ally and attempts to kidnap the Shamer and her daughter, Dina, but they escape, even though the Shamer is wounded. Dina and the grandson of the head of Clan Laclan are kidnapped and taken to Valdracu's newly built city Dracana, where she is forced to use her shamer's gift for evil to keep Valdracu from slaying his hostage.

The Serpent Gift. 2006. 9780805077704.

> Dina's father is a Blackmaster, a master of illusion and lies, but Dina joins up with him in an attempt to rescue Nico and Davin, who have been captured and taken to a neighboring country as slaves.

The Shamer's War. 2006. 9780805086560.

> Dina, now 13 years old, has discovered she has multiple gifts and puts them to use helping Nico in his fight to bring down his cousin, Drakon, who is relentlessly cruel in his plot to take control of Dunark.

Legrand, Claire.

Empirium Trilogy. [S]

It is said that there are two queens: the Sun Queen, a savior and blessed leader, and the Blood Queen, the bringer of destruction. This sprawling epic fantasy that takes place over thousands of years boasts strong female leads.

Subjects: Angels; Fate; LGBTQIA+; Prophecies; Romance

Furyborn. 2018. 9781492656623.

> Rielle has command of elemental magic, a secret that is exposed when she saves the prince. As a result, the king makes her complete a series of challenges in order to reveal whether she is the Sun Queen or the Blood Queen.

Alternating with Rielle's narrative is Eliana's, which takes place a millennium later. Eliana also has magic; hers, however, is healing magic.

Kingsbane. 2019. 9781492656654.

Rielle attempts to right the wrongs committed by her mother, while also fighting to best the dark angels threatening humanity. Eliana is forced to make a difficult change that could change the future.

Lu, Marie.

Young Elites. J S

Most people who were infected by the blood died. Some, however, like Adelina Amouteru survived and were left with its markings, and some even gained strange abilities.

Subjects: Oppression; Plagues; Secret Societies

The Young Elites. 2014. 9780399167836.

A persona non grata in normal society, Adelina finds others like her in the secretive Young Elites, a group of gifted survivors fighting against the Inquisition Axis who wants to exterminate them. Unlike some heroes, though, Adelina isn't just thirsty for justice: She wants revenge. (BFYA)

The Rose Society. 2015. 9780147511690.

Banished from the Daggers, Adelina sets about establishing her own secret group of malfettos with her sister, Violetta. Adelina continues her revenge-fueled descent into darkness.

The Midnight Star. 2016. 9780147511706.

Adelina's power—and ruthless reputation—have grown exponentially since the first book. However, her sister has left her to rejoin the Elites, and Adelina wants her back. What's more, something seems to be wrong with her powers.

Pullman, Philip.

Book of Dust. J S

This trilogy is meant to be something between a sequel and a companion series for His Dark Materials. It takes place in the same world, and the first two books, at least, still prominently feature Lyra as a character. However, whereas Lyra is an infant in the first book, in the second book, which takes place after the events of His Dark Materials, she is an adult.

Subjects: Familiars; Oxford; Spies

The Book of Dust: La Belle Sauvage. 2017. 9780375815300.

Taking place about a decade before The Golden Compass, this title is best enjoyed as a companion to that trilogy; however, it can still be read and enjoyed on its own. In this book, Lyra, heroine from His Dark Materials, is but an infant being raised by nuns in a priory. Malcolm, an upstanding young lad who works in his parents' inn, the Trout, often comes by the priory to lend a hand. When three strangers approach him and inquire about the baby, Malcolm's life begins to change. As one thing leads to another, he soon finds himself spiriting Lyra away to safety, eluding the cruel Mr. Bonneville and his hyena daemon as best he can with his trusty canoe. (BFYA, Hugo)

The Book of Dust: The Secret Commonwealth. 2019. 9780553510669.

Readers are treated to an international adventure with a grown-up Lyra in the driver's seat.

Tahir, Sabaa.

Ember in the Ashes. 🇯 🇸

The Martials, as the name indicates, are a warlike people similar in ways to the Romans. They are brutally oppressive, ruling more through fear than anything else. Part medieval fantasy, part romance, this series has been captivating readers since its first book.

Subjects: Magic Schools; Oppression; Romance

Ember in the Ashes. 2015. 9781595148049.

Laia is a member of the Scholars, who were conquered by the Martials and who still live in fear of them. They killed her parents and arrested her brother, inflaming her thirst for justice. With no one left to guide her, she seeks out the Resistance and undertakes the perilous mission of infiltrating Blackcliff Academy, a school were elite soldiers are trained. Elias is a student at Blackcliff, but he wants nothing more than to escape and leave the school and its bloody ways behind. However, he has been selected to participate in a dangerous competition, the winner of which will become emperor. Eventually, Laia and Elias meet and join forces.

A Torch Against the Night. 2016. 9781101998885.

Now allies through and through, Laia and Elias set on an adventure with the goal of liberating her brother.

A Reaper at the Gates. 2018. 9780448494500.

Laia fights for her people; Elias fights to master his new role as Soul Catcher; and the Blood Shrike fights to rescue her sister.

A Sky beyond the Storm. 2020. 9780448494531.

The dramatic conclusion to the series.

Taylor, Laini.

Strange the Dreamer Duology. 🇸

This duology has a rich, Middle Eastern–inspired world complete with its own mythology and culture, as well as an intricate plot and memorable characters.

Subjects: Dreams; Gods; Librarians; Orphans

Strange the Dreamer. 2017. 9780316341677.

Orphaned as an infant, Lazlo Strange nevertheless managed to become a librarian at the Library of Zosma, where he develops a keen interest—or obsession—with the legendary city of Weep, learning everything he can about it, including the language spoken there. When a serendipitous opportunity to travel there presents itself, he leaps at it. Weep, however, has a complicated recent history wherein humans and gods battled each other until the humans won. Some of the gods' offspring, though, have survived, and one of them, Sarai, begins appearing to Lazlo in his dreams. (BFYA, Printz Honor)

Muse of Nightmares. 2018. 9780316341714.

When their citadel was destroyed, the godspawn were thrust into a new life—even Sarai who died because, even though she's dead, she isn't gone: She is returned to this plane as a ghost by Minya. Together, Lazlo, Sarai, and friends must figure out a way to defeat the Seraphim.

White, Kiersten.

Conquerors Saga. **S**

This character-focused series boasts a historically interesting setting, taking place in Walachia and the Ottoman Empire and featuring actual historical figures, as well as a diverse cast.

Subjects: Historical Fantasy; Islam; LGBTQIA+; Medieval; Romania; Royalty; Wallachia

And I Darken. 2016. 9780553522310.

When Vlad Dracul, the prince of Wallachia, flees to the Ottoman Empire, he brings his two children, Lada and Radu. Lada, the star of the story, is essentially the teenage, female version of Vlad the Impaler. While she feels stifled as a hostage, Radu is able to find some solace in religion. Both grow close to Mehmed, heir to the Ottoman throne. (Rainbow)

Now I Rise. 2017. 9780553522358.

Lada fights for the Wallachian throne, and her brother, Radu, is sent to Constantinople as spy to help Mehmed gain control of the prominent city.

Bright We Burn. 2018. 9780553522396.

Lada, now the Prince of Wallachia, and Mehmed, Sultan of the Ottoman Empire, lock horns in a bloody battle for power and independence. Radu, friend to both, is caught in the middle.

Heroic

Extremely similar to epic fantasy, heroic has been separated out simply because it tends to focus more on a single character's journey.

Hartman, Rachel.

Tess of the Road. 2018. 9781101931288. **J** **S**

In a society with strict gender norms, Tess Dombegh is a stain on her family's reputation. However, when she gets drunk and punches her twin sister's groom on their wedding day, drastic measures are taken. Tess is to be sent to a convent; instead of going, though, she disguises herself as a boy and sets out on the road with a dragon-like quigult pal. This novel, set in the same world as *Seraphina* and *Shadow Scale* (Tess is Seraphina's stepsister), can be read on its own.

Subjects: Dragons; Gender Roles; Royalty; Trauma; Women Disguised as Men

Johnston, E. K.

The Story of Owen: Dragon Slayer of Trondheim. **2014. 9781467710664.** **M** **J** **S**

Dragons are real; they eat carbon; and they must be slain. Siobhan, a bard, narrates the story of Owen, her friend and dragon slayer, as he attempts to reclaim dragon slaying as the domain of local heroes. (BFYA, Morris Finalist)

Subjects: Bards; Canada; Dragons

Leake, Jessica.

Through the White Wood. **2019. 9780062666291.** **J** **S**

Set in 11th-century Russia, this comfortable if somewhat clichéd fantasy follows Katya, who is exiled from her village for her ice magics. Banished from her village, she is taken in by the prince, her complement, who has power over fire, and who plans to use her as a weapon.

Subjects: 11th Century; Russia

Pierce, Tamora.

Beka Cooper. **J** **S**

Hundreds of years before Alanna (from <u>Song of the Lioness Quartet</u>) was born, Beka Cooper, an orphaned 16-year-old, becomes a trainee in the Provost's Guard.

Subjects: Counterfeiting; Dogs; Journals; Kidnappings; Missing Persons; Mysteries

Terrier. 2006. 9780375838163.

Beka Cooper's strong personality and psionic powers strengthen her, despite her painful shyness. In this police procedural–like story, Beka tries to solve the kidnappings and murders of children in Tortall and works on missing persons cases involving people who were digging for fire opals. (BBYA)

Bloodhound. 2009. 9780375914690.

Promoted to Dog at the next level, a police officer, Beka, now 17, and her new temporary partner investigate a counterfeiting operation. Along the way, she finds romance.

Mastiff. 2011. 9780375814709.

Coping with complicated feelings of grief and relief, Beka is called upon to take up a dangerous, intricate, and secretive case.

Daughter of the Lioness. **M** **J** **S**

Sixteen-year-old Aly, the daughter of Tortall's famous woman knight Alanna ("the Lioness"), is at odds with her parents. They think she should be doing something with her life but don't want her to be a spy like her father.

Subjects: Gods; Nannies; Pirates; Politics; Slavery; Spies; Tricksters

Trickster's Choice. 2003. 9780375828799.

> While her mother is home from war for a visit, Aly, upset over not being allowed to follow her dreams, takes off for a few days. It seems like a good idea until she is captured by pirates and sold into slavery. Purposely getting beat up to save herself from being sold as a bed slave, she luckily ends up in the household of a Duke and his two daughters by his late wife, who was royalty of the Raka. These are the people who were conquered centuries earlier when the current ruling family overran their land. A bet with the trickster god leaves Aly trying to keep the Duke's children safe, especially his oldest daughters, who have the blood both of the current royal family and of the deposed Raka royal family in their veins. (BBYA)

Trickster's Queen. 2004. 9780375828782.

> Aly, no longer a slave, is now spymaster for the Rakas, who are trying to take back the Copper Isles. Aly uses darkling shapeshifters as some of her spies while accompanying the half-Raka future queen and her family back to the capital. (BBYA)

Magic and Wizards

Wands, Latin, and books are classic hallmarks of fantasy. A wizard's hat, for example, can be a clear symbol on a genre sticker for "fantasy." Of course, magic can happen without these things, and wizards don't have to have beards or wear robes. These books will appeal to fans of *Harry Potter* and *Lord of the Rings*.

Barnhill, Kelly Regan.

The Girl Who Drank the Moon. 2016. 9781616207465. **M** **J**

> Every year, Xan, who is revered as an evil witch but is actually a sweetheart, saves a baby, whom the townsfolk believe they are sacrificing, and places it with a loving family. One year later, however, she takes in a baby to be her own after accidentally feeding her moonlight and giving her powerful magic. She names the child Luna and raises her with help from a tiny dragon and a swamp monster. Luna's magic is an issue, and so is a witch who really is evil. (Newbery)

> **Subjects**: Mothers and Daughters; Nontraditional Family; Witches

Black, Holly.

Curse Workers. **J** **S**

> In a world that seems much like ours except for the fact that gloves are always worn, some people are curse workers, whose barehanded touch can bring luck, forgetfulness, or even death.

> **Subjects**: Mafia; Transformation

White Cat. 2010. 9781416963967.

> Cassell, the only member of his family who does not have magic, attends a boarding school. One night in his dreams, he follows a white

cat and ends up on the roof of the school. Suspected of attempting suicide, Cassell is suspended and returns to the filthy family home. One of his older brothers is away at college, one is married, and his mother is in prison for touching someone with her curse worker hands. Cassell discovers his family is hiding many secrets.

Red Glove. 2011. 9781442403406.

Cassell, a rare transformer who turned Lila into a cat, is in a pickle. On the one hand, the feds want him to become an informant, replacing his brother, Philip whose murder investigation is still active. On the other hand, the Zacharov crime boss, who happens to be Lila's father, wants Cassell to work for him. Doing either will make him an enemy of the other. In addition, he must navigate high school and deal with Lila, whom his mother cursed to love him. (BFYA)

Black Heart. 2012. 9781442403475.

It seems like everyone needs something from Cassell, whose mother is missing. Although this appears to be the end of the series, it is left open enough that another book could be added.

Clayton, Dhonielle.

Belles. **J** **S**

Legend has it that, once upon a time, the God of Sky and the Goddess of Beauty were lovers. The God of Sky, however, became jealous of the attention that the Goddess of Beauty lavished upon humans, and so he cursed them with ugliness. In response, the Goddess created the Belles, women who can magically make someone beautiful for a limited time and for a price.

Subjects: Beauty; Politics; Royalty; Sisters

The Belles. 2018. 9781484728499.

Camellia Beauregard and her sisters are Belles, magic users who can alter people's appearances. As she comes of age, the time comes to place the Belles, with the most coveted position being the one that personally tends to the royals' needs. As Camellia progresses in her role as a Belle, she comes to realize that darkness lurks behind the glitz and glam. (BFYA)

The Everlasting Rose. 2019. 9781484728482.

Queen Sophia will stop at nothing to keep Princess Charlotte from ascending to the throne. Camellia Beauregard, however, is on Charlotte's trail with help from a resistance movement, a newspaper, and more.

Owen, Margaret.

The Merciful Crow. 2019. 9781250191922. **S**

Sixteen-year-old Fie is a Crow, a social caste charged with handling plague victims and their corpses. As a Crow, Fie also has command of a morbid magic that requires the use of the bones of the dead. When her duties take her to the palace, her life is upended: The corpses are not corpses at all. They are the very much alive prince and his body double, who are fleeing from a plot against the prince's life.

Subjects: Euthanasia; LGBTQIA+; Plagues; Runaways

Pratchett, Terry.

Tiffany Aching. M J S

Magically gifted Tiffany Aching is growing up in England's chalk country when her brother is taken away, and the wee free men name her their leader. Pratchett is a master of fantasy humor, and, if readers enjoy this series, they can continue reading the other books he's written in the sprawling Discword universe.

Subjects: England; Humor; Witches

The Wee Free Men: A Story of Discworld. 2003. 9780060012366.

Armed with an iron frying pan, a nine-year-old witch named Tiffany teams up with the Nac Mac Feegle, wee blue-tattooed, hardheaded Pictsies in kilts, to rescue her kidnapped brother from the Queen of Fairyland. (BBYA)

A Hat Full of Sky: The Continuing Adventures of Tiffany Aching and the Wee Free Men. 2004. 9780060586607.

Leaving the Chalk to be tutored in witchcraft, Tiffany finds herself in some major trouble, and the Wee Free Men and Granny Weatherwax step in to save her. (BBYA, Mythopoeic Award)

Wintersmith. 2006. 9780060890315.

Winter falls in love with 13-year-old Tiffany at a dance, leaving the world in danger of an endless winter. (BBYA)

I Shall Wear Midnight. 2010. 9780061433047.

Tiffany's day-to-day life as a witch on the Chalk is not as romantic and exciting as one would think; then a new danger turns up. A trip to Ankh-Morpork, an encounter with Boffo, and a very interesting young man all come together to make this a satisfying conclusion to the Tiffany Aching saga.

Rowling, J. K.

Harry Potter. M J S

The Harry Potter series inaugurated the current popularity of fantasy and has become such a cultural touchstone in English-speaking countries that a description is hardly needed, but neither can it be overlooked. Orphaned Harry Potter lives under the stairs in the home of his aunt, uncle, and cousin, who do not like him at all. They are Muggles, people without magic who do not believe in magic, but Harry is magical. Unknown to Harry, his late parents were powerful magicians who died while fighting an evil sorcerer, but baby Harry's survival made him a legend in the wizarding world. Films have been released for every title, including two for the seventh book, *Harry Potter and the Deathly Hallows*. The order of the books is listed here for the convenience of readers. It all starts just before Harry's 11th birthday, when he is summoned to the secret Hogwarts School of Witchcraft and Wizardry. Each book covers a subsequent school year in Harry's life as he grows from child to man. (Mythopoeic Award)

Subjects: Boarding Schools; Friends; Orphans

5

Harry Potter and the Sorcerer's Stone. 1998. 9780590353403.

> Orphaned Harry, who has lived a miserable life under the stairs in his aunt's home, is summoned to Hogwarts School, where he develops a coterie of friends, makes a few enemies, and embarks on his magical adventures. (BBYA)

Harry Potter and the Chamber of Secrets. 1999. 9780439064866.

> Harry is having a perfectly terrible summer vacation away from Hogwarts when his friends rescue him in a flying car. In his second year at Hogwarts, surrounded by a close-knit group of friends, he attempts to find the mysterious chamber of secrets and faces a terrifying, time-traveling foe. (BBYA)

Harry Potter and the Prisoner of Azkaban. 1999. 9780439136358.

> When Sirius Black breaks out of the wizarding world's high-security prison, Azkaban, it is rumored that he is coming after Harry. (BBYA, Mythopoeic Award)

Harry Potter and the Goblet of Fire. 2000. 9780439139595.

> Wizard-in-training Harry Potter is entered in the Triwizard Tournament, which thrusts him into deep danger as Voldemort takes action against him. Because of the tournament, there is no Quidditch at Hogwarts this year, but Harry does get to attend the Quidditch World Cup with his friends the Weasleys. (Hugo Award)

Harry Potter and the Order of the Phoenix. 2003. 9780439358064.

> Now 15, Harry has not seen or heard from any of his Hogwarts friends over the summer vacation, but they haven't forgotten about him because *The Daily Prophet* has engaged in a massive smear campaign against him. Things go from bad to worse when he is banned from playing Quidditch. (BBYA)

Harry Potter and the Half-Blood Prince. 2005. 9780439784542.

> Voldemort and the Death Eaters are terrorizing not only the wizarding world but also the mundane Muggle world, as Harry and Dumbledore try to find a way to stop them. (BBYA)

Harry Potter and the Deathly Hallows. 2007. 9780545010221.

> With Voldemort and the Death Eaters in control of Hogwarts and the Ministry of Magic, 17-year-old Harry, Hermione, and Ron do not return to school but quest for the Horcruxes they need to find to finally defeat the evil forces. (BBYA, Norton Nebula)

Sanderson, Brandon.

The Rithmatist. 🅜 🅙 🅢

> There is still only one book in this series. Sanderson has stated that he intends to write a second book at some point, but it will likely be years before that happens. Nevertheless, the single book is popular with readers and has a unique magic system rooted in geometry and drawing with chalk.

Subjects: Chalk; Drawing; Magic Schools

The Rithmatist. 2013. 9780765338440.

> In an alternate steam-aged United States, a select group of people, called Rithmatists, can use chalk-based magic. The practical role of Rithmatists

is fending off the advances of chalklings, two-dimensional animate drawings that can kill people; however, there is also a long tradition of Rithmatist duels. Joel, the son of a chalk maker, is fiercely passionate about Rithmatism, but he himself is unable to conjure anything supernatural from chalk drawings. Nevertheless, he attends Armedius Academy, an elite school known for its Rithmatics. When students from Armedius begin to go missing, Joel and a frenemy end up getting involved in the investigation.

Stroud, Jonathan.

Bartimaeus Trilogy. M J S

In an alternate London, the government is run by magicians. (Mythopoeic Award)

Subjects: Djinn; Government

The Amulet of Samarkand. 2003. 9780786818594.

Nathaniel, a brilliant young magician's apprentice summons Bartimaeus, a djinn, to exact revenge on a powerful magician who once humiliated him by stealing the Amulet of Samarkand. (BBYA, Mythopoeic Award)

The Golem's Eye. 2004. 9780786818600.

Nathaniel, now 14, is working his way up in the government when he is assigned to track down a terrorist who is using a golem. Nathaniel enlists Bartimaeus and Kitty, a Resistance fighter, to go to Prague with him to find the golem's power source. (BBYA)

Ptolemy's Gate. 2006. 9780786818617.

Nathaniel, Kitty, and Bartimaeus join forces to fight the demons who have taken the bodies and identities of government officials. (BBYA)

World of Faerie

The Fae are fickle beings who are often powerful immortals and seldom trustworthy. The tone and atmosphere of these stories can vary widely. However, faeries, like vampires and werewolves, do share some more or less optional universal characteristics like their impish personalities, haughtiness toward lowly mortals, and sensitivity to iron.

Black, Holly.

Folk of the Air. S

When Jude Duarte and her twin were only children, their parents were killed by their half-sister's father. Afterward, she and both of her sisters were taken to the High Court of Faerie, where they have been raised by their parents' killer. Now a 17-year-old mortal living among the Fae, Jude is determined to do whatever it takes to navigate the court and make the best of her situation. Dark, brutal, and full of intrigue, Black's world, once entered, is hard to leave.

Subjects: Dark; Orphans; Palace Intrigue

5

The Cruel Prince. 2018. 9780316310314.

A perpetual outsider for being a mortal, Jude is tormented by Prince Cardan and craves the power to keep threats and bullying at bay. In order to achieve that power, she sets her sights on joining the High Court, which is currently presided over by the king and his cruel sons. (BFYA)

The Wicked King. 2019. 9780316310352.

Having successfully raised her station and having become a strong influence on King Cardan, Jude's need to deftly navigate political alliances and the potential threats to her life have nevertheless remained constant. So too has Cardan's cruelty stayed steady. It might not be so bad if she were the only person she had to care about, but she must now also do her best to ensure Oak's safety.

The Queen of Nothing. 2019. 9780316310420.

Becoming queen is an empty achievement for Jude since she was exiled by Cardan. Coping with normalcy the best she can, Jude jumps at the chance to help Taryn with a curse.

Maas, Sarah J.

A Court of Thorns and Roses. $\mathbf{S}$

Long ago, the Fae and the humans made an accord of peace that ceded immense power to the immensely powerful Fae and keeps humans and the Fae separate, for the most part. The world of the Fae is dark, often full of inscrutable dangers for mortals, as Feyre, the protagonist, discovers. However, there is also the possibility for love and more.

Subject: Intrigue

A Court of Thorns and Roses. 2015. 9781619635180.

Feyre, who is the de facto head of her family because her father suffers from debilitating grief and her layabout sisters are too self-centered to care, uses her gifted hunting skills to feed the family. However, when she accidentally kills a member of the Fae in the form of a wolf, she is stolen away into the realm of the Fae as recompense. Her life is then filled with both marvels and tedium as she is kept in the house of Tamlin, a High Fae. Their relationship is fiercely antagonistic at the beginning but evolves into a Beauty and the Beast type of romance. (BFYA)

A Court of Mist and Fury. 2016. 9781619635197.

At this point, Feyre has escaped from Under the Mountain, saved the Spring Court, and been resurrected as a High Fae. Without decades of experience, her Fae nature is foreign and hard to control. In addition, having come close to losing her, Tamlin is increasingly protective of Feyre, and it's making Feyre feel hemmed in. Due to her deal with Rhysand, High Lord of the Night Court, she leaves Tamlin once a month for a week to stay with Rhysand, where she learns more about the court.

A Court of Wings and Ruin. 2017. 9781619635203.

Feyre's shifting attention—romantic and otherwise—landed on Rhys, but she still maintains pretense with Tamlin in order to gather information. She continues to scheme against the cruel King and even returns home, where her sisters are coming to terms with being Fae themselves.

A Court of Frost and Starlight. 2018. 9781681196312.

Something of a respite from the intense action and politics of the three previous titles, this entry focuses on the Winter Solstice celebration. Some groundwork is laid for upcoming conflicts.

Stiefvater, Maggie.

Books of Faerie. **J** **S**

This contemporary series of stand-alone romantic fantasy tales, rich with music, is set in the here and now but is firmly grounded in the legends of faerie. A third book, *Requiem*, may come in the future. Stiefvater submitted a draft of it to her editor a few years after the publication of *Ballad*; however, she stated that it needed to be reworked before publication.

Subjects: Assassins; Celtic Myth; Folklore; Music; Romance

Lament: The Faerie Queen's Deception. 2008. 9780738713700.

Deirdre Monaghan, a talented, 16-year-old harpist, has debilitating stage fright, so her first meeting with flautist Luke Dillon is not auspicious, but surprisingly enough, with him by her side, her worries dissipate. Luke has been sent to Deirdre's typical suburban neighborhood by the faerie queen to assassinate her but instead has fallen in love, which puts everyone whom Deirdre cares about in peril. (BBYA)

Ballad: A Gathering of Faerie. 2009. 9780738714844.

James, Deirdre's bagpipe-playing best friend, has won a scholarship to Thornking-Ash, a music-focused boarding school. Nuala, a faerie, offers him unprecedented musical prowess, but savvy James knows that it will exact a price too high if he accepts. Meanwhile, solitary fey near the school are being assassinated.

Taylor, Laini.

Faeries of Dreamdark. **M**

Tough but tiny faeries try to save the world from being swallowed by the Dark. Taylor is planning on completing this series with a third book.

Subject: Djinn

Blackbringer. 2007. 9780399246302.

Thumb-sized fairy Magpie Windwitch is on a mission to capture all the devils that humans have released into the world, but when she comes up against Blackbringer, she realizes she may need more help than her accompanying gang of crows can provide.

Silksinger. 2009. 9780399246319.

Tiny fairy Magpie Windwitch tries to rescue Azazel, one of the five Djinn who dreamed the world into being, and his secret guardian, Whisper Silksinger, who belongs to a clan long thought extinct.

5

Urban Fantasy

Urban fantasy includes stories that take place in more modern settings—not necessarily present day but definitely not medieval either. In addition to typically using a variety of magical races or beings, a tendency toward grittiness and the noir also mark these as a class their own. Some fans of horror will find much to like here.

Bardugo, Leigh.

Six of Crows. **J**

Set in the Grishaverse, this series follows Kaz, a wily, cunning criminal with a great heart and an adept businessperson. Inej, who had been forced to be a prostitute and was once an acrobat, is a deadly assassin and silent-as-a-shadow thief. Together, along with a cast of vibrant characters, the two fight for love, peace, power, money, and other people.

Subjects: Criminals; Drugs; Heist; Orphans

Six of Crows. 2015. 9781250076960.

Six of Crows is like a fantasy version of *Ocean's Eleven*. Kaz Brekker, a leader in a gang, takes on a high-risk, high-reward job from a wealthy patron. The job, which would be the heist of the century if he can pull it off, is to break into an impenetrable fortress, break a scientist out of prison, and return the scientist to the patron. To aid him in this endeavor, he recruits a crack team of five people, each with a different skill set. (BFYA)

Crooked Kingdom. 2016. 9781250076977.

It'd be hard to call the heist a great success, but it wasn't a total failure either. Unfortunately, Inej was captured, and now Kaz and the gang want to free her. In the meantime, they also need to get even with Jan Van Eck.

Black, Holly.

Modern Faerie. **S**

Black's tales of modern faerie stand as excellent examples of urban fantasy. The stories in this series feature contemporary young women in urban settings who become involved in the affairs of the fey.

Tithe. 2002. 9780689849244.

Kaye has spent her life taking care of her mom, a talented but unsuccessful rock musician who drinks too much and hooks up with unsuitable men. After the latest boyfriend attempts to murder her mother, the two return to New Jersey to stay at Kaye's crusty grandmother's house, where as a child Kaye had faerie playmates. Hanging out with her old friend Janet, Kaye keeps hoping that her faerie friends were not just the product of an overactive imagination. One night, walking home after being attacked by Janet's boyfriend, she hears a noise in the woods and meets Roiben, a silver-haired elf knight who has been wounded. After a trip to the Seelie court under a hill, Kaye finds herself designated as a sacrifice to keep the unaffiliated fey free for seven years. This is a gruesome take on the world of faerie, along with a little romance and a generous helping of teen angst. (BBYA)

Subject: New Jersey

Valiant: A Modern Tale of Faerie. 2005. 9780786282265.

Val runs away after finding out that her mother and boyfriend are having an affair. Living in an abandoned subway stop under the city with other teen runaways, she begins using a highly addictive drug that the fey use to stave off iron sickness. (BBYA, Norton Nebula)

Subjects: Drugs; Runaways

Ironside: A Modern Faery's Tale. 2007. 9780689868207.

When Kaye declares her love for Roiben, he sets a seemingly impossible task for her.

Subject: Changelings

Chokshi, Roshani.

The Gilded Wolves. S

Fans of Leigh Bardugo's *Six of Crows* will find much to love in this series about a motley crew of misfits on a criminal quest set in a dark and gritty fantasy world. A main difference between the two is that this series takes place in real-world locations at the end of the 19th century instead of a wholly fictional world.

Subjects: 19th Century; Heist; Historical Fantasy

The Gilded Wolves. 2019. 9781250144553.

A thief and hotelier, Severin Montagnet-Alarie assembles a motley crew with disparate skills to pull off an epic heist and steal the inheritance he was denied. He was denied his inheritance when, following his father's death, he attempted to assume his place among the Order of Babel, a group of people who protect a fragment of Babel. The setting is a Gotham-esque Paris in 1889 during the hubbub leading up to the Exposition Universelle.

The Silvered Serpents. Expected 2020. 9781250144577.

Severin and his team set out on one last heist, this time in Russia.

Clare, Cassandra.

Dark Artifices. J S

The sequel to Mortal Instruments, this trilogy is intended to be read after that series, but it can also be read on its own.

Subjects: Demons, Fairies, Los Angeles

Lady Midnight. 2016. 9781442468368.

Despite the prohibition on parabatai, like Emma and Julian, from being lovers, Emma begins to develop feelings for her longtime companion and fellow Shadowhunter. In addition to navigating this intangible issue, they must also deal with a very real and immediate threat of a string of connected murders.

Lord of Shadows. 2017. 9781442468405.

> Emma's love woes continue. Julian and Emma venture into Faerie on a risky mission.

Queen of Air and Darkness. 2018. 9781442468436.

> With the Clave on the brink, Emma and Julian must put aside their romance and focus.

Infernal Devices. J S

Technically a prequel to the Mortal Instruments series, the author recommends alternating between that series and this series beginning after *City of Glass*. According to that order, one would read thus:

> Infernal Devices (Book 1): *Clockwork Angel*
>
> Mortal Instruments (Book 4): *City of Fallen Angels*
>
> Infernal Devices (Book 2): *Clockwork Prince*
>
> Mortal Instruments (Book 5): *City of Lost Souls*
>
> Infernal Devices (Book 3): *Clockwork Princess*
>
> Mortal Instruments (Book 6): *City of Heavenly Fire*

This series can also be read on its own without prior knowledge of the happenings in Mortal Instruments.

Subjects: London; Steampunk; Victorian England

Clockwork Angel. 2010. 9781481456029.

> Tessa Gray stumbles upon her true nature as a Downworlder, as well as the Shadowhunters, after being kidnapped while searching for her lost brother.

Clockwork Prince. 2011. 9781481456012.

> Tessa and her competing love interests, Will and Jem, continue their hunt for the Magister and his clockwork army.

Clockwork Princess. 2013. 9781481456012.

> Providing closure to readers, the final entry in this prequel trilogy sees Tessa coming to terms with her dual loves and a showdown with the Magister.

Mortal Instruments. S

There is much to see of the supernatural that mundanes do not see, including the Night Children, who move among them, and the Shadowhunters, who hunt them down. This popular, sprawling series was turned into a TV Series called *Shadowhunters*. There has also been a movie. The author recommends an alternative reading order to the one listed here. See the entry for Infernal Devices for more information.

Subjects: Angels; Demons; Family Secrets; Romance; Vampires; Werewolves

City of Bones. 2007. 9781416914280.

> When 15-year-old Clary Fray witnesses a killing in a club, she confronts the killers and finds out that they are Shadowhunters, people who hunt down evil and dangerous Night Children. The problem is that she shouldn't be able to see them if she is truly a mundane. And now she can't even get answers from her mother, who has been kidnapped by monsters.

City of Ashes. 2008. 9781416914297.

Now that Clary knows the identity of her father, she is set on defeating his nefarious plans, as her relationship with Simon changes and evolves.

City of Glass. 2009. 9781416914303.

When searching for a potion to cure her mother, Clary and her brother Jace face down their father in an epic battle involving werewolves, vampires, faeries, and an angel who makes allies out of enemies.

City of Fallen Angels. 2011. 9781442403543.

Just when life is beginning to take on a semblance of calm, Shadowhunters begin turning up dead. As things begin to sour, it seems that Clary may have to restore order on her own.

City of Lost Souls. 2012. 9781481456005.

Jace is kidnapped by Sebastian, Clary's brother and the protégé of their father, and the fate of the world is being threatened.

City of Heavenly Fire. 2014. 9781481444422.

Clary, Jace, Simon, and the gang have their epic showdown with Sebastian.

Ghosts of the Shadow Market. 2019. 9781534433625.

This is a collection of stories by various authors focused on Jem Carstairs and the Shadow Markets.

Clare, Cassandra, and Wesley Chu.

The Red Scrolls of Magic. 2019. 9781481495080. **J S**

The beginning of a new series in the Shadowhunters world, this title follows a magical couple, High Warlock Magnus Bane and his boyfriend Alec Lightwood. Their relaxing European vacation is cut short when they learn about—then pursue—the Crimson Hand, a demon-worshipping cult that Magnus Bane apparently founded. This is the first in a planned series called The Eldest Curses.

Subjects: Demons; Europe; LGBTQIA+; Shadowhunters; Warlocks

Gaiman, Neil.

Anansi Boys. 2005. 9780060515188. **O**

Fat Charlie Nancy (who isn't fat) was often tricked by his estranged father, who lived in America. When his dad dies, he travels to Florida and ends up at the wrong funeral. An old neighbor talks to him about the brother he never knew he had; when he returns to London, the brother, Spider, turns up on his doorstep. Charlie's fiancée, Rosey, can't tell the brothers apart, and, because she never sees them together, begins to feel a budding passion for Spider, whom she thinks is Charlie. Meanwhile, Charlie's shady boss has nefarious plans for him, and everything that can go wrong seems to. It seems the trickster god, Anansi, is involved in Charlie's life.

Subjects: London; Tricksters

McBride, Lish.

Necromancer. 🇯 🇸

This offbeat series delivers a quality combination of compelling storytelling, humor, and gore; it's like a B-movie but not quite as campy.

Subjects: Funny; Necromancy; Seattle

Hold Me Closer, Necromancer. 2010. 9780312674373.

College-dropout, fast-food-employed Sam lives the banal life nobody dreams of. Unbeknownst to him, however, he is a latent necromancer who has the power to raise the dead. Along with an oddball cast of characters, including a coworker who has lost her body and is just a talking head, he must control his powers and defeat an evil necromancer rival. (BBYA, Morris Finalist)

Necromancing the Stone. 2012. 9781250034151.

Sam continues to sort out his life, which includes new haters and new friends, as much as possible. To top things off, Douglas returns.

Schwab, Victoria.

Monsters of Verity. 🇴

In near-future America, violence creates monsters, literally, in this beautifully written duology. Specifically, three kinds of monsters are created by human violence: Corsai, a zombie-like creature that has hivemind and moves in packs; Malchai, red-eyed, vampiric monsters who feed on human blood; and, the rarest and most mysterious, Sunai, who appear human but feed on souls. Corsai are created by nondeadly violence; Malchai are made from murders; and Sunai are spawned by acts of mass violence. The monsters present the main struggle for the people of Verity but definitely not their only one.

Subjects: LGBTQIA+; Monsters; Music; Violence

This Savage Song. 2016. 9780062380852.

Verity is split in two, with North City, a stable dictatorship, ruled by Callum Harker, who is able to keep the monsters at bay, and the democratic South City, which is less stable, led by Henry Flynn. Kate Harker and August Flynn should be enemies, and, in fact, August, who is actually a Sunai, is supposed to spy on Kate. However, after a turn of events, the two end up knee-deep in an action-packed plot fighting alongside each other.

Our Dark Duet. 2017. 9780062380883.

Six months after the events in the first book, Kate and August are separated. Kate is in Prosperity, another territory, fighting monsters, while August is in Verity, taking the souls of deserving people. Kate returns, though, and the two pair up again to face the Chaos Eater, a brand-new monster that makes people act out their darkest desires, then feeds on the ensuing chaos.

Stiefvater, Maggie.

Raven Cycle. 🇯 🇸

Stiefvater conjures a world much like our own but stained here and there with vibrant magic. Blue, who is supposed to be a clairvoyant but can't see the future, and Gansey, a privileged boy with a sense of adventure, along with a score of other compelling characters, add a depth of person to a well plotted story that leaves little mystery as to why it has been such a popular series with readers. Readers just starting this series, which has been completed as a quartet, won't have to worry about waiting for the next book to be published.

Subjects: Clairvoyants; LGBTQIA+

The Raven Boys. 2012. 9780545424936.

Even though everyone else in her family can see the future, Blue can't; all she can do is amplify others' ability to prognosticate. She also has an unfortunate future in store: If she kisses her true love, that person will die. A chance—or fated—encounter with four boys who, because they attend the elite Aglionby Academy, are called Raven Boys, changes the course of her life as she is pulled into their leader Gansey's quest to awaken a sleeping Welsh king. (BFYA)

The Dream Thieves. 2013. 9780545424950.

Still on the hunt for Glendower, the Welsh king, the gang develops other problems to deal with, problems largely related to Ronan, who has the chaotic power of being able to bring items from his dreams into the waking world. What's more, the creepy Grayman seems to be sniffing around for the mysterious Greywaren. (BFYA)

Blue Lily, Lily Blue. 2014. 9780545424974.

Maintaining the momentum of the first two books, the third sees the Raven Boys and Blue still on the hunt for the sleepers, who have grown in number from one to three since the first book. Blue's mom also goes missing.

The Raven King. 2016. 9780545424998.

The final entry in the series is as full of twists, turns, and surprises as a dark forest trail. Finally, Gansey, Adam, Noah, Ronan, and Blue will find the sleeping king, but will they find what they've been looking for? In addition, Blue is still yet to kiss Gansey, who they think will die by the end of the year and who Blue believes is the love she will kill with a kiss.

Ursu, Anne.

The Lost Girl. **2019. 9780062275097.** **M** **J**

Iris and Lark are identical twins who complement each other by being analytical and creative, respectively. The have always done well when they are together, but they both struggle when, in fifth grade, they are split into separate classes. Their situation grows increasingly strange—and dire—as objects begin mysteriously disappearing and Iris begins spending time at a bizarre antique shop.

Subjects: Feminist; Siblings; Sisters; Twins

Magical Realism and Mythic Reality

This subgenre is more likely to appeal to readers of realistic fiction and literary fiction than the other members of the fantasy family. Magical realism and mythic reality feature stories in which magical happenings play a secondary or tertiary role in the narrative.

Applegate, Katherine.

Wishtree. 2017. 9781250043221. **M** **J**

A surprisingly eventful story, considering that the main character, Red, is a tree. Red isn't just any tree, though. Red is the wishtree: Every May, people write their wishes down and attach them to Red. Red is also friends with the local animals who help her help Samar, a Muslim girl who is the target of Islamophobic bigotry.

Subjects: Immigrants; Magical Nature; Muslims; Prejudice

Keil, Michelle Ruiz.

All of Us with Wings. 2019. 9781641290340. **S**

In order to escape a traumatic situation rife with sexual abuse and loss, 17-year-old Xochi runs away to San Francisco, where she becomes the live-in governess for Pallas, the daughter of a rock star living in a polyamorous household. Having fun at a Vernal Equinox party, Xochi and Pallas cast a spell that actually summons two otherworldly children who seek vengeance against those who have harmed Xochi. This title unceremoniously explores nontraditional relationships, drug use, queer identity, and more.

Subjects: Latinx; LGBTQIA+; Nontraditional Family; Runaways; Sexual Abuse

Madison, Bennett.

September Girls. 2013. 9780061255656. **O**

A few months after his mother walked out on them and slightly before the school year is over, Sam's dad spirits him and his brother away to vacation at a beach town. This beach town, however, is populated by ethereal blonde Girls who are oddly attracted to him, and he strikes up a relationship with one of them. It turns out that Sam is uniquely capable of breaking the strange curse that binds them.

Subjects: Abandonment; Curses; Mermaids

McLemore, Anna-Marie.

The Weight of Feathers. 2015. 9781250115997.

Like Shakespeare's Capulets and Montagues, the Paloma and Corbeau families are sworn enemies. In this story, however, they are also traveling performers from magical bloodlines. When a disaster thrusts Lace Paloma and Cluck Corbeau together, they fall in love with each other, making their lives even more complicated than before. (BFYA)

Subjects: Romance; Traveling Performers

When the Moon Was Ours. 2016. 9781250058669. **J** **S**

Miel, who grows roses from her wrists, and Sam, who was born a girl and lives as a boy for cultural reasons, are good friends with secrets. The four Bonner sisters, whom people call witches, antagonize Miel and Sam in their attempt to get some of the roses that grow from Miel's wrist. This atmospheric story takes place in a nameless town where the majority of people are ordinary. (BFYA, Rainbow)

Subjects: Friendship; Gender

Podos, Rebecca.

The Wise and the Wicked. 2019. 97800625699022. **J S**

Ruby, a teenager with magical genes, is blessed—and cursed—with the hereditary power of being able to see what will happen right before she dies. Of course, whether or not such fates are real or unavoidable is difficult to confirm, and there is always the hope of finding a way around it.

Subjects: Clairvoyance; Fate; Genetics

Ruby, Laura.

Bone Gap. 2015. 9780062317605. **O**

Roza, a mysterious 19-year-old Polish immigrant, had been staying with two brothers, Finn and Sean, until she disappeared. Finn knows that she was abducted, but his inability to distinguish faces leaves him unable to adequately describe the man who took her. While Finn looks for her, Roza is imprisoned in otherworldly places, unable to leave unless she marries her captor. (BFYA, NBA, Printz Award)

Subjects: Bullying; Kidnapping; Multiple Perspectives

Sedgwick, Marcus.

Midwinterblood. 2011 (2013). 9781780620091. **S**

The reader is taken through seven different time periods—beginning in the future and ending in the long distant past—as seven different, chilling stories are told about couples whose stories begin with love and end with death. Each story is connected to Blessed Fantasy, a small island in Scandinavia. This title straddles multiple genres with its magical realism lending itself to fantasy, its unsettling atmosphere to horror, and its gradual revelation to mystery. (BFYA, Printz Honor)

Subjects: Short Stories; Scandinavia

Stevenson, Noelle, et al.

Lumberjanes. **M J S**

This long-running series is stilling being published, and there's no end in sight. Five friends, Jo, April, Mal, Molly, and Ripley, are diehard besties and Lumberjanes attending a special overnight camp, Miss Quinzella Thiskwin Penniquiqul Thistle Crumpet's Camp for Hardcore Lady Types. The camp and the friends are constantly being besieged by supernatural entities, and the Lumberjanes regularly solve mysteries in order to restore order to the camp, forest, and world. It's not necessary to read these in order, but they are best experienced that way. The team of creators behind these changes periodically, so readers will notice changes in art, which can be jarring for some.

Subjects: Camps; Friends; LGBTQIA+; Outdoors

5

Lumberjanes Vol. 1: Beware the Kitten Holy. 2015. 9781608866878.

At the camp for hardcore lady types, the gang goes up against three-eyed wolves, monsters, and talking statues, all while trying to solve a mystery from which the fate of the world hangs by a thread. Right away, they show their knack for hijinks and "friendship to the max" ethos. (GGN)

Lumberjanes Vol. 2: Friendship to the Max. 2015. 9781608867370.

The gang are beseiged by velociraptors and wrestle with Jo keeping secrets. The main baddies are a boy and a girl who claim to be gods and who are competing with each other to attain ultimate power, while using the girls to do the legwork.

Lumberjanes Vol. 3: A Terrible Plan. 2016. 9781608868032.

Jo, April, Mal, Molly, and Ripley set about earning merit badges, which includes telling ghost stories, alternate dimensions, and epic failures. (GGN, Rainbow)

Lumberjanes Vol. 4: Out of Time. 2016. 9781608868605.

Wet blanket Jen continues to exert herself trying to stave off hijinks and keep the gang in line. Of course, her efforts are ultimately futile as she is separated from the group by a freak blizzard. More is learned about Rosie—who forbids the gang from trying to save Jen, a proscription they ignore—the camp, and more. (GGN)

Lumberjanes Vol. 5: Band Together. 2016. 9781608869190.

The Bandicoot Bacchanal is on the horizon, and the Lumberjanes discover a secret in the lake: Mermaid musicians. This entry also gives some backstory on the Lumberjanes' early days at camp.

Lumberjanes Vol. 6: Sink or Swim. 2017. 9781608869541.

In pursuit of a team-based merit badge, the Lumberjanes try to get Seafarin' Karen's boat back from the shapeshifting seal people called selkies, who stole it. (GGN)

Lumberjanes Vol. 7: A Bird's Eye View. 2017. 9781684150458.

The High Council is coming to inspect the camp to make sure everything is up to snuff. Of course, nothing goes according to plan as the camp is inundated by magical kittens. (GGN)

Lumberjanes Vol. 8: Stone Cold. 2018. 9781684151325.

Barney gets a true introduction to the camp when some of the campers are turned to stone and the Lumberjanes search for a cure. (GGN)

Lumberjanes Vol. 9: On a Roll. 2018. 9781608869572.

When the Yetis are displaced from their homes in the trees and, in turn, displace the Lumberjanes, it's up to the Lumberjanes to beat the Yetis in roller derby and win back their home.

Lumberjanes Vol. 10: Parents' Day. 2018. 9781684152780.

As the title suggests, the Lumberjanes' parents visit them at camp. They get a little taste of what camp is like, and the reader gets to learn a little more about the main characters.

Lumberjanes Vol. 11: Time after Crime. 2019. 9781684153251.

> Molly bargains with a mysterious bargain, and, as a result, time goes wonky. It's up to the Lumberjanes to set it back on track.

Lumberjanes Vol. 12: Jackalope Springs Eternal. 2019. 9781684153800.

> Jen gets the gang back into the swing of adventuring, and they hunt for the fabled jackalope.

West, Jacqueline.

Collectors Duology. **M** **J**

> This series is built around reflections on superstitions and the thoughtlessness with which we make wishes.

Subjects: Hearing Impaired; Secret Societies; Wishes

The Collectors. 2018. 9780062691699.

> Van, who wears hearing aids, has a stash of little things that people have dropped, lost, or forgotten about. He likes collecting those kinds of things, and when he sees a girl and a squirrel doing something similar with a coin tossed in a fountain, he wants to learn more about them. He follows them into a secret place where the Collectors live, people who collect wishes in order to protect the world from the havoc that wish magic can wreak. (Schneider Family Book Honor)

A Storm of Wishes. 2019. 9780062691729.

> Van has learned both that wishes are real and that they can have horrible, unintended consequences. In the second and final book of the series, he and the Collectors must save the world—and Pebble—from Mr. Falborg and a frightening Wish Eater.

Myth and Legend

Readers' interest in mythology is often piqued at a young age, and, with Rick Riordan's novels' popularity, stories that feature elements of mythological tales have strong appeal for many teens. Recently, a greater diversity of mythologies are informing these stories, instead of the typical Western versions from the Greeks and Romans.

Alterici, Natasha, and Rachel Deering.

Heathen. **O**

> Set in a Viking-era world, this graphic novel series takes the form of a saga about Aydis, a resilient Viking woman with unflagging confidence and the gall to take on a god. This series will be turned into a movie by the director of the *Twilight* films, so demand could shoot up when that is released.

Subjects: LGBTQIA+; Norse; Patriarchy; Vikings

Heathen: Volume 1. 2018. 9781939424181.

> For loving a mortal, Brynhild, a Valkyrie, was punished by Odin by being confined to a ring of fire atop a mountain, able to be freed only

by someone who truly loves her. Aydis, a Viking woman clandestinely exiled from her village for loving another woman, seeks Brynhild. (GGNT)

Heathen: Volume 2. 2019. 9781939424297.

Aydis, Brynhild, and Theya, goddess of love, continue their battle against Odin and his patriarchy.

Cho, Kat.

Wicked Fox. 2019. 9781984812346. **J** **S**

Gu Miyoung might look like an ordinary 18-year-old girl, but she is actually a nine-tailed fox demon. Analogous to a vampire, her survival depends on consuming the life force, or gi, of others; of course, she feeds only on those who deserve it. A wrench is thrown into her life when she saves a boy from a goblin and binds herself to him. Meeting with disapproval from her mother, Miyoung doubles down on the connection she has formed with her love interest.

Subjects: Korean Mythology; Romance

Chokshi, Roshani.

Pandava. **M** **J**

This was the first book released with Rick Riordan's Rick Riordan Presents imprint, and it has very similar appeal factors to his books, making it a solid recommendation for fans of his work. Chokshi, nevertheless, is her own author and sets herself apart from Riordan both in her writing and in the Hindu mythology see brings to the table.

Subjects: Atlanta, Georgia; Demons; Hindu Mythology

Aru Shah and the End of Time. 2018. 9781368012355.

Aru Shah lives with her mother, who is a museum curator, in Atlanta, Georgia. When she follows through on a dare to light a cursed lamp, Aru unwittingly releases a demon known as the Sleeper into the world. She also finds out that she is a special being known as a Pandava. Aru teams up with Mini, her soul sister and best friend, and a pigeon in order to foil the Sleeper and save the world.

Aru Shah and the Song of Death. 2019. 9781368013840.

Cupid's magical bow has been stolen and is being used to turn humans into zombies. To make matters worse, Aru has been framed as the thief, so now she and Mini must solve the case in order to save the world and clear her name.

Elliott, David.

Bull. 2017. 9780544610606.

This retelling of the story of Theseus and the Minotaur is presented in verse from multiple perspectives. Asterion, son of King Minos, and Queen Pasiphae, brother to Ariadne, and, most famously, the minotaur are given the protagonist's treatment while Theseus is presented as more of a brute than a hero. Each perspective is given its own poetic style. A colloquial tone keeps the poetry from feeling overly stiff and lends immediacy to the ancient tale.

Subjects: Crete; Greek Mythology; Labyrinth; Minotaur; Theseus; Verse

Friesner, Esther.

Helen of Troy Duet. **J** **S**

Helen, a Spartan princess destined for fame, is feisty and independent, wanting adventure and chafing under the restrictions placed upon her as a princess.

Subjects: Girls Dressed as Boys; Greek Mythology

Nobody's Princess. 2007. 9780375875298.

Helen of Sparta is feisty and independent as she grows up and tries to participate in the same activities as her brothers. Disguising herself as a boy, she learns how to hunt, fight, and ride horses.

Nobody's Prize. 2008. 9780375875311.

Disguised as a boy, Helen stows away on Jason's ship, the *Argo*, and sets out on her own adventure during his quest for the Golden Fleece.

Hinds, Gareth.

The Iliad. **2019. 9780763681135.** **J** **S**

A highly readable and easily absorbed retelling of Homer's classic epic about humans, gods, war, anger, love, and loss. Excellent for fans of Rick Riordan or mythology enthusiasts who find full-text translations too cumbersome to be enjoyable.

Subjects: Epic; Graphic Novels; Homer; War

The Odyssey. **2010. 9780763642662.** **J** **S**

Odysseus's journey home from the Trojan War is filled with gods, monsters, witches, and more.

Subjects: Epic; Graphic Novels; Homer

Levine, Gail Carson.

Ever. 2008. **M** **J** **S**

Olus, the Akkan god of winds, has fallen in love with Kezi, who is to be sacrificed to another god in only 30 days. But if she succeeds on a quest, Kezi may achieve immortality and be able to marry Olus.

Subjects: Human Sacrifice; Immortality

Mbalia, Kwame.

Tristan Strong Punches a Hole in the Sky. 2019. 9781368039932. **M** **J**

The eponymous hero, Tristan, is a seventh-grader from a family of boxers in Chicago. In the summer, he is sent to stay with his grandparents in Alabama, and on his way there, he reads his recently deceased friend's journal, which unleashes a host of mythological figures—and problems—into his world. Some of the figures include John Henry, Brer Rabbit, and Anansi. As the title suggests, Tristan's main task is dealing with the hole he has ripped in the sky.

Subjects: African American Folklore; African Americans; Boxing; Chicago, Illinois; West African Mythology

5

Riordan, Rick.

Percy Jackson and the Olympians. 🅼 🅹 🆂

Percy Jackson, a kid with a bent for trouble, discovers that he is a half-blood: His unknown father was a god. Since the success of this series, Riordan has become a Titan in MG and YA fantasy, even overseeing his own publishing imprint, Rick Riordan Presents.

Subjects: ADHD; Camps; Greek Mythology

The Lightning Thief. 2005. 9780786856299.

Kicked out of another school, Percy is sent to a camp for kids who are half-bloods—half-human and half-god—where he finds out more about his own history and takes on a quest to restore Zeus's lightning bolt to save humanity. (BBYA)

The Sea of Monsters. 2006. 9780786856862.

Percy Jackson, the son of Poseidon and a mortal woman, is off on a far ranging adventure with his friends, Annabeth, another half-blood, and Tyson, a Cyclops, as they try to save Camp Half-Blood, as well as Grover, a satyr who has been captured by a cyclops.

The Titan's Curse. 2007. 9781423101451.

A quest to rescue Artemis and Annabeth takes Percy, Grover, Thalia, Zoë Nightshade, and newly found half-blood Bianca on a journey across an America filled with monsters to find them and save Olympus.

The Battle of the Labyrinth. 2008. 9781423101468.

In his fourth summer at Camp Half-Blood, Percy, along with his demigod friends, ventures into the Labyrinth after discovering that it could be providing an opening for danger to penetrate the camp.

The Last Olympian. 2009. 9780739380338.

Nearly 16, Percy and friends face down the Titans in an epic battle centered in New York City, as a giant heads for the city and Olympus fights its own battles.

The Heroes of Olympus. 🅼 🅹 🆂

Although this is a sequel to the <u>Percy Jackson</u> series, which begins shortly after the events of *The Last Olympian*, and although those who know it will get more out of it, this series can be read as a stand-alone. New heroes, along with Percy and other familiar faces, face new dangers.

Subjects: Greek Mythology; Roman Mythology

The Lost Hero. 2010. 9781423113461.

Annabeth rescues three teens, Jason, Piper, and Leo, from a supernatural attack—and from the camp for troubled teens where they were staying—and brings them to Camp Half-Blood, where their divine lineage is made apparent. These newcomers are descendants of Roman variants of gods. (BFYA)

The Son of Neptune. 2011. 9781423141990.

Rounding out the prophecy of their being seven new demigods, the cast grows. Percy and crew must also rescue Death and attempt to bring the Greek and Roman camps together.

The Mark of Athena. 2012. 9781423142003.

> Although the seven heroes' primary quest is to defeat the monsters released by Gaea, they must still contend with other serious threats. In addition, Annabeth is on a mission to find the statue of Athena.

The House of Hades. 2013. 9781423146773.

> With Percy and Annabeth trapped in Tartarus, the other five must find a way to rescue them, which is anything but easy.

The Blood of Olympus. 2014. 9781423146780.

> Gaea's giants must still be defeated if the seven demigod heroes are to save the world.

Trials of Apollo. M J S

This series takes place after the events of The Heroes of Olympus. While it could make sense on its own, it is strongly encouraged to read The Heroes of Olympus first.

Subjects: Greek Mythology; LGBTQIA+

The Hidden Oracle. 2016. 9781484746417.

> Banished by Zeus, Apollo, who has the kind of proud personality one might expect from a god, finds himself on Earth as a teenager named Lester. His ultimate goal is to become his old self again; however, that is easier said than done.

The Dark Prophecy. 2017. 9781484780640.

> Lester's trials get underway as he, Leo, Calypso, and Meg set out to Indiana to restore the first of the five Oracles.

The Burning Maze. 2018. 9781484746431.

> Apollo continues to grow into his mortal coil as he and Meg undertake navigating the labyrinth in order to restore an oracle and progress in their task of conquering the evil Roman emperors.

The Tyrant's Tomb. 2019. 9781484746448.

> The wicked Triumvirate threatens Camp Jupiter, where Lester and friends prepare for a final showdown. The task, however, is less straightforward than it appears.

Roanhorse, Rebecca.

Race to the Sun. 2020. 9781368024662. M J

> The first in what will likely be a series for the Rick Riordan Presents imprint, Race to the Sun takes place in New Mexico and follows Nizhoni Begay, a seventh-grader, who is related to Navajo gods.

Subjects: Navajo; New Mexico

Tucholke, April Genevieve.

The Boneless Mercies. 2018. 9781250211507. J S

> Essentially a retelling of Beowulf with updated, feminist sensibilities, this is the story of Frey and three other Boneless Mercies, people who execute

mercy killings for a community. The life of a Boneless Mercy is uneventful and attains little glory. Frey, however, is not satisfied with such a life and recruits her friends to fight the vicious Blue Vee Beast who is wreaking havoc nearby. If they are victorious, their story will be retold for generations, and they will earn enough money to retire from the Mercy profession.

Subjects: Beowulf; Feminist

Wees, Alyssa.

The Waking Forest. 2019. 9780525581161. **J** **S**

Dark and surreal, Rhea Ravenna lives somewhere between the world of dreams and the waking world. In another world, there are woods where the Witch of Wishes lives, granting wishes for the price of taking away the wisher's pain. The action begins when Rhea's family begins to disappear and her world and witches crash into each other.

Subjects: Foxes; Wishes; Witches

Fairy Tales

Composing and enjoying reimaginings and retellings of familiar stories is deeply human, captivating our fascination with the familiar being made unfamiliar. Readers who enjoy these stories should look for "retold classics" in the subject index to find more items like these in different genres.

Donnelly, Jennifer.

Stepsister. 2019. 9781338268461. **J** **S**

Personifications of Fate and Chance wager against each other regarding the future of Isabelle de la Paumé, who cut off her own toes in order to fit her foot into the glass slipper. Of course, her sacrifice was for naught as her stepsister, Ella, won the prince's hand. However, Isabelle's future is still an unsettled matter. She could end up living a miserable life of alienation as a disgraced and disfigured woman. She could find herself and be redeemed. The power is in her hands—or is it in Fate's and Chance's?

Subjects: Cinderella; Redemption; Retold Classics; Self-harm

Flinn, Alex.

Beastly. 2007. 9780060874162. **J** **S**

Conceited Kyle Kingsbury turns into a hideous beast after playing a cruel prank on a new, goth-looking girl at his school. One unthinking act of kindness allows him an opportunity for redemption and to turn back into himself; but he will have to be kissed by his own true love within two years for that to happen. In his beastly form, the chances don't look too likely.

Subjects: Beauty and the Beast; Retold Classics

Hale, Shannon.

Princess Academy. 2005. 9781582349930. **M** **J**

The residents of Mount Eskel eke out a subsistence living by quarrying linder, a rare and beautiful stone that is found nowhere else in the kingdom and trading it for foodstuffs when rare traders come through. When the priests forecast that the crown prince will marry a girl from Mount Eskel, all the girls from Miri's village are sent to a Princess Academy to be trained for a year before meeting the prince. While there, Miri learns just how valuable linder really is, and she discovers her talent for Quarry-speak, a kind of telepathy. The prince visits and the day after he leaves, bandits arrive. (Newbery Honor)

Subjects: Princesses; Telepathy

Kemmerer, Brigid.

A Curse So Dark and Lovely. 2020. 9781681195100. **J** **S**

Harper's normal life as a teen in D.C. is upended when she is transported to Emberfell, an enchanted parallel world where magic is real. There she meets Prince Rhen, who has a devastating curse: He is transformed into a savage monster every fall. The only way to break the curse is for someone to fall in love with him. Will Harper be the one to do it?

Subjects: Beauty and the Beast; Curses

Moskowitz, Hannah.

Teeth. 2013. 9781442449466. **S**

More inspired by folklore than a fairy tale, this novel nevertheless has the feel of a modern fairy tale. Rudy and his family move to a magical island, where his parents hope to find a way to cure his brother's cystic fibrosis. Special Enki fish are purported to be just such a cure, so Rudy catches them to feed to his brother. Things get complicated, though, when Rudy befriends a half-fish, half-human boy named Teeth. (BFYA)

Subjects: Brothers; Cystic Fibrosis

Novik, Naomi.

Spinning Silver. 2018. 9780399180989. **S**

This beautiful retelling of *Rumpelstiltskin* takes its cues as much from the fairy tale it reworks as it does from Eastern European folklore and modern sensibilities. Born into a family of moneylenders, Miryem takes over her family's business when she grows frustrated with her father's unwillingness to collect from his borrowers, even when it means discomfort for his own family. Her prowess and turning small loans into big returns don't earn her many friends and attract the attention of the Staryk, a sort of mysterious winter Fae. (Alex Award)

Subjects: Abuse; Eastern European; Elves; Jews

Alternate and Parallel Worlds

Stories under this heading tell of other worlds that exist mysteriously alongside our own, and these worlds normally have special entryways or rules for admittance. The worlds can be eerily identical to the normal world or wildly different, halcyon or eldritch, open or forbidden. Readers drawn to these stories may also be interested in science fiction dealing with simulated reality or parallel dimensions.

Haddix, Margaret Peterson.

The Strangers: Greystone Secrets #1. 2019. 9780062838377. **M** **J**

Secrets, twists, and turns abound in this mystery-centric series opener. Chess, Emma, and Finn are three siblings with a normal life and a normal mom, until one day when they encounter news of what appear to be their doppelgangers. Three children with similar names and identical ages go missing at about the same time their mother goes away on a trip. The siblings investigate and try to uncover the truth, whatever it may be. This is the first in a planned series.

Subjects: Multiple Perspectives; Siblings

Heilig, Heidi.

The Girl from Everywhere. **J** **S**

Get ready to embark on a quest that combines sailing, time travel, and fantasy to tell the story of Nix and her long-suffering father, Slate.

Subjects: Grief; Hawaii; Maps; Sailing; Time Travel

The Girl from Everywhere. 2016. 9780062380760.

Sixteen-year-old Nix has spent 16 years journeying through time and space with her father, who is struggling under the weight of his grief, as he hunts for a map that will lead them back to Hawaii before Lin, her mother and his wife, died. His hope is to prevent her untimely end. (BFYA)

The Ship beyond Time. 2019. 9780062380784.

Now the captain of the *Temptation*, Nix leads the crew to a legendary land, hoping to find a way to prevent the death of the person she has finally realized she loves, Kash.

Leno, Katrina.

You Must Not Miss. 2019. 9780316449779. **S**

Magpie Lewis escapes her miserable life—her mother's drinking, her father's affair, being slut shamed, and losing her best friend—by writing about a fantasy world called Near. She literally writes Near into existence. At first an innocent retreat, it quickly becomes something darker.

Subjects: Family; LGBTQIA+; Mental Illness; Sexual Abuse

Okorafor, Nnedi.

Akata Witch. **J** **S**

Sunny Nwazue, a 12-year-old girl living in Nigeria, is different in a lot of ways. She was born in America, has albinism, and is a Leopard person, which means that she, unlike the Lambs of the world, can use magic and travel to the wondrous, bustling city of Leopard Knocks.

Subjects: Albinism; Immigrants; Nigeria

Akata Witch. 2011. 9780142420911.

Forced to keep her abilities secret from all but fellow Leopards, Sunny lives a dual life split between the mundane world and the magical world. It's difficult to do, but she has great friends and enjoys learning about magic and the new world she's entered. The stakes ramp up when she and three of her Leopard friends take on a serial killer, Okotoko the Black Hat. (Bloomer)

Akata Warrior. 2017. 9780142425855.

Sunny has had a year to develop her skills with magic, but she is still gradually uncovering the mysteries of the Leopard world. Nevertheless, she and her friends face an apocalyptic threat with the future of humanity on the line. (Hugo)

Papademetriou, Lisa.

Dreamway. 2019. 9780062371119. **M**

Stella, normally not one to believe in fantasies, follows a talking mouse to the Dreamway, a network of railways for the dreaming, in order to rescue her twin brother from the Nightmare Line and return him to his normal self in the real world.

Subjects: Disabilities; Mental Illness; Twins

Wilde, Fran.

Riverland. 2019. 9781419733727. **M** **J**

An exploration of trauma and dissociative escapism as experienced by two sisters, Eleanor, who is in middle school, and Mary, her little sister. The sisters believe small acts of magic happen around them, and then they are submerged in a sort of wonderland that takes the form of a river (hence the title).

Subjects: Domestic Abuse; Sisters

Sam's Picks

- Bardugo, Leigh. <u>Six of Crows.</u>
- Okorafor, Nnedi. <u>Akata Witch</u>.
- Pratchett, Terry. <u>Tiffany Aching.</u>
- Pullman, Philip. <u>Book of Dust</u>.
- Stevenson, Noelle, et al. <u>Lumberjanes</u>.

5

Appendix A: Alternate Formats

Graphic Novels

Allison, John, Christine Larsen, and Sarah Stern. *By Night*.

Alterici, Natash, and Rachel Deering. <u>Heathen</u>.

Anderson, Laurie Halse. Illustrated by Emily Carroll. *Speak: The Graphic Novel*.

Brallier, Max, and Douglas Holgate. *The Last Kids on Earth*.

Carroll, Emily. *Through the Woods*.

Chmakova, Svetlana. *Awkward*.

Chmakova, Svetlana. *Brave.*

Chmakova, Svetlana. *Crush.*

Detective Comics: 80 Years of Batman.

Doctorow, Cory, and Jen Wang. *In Real Life*.

Ennis, Garth, Steve Epting, and Elizabeth Breitweiser. *Sara*.

Hicks, Faith Erin. *Friends with Boys*.

Hinds, Gareth. *The Iliad*.

Hinds, Gareth. *The Odyssey*.

Keenan, Sheila. *Dogs of War*.

Jamieson, Victoria. *All's Faire in Middle School*.

Jamieson, Victoria. *Roller Girl*.

Panetta, Kevin. Illustrated by Savanna Ganucheau. *Bloom*.

Priest, Cherie, and Tara O'Connor. *The Agony House*.

Smallwood, Greg, Megan Smallwood, and Jack Morelli. *Vampironica*.

Stevenson, Noelle, et al. <u>Lumberjanes</u>.

Tamaki, Mariko. Illustrated by Rosemary Valero-O'Connor. *Laura Dean Keeps Breaking Up with Me*.

Telgemeier, Raina. *Drama*.

Tynion, James, IV, and Eryk Donovan. *Memetic*.

Walden, Tillie. *On a Sunbeam*.

Whedon, Joss, Jordie Bellaire, Dan Mora, and Raul Angulo. *Buffy the Vampire Slayer: Vol. 1: High School Is Hell.*

Wild, Ailsa, et al. *The Invisible War: A World War I Tale of Two Scales.*

Novels in Verse

Acevedo, Elizabeth. *The Poet X.*

Alexander, Kwame. *Booked.*

Alexander, Kwame. *The Crossover.*

Alexander, Kwame. *Rebound.*

Crossan, Sarah. *One.*

Elliott, David. *Bull.*

Frost, Helen. *Keesha's House.*

Reynolds, Jason. *Long Way Down.*

Epistolary Novels/Diaries/E-mails

Davis, Jenny Fran. *Everything Must Go.*

Dellaira, Ava. *Love Letters to the Dead.*

Kisner, Adrienne. *Dear Rachel Maddow.*

McCarthy, Cori, and Amy Rose Capetta. Illuminae Files.

Menon, Sandhya. *From Twinkle, with Love.*

Moskowitz, Hannah, and Kat Helgeson. *Gena/Finn.*

Quintero, Isabel. *Gabi, a Girl in Pieces.*

Schlitz, Laura Amy. *The Hired Girl.*

Stone, Nic. *Dear Martin.*

Thomas, Leah. *Because You'll Never Meet Me.*

Verano, M. Diary of a Haunting.

Wein, Elizabeth. Code Name Verity.

Scrapbooks

Anthony, Jessica, and Rodrigo Corral. *Chopsticks.*

Short Stories

All Out: The No-Longer-Secret Stories of Queer Teens throughout the Ages.

Carroll, Emily. *Through the Woods.*

Dayton, Arwen Elys. *Stronger, Faster, More Beautiful.*

Keenan, Sheila. *Dogs of War.*

Let It Snow: Three Holiday Romances.

Meet Cute: Some People Are Destined to Meet.

My True Love Gave to Me: Twelve Holiday Stories.

Sedgwick, Marcus. *Midwinterblood.*

Summer Days and Summer Nights: Twelve Love Stories.

Three Sides of a Heart: Stories About Love Triangles.

Appendix B: Multicultural Interest

Black/African American

Alexander, Kwame. *Booked.*

Alexander, Kwame. *The Crossover.*

Alexander, Kwame. *Rebound.*

Alexander, Kwame. *Solo.*

Anderson, Laurie Halse. <u>Seeds of America</u>.

Anderson, M. T. <u>The Astonishing Life of Octavian Nothing, Traitor to the Nation</u>.

Bolden, Tonya. *Crossing Ebenezer Creek.*

Bolden, Tonya. *Saving Savannah.*

Booth, Coe. *Tyrell.*

Clayton, Dhonielle. <u>Belles.</u>

Dellaira, Ava. *In Search of Us.*

Draper, Sharon. *Copper Sun.*

Emezi, Akwaeke. *Pet.*

Ireland, Justina. *Dread Nation.*

Lester, Julius. *Day of Tears: A Novel in Dialogue.*

Mbalia, Kwame. *Tristan Strong Punches a Hole in the Sky.*

Mosley, Walter. *47.*

Reynolds, Jason. *Ghost.*

Reynolds, Jason. *Long Way Down.*

Rinaldi, Ann. *An Unlikely Friendship: A Novel of Mary Todd Lincoln and Elizabeth Keckley.*

Rinaldi, Ann. *Come Juneteenth.*

Schmidt, Gary D. *Lizzie Bright and the Buckminster Boy.*

Shabazz, Ilyasah. *X.*

Smith, Sherri L. *Flygirl.*

Stone, Nic. *Dear Martin.*

Thomas, Angie. *The Hate U Give.*

Thomas, Angie. *On the Come Up.*

Volponi, Paul. *Final Four.*

Asian American

Gilbert, Kelly Loy. *Picture Us in the Light.*

Goo, Maureen. *Somewhere Only We Knew.*

Goo, Maureen. *The Way You Make Me Feel.*

Han, Jenny. <u>The Lara Jean Series</u>.

Henry, Katie. *Heretics Anonymous.*

Kadohata, Cynthia. *Kira-Kira.*

Lee, Stacey. *The Downstairs Girl.*

Lee, Stacey. *Outrun the Moon.*

Menon, Sandhya. *When Dimple Met Rishi.*

Menon, Sandhya. *There's Something About Sweetie.*

Menon, Sandhya. *From Twinkle, with Love.*

Rowell, Rainbow. *Eleanor and Park.*

Safi, Aminah Mae. *Tell Me How You Really Feel.*

Strohm, Stephanie Kate. *Love à la Mode.*

Wen, Abigal Hing. *Loveboat, Taipei.*

Yang, Kelly. *Front Desk.*

Yoon, David. *Frankly in Love.*

Yoon, Nicola. *The Sun Is Also a Star.*

Latinx

Acevedo, Elizabeth. *The Poet X.*

Acevedo, Elizabeth. *With the Fire on High.*

Alsaid, Adi. *North of Happy.*

Capo Crucet, Jeanine. *Make Your Home among Strangers.*

Flores-Scott, Patrick. *American Road Trip.*

Hernandez, Carlos. *Sal & Gabi Break the Universe.*

Keil, Michelle Ruiz. *All of Us with Wings.*

Longo, Jennifer. *Six Feet over It.*

Pfeffer, Susan Beth. Last Survivors/Moon Crash/Life as We Knew It.

Quintero, Isabel. *Gabi: A Girl in Pieces.*

Saenz, Benjamin Alire. *Aristotle and Dante Discover the Secrets of the Universe.*

Safi, Aminah Mae. *Tell Me How You Really Feel.*

Sanchez, Alex. *The God Box.*

Sanchez, Erika L. *I Am Not Your Perfect Mexican Daughter.*

Spalding, Amy. *The Summer of Jordi Pérez.*

Stork, Francisco X. *Disappeared.*

Yoon, Nicola. *The Sun Is Also a Star.*

Native American and First Nations

Dimaline, Cherie. *The Marrow Thieves.*

Heilig, Heidi. The Girl from Everywhere.

Roanhorse, Rebecca. *Race to the Sun.*

Mixed Race

Allison, John, Christine Larsen, and Sarah Stern. *By Night.*

Callender, Kacen. *This Is Kind of an Epic Love Story.*

Han, Jenny. The Lara Jean Series.

Maniscalco, Kerri. Stalking Jack the Ripper.

Reynolds, Jason. *Miles Morales.*

Safi, Aminah Mae. *Tell Me How You Really Feel.*

Stone, Nic. *Odd One Out.*

Yoon, Nicola. *The Sun Is Also a Star.*

Other Countries

African Countries and Culture

Adeyemi, Tomi. <u>Legacy of Orïsa</u>.

Alexander, Kwame. *Solo*.

Hartley, A. J. <u>*Alternative Detective*</u>.

Okorafor, Nnedi. <u>*Akata Witch*</u>.

Asian Countries and Culture

Alkaf, Hanna. *The Weight of Our Sky*.

Cho, Kat. *Wicked Fox*.

Chokshi, Roshani. <u>Pandava</u>.

Chupeco, Rin. <u>The Girl from the Well</u>.

DeWoskin, Rachel. *Someday We Will Fly*.

Goo, Maureen. *Somewhere Only We Knew*.

Gratz, Alan. *Samurai Shortstop*.

He, Joan. *Descendant of the Crane*.

Kawahara, Reki. *Sword Art Online 1: Aincrad*.

Khorram, Adib. *Darius the Great Is Not Okay*.

Lawrence, Caroline. <u>The Roman Mysteries</u>.

Lee, Yoon Ha. *Dragon Pearl*.

Lu, Marie. <u>Warcross</u>.

McCulloch, Joy. *Blood Water Paint*.

Meyer, Caroline. *Duchessina*.

Pon, Cindy. <u>Want</u>.

Rogers, Meghan. *Crossing the Line*.

Wen, Abigal Hing. *Loveboat, Taipei*.

Australia

Abdel-Fattah, Randa. *Does My Head Look Big in This?*

Crowley, Cath. *Graffiti Moon*.

Crowley, Cath. *Words in Deep Blue*.

Marchetta, Melina. *The Piper's Son*.

Marchetta, Melina. *Saving Francesca*.

Marney, Ellie. The Every Series.

Plozza, Shivaun. *Tin Heart*.

Silvey, Craig. *Jasper Jones*.

Zusak, Markus. *Bridge of Clay*.

Zusak, Markus. *I Am the Messenger*.

Canada

Bradley, Alan. *As Chimney Sweepers Come to Dust*.

Johnston, E. K. *Exit, Pursued by a Bear*.

Johnston, E. K. *The Story of Owen: Dragon Slayer of Trondheim*.

Marshall, Kate Allie. *I Am Still Alive*.

McNamee, Graham. *Acceleration*.

McNamee, Graham. *Defender*.

Scarrow, Kristine. *The Gamer's Guide to Getting the Girl*.

Storm, Jo. *Snowhook*.

Younge-Ullman, Danielle. *Everything Beautiful Is Not Ruined*.

European Countries

Alterici, Natash, and Rachel Deering. Heathen.

Carter, Ally. The Heist Society Series.

Chokshi, Roshani. The Gilded Wolves.

Elliott, David. *Bull*.

Fiore, Kelly. *Taste Test*.

Forman, Gayle. *Just One Day*.

Forman, Gayle. *Just One Year*.

Gratz, Alan. *Projekt 1065*.

Hartnett, Sonya. *The Silver Donkey*.

Hesse, Monica. *Girl in the Blue Coat*.

Iturbe, Antonio. *The Librarian of Auschwitz*.

Johnson, Maureen. *13 Little Blue Envelopes*.

Killeen, Matt. *Orphan Monster Spy*.

Leake, Jessica. *Through the White Wood.*

Lindner, April. *Love, Lucy.*

Novik, Naomi. *Spinning Silver.*

Peet, Mal. *Tamar.*

Perkins, Stephanie. *Anna and the French Kiss.*

Perkins, Stephanie. *Isla and the Happily Ever After.*

Rae, Kristin. *Wish You Were Italian.*

Ruby, Laura. *Bone Gap.*

Sedgwick, Marcus. *Midwinterblood.*

Sepetys, Ruta. *Between Shades of Gray.*

Sepetys, Ruta. *The Fountains of Silence.*

Stead, Rebecca. *First Light.*

Strohm, Stephanie Kate. *Love à la Mode.*

Wein, Elizabeth. *Code Name Verity.*

Wilson, Kip. *White Rose.*

Yolen, Jane. *Mapping the Bones.*

Zusak, Markus. *The Book Thief.*

Great Britain

Albright, Emily. *The Heir and the Spare.*

Auxier, Jonathan. *Sweep.*

Avi. Crispin.

Avi. *The Traitors' Gate.*

Barter, Catherine. *Troublemakers.*

Bradley, Alan. The Flavia de Luce Mysteries.

Bradley, Kimberly Brubaker. *The War I Finally Won.*

Bradley, Kimberly Brubaker. *The War That Saved My Life.*

Carter, Ally. *Heist Society.*

Cavallaro, Brittany. *The Last of August.*

Cavallaro, Brittany. *A Question of Holmes.*

Cook, Eileen. *You Owe Me a Murder.*

Dowd, Siobhan. *The London Eye Mystery.*

Author/Title Index

Abdel-Fatteh, Randa, 11
Abrahams, Peter, 97–98
Abundance of Katherines, An, 11, 24
Acceleration, 111
Acevedo, Elizabeth, 1, 38, 46
Acosta, Daniel, 52
Adeyemi, Toni, 182
Adoration of Jenna Fox, The, 161
Aftershock, 123
Afterward, The, 187
Agony House, The, 149
Ahmadi, Arvin, 163
Ahmed, Samira, 165
Airborn, 168
Airborn Adventures, 168
Akata Warrior, 217
Akata Witch, 216–217
Akata Witch, 217
Alameda, Courtney, 133
Albertalli, Becky, 15, 91
Albright, Emily, 77
Alex & Eliza, 49
Alex Rider Series, 120–121
Alexander, Kwame, 1, 17
Ali, S.K, 2
Alkaf, Hanna, 67
All for One, 49
All Is Fair, 70
All of Us with Wings, 206
All Out: The No-Longer-Secret Stories of
Queer Teens throughout the Ages, 66
All Unquiet Things, 100
All's Faire in Middle School, 35
Allen, Sarah Addison, 33
Allies of the Night, 141
Allison, John, 165
Along for the Ride, 24
Alsaid, Adi, 22, 224
Also Known As, 114
Alterici, Natasha, 209–210
Alternative Detective, 168
Always and Forever, Lara Jean, 88
Amateurs, The, 102

Amber Fang: Hunted, 141
Amelia Anne Is Dead and Gone, 111
American Road Trip, 35
Amity, 128
Amulet of Samarkand, The, 197
Amy and Roger's Epic Detour, 84, 95
Anansi Boys, 203
And I Darken, 191
And Then There Were Four, 113
And We Stay, 31
Anderson, Laurie Halse, 13, 48
Anderson, M. T., 48–49, 170
Andrews, Jan, 52
Angel, 161
Angulo, Raul, 128
Anna, 130
Anna and the French Kiss, 89, 90, 94
Anna Dressed in Blood, 130
Anstey, Cindy, 60
Anthony, Jessica, 107
Applegate, Katherine, 206
Arc of a Scythe, 175
Archenemies, 153
Arden, Katherine, 126
Aristotle and Dante Discover the Secrets of the
Universe, 10
Ark Angel, 121
Aru Shah and the End of Time, 210
Aru Shah and the Song of Death, 210
As Chimney Sweepers Come to Dust, 104
As I Descended, 148
Ashes, 143
Ashes, 143
Ask and the Answer, The, 175
Ask the Passengers, 9
Assassins of Rome, The, 62
Astonishing Life of Octavian Nothing, Traitor
to the Nation, The, 48
At the Edge of the World, 61
Attack of the Fiend, 146
Audacity, 53
Audrey, Wait!, 2
Aurora Rising, 155

Autoboyography, 92
Auxier, Jonathan, 60, 129
Avi, 49, 61, 67, 129
Awakened, 137
Awkward, 30
Ayarbe, Heidi, 40

Bacigalupi, Paolo, 143, 177
Backman, Frederick, 17
Bad Decisions Playlist, The, 16
Ballad: A Gathering of Faerie, 199
Band Together, 208
Baratz-Logsted, Lauren, 80
Bardugo, Leigh, 94, 152, 182–183, 200, 217
Barker, Michelle, 67
Barnhill, Kelly Regan, 193
Barter, Catherine, 119
Barthelmess, Nikki, 39
Bartimaeus Trilogy, 197
Batman: Nightwalker, 152
Battle for Skandia, The, 186
Battle of the Labyrinth, The, 212
Beartown, 17
Beastly, 214
Beastly Bones, 150
Beatty, Robert, 135
Beauty Queens, 115
Because You'll Never Meet Me, 163
Before the Devil Breaks You, 104
Beggar of Volubilis, The, 63
Behemoth, 169
Behind the Curtain, 98
Beka Cooper, 192
Bellaire, Jordie, 128
Belle Sauvage, La, 189
Belles, 194
Belles, The, 194
Bennett, Jenn, 68, 77
Benway, Robin, 2, 34, 114
Berquist, Emma, 129
Berry, Julie, 61, 68, 75
Bérubé, Amelinda, 130, 133
Betrayed, 137
Better Nate Than Ever, 19–21
Better Nate Than Ever, 19
Between Shades of Gray, 72
Beware the Kitten Holy, 208
Bick, Ilsa J., 143
Bird's Eye View, A, 208
Bitter Kingdom, The, 184
Bitterblue, 185
Bittersweet, 23

Black, Holly, 94, 126, 136, 154, 193–194, 197–198, 200–201
Black Heart, 194
Black Light Express, 158
Blackbringer, 199
Blake, Kendare, 130, 154, 183
Bliss, Bryan, 11
Block, Francesca Lia, 94
Blood of Olympus, The, 213
Blood Promise, 138
Blood Water Paint, 64
Bloodhound, 192
Bloody Jack: Being an Account of the Curious Adventures of Mary "Jacky" Faber, Ship's Boy, 65
Bloody Mary, 131
Bloom, 22, 93
Blue Lily, Lily Blue, 205
Bluff, 21
Blume, Judy, 52
Blundell, Judy, 53,
Bohjalian, Chris, 40
Bolden, Tonya, 49, 53
Bone Gap, 36, 207
Bone Magician, The, 147
Boneless Mercies, The, 213
Book of Dust, 189–190
Book of Dust: La Belle Sauvage, The, 189
Book of Dust: The Secret Commonwealth, The, 190
Book of Shadows, 152
Book Thief, The, 74
Booked, 17
Books of Ember, 177–178
Books of Faerie, 199
Booth, Coe, 41
Boston Jacky: Being an Account of the Further Adventures of Jacky Faber, Taking Care of Business, 66
Bowman, Erin, 148
Boy at the Top of the Mountain, The, 68
Boy in the Striped Pajamas, The, 68
Boy Meets Boy, 92
Boyne, John, 68
Bradley, Alan, 103–104
Bradley, Kimberly Brubaker, 69
Brallier, Max, 133
Brandon, James, 53
Brashares, Ann, 88
Brave, 30
Bray, Libba, 94, 104, 115
Breaking Dawn, 139

Breathe, Annie, Breathe, 82
Breitweiser, Elizabeth, 70, 75
Brides of Rollrock Island, The, 147
Bridge of Clay, 35, 37
Bright We Burn, 191
Brightly Burning, 173
Brown, Jaye Robin, 8
Brown, Peter, 165
Buffy the Vampire Slayer: Vol. 1: High School Is Hell, 128
Bull, 210
Bunheads, 20
Burkhart, Jessica, 80
Burn Baby Burn, 56
Burned, 137
Burning Bridge, The, 185
Burning Maze, The, 213
Button War, The, 67
By Night, 165, 181

Cai, Rovina, 128
Calpurnia Tate, 50
Can't Get There from Here, 41
Capetta, Amy Rose, 156
Capó Crucet, Jennine, 5
Capturing the Devil, 64
Cardturner, 21
Carlton, Susan Kaplan, 53
Carmilla, 142
Carroll, Emily, 13, 126
Carson, Rae, 94, 184
Carter, Ally, 114–115, 119–120
Case for Jamie, The, 98
Case of the Bizarre Bouquets, The, 106
Case of the Cryptic Crinoline, The, 106
Case of the Gypsy Goodbye, The, 106
Case of the Left-Handed Lady, The, 106
Case of the Missing Marquess, The, 106
Case of the Peculiar Pink Fan, The, 106
Cashore, Kristin, 184–185
Cast, Kristin, 136–138
Cast, P. C., 136–138
Catching Fire, 173
Catching Jordan, 82
Catwoman: Soulstealer, 152
Cavallaro, Brittany, 98
Center of the Universe, The, 36
Chains, 48
Changes in Latitudes, 36
Chaos Walking, 174–175
Character, Driven, 27
Charaipotra, Sona, 19

Charioteer of Delphi, The, 63
Charlotte Holmes Mysteries, The, 98
Charm and Strange, 109
Chayil, Elishes, 11
Cheerleaders, The, 103
Children of Blood and Bone, 182
Children of Virtue and Vengeance, 182
Chmakova, Svetlana, 30
Cho, Kat, 210
Chokshi, Roshani, 201, 210
Chopsticks, 107
Chosen, 137
Chu, Wesley, 203
Chupeco, Rin, 130
Cinder, 171
Cirque du Freak, 140–141, 144
Cirque du Freak: A Living Nightmare, 140
City of Ashes, 203
City of Bones, 202
City of Ember, The, 178
City of Fallen Angels, 202–203
City of Glass, 202–203
City of Heavenly Fire, 202–203
City of Lost Souls, 202–203
Clare, Cassandra, 94, 201–203
Clash of the Demons, 146
Clayton, Dhonielle, 19, 94, 194
Climbing the Stairs, 73
Cline, Ernest, 164
Clockwork Angel, 202
Clockwork Prince, 202
Clockwork Princess, 202
Close Your Eyes, Hold Hands, 40
Coben, Harlan, 98–99
Code Name Verity, 73, 74, 123
Cohn, Rachel, 15
Colbert, Brandy, 94
Cold Legacy, A, 135
Coldest Girl in Coldtown, The, 136
Collectors, The, 209
Collectors Duology, 209
Collins, Suzanne, 172–173
Colossus of Rhodes, The, 62
Come Juneteenth, 51
Coming Up for Air, 83
Complicit, 109
Compromised, 40
Condie, Ally, 167
Confusion of Princes, A, 157
Conquerors Saga, 191
Contagion, 148
Contagion, 125, 148

Conviction, 3
Cook, Eileen, 107
Copper Sun, 50
Corral, Rodrigo, 107
Court of Frost and Starlight, A, 199
Court of Mist and Fury, A, 198
Court of Thorns and Roses, A, 198
Court of Thorns and Roses, A, 198–199
Court of Wings and Ruin, A, 198
Cracker! The Best Dog in Vietnam, 55
Creeping Shadow, The, 151
Cress, 171
Cribbs, Gia, 107
Crispin, 61
Crispin: At the Edge of the World, 61
Crispin: The Cross of Lead, 61
Crispin: The End of Time, 61
Crocodile Tears, 121
Crooked Kingdom, 200
Cross, Julie, 78
Cross Fire, 171
Cross My Heart and Hope to Spy, 119
Cross of Lead, The, 61
Crossan, Sarah, 34
Crossing Ebenezer Creek, 49
Crossing the Line, 122
Crossover, The, 17
Crowder, Melanie, 53, 69
Crowley, Cath, 14, 42, 46
Crown of Embers, The, 184
Cruel Prince, The, 198
Crush, 30
Crutcher, Chris, 39
Crying Laughing, 4
Cupala, Holly, 41
Curious World of Calpurnia Tate, 50
Curse of the Bane, 146
*Curse of the Blue Tattoo: Being an Account
    of the Misadventures of Jacky Faber,
    Midshipman and Fine Lady*, 65
Curse So Dark and Lovely, A, 215
Curse Workers, 193–194

Dairy Queen, 18
Dairy Queen, 18
Darius the Great Is Not Okay, 6
Dark Artifices, 201–202
Dark beneath the Ice, 130
Dark Descent of Elizabeth Frankenstein, The,
    135
Dark Prophecy, The, 213
Darkling Plain, A, 181

Dashner, James, xii
Daughter of the Lioness, 192–193
Davis, Jenny Fran, 24
Day of Tears: A Novel in Disguise, 51
Dayton, Arwen Elys, 159
de la Cruz, Melissa, 49
de la Peña, Matt, 94
Dead and the Gone, The, 180
Deadlock, 123
Deadly Curious, 60
Dear Martin, 7
Dear Rachel Maddow, 22
Deaver, Mason, 8
Deering, Rachel, 209–210
Defender, 101
Defending Taylor, 83
Delaney, Joseph, 145–147
Dellaira, Ava, 34, 42
Descendant of the Crane, 187
Descent, 116
Dessen, Sarah, 2, 24, 34, 40
Destined, 137
Detective Comics: 80 Years of Batman, 152
Devlin, Calla, 54
Devoted, 13
Devouring Gray, The, 126
DeWoskin, Rachel, 69
Diabolic, The, 159
Diabolic, The, 159–160
Diamond of Darkhold, The, 178
Diary of a Haunting, 151
Diary of a Haunting, 151–152
Dill, Julie, 21
Dimaline, Cherie, 173
Dire King, The, 150
Disappearance of Sloane Sullivan, 107
Disappeared, 112
*Disreputable History of Frankie Landau-
    Banks, The*, 3
Diviners, The, 104
Diviners Series, The, 104
Doctorow, Cory, 21, 155
Does My Head Look Big in This?, 11
Dogs of War, 55
Doktorski, Jennifer, 78
Doll, Jen, 30
Doll Bones, 126, 154
Dolphins of Laruentum, The, 62
Donne, Alexa, 173
Donnelly, Jennifer, 54, 104, 123, 214
Donovan, Eryk, 145, 154

Don't Breathe a Word, 41
Don't Judge a Girl by Her Cover, 119
Dowd, Siobhan, 99
Down among the Sticks and Bones, 128
Down the Rabbit Hole, 97
Downstairs Girl, The, 50
Dragon Pearl, 156
Drama, 20
Dramarama, 20
Draper, Sharon, 50
Dread Nation, 143, 154
Dreadnought, 122
Dream Thieves, The, 205
Dreamway, 217
Duchessina: A Novel of Catherine de' Medici, 64
Ducie, Joe, 173
D.U.F.F.: Designated Ugly Fat Friend, The, 89
Dugan, Jennifer, 92
Dumplin', 4, 89
Duncan, Emily A., 185
DuPrau, Jeanne, 177–178

Eagle Strike, 121
Earth Flight, 174
Earth Girl, 174
Earth Girl, 174
Earth Star, 174
Earth, My Butt, and Other Big Round Things, The, 27
Echo Falls Mysteries, The, 97–98
Eclipse, 139
Edwards, Janet, 174
Eleanor and Park, 15
Elephant Run, 72
Elliott, David, 210
Ember in the Ashes, 190
Ember in the Ashes, 190
Emezi, Akwaeke, 133
Emperor of Any Place, The, 60
Emperor of Nihon-Ja, The, 186
Empirium Trilogy, 188–189
Empress, The, 160
Empty Grave, The, 151
End of Time, The, 61
Enemies of Jupiter, The, 62
Ennis, Garth, 70, 75
Enola Holmes Mysteries, 106
Epitaph Road, 179
Epting, Steve, 70, 75
Erak's Ransom, 186
Escape Velocity, 122

Escaping from Houdini, 64
Ever, 211
Everlasting Rose, The, 194
Every Breath, 101
Every Move, 101
Every Series, The, 101
Every Word, 101
Everything Beautiful Is Not Ruined, 37
Everything But the Truth, 80
Everything, Everything, 45
Everything Must Go, 24
Everything You Want Me to Be, 111
Evil Star, 127
Evolution of Calpurnia Tate, The, 50
Exit, Pursued by a Bear, 31, 46
Exo, 170–171
Exo, 171
Extraordinary Means, 45
Extras, 177

Faeries of Dreamdark, 199
Falkner, Brian, 169
Fama, Elizabeth, 115, 123, 134
Fame, Fate, and the First Kiss, 87
Fang, 161
Fangirl, 14, 46
Far from the Tree, 34
Fat Kid Rules the World, 15
Fault in Our Stars, The, 43
Fear, 179
Federle, Tim, 19–20, 94
Feinstein, John, 17
Field Notes on Love, 85
Final Fall, 102
Final Four, 19
Final Warning, The, 161
Finding Felicity, 26
Finnegan, Amy, 80
Fiore, Kelly, 23. *See also* Stultz, Kelly Fiore
Fire, 184
Fire and Thorns, 184
Firebrand, 168
Firefight, 154
First Frost, 33
First Light, 167
First Part Last, The, 37, 38
Five Dark Fates, 183
Five, Six, Seven, Nate!, 20
Flack, Sophie, 20
Flanagan, John, 185–186
Flavia de Luce Mysteries, 103–104
Flinn, Alex, 30, 214

Flores-Scott, Patrick, 35
Flygirl, 59
Folk of the Air, 197–198
Fool Me Twice, 81
Forge, 48
Forman, Gayle, 42, 78–79, 94, 95
47, 51
Found, 99
Fountains of Silence, The, 47, 72, 75
Fox Forever, The, 162
Fox Inheritance, The, 162
Foxlee, Karen, 54
Frankly in Love, 7
Fredericks, Mariah, 99
Freitas, Donna, 43
Friend, Natasha, 43
Friends with Boys, 35
Friendship to the Max, 208
Friesner, Esther, 211
From Twinkle, with Love, 84
From You to Me, 44
Front and Center, 18
Front Desk, 7
Frost, Helen, 41
Frostbite, 138
Fugitive from Corinth, The, 62
Furyborn, 188

Gabi, a Girl in Pieces, 6
Gaiman, Neil, 131, 166, 203
Gallagher Girls Series, 119–120
Gamer's Guide to Getting the Girl, 118
Ganucheau, Savanna, 93
Garretson, Dee, 70
Gatekeepers, The, 127
Gemina, 157
Gena/Finn, 3
Gentleman's Guide to Vice and Virtue, The, 63
Genuine Fraud, 109
Georgia Peaches and Other Forbidden Fruit, 8
Ghost, 18
Ghostly Echoes, 150
Ghosts of the Shadow Market, 203
Gidwitz, Adam, 186
Gilbert, Kelly Loy, 3, 5
Gilded Wolves, The, 201
Gilded Wolves, The, 201
Girard, M.-E., 9
Girl from Everywhere, The, 216
Girl from Everywhere, The, 216
Girl from the Well, The, 130–132
Girl from the Well, The, 130

Girl Gone Viral, 163
Girl I Used to Be, The, 108
Girl in the Blue Coat, 70
Girl in the Park, The, 99
Girl Is Murder, The, 105
Girl Is Trouble, The, 105
Girl Mans Up, 9
Girl of Fire and Thorns, The, 184
Girl of Nightmares, 130
Girl Underwater, 116, 124
Girl Who Drank the Moon, The, 193
Girl Who Was Supposed to Die, The, 108
Girls of July, 30
Gladiators from Capua, The, 62
God Box, The, 13
Godless, 11
Going, K. L., 15
Golden Tresses of the Dead, The, 104
Golem's Eye, The, 197
Goliath, 169
Gone, 178
Gone, 178–179
Goo, Maureen, 24, 79
Gospel of Winter, The, 56
Graceling, 184
Graceling, 184–185
Graffiti Moon, 14, 46
Grandmaster, 21
Grant, Michael, 178–179
Grasshopper Jungle, 181
Gratz, Alan, 61, 70
Grave's a Fine and Private Place, The, 104
Graveyard Book, 131
Gravity of Us, The, 22
Great Alone, The, 115
Green, John, 11, 24, 43–44, 94, 99
Greenland, Shannon, 120
Gregorio, I. W., 9
Grisha Trilogy, 182–183
Guardian, 168

Haddix, Margaret Peterson, 216
Hahn, Mary Downing, 131
Haines, Kathryn Miller, 105
Hale, Shannon, 214
Halpern, Sue, 31
Halt's Peril, 186
Han, Jenny, xii, 88, 94
Hand on the Wall, The, 100
Hannah, Kristin, 115
Harbor Me, 33
Harlem Summer, 56

Harry Potter, xiv, 139, 181, 193, 195–196
Harry Potter and the Chamber of Secrets, 196
Harry Potter and the Deathly Hallows,
    196
Harry Potter and the Goblet of Fire, 196
Harry Potter and the Half-Blood Prince, 196
Harry Potter and the Order of the Phoenix,
    196
*Harry Potter and the Prisoner of
    Azkaban*, 196
Harry Potter and the Sorcerer's Stone,
    196
Hartley, A. J., 168
Hartman, Rachel, 187, 191
Hartnett, Sonya, 70
*Hat Full of Sky: The Continuing Adventures
    of Tiffany Aching and the Wee Free
    Men, A*, 195
Hate U Give, The, 7, 133
Hattie Big Sky, 56
Haunting of Gabriel Ashe, The, 134
Hautman, Pete, 11, 25
Hawkins, Rachel, 79, 92
He, Joan, 187
Hearts Made for Breaking, 83
Heath, Jack, 108
Heathen, 209–210
Heathen: Volume 1, 209
Heathen: Volume 2, 210
Heavy Metal and You, 15
Heilig, Heidi, 216
Heir and the Spare, The, 77
Heist Society, 114
Heist Society Series, 114
Helen of Troy Duet, 211
Helgeson, Kat, 3
Hello, Goodbye, and Everything in Between,
    85
Henry, April, 108
Henry, Katie, 12, 46
Hepler, Heather, 44
Her Dark Curiosity, 134
Her Royal Highness, 79, 92
Here There Are Monsters, 133
Heretics Anonymous, 12, 46
Herman, Chrstine Lynn, 126
Hernandez, Carlos, 166
Heroes of Olympus, The, 212–213
Hesse, Monica, 54, 70
Hicks, Faith Erin, 35
Hidden, 138
Hidden Oracle, The, 213

Higgins, F. E., 147
High School Is Hell, 128
Highly Illogical Behavior, 32
Hinds, Gareth, 211
Hinton, S. E., 35,
Hired Girl, The, 58
Hitchcock, Bonnie-Sue, 55
*H.I.V.E.: Higher Institute of Villainous
    Education*, 122
H.I.V.E. Series, 122–123
Hold Me Closer, Necromancer, 204
Holgate, Douglas, 133
Hollow Boy, The, 151
Holt, K. A., 44
Homeland, 155
Horowitz, Anthony, 118, 120–121, 127
Host, The, 172
Hostage Three, 117
Hot Dog Girl, 92
House of Hades, The, 213
House of Night, 136–138
House of One Thousand Eyes, The, 67
How My Summer Went up in Flames, 78
How to Disappear, 112
How to Save a Life, 39
How We Roll, 43
*How Zoe Made Her Dreams (Mostly) Come
    True*, 90
Hubbard, Jenny, 31
Hubbard, Mandy, 80–81
Hullmetal Girls, 158
Hundred Oaks Series, The, 82–83
Hunger, 178
Hunger Games, 172–173
Hunger Games, The, 154, 172
Hungry City Chronicles, 180–181
Hunted, 137
Hunters of the Dusk, 141
Hunting Prince Dracula, 64
Hush, 11
Hutchinson, Shaun David, 170

I Am Alice, 147
I Am Grimalkin, 147
I Am Half-Sick of Shadows, 103
I Am Not Your Perfect Mexican Daughter, 6
I Am Still Alive, 117
I Am the Messenger, 29
I, Claudia, 110
I Hunt Killers, 110
I Shall Wear Midnight, 195
I Wish You All the Best, 8

I Woke Up Dead at the Mall, 1, 36
Icebound Land, The, 185
I'd Tell You I Love You, But Then I'd Have to Kill You, 119
If I Stay, 42
If Only . . . Series, 80–81
Iliad, The, 37, 211
I'll Give You the Sun, 14
Illuminae, 157
Illuminae Files, The, 156–157
Immunity, 148
In Darkness, 117
In Real Life, 21
In Search of Us, 34
In the Belly of the Bloodhound: Being an Account of a Particularly Peculiar Adventure in the Life of Jacky Faber, 65
In the Neighborhood of True, 53
In the Shadow of Blackbirds, 132
In the Unlikely Event, 52
Infernal Devices, 202
Infernal Engines, 181
Inquisitor's Tale, Or, The Three Magical Children and Their Holy Dog, The, 186
Internment, 165
InterWorld, 166
Into the Dark, 98
Invisible War: A World War I Tale of Two Scales, 74
Ireland, Justina, 143, 148, 154
Iron River, 52
Ironside: A Modern Faery's Tale, 201
Isla and the Happily Every After, 89
Iturbe, Antonio, 71

Jackaby, 150
Jackaby, 150
Jackalope Springs Eternal, 209
Jackson, Tiffany, 100
Jamieson, Victoria, 18, 35
Jarzab, Anna, 12, 46, 100
Jasper Jones, 106
Jenna Fox Chronicles, 161–162
Jesse's Girl, 82
Johnson, Angela, 37, 38
Johnson, Maureen, 25, 94, 100, 124
Johnston, E. K., 31, 46, 94, 187, 192
Johnston, Tim, 116
Just Like the Movies, 81
Just One Day, 78, 95
Just One Year, 79

Kaaberbøl, Lene, 188
Kade, Stacey, 26
Kadohata, Cynthia, 55
Kalmar, Daphne, 55
Kaplan, Ariel, 26
Kaufman, Amie, 155
Kawahara, Reki, 164
Keenan, Sheila, 55
Keeping Corner, 72
Keesha's House, 41
Keil, Michelle Ruiz, 206
Kells, Claire, 116, 124
Kelly, Jacqueline, 50
Kemmerer, Brigid, 215
Kenneally, Miranda, 82
Kennedy, Katie, 26
Kephart, Beth, 116
Keplinger, Kody, 89
Khorram, Adib, 6
Kiely, Brendan, 56
Killeen, Matt, 71
Killers of the Dawn, 141
Kincaid, S. J., 159–160
King, A. S., 9, 31
King, Stephen, 109
King of Crows, The, 104
King of Scars, 183
Kingdom on the Waves, The, 49
Kings of Clonmel, 186
Kingsbane, 189
Kira-Kira, 55
Kisner, Adrienne, 22
Kissing in America, 28
Klages, Ellen, 18
Klass, David, 21
Klein, Jen, 83
Knife of Never Letting Go, The, 174
Konigsberg, Bill, 10
Kraus, Daniel, 127
Kristoff, Jay, 155
Krovatin, Christopher, 15
Kuehn, Stephanie, 109, 116
Kurtagich, Dawn, 128

LaCour, Nina, 26, 94
Lady Midnight, 201
Lady Rogue, The, 68
Lady's Guide to Petticoats and Piracy, The, 63
Lair of Dreams, 104
Lake, Nick, 117
Lake of Souls, The, 141
Lament: The Faerie Queen's Deception, 199

Lanagan, Margo, 147
Landers, Melissa, 156, 181
Landscape with Invisible Hand, 170
Lara Jean Series, The, 88
Larsen, Christine, 165, 181
Larson, Kirby, 56
Last Days, The, 142
Last Kids on Earth, The, 133
Last of August, The, 98
Last Olympian, The, 212
Last Sacrifice, 139
Last Survivors/Moon Crash/Life as We
     Knew It, 179–180
Last Voyage of Poe Blythe, 167
Laura Dean Keeps Breaking Up with Me, 32
Lauren, Christina, 92
Lawrence, Caroline, 62–63
Leah on the Offbeat, 15
Leake, Jessica, 192
Learning to Swear in America, 26
Lee, Fonda, 170–171
Lee, Mackenzie, 63
Lee, Stacey, 50, 56
Lee, Yoon Ha, 156
Legacy of Orïsa, 182
Legrand, Claire, 149, 188–189
Lenny's Book of Everything, 54
Leno, Katrina, 216
Lester, Julius, 51
Let It Snow: Three Holiday Romances, 94
Leviathan, 169
Leviathan Trilogy, 169
Levine, Gail Carson, 211
Levithan, David, 10, 15, 92, 94, 131
Librarian of Auschwitz, The, 71
Lies, 179
Life As We Knew It, 180
Liggett, Kim, 149
Light, 179
Lightning Thief, The, 212
Like a Love Story, 57
Lindner, April, 83
Little Brother, 155
Little Brother, 155
Lizzie Bright and the Buckminster Boy, 58
Lock and Key, 40
Lock and Mori, 102
Lock and Mori Mysteries, The, 102
Lockhart, E., 3, 20, 109–110
Lockwood & Co., 150–151
Lola and the Boy Next Door, 90
London Eye Mystery, The, 99

Long Way Down, 28, 132
Longo, Jennifer, 32
Looking for Alaska, 25
Lord of Shadows, 202
Lord of the Shadows, 141
Losers Bracket, 39
Lost Girl, The, 205
Lost Hero, The, 212
Lost Stories, The, 186
Love & War, 49
Love à la Mode, 23
Love and Gelato, 86
Love Letters to the Dead, 42
Love, Lucy, 83
Loveboat, Taipei, 87
Lovely War, 68, 75
Lu, Marie, 152, 164, 189
Lubar, David, 27
Lucy Variations, The, 16
Lumberjanes, 207–209, 217
Lumberjanes Vol. 1: Beware the Kitten Holy,
     208
Lumberjanes Vol. 10: Parents' Day, 208
Lumberjanes Vol. 11: Time after Crime, 209
*Lumberjanes Vol. 12: Jackalope Springs
     Eternal,* 209
Lumberjanes Vol. 2: Friendship to the Max,
     208
Lumberjanes Vol. 3: A Terrible Plan, 208
Lumberjanes Vol. 4: Out of Time, 208
Lumberjanes Vol. 5: Band Together, 208
Lumberjanes Vol. 6: Sink or Swim, 208
Lumberjanes Vol. 7: A Bird's Eye View, 208
Lumberjanes Vol. 8: Stone Cold, 208
Lumberjanes Vol. 9: On a Roll, 208
Lunar Chronicles, 171–172
Lyga, Barry, 110

Maas, Sarah J., 152, 198–199
Mackler, Carolyn, 27
Made You Up, 45
Madison, Bennett, 206
Madman's Daughter, The, 134
Madman's Daughter Trilogy, 134–135
Mafi, Tahereh, 12
Maisie Dobbs, 106
Make Your Home among Strangers, 5
Malone, Jen, 36
Man from Pomegranate Street, The, 63
Maniscalco, Kerri, 63, 75
Mapping the Bones, 74
Marchetta, Melina, 28

Mark of Athena, The, 213
Mark of the Golden Dragon: Being an Account of the Further Adventures of Jacky Faber, Jewel of the East, Vexation of the West, and Pearl of the South China Sea, The, 66
Marked, 136
Marly's Ghost, 131
Marney, Ellie, 101
Marrow Thieves, The, 173
Marshall, Kate Allie, 117
Martian, The, 118, 167, 181
MARY: The Summoning, 132
MARY: Unleashed, 132
Mastiff, 192
Mathieu, Jennifer, 13
Matson, Morgan, 84, 95
Max, 161
Maximum Ride, 160–161
Maximum Ride Forever, 161
Maximum Ride: Saving the World and Other Extreme Sports, 161
Maximum Ride: School's Out—Forever, 160
Maximum Ride: The Angel Experiment, 160
Mbalia, Kwame, 211
McBride, Lish, 204
McCarthy, Cori, 156
McCaughrean, Catherine, 117
McCoy, Mary, 110
McCreight, Kimberly, 110
McCullough, Joy, 64
McDonald, Christina, 111
McGuire, Seanan, 128
McLemore, Anna-Marie, 206
McNamee, Graham, 101, 111, 124
McNaughton, Danielle, 133
Mead, Richelle, 138–139
Medina, Meg, 56
Meet Cute: Some People Are Destined to Meet, 94
Mejia, Mindy, 111
Memetic, 145, 154
Menon, Sandhya, 84, 95
Merciful Crow, The, 194
Meyer, Carolyn, 64
Meyer, L. A., 65–66
Meyer, Marissa, 153, 171–172
Meyer, Stephenie, 139
Mickey Bolitar Series, The, 98–99
Midnight Star, The, 189
Miles Morales, 153
Miller, Sarah, 51

Mind Games, 102
Miss Spitfire: Reaching Helen Keller, 51
Missing, Presumed Dead, 129
Mississippi Jack: Being an Account of the Further Waterborne Adventures of Jacky Faber, Midshipman, Fine Lady, and Lily of the West, 65
Mitchell, Saundra, 66
Mockingjay, 173
Modern Faerie, 200–201
Monahan, Hillary, 131–132
Monday's Not Coming, 100
Money Boy, 42
Money Run, 108
Monster, 179
Monsters, 143
Monsters of Men, 175
Monsters of Verity, 204
Monstrous Beauty, 134
Montague Siblings, 63
Moon Crash, 179–180
Mora, Dan, 128
More Happy Than Not, 162
Morelli, Jack, 142, 154
Morpurgo, Michael, 71
Mortal Coil, 162
Mortal Engines, 180
Mortal Instruments, 201–203
Moskowitz, Hannah, 3, 215
Mosley, Walter, 51
Mr. Mercedes, 109
Murdock, Catherine Gilbert, 18
Murphy, Julie, 4, 89, 94
Muse of Nightmares, 191
My Bonny Light Horseman: Being an Account of the Further Adventures of Jacky Faber, in Love and War, 65
My True Love Gave to Me: Twelve Holiday Stories, 94
Myers, Walter Dean, 56
Myracle, Lauren, 94

Nate Expectations, 20
Nazemian, Abdi, 57
Neanderthal Opens the Door to the Universe, 4
Necromancer, 204
Necromancing the Stone, 204
Necropolis, 127
Nelson, Jandy, 14
Nemesis, The, 160
Ness, Patrick, 174–175

Nest, The, 149
Never Say Die, 121
Nevermore, 161
New Moon, 139
Night Gardener, The, 129
Night of the Soul Stealer, 146
Night Olivia Fell, 110–111
Nightrise, 127
Nightshade, 121
Nix, Garth, 94, 157
No Parking at the End Times, 11
Nobody's Princess, 211
Nobody's Prize, 211
Nolan, Han, 38
None of the Above, 8–9
North of Happy, 22
Northern Light, A, 54, 104, 123
Norton, Preston, 4
Not If I Save You First, 114
Not in the Script, 80
Notes from My Captivity, 117
Novik, Naomi, 215
Now I Rise, 191

O'Connor, Tara, 149
Oblivion, 127
Obsidio, 157
Ockler, Sarah, 23
Odd One Out, 94
Odyssey, The, 37, 211
Off Season, The, 18
Okay for Now, 58, 75
Okorafor, Nnedi, 216–217
Oliver, Lauren, 160
On a Roll, 208
On a Sunbeam, 159, 181
On the Come Up, 16
On the Fence, 87
Once & Future, 156
Once and for All, 24
One, 34
One Dark Throne, 183
Only the Good Spy Young, 120
Openly Straight, 10
Oppel, Kenneth, 149, 168
Opposite of Hallelujah, The, 12, 46
Or Give Me Death, 51
Orbiting Jupiter, 38
Orphan Monster Spy, 71
Ostow, Micol, 128
Our Dark Duet, 204
Out of Darkness, 57

Out of Left Field, 18
Out of Salem, 140
Out of Sight, Out of Time, 120
Out of the Easy, 58, 105
Out of Time, 208
Outrun the Moon, 56
Outsiders, The, 35
Overlord Protocol, The, 122
Owen, Margaret, 194
Owens, Delia, 105
Owls Have Come to Take Us Away, The, 172

P.S. I Still Love You, 88
Pandava, 210
Panetta, Kevin, 93
Papademetriou, Lisa, 217
Paper Towns, 99
Parents' Day, 208
Park, Kathy, 117
Parker, Natalie C., 94
Pasadena, 112
Passion of Dolssa, The, 61
Patel, Sonia, 57
Patneaude, David, 179
Patterson, James, 160–161
Paulsen, Gary, 170
Pearl Thief, The, 74
Pearson, Mary E., 161–162
Peeps, 142
Peeps, 142
Peet, Mal, 71
People of Sparks, The, 178
Percy Jackson and the Olympians, 181, 212
Pérez, Ashley Hope, 57
Perfect Scoundrels, 114
Perini, Mark, 78
Perkins, Mitali, 57
Perkins, Stephanie, x, 89–90, 94
Pet, 133
Petty, Heather, 102
Pfeffer, Susan Beth, 179–180
Picture Us in the Light, 5
Pierce, Tamora, 192–193
Piper's Son, The, 28
Pirates of Pompeii, The, 62
Pitch Dark, 125, 133
Pizza, Love, and Other Stuff That Made Me Famous, 23
Plague, 179
Please Ignore Vera Dietz, 31
Plozza, Shivaun, 44
Plus One, 115, 123

Poblocki, Dan, 134
Podos, Rebecca, 207
Poet X, The, 1
Point Blank, 120
Pon, Cindy, 166–167
Possession, 151
Pox Party, The, 48
Pratchett, Terry, 195, 217
Predator's Gold, 180
Pregnant Pause, 38
Pretties, 176
Priest, Cherie, 149
Prince in Disguise, 86
Princess Academy, 214
Private Peaceful, 71
Prodigy, The, 17
Projekt 1065, 70
Prophet from Ephesus, The, 63
Prophet of Yonwood, The, 177
Ptolemy's Gate, 197
Puddin', 4
Pullman, Philip, 189–190, 217

Queen of Air and Darkness, 202
Queen of Nothing, The, 198
Question of Holmes, A, 98
Quick, Matthew, 41
Quiet You Carry, The, 39
Quintero, Isabel, 6

Rabb, Margo, 28
Race to the Sun, 213
Racing Savannah, 82
Rae, Kristin, 81
Rage of the Fallen, 146
Railhead, 157
Railhead, 157–158
Ranger's Apprentice, 185–186
Rani Patel in Full Effect, 57
*Rapture of the Deep: Being an Account of the
    Further Adventures of Jacky Faber,
    Soldier, Sailor, Mermaid, Spy*, 66
Raven Boys, The, 205
Raven Cycle, 33, 204–205
Raven King, The, 205
Raven's Gate, 127
Raven's Tale, The, 135
Ready Player One, 164
Reaper at the Gates, A, 190
Rebound, 17
Reckoners Trilogy, 153–154
Reconstructing Amelia, 110–111

Red Girl, Blue Boy, 80
Red Glove, 194
Red Herring Without Mustard, A, 103
Red Scrolls of Magic, The, 203
Redeemed, 138
Redshirts: A Novel with Three Codas, 158
Reeve, Philip, 157–158, 180–181
Renegades, 153
Renegades, 153
Replica, 160
Replica, 160
Rest of the Story, The, 34
Revealed, 138
Revenge of the Witch, 146
Revolver, 112
Reynolds, Jason, xiii, 18, 28, 132, 153
Rig, The, 173
Rinaldi, Ann, 51
Ringer, 160
Riordan, Rick, 182, 210, 212–213
Rise of the Huntress, 146
Rithmatist, The, 196–197
Rithmatist, The, 197
Ritter, William, 150
Riverland, 217
Road Tripped, 25
Roanhorse, Rebecca, 213
Rogers, Meghan, 122
Rogue, 123
Roller Girl, 18
Roman Mysteries, The, 62
Rose Society, The, 189
Rose Under Fire, 73
Rosenfield, Kat, 111
Roth, Veronica, 94
Rotters, 127
Rowell, Rainbow, 14–15, 46, 94
Rowling, J. K., 195–196
Royals, 79
Rubens, Michael, 16
Rubin, Lance, 4
Ruby, Laura, 36, 207
Ruin and Rising, 183
Ruins of Gorlan, The, 185
Rules of Survival, 113
Run, Hide, Fight Back, 108
Ruse, 167
Russian Roulette: The Story of an Assassin,
    121

Sachar, Louis, 21
Sacrifice Box, 150

Sadie, 102, 124
Saenz, Benjamin Alire, 10
Safi, Aminah Mae, 93
Saints and Misfits, 2
Sal & Gabi Break the Universe, 166
Sales, Leila, 16
Salt to the Sea, 72
Samurai Shortstop, 61
Sanchez, Alex, 6, 13
Sánchez, Erika, 6
Sanderson, Brandon, 153–154, 158,
    196–197
Sara, 70, 75
Saving Francesca, 28
Saving Savannah, 53
Sawkill Girls, 149
Scalzi, John, 158, 162
Scarlet, 171
Scarrow, Kristine, 118
Schlitz, Laura Amy, 58
Schmidt, Gary D., 38, 58, 75
Schneider, Robin, 45
Schrieve, Hal, 140
Schumacher, Julie, 32
Schwab, Victoria, 204
Scorpia, 121
Scorpia Rising, 121
Scream Site, 148
Screaming Staircase, The, 150
Scribes from Alexandria, The, 63
Scythe, 175
Sea of Monsters, The, 212
Seconds Away, 99
Secret Commonwealth, The, 190
Secrets of Vesuvius, The, 62
Sedgwick, Marcus, 112
Seeds of America, 48
Seer of Shadows, The, 49, 129
Sepetys, Ruta, xii, 58, 72, 75, 105
September Girls, 206
Serafina, 135–136
Serafina and the Black Cloak, 136
Serafina and the Seven Stars, 136
Serafina and the Splintered Heart, 136
Serafina and the Twisted Staff, 136
Seraphina, 187
Seraphina, 187, 192
Serious Moonlight, 77
Serpent Gift, The, 188
17 & Gone, 113
Shabazz, Ilyasah, 59
Shade of the Moon, The, 180

Shadow, 143
Shadow and Bone, 182
Shadow Kiss, 138
Shadow Scale: A Companion to Seraphina,
    187, 192
Shamer Chronicles, 188
Shamer's Daughter, 188
Shamer's Signet, 188
Shamer's War, The, 188
Shan, Darren, 140–141, 144
Sheehan, Judy, 1, 36
Shelter, 99
Shepard, Sara, 94, 102
Shepherd, Gail, 59
Shepherd, Megan, 134
Sherwood, 67
Sheth, Kashmire, 72
Ship beyond Time, 216
Ship Breaker, 177
Shusterman, Neal, 175, 181
Siege and Storm, 183
Siege of Macindaw, 186
Silksinger, 199
Silvera, Adam, 91, 162
Silver Donkey, The, 70
Silvered Serpents, The, 201
Silvey, Craig, 106
Simon vs. the Homo Sapiens Agenda, 15, 91
Sink or Swim, 208
Sirens of Surrentum, The, 62
Sisterhood of the Traveling Pants, 31, 88
Six Feet Over It, 32
Six of Crows, 200, 217
Six of Crows, 200–201
Skeleton Key, 121
Skrutskie, Emily, 158
Sky beyond the Storm, A, 190
Skybreaker, 168
Skyward, 158
Skyward, 158
Slade, Arthur, 141
Slave Girl from Jerusalem, The, 63
Slayer, 129
Slither, 147
Small Spaces, 126
Smallwood, Greg, 142, 154
Smallwood, Megan, 142, 154
Smart Girls Get What They Want, 90
Smell of Other People's Houses, The, 55
Smith, Andrew, 181
Smith, Jennifer E., 4, 85–86, 95
Smith, Roland, 72

Smith, Ronald L., 172
Smith, Sherri L., 59, 112
Snakehead, 121
Snowhook, 118
Solo, 1
Solomon, Rachel Lynn, 5
Someday We Will Fly, 69
Somewhere Only We Knew, 79
Son of Neptune, The, 212
Song of the Lioness Quartet, 192
Sons of Destiny, 141
Sorcerer in the North, 186
Sorta Like a Rock Star, 41
Spalding, Amy, 93, 95
Speak: The Graphic Novel, 13
Speaking from among the Bones, 104
Specials, 177
Spinning Silver, 215
Spirit Bound, 139
Spook's Blood, The, 147
Spook's Revenge, The, 147
Spooner, Meagan, 67
Springer, Nancy, 106
Stalking Jack the Ripper, 63–64
Stalking Jack the Ripper, 64, 75
Stamper, Phil, 22
Stamper, Vesper, 73
Stampler, Helen Redisch, 112
Starclimber, 168
Starfall, 156
Starflight, 156
Starflight Duology, 156, 181
Starsight, 158
Station Zero, 158
Statistical Probability of Love at First Sight, The, 85, 95
Stead, Rebecca, 167, 170
Stealing Parker, 82
Steelheart, 153
Steeplejack, 168
Stepsister, 214
Stern, Sarah, 165, 181
Stevenson, Noelle, 207–209, 217
Stewart, Martin, 150
Stiefvater, Maggie, 33, 199, 204
Stitch in Time, A, 55
Stone, Nic, 7, 94
Stone Cold, 208
Stork, Francisco X., 112
Storm, Jo, 118
Storm of Wishes, A, 209
Stormbreaker, 118, 120

Story of Owen: Dragon Slayer of Trondheim, The, 192
Strange the Dreamer Duology, 190–191
Strange the Dreamer, 190
Strangers: Greystone Secrets #1, The, 216
Strasser, Todd, 41
Strohm, Stephanie Kate, 23
Strohmeyer, Sarah, 86, 90
Stronger, Faster, More Beautfiul, 159
Stroud, Jonathan, 150–151, 197
Study in Charlotte, A, 98
Stultz, Kelly Fiore, 81. *See also* Fiore, Kelly
Suffering, The, 131
Suma, Nova Ren, 113
Summer Days and Summer Nights: Twelve Love Stories, 94
Summer Hours at the Robbers Library, 31
Summer of Jordi Perez (and the Best Burger in Los Angeles), The, 93, 95
Summers, Courtney, 102, 124
Sun Is Also a Star, The, 8
Survival Kit, The, 43
Suvada, Emily, 162
Sweep: The Story of a Girl and Her Monsters, 60
Sweetness at the Bottom of the Pie, The, 103
Sword Art Online 1: Aincrad, 164

Tahir, Sabaa, 94, 190
Talley, Robin, 148
Tamaki, Mariko, 32
Tamar: A Novel of Espionage, Passion, and Betrayal, 71
Taste Test, 23
Taylor, Laini, 94, 190–191, 199
Teeth, 215
Teeth in the Mist, 128
Telgemeier, Raina, 20
Tell Me How You Really Feel, 93
Tell Me Something Real, 54
Tempted, 137
Terrible Plan, A, 208
Terrier, 192
Tess of the Road, 191
There's Something About Sweetie, 84, 95
These Shallow Graves, 105
Thieves of Ostia, The, 62
Things I Can't Forget, 82
13 Little Blue Envelopes, 25
This Cruel Design, 163
This Is Kind of an Epic Love Story, 91
This Is My Brain on Boys, 86

This Is the Story of You, 116
This Is What Happy Looks Like, 86
This Mortal Coil, 163
This Savage Song, 204
This Song Will Save Your Life, 16
Thomas, Angie, 7, 16
Thomas, Kara, 103
Thomas, Leah, 163
<u>Three Dark Crowns,</u> 183
Three Dark Crowns, 183
Three Sides of a Heart: Stories About Love Triangles, 94
Thrice the Brinded Cat Hath Mew'd, 104
Through the White Wood, 192
Through the Woods, 126
Thunderhead, 175
<u>Tiffany Aching,</u> 195, 217
Time after Crime, 209
Time Hackers, The, 170
Tin Heart, 44
Tiny Pretty Things, 19
Titan's Curse, The, 212
Tithe, 200
T-Minus, 120
To All the Boys I've Loved Before, 88
To See the Stars, 52
Toll, The, 175
Tomorrow Code, The, 169
Took, 131
Torch Against the Night, A, 190
Traitors' Gate, The, 61
<u>Trials of Apollo,</u> 213
Trials of Death, 140
Trickster's Choice, 193
Trickster's Queen, 193
Tristan Strong Punches a Hole in the Sky, 211
Tromly, Stephanie, 103
Trouble Is a Friend of Mine, 103
Troublemakers, 119
True History of Lyndie B. Hawkins, The, 59
Truly Devious, 100, 124
<u>Truly Devious Mysteries, The,</u> 100
Tucholke, April Genevieve, 213
Tunnels of Blood, 140
Turrisi, Kim, 142
Turtles All the Way Down, 43
Twelve Tasks of Flavia Gemina, The, 62
<u>Twilight,</u> xvi, 125, 139, 209
Twilight, 139
Two Boys Kissing, 10
Two Dark Reigns, 183
Tynion, James, 145, 154

Tyrant's Tomb, The, 213
Tyrell, 41

Uglies, 176
<u>Uglies Series,</u> 176–177
Unbearable Book Club for Unsinkable Girls, The, 32
Unclaimed Baggage, 30
Uncommon Criminals, 114
Under the Jolly Roger: Being an Account of the Further Nautical Adventures of Jacky Faber, 65
UnDivided, 176
Unfortunates, The, 149
Uninterrupted View of the Sky, An, 69
United We Spy, 120
Universe Is Expanding and So Am I, The, 27
Unlikely Friendship: A Novel of Mary Todd Lincoln and Elizabeth Keckley, An, 51
UnSouled, 176
Untamed, 137
UnWholly, 176
Unwind, 176
<u>Unwind Dysology,</u> 175–176
Ursu, Anne, 205

Valero-O'Connor, Rosemary, 32
Valiant: A Modern Tale of Faerie, 201
Vampire Academy, 138
<u>Vampire Academy,</u> 138–139
Vampire Mountain, 140
Vampire Prince, The, 140
Vampire's Assistant, The, 140
Vampironica, 142, 154
Van Draanen, Wendelin, 29
Vanishing Stair, The, 100
Venkatraman, Padma, 73
Verano, M., 151–152
Very Large Expanse of Sea, A, 12
Vicious Cure, A, 163
Villain, 179
Viva Jacquelina! Being an Account of the Further Adventures of Jacky Faber, Over the Hills and Far Away, 66
Volponi, Paul, 19
Voros, Ria, 36

Wake of the Lorelei Lee: Being an Account of the Further Adventures of Jacky Faber, on Her Way to Botany Bay, The, 66
Waking Forest, The, 214
Walden, Mark, 122–123

Walden, Tillie, 159, 181
Wang, Jen, 21
Want, 166
Want, 166–167
War Horse, 71
War I Finally Won, The, 69
War Outside, The, 54
War That Saved My Life, The, 69
War That Saved My Life, The, 69
Warcross, 164
Warcross, 164–165
Wardstone Chronicles, The, 145–147
Way You Make Me Feel, The, 22, 24
We Are Okay, 26
We Are the Ants, 170
We Regret to Inform You, 26
We Were Beautiful, 44
We Were Liars, 110
Wednesday Wars, The, 58
Wee Free Men: A Story of Discworld, The,
    195
Weed that Strings the Hangman's Bag, The,
    103
Wees, Alyssa, 214
Weight of Feathers, The, 206
Weight of Our Sky, The, 67
Wein, Elizabeth, 73, 123–124
Weir, Andy, 118, 167, 181
Welch, Jenna Evans, 86
Wen, Abigal Hing, 87
Werlin, Nancy, 113
West, Jacqueline, 209
West, Kasie, 87
Westerfeld, Scott, 142, 169, 176–177
Whaley, John Corey, 32
What Happened to Goodbye, 2
What I Saw and How I Lied, 53
What If It's Us, 91
What the Night Sings, 73
What You Always Wanted, 81
Whedon, Joss, 128
When Dimple Met Rishi, 84
When I Am Through with You, 116
When the Moon Was Ours, 206
When You Reach Me, 170
Where the Crawdads Sing, 105
Whispering Skull, The, 151
White Cat, 193
White Darkness, 117
White Rose, 74
White, Ellen Emerson, 19
White, Kiersten, 129, 135, 191

Wicked Fox, 210
Wicked King, The, 198
Wicked Saints, 185
Wild, Ailsa, et al., 74
Wild Bird, 29
Wild Hearts, 80
Wild Robot Escapes, The, 166
Wild Robot, 165–166
Wild Robot, The, 165
*Wild Rover No More: Being the Last Recorded
    Account of the Life & Times of Jacky
    Faber,* 66
Wildcard, 165
Wilde, Fran, 217
Williams, Kathryn, 23
Wilson, Kip, 74
Windfall, 4
Winspear, Jacqueline, 106
Winter, 172
Winters, Cat, 132, 135
Wintersmith, 195
Wise and the Wicked, The, 207
Wish You Were Italian, 81
Wishtree, 206
With the Fire on High, 22, 38, 46
Wolf Hollow, 59
Wolk, Lauren, 59
Wonder Woman: Warbringer, 152
Woodson, Jacqueline, 33
Words in Deep Blue, 42
World We Live In, The, 180
Wrath of the Bloodeye, 146
Wynne-Jones, Tim, 60

X, 59

Yang, Kelly, 7
Yee, Paul, 42
Yolen, Jane, 74
Yoon, David, 7
Yoon, Nicola, 8, 45
You before Anyone Else, 78
You Bring the Distant Near, 57
You Must Not Miss, 216
You Owe Me a Murder, 107
You'll Miss Me When I'm Gone, 5
Young Elites, 189
Young Elites, The, 189
Younge-Ullman, Danielle, 37

Zappia, Francesca, 45
Zarr, Sara, 16, 39

Zero Hour, 123
Ziggy, Stardust & Me, 53
Zoe's Tale, 162
Zom-B, 144
Zom-B, 144–145
Zom-B Angels, 144
Zom-B Baby, 144
Zom-B Bride, 145
Zom-B City, 144

Zom-B Clans, 145
Zom-B Family, 145
Zom-B Fugitive, 145
Zom-B Gladiator, 144
Zom-B Goddess, 145
Zom-B Mission, 145
Zom-B Underground, 144
Zombie Baseball Beatdown, 143
Zusak, Markus, 29, 37, 74

Subject Index

1600s, 64
1830s, 51
1872, 49, 129, 134
1880s, 106
1890s, 50, 61, 105
1900s, 53, 135
1910s, 132
1920s, 55, 56
1940s, 53, 59, 73
1950s, 52, 55, 59, 72, 103, 105, 170
1960s, 58
1970s, 53, 54, 55, 170
1980s, 10, 15, 59, 67, 82, 150, 164
1980s pop culture, 164
1990s, 7, 10, 57, 140

Abandonment, 40, 69, 170, 206
Abductions, 170, 172
Abortion, 31, 82
Abuse, 2, 11, 15, 38, 39, 49, 56, 57, 59, 68, 69,
        100, 102, 113, 144, 177, 206, 215, 216,
        217
Abusive parents, 58
Accidents, 6, 40, 43, 78, 111, 161
Action-adventure, 113–115, 185
Active shooter, 108
Activism, 21–22, 53, 74
ADHD, 91, 212
Adirondacks, 31, 54, 105
Adoption, 2, 34, 39, 127
Adventure, 29, 113–123, 127, 155–159, 168,
        185–186
Adventure therapy, 29
Advice columns, 50
African American folklore, 211
African Americans, 2, 7, 16, 17, 18, 19, 29, 41,
        48, 50, 51, 52, 58, 59, 94, 211
Agnostics, 12
Agoraphobia, 33
AIDS epidemic, 10, 57
Airplanes, 86. *See also* Pilots; Plane crashes
Alabama, 25, 30, 211
Alaska, 55, 115, 116, 117

Albigenses, 61
Albinism, 159, 216
Alcoholism, 59
Alex Award, 107, 118, 128, 164, 167, 215
Alien abductions, 172
Aliens, 133, 157, 158, 170–172
All American Girls Professional Baseball
        League, 18
Alopecia, 43
ALS, 4
Alternate dimension, 166, 208
Alternate formats, 51, 149, 151, 156, 163
Alternate history, 115, 143, 169
Alternative rock music, 15
Alternative schools, 24
Amazon rainforest, 123
American Revolution, 48
Amherst, Massachusetts, 31
Amnesia, 81, 108, 109, 161
Amputees, 43
Amsterdam, 43, 70, 79
Amusement parks, 90, 92
Amyotrophic lateral sclerosis, 4
Anagrams, 25
Anchorage, 180–181
Angels, 188, 202
Animal protagonist, 71
Animals, 50, 134, 166
Anime, 164
Antarctica, 117, 161
Anti-Semitism, 53, 54, 105
Anxiety, 26, 33, 44
Apocalypse, 142, 181. *See also*
        Postapocalypse
Apprentices, 49, 64, 128, 129, 146, 168, 175,
        180, 185, 187, 197
Archaeology, 174
Archiverse, 142
Arctic Circle, 112
Aristocracy, 70
Arkham Asylum, 152
Art, 6, 9, 13–14, 25, 27, 30, 38, 44, 58, 64, 81,
        98, 115

Art forgery, 98
Art theft, 114
Arthurian, 156
Artificial intelligence, 122–123
Asian Americans, 55. *See also* Chinese
        Americans; Korean Americans
Asian influence, 187
Assassins, 62, 108, 123, 180, 199
Assumed identity, 108
Asteroids, 26, 179
Astronauts, 22, 118, 167
Astrophysics, 37
Atheists, 12
Atlanta, 8, 15, 50, 53, 89, 210
Auschwitz, 68, 71
Australia, 11, 14, 28, 29, 37, 42, 44, 66, 101,
        106, 121
Austria, 114
Autism spectrum, 43, 90, 99
Autopsies, 64

Bakeries, 93
Baking, 23
Ballet, 18, 19, 20
Baltimore, 58, 93, 143
Barcelona, 90
Bards, 192
Baseball, 3, 18, 19, 58, 61, 82, 99, 143
Basketball, 17, 18, 19, 39, 101
Battle Royale, 172
BBYA, 3, 12, 15, 18, 25, 27, 29, 38, 41, 43,
        48–51, 53, 54, 56, 58, 59, 61, 65, 71, 72,
        73, 74, 92, 99, 105, 113, 117, 121, 131,
        134, 139, 142, 146, 155, 162, 168, 169,
        170, 172, 173, 174, 176, 177, 180, 181,
        184, 185, 192, 193, 195, 196, 197, 199,
        200, 201, 204, 212
Beauty, 176, 194
Beauty and the Beast, 198, 214, 215
Beauty pageants, 89, 115
Beowulf, 214
Bereavement, 117
Bergen-Belsen, 73
Berghof, 68
Berlin, Germany, 68, 70, 98
Best friends, 83, 90
Betrayal, 49, 54, 71
BFYA, 1, 2, 3, 4, 6, 7, 8, 9, 10, 11, 14, 15, 16, 17,
        18, 19, 21, 26, 27, 28, 29, 31, 32, 33, 34,
        35, 36, 37, 38, 39, 43, 44, 45, 48, 49, 54,
        56, 57, 58, 59, 60, 61, 63, 64, 66, 68, 70,
        71, 72, 73, 79, 84, 89, 90, 93, 100, 103,
        104, 105, 109, 110, 112, 113, 117, 132,
        134, 136, 147, 149, 150, 154, 157, 159,
        162, 164, 168, 170, 171, 173, 175, 182,
        184, 187, 189, 190, 191, 192, 194, 195,
        200, 205, 206, 207, 212, 215, 216
Bicycles, 24
Big business, 143
Billionaires, 164
Bioengineering, 159–163, 169
Biographical fiction, 51, 52
Biological warfare, 108
Biomedical, 161
Biracial, 34, 78, 88, 91, 93, 94
Black humor, 110
#BlackLivesMatter, 7
Blackmail, 107
Blind, 21, 51
Blizzards, 118
Blogs, 151
Blood magic, 185
Bloomer, Amelia (List), 2, 6, 9, 14, 28, 31, 50,
        57, 63, 64, 85, 89, 105, 217
Boarding school, 3, 7, 10, 24, 25, 31, 45, 65,
        71, 89, 90, 92, 98, 100, 109, 119, 136,
        195
Body horror, 144, 150
Body image, 4, 27, 89
Body modification, 159
Body positivity, 15, 93
Bodyguards, 159
Bolivia, 69
Book clubs, 32
Books, 71, 74, 101
Bookstores, 42
Boston, 49, 65–66, 116, 161
Botany, 118
Boulder, Colorado, 10
Bounty hunters, 164
Boxing, 211
Boy next door, 87, 90
Brain tumors, 143
Breakdancing, 13
Breakups, 25
Bridge, 21
Broadway, 19–20, 91
Brooklyn, 11, 38, 110
Brothers, 3, 35, 36, 37, 71, 87
Brothers and sisters, 16, 35, 99, 109, 113, 215.
        See also Siblings
Buffy the Vampire Slayer, 128–129
Bullying, 9, 17, 30, 54, 59, 110, 170, 207
Burma, 72

Cab drivers, 29
California, 3, 5, 7, 8, 23, 24, 28, 32, 34, 35, 52,
    83 84, 85, 93, 100, 109, 110, 112, 116,
    132, 155, 161, 178, 201
Camp, 20, 31, 38, 82, 207, 212
Camping, 116
Canada, 31, 60, 104, 117, 118, 192
Cancer, 43, 55
Cape Cod, 110
Cards, 21
Cars, 25
Cartoonists, 85
Casinos, 21
Cataplexy, 109
Catherine, Queen of France, 64
Catholic church, 1, 12, 56
Catholic schools, 12
Catholicism, 58, 61
Cats, 135
Caves, 149
Celebrities, 56
Celtic myth, 199
Chalk, 196
Changelings, 201
Charter schools, 161
Chassidic Jews, 11
Cheating, 110
Cheerleading, 31, 93, 103
Chefs, 23
Chemistry, 103
Cherokees, 136
Chess, 21
Chicago, 5, 6, 85, 115, 211
Child brides, 72
Child labor, 60
Chinese Americans, 6, 7, 50, 56, 87
Chinese immigrants, 42
Christian life, 13
Christmas, 94
Churches, 58
Cinderella, 171, 214
Circuses, 140
Civil rights, 59
Civil war, 49, 143
Clairvoyance, 207
Clairvoyants, 205
Class struggle, 166
Climate change, 173, 179
Clones, 160
Cold cases, 100, 102
College, 3, 5, 14, 26, 27, 35, 77, 79, 84, 85, 88, 90
College admissions, 26

Colonies, 51, 162
Colonization, 171
Colorado, 10, 84, 102, 116
Coma, 111, 161
Comedy, 4
Comics, 15, 152, 153
Coming out, 10
Coming-of-age, 106
Communes, 48
Community service, 31
Competition, 19, 20, 164
Computers, 170
Concentration camps, 68, 71, 73, 74
Conjoined twins, 34
Connecticut, 56, 78, 97, 98
Conspiracy theories, 113
Contests, 23
Cooking, 22–23, 38
Coretta Scott King Award, 17, 50, 51, 59
Corporate espionage, 115
Corruption, 175
Costumes, 90
Counterfeiting, 192
Country music, 83
Cousins, 34, 90, 99, 110
Crete, 210
Criminals, 114, 122, 123, 200
Cryptography, 70
Crystal City, Texas, 54
Cuba, 121, 166
Cuban Americans, 5
Cupcakes, 23
Cupertino, California, 6
Curses, 206, 215
Cyber punk, 171
Cyborgs, 158, 171
Cystic fibrosis, 153, 215

Dance, 4, 19, 20, 78, 81, 87
Dancers, 65, 78
Dark, 183, 197
Dark fantasy, 185
Date rape, 27, 31
Dating, 8, 86, 88
Dating violence, 111
DC Comics, 152–153
Deaf, 51
Death, 29, 37, 42–45, 51, 74, 112, 131, 147, 175
Deception, 188
Demons, 146, 201–203, 210
Denver, 85
Deportation, 8

Depression, 6, 28, 41
Desert, 113
Desert islands, 115
Deserters, 70
Desis, 84, 85
Detective, 60, 168
Dhampirs, 138
Diabetes, 113, 166
Diaries, 58, 87, 151. *See also* Journals
Dickinson, Emily, 31, 40
Dictators, 174
Diners, 44, 78
Disabilities, 69, 129, 163, 217
Distant future, 174
Diving, 66
Divorce, 2, 16, 17, 24, 36, 42, 86, 89
Djinn, 197, 199
DJs, 16, 41
Dogs, 55, 117, 174, 192
Dogsleds, 118
Dolls, 126
Dolly Parton, 89
Domestic abuse, 217
Domestic terrorism, 120
Donkeys, 70
Double agents, 119, 122
Dr. Jekyll and Mr. Hyde, 134
Drag queens, 89, 92
Dragons, 187, 188, 192
Drama camp, 20
Drawing, 196
Dreams, 173, 190
Drug use, 56, 63, 159
Drummers, 15
Dungeons, 188
Dysfunctional families, 11, 113
Dystopia, 136, 153, 172–177

Earthquakes, 56, 117
East Germany, 68
Eastern European, 72, 215
Ebenezer Creek, 49
Ecology, 160
Economic inequality, 170
Edgar Award, 29, 99, 102, 108, 111, 132, 148
Education, 51
Egypt, 62
Eighteenth century, 48, 50, 51, 63
El Paso, Texas, 10
Elephants, 72
Eleventh century, 192
Elizabeth, New Jersey, 52

Elves, 215
E-Mails, 22
Emancipation, 49
Emily Dickinson, 31, 40
Engineers, 167
England, 60, 61, 65, 69, 71, 77, 85, 86, 98, 101, 103, 107, 127, 129, 195, 202
Entertainment, 170
Environmental, 169
Epic, 68, 211
Epic fantasy, 182–191
Epistolary novels, 3, 22, 24, 42, 84
Espionage, 71, 73, 115, 118–123, 155, 160
Eugenics, 58
Europe, 25, 68, 79, 84, 203
Evangelical Christians, 8, 11
Exploitation, 21, 176
Exploration, 66, 168

Facial disfigurement, 44
Factory farms, 143
Faerie, 197–202
Fairies, 201
Fairy tales, 126, 171, 214–215
Faith, 1, 4, 8, 10–13
Falconry, 83
False identity, 110, 112
Fame, 2, 187
Familiars, 189
Family, 2, 4, 5, 6, 7, 28, 29, 32, 33–37, 56, 57, 59, 60, 87, 103, 109, 117, 119, 128, 131, 149, 193, 206, 216
Family problems, 89
Family secrets, 14, 37, 202
Family violence, 18
Famine, 179
Fanfiction, 3, 14
Farming, 18
Fashion, 24, 78, 90, 93
Fate, 188, 207, 214
Fathers, 38, 112
Fathers and daughters, 4, 84, 87, 105, 117
Fathers and sons, 2, 3, 16, 17, 21, 27, 128
Faust, 128
Female athletes, 18, 39, 83. *See also* Women in sports
Feminism, 24
Fentress, Texas, 50
Figure skating, 23
Film, 7, 45, 88, 89, 120, 139, 140, 160, 172, 173
Filmmaking, 84

First ladies, 52
First love, 13, 27, 45, 92, 93, 115
First-generation college students, 5
Flight, 168
Florence, Italy, 64, 81, 87
Flying, 160. *See also* Pilots
Folklore, 60, 67, 130, 135, 199, 211
Food trucks, 24
Football, 18, 82
Forensic science, 64, 100, 101, 110
Fort Mose, Florida, 50
Foster care, 34, 38–41, 74, 127, 133
Founding fathers, 49
Fourteenth century, 61
Foxes, 156, 214
France, 61, 64, 70, 71, 73, 114, 123, 186
Franco, Francisco, 72
Frankenstein, 134, 135
Freedoms, 155
Friends, 2, 4, 6, 10, 15, 26, 27, 28, 29–33, 35,
        36, 39, 44, 62, 67, 85, 89, 90, 107, 112,
        126, 129, 140, 195, 207
Friendship, 4, 10, 18, 20, 29–33, 56, 73, 78,
        81, 83, 88, 102, 109, 113, 134, 163, 165,
        181, 207, 208
Fugitives, 156
Funny, 133, 143, 158, 204. *See also* Humor
Future, 161, 170, 174

Gadgets, 108, 120
Gambling, 21
Gaming, 118. *See also* Role-playing games;
        Video games
Gangs, 35
Gay dads, 90
Geeks, 26
Gender, 8–10, 179, 207
Gender roles, 50, 192
Gentrification, 149
Georgia, 8, 49, 51, 55, 210
Germany, 68, 70, 71, 74, 161
GGN (Great Graphic Novels List), 14, 20,
        21, 30, 32, 35–36, 55, 126, 208
Ghana, 2, 57
Ghosts, 22, 29, 35, 36, 49, 113, 129–132, 203
Girlfriends, 25
Girls dressed as boys, 65, 211. *See also*
        Women disguised as men
Global warming, 167
Goddess worship, 136
Gods, 68, 190, 192
Gold, 170

Golems, 60, 197
Golf, 17
Gory, 130
Gotham City, 152–153
Gothic, 128, 151, 173
Government agencies, 175
Government, 197
Goya, Francisco, 66
Graffiti, 14, 38
Grandmothers, 44, 136
Grandparents, 6, 27, 80
Graphic novels, 13, 18, 21, 30, 32, 35, 36, 55,
        70, 74, 93, 126, 129, 133, 142, 145, 149,
        152, 159, 165, 211
Graves, 128
Graveyards, 32
Great River Road, 25
Greece, 62
Greek gods, 68
Greek mythology, 210–213
Greenland, 167
Grief, 4, 6, 14, 17, 22, 25, 27, 28, 32, 37, 39,
        42–44, 54, 55, 60, 67, 68, 82, 84, 87, 112,
        117, 126, 128, 132, 153, 166, 216
Grishaverse, 182–183, 200
Gross, 133
Guilt, 44, 149
Guinness Book of World Records, 10
Gun violence, 7
Guns, 132

Hackers, 155, 162, 164, 170
Haiti, 117
Hamburgers, 93
Hamilton, Alexander, 49
Handicaps, 51, 174. *See also* Disabilities
Harlem, 1, 56
Harlem Renaissance, 56
Hate crimes, 53
Hawaii, 57, 216
Health conditions, 54
Hearing impaired, 78, 91, 209
Heart transplants, 44
Heavy metal music, 15
Heist, 114, 155, 200–201
Henri II, King, 64
Heroes, 29, 212–213
Heroic fantasy, 191–193
Hidden identity, 61
High school, 2, 4, 14, 15, 27, 31, 35, 82,
        83, 90, 91, 100, 103, 128. *See also*
        Boarding schools; Prep schools

High school graduation, 14
Hijab, 11, 13
Hindu mythology, 210
Hip-hop, 16, 57
Historical fantasy, 191, 201
Historical fiction, 47–76, 103, 129, 134, 135, 150
Hitler, Adolf, 68
Hockey, 17, 23
Hollywood, 2, 80, 87
Holocaust, 68, 71, 73, 74
Homelessness, 11, 40–42, 101
Homer, 211
Homeschooling, 13, 31, 35
Homesteading, 56, 116
Homophobia, 53, 162
Hong Kong, 79, 127
Horse racing, 82
Horses, 71, 80, 81
Hotels, 41, 78, 80, 105
Houston, 22, 81
Human sacrifice, 211
Humor, 4, 24, 26, 27, 36, 86, 92, 103, 110, 115, 119, 165, 195. *See also* Funny
Huntington's disease, 5, 113
Hurricanes, 116

Ice hockey, 17, 23
Idaho, 40, 151
Identity, 1–23, 108, 110, 112, 160
Identity theft, 108
Illness, 54
Illustrated, 73. *See also* Graphic novels
Imagination, 134
Immigrant experience, 143
Immigrants, 7, 42, 52, 54, 56–57, 143, 206, 216
Immigration, 7, 33, 113
Immortality, 162, 211
Immunodeficiency, 45
Improv, 4
Incarceration, 33
Incest, 57
Indentured servants, 50
Independence, 56, 73
India, 72, 73
Indian Americans, 57, 84, 85
Indonesians, 127
Inquisition, 61, 66, 186, 189
Insects, 181
Internet culture, 148
Intersex, 9

Intrigue, 171, 187, 197, 198
Inventors, 90
Iowa, 128, 143, 181
Iran, 6, 12
Islamophobia, 165
Islands, 22, 110, 115, 116, 122
Isolation, 148
Israelis, 5
Istanbul, 68, 169

Jamaican Americans, 8
Jane Eyre, 173
Japan, 54, 61, 69, 72, 122, 131, 164
Japanese Americans, 55, 78
Japanese folklore, 130
Jazz, 17
Jekyll & Hyde, 134
Jewish diaspora, 53, 69
Jewish folklore, 60
Jews, 5, 69, 70, 74, 93, 105
Jockeys, 37
Journalism, 4, 148
Journals, 192. *See also* Diaries
Jugglers, 61
Juneteenth, 51

Keckley, Elizabeth, 51–52
Keller, Helen, 51
Kidnapping, 36, 107, 113, 116, 123, 192, 207
Kissing, 10, 28
Knights, 187
Korea, North, 122
Korean Americans, 8, 12, 15, 23, 24, 79, 88
Korean mythology, 210
K-pop, 79
Kuala Lumpur, Malaysia, 67

LA Times Book Prize, 1, 6, 7, 10, 29, 110, 115, 132
Labor camps, 72
Labor issues, 52
Labor unions, 54
Labyrinth, 210, 212
Lakes, 34
Lambda Award, 9, 10, 19, 91, 92, 162
Latinx, 5, 6, 13, 22, 38, 93, 94, 113, 166, 179, 206
Latter Day Saints, 92
Leningrad, 70
Letters, 7, 42, 77, 88, 163

LGBTQIA+, 3, 4, 6, 8, 9, 10, 12 13,14, 15, 19,
    32, 33, 41, 42, 53, 57, 63, 66, 79, 82, 90,
    91, 92, 93, 94, 125, 127, 130, 133, 140,
    142, 145, 148, 149, 156, 159, 162, 170,
    181, 187, 188, 191, 194, 203, 204, 205,
    206, 207, 209, 213, 216
Librarians, 39, 41, 71, 190
Libraries, 31
Light novels, 164
Lincoln, Mary Todd, 51–52
Literary, 70, 71
Lithuania, 72
Little League, 18
London, 60, 61, 65, 66, 69, 79, 99, 101, 102,
    106, 107, 110, 114, 119, 134, 144, 145,
    150, 151, 180, 181, 197, 202, 203
Loneliness, 134
Long Island, New York, 58
Los Angeles, 24, 87, 93, 110, 201
Lost articles, 30
Lottery, 5
Love letters, 42
Love triangles, 94, 172
Loyalty, 73

Macbeth, 148
Machines, 169
Mad scientists, 160
Madrid, Spain, 72
Mafia, 193
Magic, 128, 185, 193–196, 203
Magic schools, 190, 196
Magical nature, 206
Magical realism, 14, 22, 33, 36, 68, 118,
    205–209
Magicians, 78, 147
Maine, 38, 58, 86
Malcolm X, 59
Mall of America, 36
Malls, 36, 108, 118
Manga, 164
Manhattan, 15, 20, 105, 170
Manhood, 29
Maps, 99, 216
Marathons, 82
Marriage, 38
Mars, 118, 167
Mars mission, 22
Martha's Vineyard, 109, 110
Marvel Comics, 152–153
Marysville, New York, 58
Masculinity, 132

Massachusetts, 10, 31, 43
Matchmaking, 84, 85, 86
#MeToo, 2, 14, 17, 27, 31
Medical horror, 134, 135
Medieval, 67, 184, 191
Melbourne, Victoria, Australia, 11, 101
Memes, 145
Memory, 162, 172
Memory loss, 74
Mental illness, 3, 12, 45, 51, 67, 68, 107, 109,
    113, 130, 149, 216, 217
Mermaids, 134, 206
Metafiction, 158
Mexican Americans, 6, 10, 32, 35, 52, 93,
    178
Mexico, 6, 22, 36, 54, 110, 112, 113
Miami, 5
Mid-Atlantic Coast, 93
Middle ages, 186
Middle passage, 50
Middle school, 17, 18, 20, 30, 33, 35, 36
Minister's children, 58
Minnesota, 25, 36, 111
Minor League Baseball, 19
Minotaur, 172, 210
Missing girls, 99, 100, 101, 102, 103, 105, 113
Missing persons, 37, 44, 59, 70, 99, 106, 133,
    148, 164, 192. *See also* Missing girls
Mississippi River, 25, 65
Missouri, 53
Mob, 105
Mobsters, 56
Modeling, 78
Monsters, 60, 127, 132–135, 204, 212
Montana, 56, 138
Moon, 179, 180
Mormons, 92
Moroi, 138–139
Morris Award, 6, 7, 91, 109
Morris finalist, 2, 3, 9, 11, 54, 55, 57, 64, 72,
    73, 163, 182, 184, 187, 204
Mortality, 175
Motels, 7, 34
Mothers and daughters, 33, 37, 40, 54, 69,
    77, 80, 82, 87, 89, 105, 110, 111, 193
Mothers and sons, 91
Movie stars, 86
Movies, 81, 87–89, 93
Multigenerational families, 38
Multiple perspectives, 51, 57, 72, 128, 185,
    186, 207, 216
Munich, Germany, 74

Murder, 36, 41, 53, 54, 99, 100, 101, 102, 103, 105, 107, 108, 110, 111, 113, 116, 134, 188
Murder trials, 53
Murder-suicide, 134
Muses, 135
Music, 2, 14–16, 28, 37, 83, 199, 204
Musical theater, 19–20, 84
Musicians, 16, 43, 56, 73, 187
Muslims, 2, 11, 13, 25, 165, 206
Mutations, 178
Mysteries, 62, 64, 97–107, 130, 150, 168, 187, 192
Mystery writers, 78
Mythopoeic Award, 126, 184, 186, 195, 196, 197

Nannies, 192
Napa, California, 23
Narcolepsy, 78
NASA, 22, 26
Nashville, Tennessee, 82–83
National Book Award, 1, 3, 6, 7, 10, 12, 13, 29, 48, 53, 58, 64, 91, 113, 132, 177, 207
Native Americans, 53, 55, 127, 139, 143, 173
Natural history, 105
Navajo, 213
Nazi Youth, 70
NCAA tournament, 19
Near future, 161
Nebraska, 14
Necromancers, 204
Negro League Baseball, 18
Nevada, 39, 40
New adult, 78, 79
New England, 92, 128, 134, 150. *See also* Maine; Massachusetts; New Hampshire; Vermont
New family member, 149
New Hampshire, 31
New Jersey, 52, 78, 99, 116, 200
New kid, 134
New London, Texas, 57
New Mexico, 35, 213
New Orleans, 58, 59, 65, 105, 149
New York (City), 1, 8, 15, 19–20, 27, 28, 41, 44, 49, 56, 57, 78, 90, 91, 104, 105, 110, 114, 129, 142, 154, 179, 180, 212
New York State, 5, 23, 24, 26, 27, 58, 103, 126
New Zealand, 169
Newspapers, 50
Nigeria, 216

Nineteenth century, 49, 51, 60, 64, 129, 134, 135, 150, 168, 201
Ninjas, 122
Nobility, 64
Nonbinary, 9
Nontraditional family, 193, 206
Nonviolent activism, 74
Norse, 209
North Africa, 62, 65
North Carolina, 2, 9, 24, 105, 135, 177
Norton Nebula Award, 182, 196, 201
Novel writing, 92
Nuclear disasters, 40
Nuclear power, 178
Nuns, 12,
Nurses, 74

Obesity, 15, 38
Obituaries, 25
Obsessive compulsive disorder (OCD), 44, 67
Occult, 126–129
Ohio, 54
Oklahoma, 21, 35, 136
Omaha, 15, 137
Online dating, 86
Oppression, 68, 72, 171, 189, 190
Optimism, 41
Oregon, 36, 43, 108, 140
Orphans, 56, 60, 61, 64, 68, 71, 127, 129, 131, 133, 167, 176, 182, 190, 195, 197, 200
Orthodox Judaism, 11, 58
Ostia, 62
Out of body experiences, 43
Outdoors, 207
Oxford, England, 77, 98, 101, 189

Pacific Railroad, 52
Pacts, 150
Pagans, 12
Painting, 14, 170
Palace intrigue, 197
Palm Beach, Florida, 53
Paparazzi, 80
Parallel worlds, 128, 165–167, 215–217
Paranoid schizophrenia, 45
Paranormal, 68, 125–154, 178
Paranormal abilities, 178
Parasites, 142
Parents, 9, 34, 38, 58
Paris, 23, 65, 79, 89, 90, 201
Parton, Dolly, 89

Pasadena, California, 26, 112
Patriarchy, 209
Pennsylvania, 9, 10, 19, 20, 59, 179, 180
Performers, 69, 206
Persian Americans, 6, 93
Phippsburg, Maine, 58
Photography, 49, 72, 79, 93, 129
Piano players, 16, 107
Pilots, 59, 123, 158
Pirates, 63, 65, 66, 117, 156, 168, 192
Pittsburgh pirates, 19
Pizza, 23, 32
Plagues, 148, 158, 162, 179, 189, 194
Plane crash, 52, 115, 116
Playlists, 15, 31, 83, 84, 93
Plus size, 27
Podcasts, 102
Poe, Edgar Allan, 66, 135
Poetry, 1, 8, 31
Poisons, 103
Poker, 21
Poland, 37, 67, 68, 114
Police brutality, 7
Politics, 22, 80, 110, 183, 188, 192, 194
Pollution, 166
Pompeii, 62
Portals, 127
Portland, Oregon, 43, 108
Portuguese Americans, 9
Postapocalyptic, 133, 143, 169, 173, 177–181
Poverty, 21, 55
Power couples, 49
Pranks, 3, 44, 99, 170
Pregnancy, 6, 34, 37–39, 41
Prejudice, 13, 50, 52, 53, 56, 57, 63, 74, 140,
    143, 144, 153, 206
Prep schools, 15, 26, 28, 99, 110
President of the United States, 120
Presidential campaigns, 80
Priests, 56
Princes, 77, 79, 86, 157, 184, 191, 198, 202, 215
Princesses, 92, 156, 171, 184, 185, 187, 194,
    202, 211, 214, 215
Printz Award, 1, 14, 25, 27, 36, 38, 117, 177,
    207
Printz Honor, 3, 7, 8, 10, 15, 25, 27, 29, 31, 32,
    41, 48, 54, 57, 58, 61, 73, 74, 105, 110,
    112, 132, 168, 175, 181, 191, 207
Prison, 69, 173
Private investigators, 107
Privateers, 65
Privilege, 149

Prohibition era, 104
Prom, 81
Prophecies, 152, 188
Prosthetics, 43
Prostitution, 59, 105
Provo, Utah, 92
Psychic abilities, 104
Psychics, 130
Psychological suspense, 110, 112
Psychology, 33
PTSD, 31, 35, 59, 101, 115, 116
Publicity, 79
Punk rock, 15
Puzzles, 164

Quarks, 109
Quiverfull, 13
Quiz bowl, 92

Race, 29, 133
Racism, 7, 68, 106, 144, 153
Rainbow Book List, 3, 6, 8, 9, 10, 32, 33, 63,
    93, 104, 148, 170, 191, 207, 208
Rape, 6, 14, 17, 27, 31, 68
Rappers, 16
Rapture, 11
Rapunzel, 171
Rare books, 101
Rats, 142
Real estate development, 80
Reality TV, 22, 23, 172, 173
Rebellion, 176
Recipes, 23
Redemption, 214
Refugees, 69, 72, 177
Religion, 3, 12, 61, 186. See also Faith
Renaissance Faires, 35–36
Reno, Nevada, 39
Reporters, 105, 113
Resistance movements, 71, 74, 115, 153, 165,
    190, 197
Resorts, 54, 105
Restaurants, 2, 22. See also Cooking
Retold classics, 110, 134, 135, 148, 171, 173,
    214
Revenge, 28, 29, 112, 132, 153
Revolution, 48, 153, 156, 166
Riverboats, 65
Road trips, 25, 28, 35, 78, 84, 85
Robin Hood, 67
Robots, 165–166
Rock music, 2, 15, 16

Rock musicians, 16
Role-playing games, 21, 126
Roller Derby, 18
Roman Mythology, 212–213
Romance, 15, 23, 24, 77–95, 107, 114, 139, 159,
    173, 188, 190, 199, 202, 206, 210
Romania, 64, 191
Rome, 62–64, 110
Roommates, 92
Royalty, 77, 79, 86, 92, 156, 182, 183, 184, 187,
    191, 192, 194
Runaways, 40–42, 50, 176, 194, 201, 206
Runners, 18, 82, 84, 116
Russia, 53–54, 117, 118, 192, 201
Russians, 26, 67, 70, 72, 114, 115, 121

Sad stories, 51. See also Grief
Sailing, 36, 65, 216
Salem, Oregon, 140
San Diego, California, 54, 132
San Francisco, 11, 26, 27, 36, 56, 84, 85, 90,
    121, 155, 206
San Francisco Bay Area, 18
San Gabriel, 52
San Juan Islands, 22
Santa Cruz, 36
Saskatchewan, 118
Scandinavia, 207
Scavenging, 177
Schneider Family Book Awards, 69, 209
Scholars, 48, 190
School politics, 22, 110
School shootings, 24
School tragedy, 57
Schools, 122. See also Boarding schools;
    Charter schools; High schools;
    Magic schools; Middle school; Prep
    schools; Private schools
Schuyler, Eliza, 49
Science, 26, 30, 50, 64, 86
Science fiction, 51, 142, 148, 154–181
Scientific, 168
Scotland, 79, 86, 92, 135
Scrapbook, 107
Sculpture, 14
Seamstresses, 52
Seattle, 27, 41, 77, 78, 80, 91, 139, 179, 204
Secret codes, 72
Secret identities, 153
Secret service, 114, 115, 120
Secret societies, 3, 189, 209
Secrets, 87

Seers, 49
Self-esteem, 26, 27, 29
Self-harm, 214
Self-image, 159
Selkies, 147, 208
Serial killers, 56, 104, 109, 110, 111, 147, 150,
    217
Servants, 50, 58, 129
Sestinas, 41
Sex, xii, 27, 89
Sextuplets, 85
Sexual abuse, 2, 11, 49, 56, 57, 67, 68, 206,
    216
Sexual identity, 8–10, 15, 187
Sexual violence, 64
Sexuality, 8–11, 53, 74, 91, 187
Shadowhunters, 202–203
Shakespeare, 58, 78, 79, 101, 148
Shanghai, 69
Shapeshifters, 135, 147, 187, 193
Shelley, Mary, 134–135
Sherlock Holmes, 98, 101–102, 106
Shipwrecks, 63, 72, 168
Shopping malls, 36, 108, 118
Short stories, 55, 66, 94, 126, 207
Siberia, 118, 123, 138, 139
Siblings, 9, 54, 61, 63, 128, 129, 131, 156,
    179, 182, 205, 216. See also Brothers;
    Brothers and sisters; sisters
Simulated reality, 164
Singing, 37
Single mother, 170
Single parents, 34
Single-sex societies, 174
Sisters, 5, 6, 12, 33, 34, 40, 42, 44, 51, 55, 86,
    88, 133, 183, 194, 205, 217
Sixteenth century, 64
Slam poetry, 1
Slavery, 48, 50, 51, 143, 192
Slaves, 52, 63, 135
Small towns, 10, 32, 36, 97, 106, 111
Snipers, 70
Snow, 94, 118
Snow White, 171–172
Soccer, 17, 83
Social anxiety, 26
Social classes, 80
Social media, 91, 93, 136, 151
Social workers, 39
Somalia, 117
Sonnets, 41
Sounds, 133

South Africa, 168
South Asians, 93
South Carolina, 48, 50
South Pole, 117
Southern California, 8
Space, 133
Space colonies, 162
Space opera, 156–157
Spain, 38, 72
Spanish influenza, 132
Spanish inquisition, 66
Special abilities, 150
Special needs, 54
Spies, 65, 70–71, 73, 114, 119–123, 166, 189, 192
Sports, 16–19, 87
St. Augustine, Florida, 50
Stanford, 19, 116, 148
Steampunk, 167–169, 202–203
Stepfamilies, 24, 39
Stepmothers, 86
Stonewall Awards, 6, 10, 14, 19, 20, 63
Storms, 116, 118
Stranded, 116, 118, 167
Street art, 14, 38
Strigoi, 138–139
Suffragists, 53
Suicide, 4, 15, 16, 25, 31, 105, 110, 134, 162, 170
Sullivan, Annie, 51
Summer, 16, 17, 20, 22, 24, 25, 30, 32, 34, 35, 44, 56, 78, 79, 81, 82–84, 86, 87, 90, 92, 93, 98, 110, 111
Summer jobs, 24, 30, 92, 93
Summer romance, 24, 81, 82, 84, 87, 90, 91, 93, 94
Summoning, 132
Super villains, 122, 153
Supernatural, 60, 130, 131, 145, 146, 197, 202, 207, 212
Surveillance, 155
Survival, 29, 37, 72, 105, 107, 114–118, 123, 133, 143, 162, 166, 167, 177, 179
Suspense, 107–113, 116, 144, 155
Sussex, England, 98
Sweden, 17
Swimming, 39, 83, 116
Sydney Taylor Award, 5, 60

Tabloids, 80
Taipei, 87, 166
Tattoos, 130, 136

Taxidermy, 55
Teachers, 51
Teen fathers, 38
Teen mothers, 38
Teen pregnancy, 34, 37–39
Teen spies, 120. *See also* Spies
Teenage boys, 27
Teenage girls, 111
Telepathy, 215
Television shows, 80. *See also* Reality TV
Tennessee, 25, 59, 82, 83, 86
Tennis, 109
Tense, 56
Terrorism, 53, 118–122
Terrorists, 115, 117
Texas, 4, 10, 13, 22, 50, 51, 54, 57, 89
Theater, 19–21, 31, 84, 91, 98
Theseus, 210
Thieves, 108, 157
Thriller, 113–123, 130
Tigers, 182
Time travel, 51, 127, 169–170, 216
Tokyo, Japan, 61
Toronto, 42, 101, 111
Torture, 116, 144
Toxic relationships, 32
Trains, 85, 157
Traitors, 123
Transformation, 193
Trauma, 57, 110, 192. *See also* PTSD
Travel, 25. *See also* Road trips
Traveling performers, 206
Treasure, 66
Trench warfare, 71
Triangle Shirtwaist Factory, 52
Tricksters, 192, 203
Triplets, 183
Truth, 188
Tuberculosis, 45
Tulsa, Oklahoma, 136, 137
Turkey, 62
Tuscany, 86, 87
Twentieth century, 51–60, 67–75
Twins, 11, 14, 17, 34, 74, 127, 129, 205, 217

U.S. Internment Camps, 54, 165
Uncles, 21
Underground cities, 158, 177
Undocumented immigrants, 143
Unreliable narrator, 27, 45, 107, 109, 110
Urban fantasy, 129, 200–205
Urban legends, 132

Utah, 29, 92
Utopias, 167, 172–177

Valentine's Day, 131
Vampires, 135–142, 202–203
Vegans, 44
Vermont, 40, 55, 100, 109
Verse novels, 1, 17, 34, 41, 64, 74, 132, 210
Veterans, 53, 59
Victorian England, 60, 202, 203
Video games, 164
Vietnam War, 55, 58
Vietnamese Australians, 106
Vikings, 209–210
Viola players, 5
Virginia, 26, 148
Virtual reality, 163–164
Vitiligo, 41
Vlad the Impaler, 64, 68, 191
Volcanoes, 122

Walden Award, 7, 8, 10, 29, 55, 132
Wales, 128
Wallachia, 191
War on drugs, 69
Warlocks, 203
Washington, D.C., 23, 53, 100, 120
Washington State, 22, 35, 81, 139
Wasps, 149
Web development, 84, 85
Web series, 142
Weddings, 24, 86

Wells, H.G., 134
Werewolves, 135, 139, 202
West Africa, 182
West African mythology, 211
Widows, 72
Wilderness, 114, 115
Wilderness survival, 29, 37, 118
Winter, 94
Wisconsin, 18, 116
Wishes, 209, 214
Witchcraft, 127, 145–148, 195, 196
Witches, 193, 195, 214, 216–217
Witness protection, 107
Women disguised as men, 192. *See also* Girls dressed as boys
Women in sports, 19. *See also* Female athletes
Women's Temperance Movement, 66
Word play, 54, 105
Words, 17
World War I, 55–56, 68, 70, 71, 74, 106, 107, 132, 169
World War II, 54, 55, 58, 59, 60, 67, 68, 69, 70, 71, 72, 73, 74, 123
Writers, 56, 78

X, Malcolm, 59
Xenophobia, 54, 165

Yachts, 117

Zombies, 136, 142–145

About the Authors

SARAH FLOWERS is a retired librarian from California and a past president of the Young Adult Library Services Association (YALSA), a division of the American Library Association. She has served on several YALSA book award committees. She is author of several books on teen services, most recently *Crash Course in Young Adult Services* (Libraries Unlimited, 2017).

SAMUEL STAVOLE-CARTER is the Community Engagement Specialist: Youth Services for Shaker Heights (OH) Public Library. A member of YALSA's Great Graphic Novels for Teens 2021 committee, he also serves on YALSA's The Hub Advisory Board. He is coauthor of *Genreflecting: A Guide to Popular Reading Interests*, 8th edition (with Diana Tixier Herald, Libraries Unlimited, 2019).

Ingram Content Group UK Ltd.
Milton Keynes UK
UKHW050158070423
419791UK00010BA/118